How Sweet the Sound

HOW SWEET THE SOUND

Music in the Spiritual Lives

of Americans

DAVID W. STOWE

HARVARD UNIVERSITY PRESS
Cambridge, Massachusetts
London, England
2004

Publication of this book has been supported
through the generous provisions of the
Maurice and Lula Bradley Smith Memorial Fund.

I gratefully acknowledge permission to use the following:

Lines from "Come Sunday" by Duke Ellington;
copyright © 1946 (renewed) by G. Schirmer, Inc.;
international copyright secured; all rights reserved.

"Precious Lord, Take My Hand"; words and music by
Thomas A. Dorsey; copyright © 1938 by Unichappell Music, Inc.;
copyright renewed; international copyright secured;
all rights reserved; used by permission; Warner Bros.
Publications U.S., Inc., Miami, FL 33104.

An earlier version of Chapter 4 was published in *AIQ*, vol. 16, September 2003;
used by permission of the University of Rhode Island.

An earlier version of Chapter 9 was published in *Esoterica*, vol. 5, 2003.

Book design by Gwen Nefsky Frankfeldt

Library of Congress Cataloging-in-Publication Data

Stowe, David W. (David Ware)
How sweet the sound : music in the spiritual lives of Americans /
David W. Stowe.
p. cm.
Includes bibliographical references and index.
ISBN 0-674-01290-9 (hardcover : alk. paper)
1. Sacred songs—United States—History and criticism.
2. Church music—United States.
3. Music—Religious aspects. I. Title.
ML2911.S76 2004
781.7'00973—dc22 2003067543

For Henry and Caroline

Acknowledgments

This book germinated in Japan and came to fruition in Michigan. Sounds that have been with me since earliest memory somehow took on a fresh significance while I was living in the very different soundscape of Kyoto. My first opportunity to think about sacred music in American history came as an invitation to teach a course in religious history at Doshisha University; for supporting me there I thank Takenaka Masao and Mori Koichi; Sekiya Naoto, who was a joy to teach with; and Sakashita Fumiko, who provided diligent assistance. To my colleagues at Doshisha's Graduate School of American Studies, especially Hosoya Masahiro, Sasaki Takashi, and Ikeda Keiko, I want to express my deep gratitude: *o-sewa ni narimashita*. In addition, generous research funds from Doshisha helped me begin building the library of recordings and books that has proved essential to grasping these elusive forms.

At Michigan State University, a timely intramural research grant paid for the purchase of diverse research materials and funded an essential eight-month respite from teaching. Fortuitous teaching assignments presented additional opportunities to collect samples and refine themes. Both institutions provided travel grants to present my research at conferences and symposia in the United States, Japan, and the Netherlands. The MSU library proved to be an unexpected treasure trove of sources for my research. I'm especially grateful to the staff of the Fine Arts Library and of interlibrary loan, which never once let me down. Erik Green, a student in the Honors College, has assisted in various ways during the latter stages of preparing the manuscript. Special thanks to Doug Noverr, without whose support and leadership over the last several years this project (and much else) would have turned out differently.

My path through the tangled thickets of sacred song has been guided by suggestions and insights from numerous friends, colleagues, acquaintances, students, and passing strangers. Here I can acknowledge only the support of those who kindly read drafts of chapters, and in many cases shared materials and offered substantial advice and criticism as well: Christopher Chase, Phil Deloria, Amy DeRogatis, John Eulenberg, Charles and Elizabeth Hambrick-Stowe, Craig Kleinman, Hans Krabbendam, Malcolm Magee, Steve Rohs, Christopher Shannon, and Arthur Versluis. Scholars in several countries responded to my requests for assistance on particular musicians or pieces, including John S. Andrews, David Brady, Jon Butler, Esther Rothenbusch Crookshank, Neil Dickson, Bruce Hindmarsh, Patrick LeBeau, Pat McConeghy, Eisho Nasu, Richard Payne, Ian Randall, and Yoshida Ryo. My father cheerfully located, copied, and sent some of my first sources while I was living in Japan; I regret that he did not live to see the book's completion.

My editor, Joyce Seltzer, has exerted a gracious professional presence throughout, tactfully but insistently prodding both author and manuscript. Ann Hawthorne's gimlet-eyed scrutiny of the text saved me from many errors. Linda, Henry, and Caroline have shared in every page of this book, on both sides of the Pacific. It would not have been worth doing without them. I dedicate it to my children, inheritors of a new sacred soundscape.

Contents

How Sweet the Sound

Introduction

> The growth, development and future of all our religious ideals
> rests largely with our hymnology. The songs of a nation will in the
> long run make the nation.
>
> —Benjamin F. Crawford

On 5 July 1852 Frederick Douglass stepped to the podium of Corinthian Hall in Rochester, New York, to deliver one of the most celebrated speeches ever delivered in the United States. "What to the slave is the Fourth of July?" is the question he put to the packed audience. For enslaved African Americans, which Douglass had been for most of his life, Independence Day was a holiday that heightened the contradictions; in celebrating American freedom, it underscored the bondage of a substantial portion of its population. "The rich inheritance of justice, liberty, prosperity, and independence, bequeathed by your fathers, is shared by you, not by me," he thundered. "The sunlight that brought life and healing to you, has brought stripes and death to me." In short: "This Fourth of July is *yours*, not *mine*. *You* may rejoice, *I* must mourn."[1]

Douglass likened the United States to another unnamed nation, one "whose crimes, towering up to heaven, were thrown down by the breath of the Almighty, burying that nation in irrecoverable ruin!" Then he intoned what he called "the plaintive lament of a peeled and woe-smitten people," the first six verses of a Hebraic psalm.

> By the rivers of Babylon, there we sat down. Yea! we wept when we remembered Zion. We hanged our harps upon the willows in the midst thereof. For there, they that carried us away captive, required of us a song; and they who wasted us required of us mirth, saying, Sing us one of the songs of Zion. How

can we sing the Lord's song in a strange land? If I forget thee, O Jerusalem, let my right hand forget her cunning. If I do not remember thee, let my tongue cleave to the roof of my mouth.[2]

Psalm 137 has been the basis for countless religious songs over the centuries. The Puritans' *Bay Psalm Book* of 1640 had one, with its distinctive twisted syntax. Isaac Watts somehow failed to include it in his pathbreaking psalm collection of 1719, but later revisers of Watts corrected the omission. Taken together these psalm collections would dominate the worship music of a great majority of church-minded Americans until well into the nineteenth century. The Boston composer William Billings wrote his own typically patriotic version of the psalm, substituting British for the Babylonian oppressors and Bostonians for the Israelites. As recently as 1995, country rock singer Steve Earle recorded a version of Psalm 137 called "Rivers of Babylon."

For a peculiarly Bible-reading, psalm-singing populace, the metaphor Douglass chose has been a potent one. His own people, enslaved Africans, were the children of Israel, he asserted, and those who conspired to keep them down, either actively as slaveholders or indirectly as people who profited from the slave system, were Babylonian oppressors. The passage he chose was particularly close to the bone of a nation peopled largely by immigrants, exiles, captives, and castoffs. Rife as it is with Judeo-Christian imagery, the psalm could just as easily convey the experience of the myriad non-Christians who have come to or found themselves living in the United States: how to sing their own sacred songs in a land so dominated by one version of the divine. Songs of Zion—sacred songs—were crucial equipment for living in these circumstances, but the circumstances could make the voicing of those very songs difficult. They sounded out of place. They invited mockery. They were not always easy to remember.

THE United States has often been called "a Christian nation," a label that in recent decades has generated some indignant dissent. But survey results bear out that Americans are in fact the most God-believing, prayer-uttering, Bible-revering, church-attending society of the modern capitalist democracies. And by a large majority, those Americans believe in the God of the holy trinity and attend Christian churches. The evidence shows that rather than becoming more secular, the United States is as believing a nation as it has ever been. And despite a detectable waxing and waning of religious zeal over the centuries, it has always been a believing place. Native peoples were characteristically devoted to religious practices inseparable from other aspects of life. European exploration, settlement, and conquest had multiple motives, but Spain, France, and England all poured substantial resources into Christianizing the Amerindians. Certainly the European imperial presence would have been very different without the resources and commitments of the missionaries who were among the earliest presences on the continent.

Music has always been central to the ways in which Americans have thought about and practiced their religion. The links between music and the sacred extend far back, of course, into the dim recesses where history becomes myth. There is every reason to believe that the origins of music lie in the rituals of worship, and that among many cultures, the practice of worship has been and continues to be inextricable from music. Everything we know about the religious practices of Native Americans before European contact suggests that music—in the form of songs, chants, percussion—was integral to the practice of religion. And in the centuries since Europeans began exerting an impact on North America, it is clear that musical expression, generally in the form of hymns, has been at the heart of the religious experience.

Music plays a variety of roles in religious life. It is most obviously a means of communication with the divine: a mechanism for expressing praise and thanksgiving, for petitioning for mercy, protection, and power. And music, often combined with dance or physical movement and pursued in circumstances that raise the psychic stakes, serves to elevate the worshipper to a heightened or ecstatic state in which the presence of the divine is keenly felt. The social aspects are equally important. By linking together worshippers in pursuit of a common purpose, music also creates the sense of a worship community; it fuses a collection of individuals into the collective that has most often been the appropriate mode of address toward the divine. And music serves as the carrier of creeds and core beliefs. Every time a worshipper sings a hymn, she is essentially professing a creed or testifying to her faith, at once internalizing and making public the teachings expressed by the song (which itself has been adopted by the collective as an appropriate expression of what the community chooses to believe). Sacred songs are extraordinary in their capacity to compress and epitomize the most fundamental ideas of a faith community. In fact those who attempt to study religion without paying adequate attention to its sacred song run the risk of missing some key components of those belief systems.

Sacred songs are densely layered artifacts, gathering additional meanings over time. Hymns are at once intensely personal yet eminently social documents. Whether they emerge autochthonously from collective worship or are penned privately in a pastoral study, sacred songs are performed, experienced, and rewritten in the intense crucible of religious experience. Hymns can be remarkable linguistic and musical palimpsests.

They are revised formally by hymnbook editors, compilers, translators, and ecclesiastical authorities. Informally they are altered by worship leaders, music directors, organists, soloists, and congregations who adapt them over time, and parodists who convert familiar songs to new, sometimes widely divergent, ends. Words are often created independently of music, producing an even more complexly determined artifact. Texts are set and reset to melodies that themselves evolve over time. Sometimes hymn writers compose words inspired by particular tunes, while composers create original music for favorite texts.

These texts are the point at which Judaism enters and animates the worship of this churchgoing nation. The Hebrew Bible is of course the foundation of the New Testament, the Christian gospels, and the elaborate theological superstructure that has followed. We would expect some continuities, since the Christian church has seen itself as fulfilling and completing the work of the Hebrew Bible. But in surveying the range of psalms, hymns, and other sacred songs that have emerged on American soil over the last several hundred years, one is struck by the frequency with which Hebrew images, metaphors, and stories appear: the River Jordan and the land of Canaan; the language of Jerusalem, Zion, and Israel; Egyptian bondage and Babylonian captivity; the social criticism of the prophets; the panoply of human emotions explored by the Psalms of David, which have served as the model for so much Christian music. And somewhat at cross-purposes to all this, Judaism has left another inheritance: the fear of music's unpredictable powers, the suspicion that music has the potential to lead one astray. In the range of American sacred music, the figure and language of Jesus Christ have formed a relatively small part. That said, many of the teachings and parables attributed to Christ, not to mention the images and metaphors attached to him, are themselves drawn from antecedents in the Hebrew Bible. Old Testament phrases, images, and stories are what have made American sacred music so adaptable, so readily exchanged across boundaries of ethnicity, race, and religion that have proved more resistant to the flow of other cultural currencies.

And so the sacred music of this Christian nation is deeply accented by the traditions and forms of Judaism, a religion that has never included more than 4 percent of the U.S. population. But Protestant Christianity has exerted its own profound influence, not just on American Jews but on the practices of non-Christians ranging from Native Americans to Buddhists and Hindus. Practitioners of religions that traditionally do not organize themselves into local communities that meet regularly find themselves adapting to the United States by organizing themselves into the equivalent of parishes or congregations and holding weekly worship. Musically speaking, an analogous process has taken place: a musical isomorphism toward hymnody. While music is a nearly universal aspect of religious practice, hymns are not; they are a relatively late innovation even within Christianity. But they have been an exceptionally useful one, with the result that Protestant-style hymns have become a part of many non-Christian worship ceremonies, ranging from Native to Buddhist to Jewish. With some exceptions, the history of American sacred music looks like a series of footnotes to the great Protestant hymn writers of the eighteenth century. Which is not to say that those footnotes don't introduce significant variations of emphasis and technique.

There is no better way of navigating American history than by tracing the religious propensity of Americans, the role of music in worship, and the fund of texts and metaphors provided by Judaism. Sacred music doesn't explain American history. But it does allow access to the ways in which many Americans have understood and coped with their history. The implications of this relationship between faith, music, and social change extend far beyond what people do in church or synagogue on the sabbath, or in the informal devotionals that take place in the homes or neighborhoods of the pious. The interplay of beliefs and sacred songs has deeply marked the complex container of differences that we call American culture. Like any diverse society, the United States is a congeries of cultures in motion: ethnic cultures, regional cultures, religious cultures, occupational cultures, racial cultures, political cultures. Along with the imperatives of a market economy, religious conviction has been a major energy source driving the social and cultural collisions that have animated and directed the course of American history. And music—particularly sacred music—has been a crucial medium by which individuals and social groups have encountered, struggled against, learned from, and accommodated to other individuals and groups. By singing and making music, Americans wear their spiritual hearts on their sleeves.

Before I attempt to sketch the specific processes that have shaped the development of American sacred music, some definitions are in order. By *America*, I refer primarily to North America, most often the United States, but always with an understanding that the music discussed in this book was under way long before there was a United States, that the boundaries of that nation have shifted dramatically over the past two hundred–plus years, and that what we think of as America has been shaped and given substance by people who through historical contingency have ended up in other nations: most obviously the Caribbean countries, Mexico, and Canada, but other nations as well. By *sacred*, I mean that which is concerned with ultimate realities that transcend the here and now. The words *reli-*

gious and *spiritual* are closely aligned, and at times will better fit the musics under discussion. *Religious,* however, conveys a sense of the formal and the organized aspects of the world religions that are always capitalized and that constitute settled systems of beliefs. *Spiritual* suggests the other end of the continuum of the sacred: experiences of contact with the divine or the transcendent that may be attained through the auspices of organized systems or institutions of worship, but may be pursued informally or individually as well. By *music,* I mean humanly organized sound. It used to be enough to say "organized sound," but scientists have recently determined that animals produce sound that by all rights deserves the label music. Of course, human beings regularly produce sound that isn't usually considered music; recent studies have investigated the historical meanings of soundscapes, the significance of the easily forgotten sonic world on the people who lived amid those sounds.[3] But music is organized and intentional, even if the sonic product is ultimately not labeled as music by those who produce it: Muslims, for example, reject the term *music* for their extraordinary melodic calls to prayer and cantillation of the Qur'an. In sum, in writing about American sacred music, I mean to emphasize the United States within America, the religious within the spiritual, and music within sound.[4]

Rather than attempting a comprehensive survey of all sacred musics that have appeared or developed in North America, or even the United States, the following chapters present exemplary interlinked case studies to convey something of the range of religious and musical expression. At most two degrees of separation distinguish these songs and composers from one another; American sacred music begins to sound more like a coherent conversation than like a sonic Tower of Babel. No sampling of artists, songs, or recordings could be fully representative, but the ones ahead give a sense of the larger whole, and of the historical processes that have driven the development of American sacred music: origins, destinations, collisions, and boundaries.

Origins calls attention to the diasporic roots of American sacred musics, the way in which people from Europe, Africa, and Asia have brought with them from their places of origin religious belief systems and accompanying musical practices. The first wave of settlers probably arrived from Asia at least 15,000 years ago (and perhaps much earlier), followed much later by European Americans, who settled in the Caribbean, Mesoamerica, and the eastern seaboard of North America. Africans were forcibly transported to these same regions shortly afterward. Many other waves of migration have occurred in the decades before the Civil War, the turn of the nineteenth century, and since 1965. Taking North America as the geographic reference point, *destinations* refers to the outward flow of beliefs and musical practices to various points around the globe, sometimes back to their regions of origin. Streams of two-way cultural exchange have existed since the earliest days of European colonization, and before, among Native peoples. While the rate of exchange has accelerated since the second half of the twentieth century, the process is best understood as a series of cultural inhalations and exhalations, often linked to Protestant revivals. Sacred music flowed rapidly within the Anglophone world at the time of the Awakenings of the mid-1700s and early 1800s, and again after the Civil War. Revival hymns, gospel songs, African-American concert spirituals, and various forms of gospel blues and Pentecostal music have been major cultural exports from America.

Like *origins* and *destinations, collisions* and *boundaries* represent different facets of a dialectical social process. As Asians, Africans, and Europeans streamed into the Americas, they collided with groups practicing different religions and different musics. Beginning in the late fifteenth century, Europeans encountered Native peoples along the Atlantic coast in what they immediately took to calling New Spain, New England, and New France. Contacts with enslaved Africans by both groups began early in the seventeenth century. The process continued mainly in the coastal cities with the arrival of Irish in the antebellum period; Chinese, Japanese, Russian Jews, and a variety of southern and eastern Europeans in the decades around the turn of the twentieth century; and a myriad of nationalities since the revising of immigration restrictions in 1965. These contacts were sometimes violent, sometimes peaceful, often a mix of the two. Some social boundaries were dissolved while new ones were erected. People sometimes borrowed and adapted in response to differences they encountered; at other times they consolidated their sense of difference. The story of sacred music, like many others that have been told about America, is one of cross-pollination and syncretism taking place amid encounters marked by conquest and exploitation. Out of these social collisions, cultural boundaries have been challenged, redefined, reinforced, and sometimes dissolved. The musical results include Amerindian hymns, Shaker gift songs, Methodist hymns, shape-note singing, African-American spirituals, gospel songs, klezmer, and sacred jazz, to name a few.

The term and process of *crossover* capture the dynamics of religious and musical exchange. Writers about popular music use the term to describe a form of music that originates in one demographic sector and finds an enthusiastic audience in another, sometimes unexpected place. Motown (or rap) might stand as the paradigmatic crossover music, created by urban blacks but enjoying enormous popularity among suburban whites. The whole of American popular music might be told as a story of crossover, and so too that of sacred music. Because the creation of boundaries is so central to religious experience, crossover provides a useful shorthand for analyzing the complex interactions within American sacred music. Since religious beliefs are among the most prized cultural possessions of ethnic and racial communities, the crossing into other religious traditions, or different denominations within the same religion, to borrow musical forms or style is of central importance. Buddhist hymns are one product, Indian peyote songs another. Likewise, artists schooled in sacred music have crossed over into secular music-making, and have sometimes crossed back; composers of hymn tunes and gospel songs have borrowed techniques and melodies from secular music. Protestant music from the hymns of Charles Wesley to contemporary praise-and-worship songs are the result, as are the careers of artists like Sister Rosetta Tharpe, Elvis Presley, James Brown, Amy Grant, and Bob Dylan. The popularity of quasi-spiritual songs like "Amazing Grace" is another instance.

Closely related to the crossover between sacred and secular is that between commercial and noncommercial: between music created to extract earnings from a paying audience, and music created to edify and incite the religious fervor of participants, and bind them more tightly into a community of faith. Whether the deacon takes a collection or the promoter sells tickets can make an important difference. What ordinary people do during worship is most important, but what religious folk purchase or consume in less active circumstances is not irrelevant. Another subtle boundary is that separating art from ritual: music intended to be experienced by a passive spectator in contrast to music geared toward participation in which all present—whether singing or playing instruments—are brought into a quickened state of contact with the transcendent or the divine. Can music sacralize a secular space, as when John Coltrane played his spiritually charged music in nightclubs, or can inappropriate music profane a sacred space, as some critics of black gospel have complained? Sacred music is always a performance within a performance; even if no spectators are present, there is an audience.

A final area of crossover in sacred music involves male and female. In the Abrahamic faiths—Judaism, Christianity, Islam—praying and interpreting scripture have traditionally been off-limits to women. Because music is closely associated with prayer, sacred song has been proscribed for women in certain circumstances; Orthodox Jews, for example, fear the siren-song power of the female voice to inspire licentious thoughts among men. But the general tendency in sacred music has been toward inclusion and participation. Women have gained access through song to realms of religious practice that were otherwise barred to them. Beginning in the nineteenth century, evangelical Protestants, along with sects like the Shakers, provided musical openings for women, who colonized the nascent Sunday school movement. They set the tone for the gospel songs that remade the sound of Protestant worship after the Civil War. African-American gospel music hinged on the contributions of women, as did the worship music of Pentecostals. This doesn't mean, of course, that women were unconstrained in the musical realm, only that musical worship provided a space of relative autonomy that women were sometimes able to leverage for the purpose of increasing their authority in their respective communities of faith.

The term *crossover,* in its many forms, musical and social, tends to suggest peaceful, empathic sharing, a form of liberal multiculturalism in which everyone is enriched by listening to and learning from those who are different. But the examples of crossover that emerge in the chapters ahead are far from an entirely peaceful exchange. Boundaries are surveilled and enforced by those who have an interest in maintaining them. Native American sacred musics are bound up with genocide and cultural dispossession. African-American musics emerged against a backdrop of chattel slavery, religious Holocaust, and racial apartheid enforced by state-sanctioned terror. Jewish music in America developed directly out of diasporas driven by persecution and forced emigration, from Spain in the late fifteenth century, Russia in the late nineteenth century, and Nazi Germany. Moravians, Shakers, and Mormons created their music out of experiences of intolerance and persecution. American Buddhist music was shaped by nativism and exclusion beginning after the Civil War and exacerbated by World War II. Even culturally dominant Protestant music was forged in the crucible of religious persecution, revolutions, and war. Music has created bridges, to be sure, but bridges often erected in the face of dispersion and death. Sacred music is the scar tissue, fascinating and eerily beautiful, that forms over deep trauma cauterized by spirit and hope.

SAN JUAN is a small Tewa-speaking community in northern New Mexico, located along the upper Rio Grande River roughly equidistant between Albuquerque to the southwest and the Colorado border to the north. About fifty miles to the northeast lies Taos. Every year on Christmas Eve a group of about eighteen residents of San Juan Pueblo perform a pantomimed ceremony called the *matachines,* which begins after morning Mass, moves in procession from church to graveyard and through the plazas, and is repeated at various locations through Christmas Day. There are four central characters in the wordless forty-five-minute dance-drama. The most imposing figure is called *El Monarca,* the king; his partner is a small girl known as *La Malinche,* dressed in white with a diadem and high moccasins. They are joined by *El Toro,* a young boy wearing rawhide and a horned helmet, and by two clownish *Abuelos,* or grandfathers, who wear conical headpieces with painted-on faces. Completing the ensemble are ten or twelve male dancers arranged in two files and wearing masks, headdresses, and multicolored ribbons down their backs. The *matachines* begins with a musical procession, played by the two musicians, a violinist and a guitarist, who perform a series of simple songs throughout the drama. Over the course of the dance, El Monarca and La Malinche perform several movements, exchanging a rattle and a trident, while the Abuelos control the rambunctious Toro by wrestling to the ground, killing and finally castrating him. Interwoven through this drama the *danzantes* perform a variety of choreographed interweaving and crossover steps. The dance ends with a recessional, performed to the same musical piece as the opening procession.

How did the *matachines* dance originate, and what does it mean? The answers are complex, and illuminate the themes and processes that have been sketched above and will be developed in the chapters that follow. The *matachines* condenses in one dance many of the features and processes that have been important and distinctive about sacred music in America. Despite the conspicuous Native features visible in San Juan and other pueblos, the dance is of European origin, descended from the ancient Roman sword dances that were grudgingly tolerated to greater and lesser degrees by ecclesiastical authorities suspicious of their potential for burlesque and social criticism. The term *matachín* itself has a long and far-flung etymology. The Italian *matto* means fool or madman; *mattacinos* refers to fantastically costumed sword dancers of the sixteenth and seventeenth centuries. Another possible source is the Arabic *mutawajjihin,* to assume a mask. The root is also similar to the Spanish *matar,* to kill, which comes in turn from the Persian word for death, *mat* (source of chess's *checkmate*). Interestingly, the second half of the word is similar to the Persian *chine* or *chini,* which refers to China; possibly the *mattacinos* originated in comic performances of adventures of Marco Polo, who had returned from China with what were thought to be outlandish tales suitable for burlesque.[5]

Fools, masks, and death: all are present in the San Juan *matachines.* And there is another important ingredient: the legacy of conquest. The first reference to the dance in the Americas comes from Bernal Díaz, a Spanish soldier present with Cortés during their entrance to Tenochtitlán in 1519. "One part of the city was entirely occupied by Montezuma's dancers of different kinds," wrote Díaz, "some of whom bore a stick on their feet, others flew in the air, and some danced like those in Italy called by us *Matachines*." Within two years Moctezuma had been reduced to a puppet ruler, ultimately stoned to death by fellow Aztecs, and Tenochtitlán subdued. In this context the historical-etymological trail becomes more complex, because the *matachines* as practiced across southern Europe bears an obvious family resemblance to another dance: *Los Moros y Cristianos,* a mock combat celebrating the victory of the Christians over the Turks and, later, the Moors. In the religious drama, the Cross is stolen by the Moors, recaptured by heroic Christian soldiers, and finally accepted by the submissive infidels. Though distinct from the *matachines*, the mock combat *auto sacramental* determined the associations that the other dance would have. Further complicating the genealogy, similar dances are performed in North Africa as part of rituals aimed at producing rain. And the *matachines* shares important features with ritual dramas indigenous to Mesoamerica.[6]

As Spanish colonizers continued to arrive in Mexico and points north, they brought with them the songs, poems, dramas, and dances of Iberia. The *matachines* migrated slowly northward from central Mexico to the northern Rio Grande with the Spanish and Mexican Indians who gradually established settlements through the region. A conquistador named Don Juan de Oñate modeled himself on Cortés, pressing into service the same displays of pomp and circumstance that had served the earlier soldier in his conquest of the Aztecs. When he reached the village of Ohke in 1598, he renamed it San Juan de los Caballeros and staged a performance of *Los Moros y Cristianos;* afterward local Natives were required to swear obedience to the Franciscans with whom they returned to their pueblos. These Catholic missionaries quickly picked up on the potential of music and dance to facilitate the spread of Christianity among Native peoples, building on their love of the sights and sounds of pageantry. There were areas of cultural overlap that contributed to the survival of the *matachines* among Pueblos: La Malinche resembled the White Corn Goddess, a Tewa deity who also had affinities to the Virgin Mary. The Franciscans also took advantage of the fact that Advent and Christmas coincided with the beginning of the Pueblo winter cycle, the six-month half of its ritual year that began with the winter solstice and was devoted to the celebration of animal life and hunting, both key to winter subsistence. During the same days in mid-December when Pueblos prepared for the winter solstice, the Franciscans staged a series of dance dramas commemorating the stories of Mary, Joseph, and the shepherds.[7]

Though Pueblo people who actually perform the *matachines* are reluctant to offer interpretations of it, ethnographers describe it as an allegory of colonization and conquest, a "beautiful dance of subjugation." But it is also a means of seizing and symbolically inverting that same history. The characters have both Christian and aboriginal associations. La Monarca symbolizes Moctezuma, while La Malinche has obvious associations with Doña Marina, a Mayan woman of noble birth who became the first Native American convert and Cortés' interpreter, confidante, and mistress. She is remembered both as a traitor to her people and as the mother of a new people, *los mestizos*. The interplay between El Monarca and La Malinche, then, is a kind of conversion narrative, as El Monarca gropes toward Christian belief with the assistance of La Malinche. One outcome is the conquest and castration of El Toro, who is associated with humans' baser drives and instincts. Paired with El Toro are the Abuelos, who symbolize the wisdom of elders. The ten or twelve *danzantes* are taken to represent Christ's apostles, but also a platoon of soldiers. Cortés ritually welcomed a group of twelve Franciscan "Apostles" to Mexico in 1524 in front of an audience of Native peoples, symbolizing the arrival of a new regime of Christendom in the New World. Oñate reenacted the same public ritual with a contingent of twelve friars he brought with him when he entered New Mexico in 1598, in the expectation that the conquest of New Mexico would follow the same script as the earlier conquest of Mexico. Presented at Christmastime by Amerindians, many of whom are devout Catholics, the *matachines* offers an ambivalent celebration of the coming of Christianity shadowed by the history of conquest that accompanied it.[8] It is a kind of answer to the question put by Psalm 137: how to sing the Lord's song in a strange land.

Pueblo Indians are not the only group to perform *matachines*. The dance is performed widely by Mexicanos as well, with the same characters and plot but different symbolic associations. Historically, communities like San Juan, where the *matachines* continues to be performed, lay at the northern frontier of the Spanish New World empire. For more than four centuries the region's history has been deeply sedimented by the interactions of three major populations: the Pueblo; the Hispano population left by the Spanish conquest; and the Anglos from the north. San Juan was the first site of Spanish settlement in the region; its Tewa-speaking people played a major role in the Pueblo revolt of 1680, whose best-known leader, Popé, was from San Juan. Twelve years later the region was reconquered by an expedition led by Diego de Vargas. Throughout the eighteenth century, with Pueblos subdued, Spain sought to protect its lucrative silver-producing holdings in northern New Spain against nomadic Apaches and Comanches. The end of the Seven Years' War in 1763 gave Spain France's trans-

Mississippi western holdings and put Spain in direct rivalry with the English who controlled territory to the east. The year 1821 brought Mexico independence from Spain, but also opened the upper Rio Grande valley to aggressive Anglos; by 1846 the United States had annexed New Mexico. The following year, Taos was the site of another revolt, this time of Mexicanos attempting to throw off Anglo occupiers from the north.[9]

This history helps explain differences in Pueblo and Mexicano enactments and understandings of the *matachines*. Though they have shared a history, they exist on different sides of the boundary that separates the colonizing Spanish from the colonized Natives. Just as history is usually written by the victors, so the *matachines* has been scripted by the victors, at least in terms of the basic narrative and characters. For Pueblos, the *matachines* is at some level a symbol of subjugation, both military and religious, even if it has come to include oppositional meanings. The conversion of La Monarca and the castration and death of El Toro express these accents. Among Mexicanos, the parallel between the Moors and the Native Indians—neither European, civilized, nor Christian—is remembered and acted out with less ambivalence. Mexicanos are, after all, descendents of the Spanish conquerors (themselves conquered in due time by Anglos from the north). La Monarca is generally associated with Cortés rather than Moctezuma. Even the stories that the two groups tell about the origin of the *matachines* are different. Many Pueblos hold to the "Montezuma legend," the idea that the Aztec leader brought the dance north from Mexico. Mexicanos stress instead the Spanish origin of the dance, claiming that it was introduced to the northern Rio Grande by the conquering Oñate or de Vargas.[10]

Sometimes more clearly than the eye, the ear reveals differences in how these distinct but interlinked communities have adopted and adapted this ancient Old World ritual. While each pueblo and village performs its own variations, the pantomimed dance-drama usually makes use of about a half-dozen songs, played on violin and guitar. The tunes are simple, repetitive vamps, combining triplet and duplet figures in skipping rhythms that fit the dance steps they accompany. The melodies closely resemble those used for Italian *Morisque* and *Bouffons* sword dances, as well as Castilian dances of northeast Spain.[11] The songs are part of a larger field of Iberian music that was transported and developed gradually over the centuries in New Spain, including *romances, canciones,* and *corridos.*

Matachines songs symbolize the role that music plays in cultural crossover, in the dissolution and erection of boundaries. For the Pueblos, the *matachines* is unique in that it is the only regular ceremony in which European instruments and musical forms are used. Moreover, unlike the indi-

viduals selected as dancers, who are always Pueblos, the guitarist and vio-
linist are frequently Mexicanos, hired musicians who sometimes return
regularly over decades to play their part in the performance. This event
provides a rare avenue of overlap in two ethnic groupings, Pueblo and
Hispano, who exist in close proximity but maintain relatively separate
existences. *Matachines* music thus represents cultural exchange in various
guises: technologically, in the material forms used to play the music;
socially, in the individuals who play the instruments; and formally, in
the musical features of the songs themselves. Despite this exchange,
matachines songs help establish the differences in how the ceremony is
performed. Pueblos often include percussion and rattles not present in
Mexicano performances. In some pueblos, the *matachines* is performed using a male chorus and drum in place of the stringed instruments. At San
Juan, the Christmas Day *matachines* is followed on 26 December by the
pueblo's traditional Turtle dance, as if to underscore the contrast between
the borrowed and the indigenous traditions.[12]

THE *matachines* is only one example among numerous possibilities, but it
crystallizes many of the themes and processes pursued in the following
chapters. We see both how closely music is integrated into other aspects of
religious practice, and the ambiguities inherent in the very category of "sacred music." To what extent is the *matachines* a musical performance, let
alone a form of sacred music? In what sense can we consider it as American? The dance-drama clearly has its roots in a version of Spanish history
inseparable from the history of European religion, and it came to play a
part in the religious world of Catholic Christians, Spanish and Native
alike. Its ability to survive social and political disruptions since the sixteenth century testifies to a connection between the *matachines* and Native
spiritual traditions as well. In fact, it seems that its popularity among
Pueblos who abandoned polyphonic church music with the collapse of the
missions helped the drama survive among Mexicano villages as well.[13]

As a component of a dance-drama, *matachines* music reveals what is often the case among American sacred musics: that music and dance are inextricably bound. In the same way, it is impossible to distinguish ritual
from performance, collective participation from spectacle. The *matachines*
operates at various levels at the same time, holding different meanings for
its performers, for clergy, politicians, and members of the local community
who organize and attend, and for the tourists bussed in to witness a colorful spectacle. The performance disrupts boundaries of nation, religion,
ethnicity, even sexuality; roughly half the communities that perform the
matachines feature the character *Abuela*, a cross-dressed man who plays

Abuelo's clowning spouse and conspicuously gives birth to a doll of inde-
terminate ethnic ancestry (this in a season celebrating a virgin birth).[14]

And so, the *matachines* is a product of cultural exchange, but an exchange premised on naked power and brute force, not on cheery syncretism or multicultural empathy. Religious song is a response to power,
equipment for living under adverse conditions, but also an instrument of
power. It originated as part of a ruthless imperial strategy: to regularly remind the conquered of their status by making them act out a story of their
own subjugation. All the better if those subjects came to embrace it willingly. The people, however, embrace it not for its original intention, but for
its ability to contest, even to parody, that conquest; and for a host of other
reasons as well. Like so many cases in the pages that follow, sacred song is
a residue of forced removal, conquest, and exile. We see this most readily
in African-American sorrow songs and Amerindian Ghost Dance songs,
but also in the diverse hymns and gift songs of German-speaking Moravians, Shakers, Mormons, and Jews—all religious exiles from their respective homelands—and in the Buddhist hymns that bear traces of racial
exclusion, internment, and ethnic cleansing. The *matachines*, which began
at the turn of the sixteenth century as the ritual of a Native people subjugated by Spanish conquerors, became during the nineteenth century the
ritual of two peoples, Pueblos and Mexicanos, subjugated in different
ways by the dominant Anglo culture of the United States. And the dance-
drama continues to be infused with meanings from contemporary social
and political struggles over the age-old issues of land use and water rights,
as the northern Rio Grande faces continuing encroachment from the outside, driven now by the lucrative industries of tourism and retirement living.[15]

To understand why the *matachines* continues to be performed in certain
Pueblo and Mexicano communities and not others, and the particular timing and details of the performance, requires close attention to the local.
There is nothing more local than the feast day of a village's patron saint.
But the fact that the dance is performed at all suggests with equal vigor
the need to pursue historical work with the broadest possible geographic
frame. The *matachines* is the product of the most inclusive sort of transnational, even transoceanic history, drawing elements and meanings from
historical developments in the Middle East and Iberia through central and
northern Mexico into what has become the southwestern region of the
United States. In the past decade historians have redoubled their efforts to
step outside the analytical boundaries of the nation-state that have defined
the unit of historical study in recent generations, and to analyze the movements and processes that move across nations and continents. Their exam-

ple encourages us to rethink familiar national narratives by adopting a simple dictum: to follow the people, the money, the ideas, the things, all of which have a stubborn tendency to ignore national boundaries.[16] Also, to follow the songs, especially the religious ones. Organized religion is among the most transnational of all social phenomena.

The same logic explains the rather sprawling temporal frame of the following chapters. Though the narrative ranges widely over several centuries, my intention has not been to write a synthesis of American history through its hymns. Often—not always—sacred music is a dilatory eddy in one of the slowest-moving of all social products in the stream of human history. Because religious practice and music tend to be innately conservative and resistant to change, a broad temporal frame enables us to grasp patterns in how musical forms have developed. A surprising number of the spiritual songs performed by Americans in the twentieth and even the twenty-first centuries are directly linked to what their forebears sang two or three centuries earlier. People living through history experience it through different temporalities, both as part of specific communities and as individuals whose experience of change is not unitary.[17] Some experienced time as cyclical, others experienced it as linear. Many who created and performed this music, it can safely be said, were living in but not of their time. Some considered themselves the offspring of the children of Israel. Others thought they were living in biblical End Time, or that they had already entered the millennium. To these subjects we now turn.

CHAPTER ONE

O for a Thousand Tongues to Sing

> Next to theology, I give a place to music: for thereby all anger is
> forgotten, the devil is driven away, and melancholy, and many
> tribulations, and evil thoughts are expelled. It is the best solace for
> a desponding mind.
>
> —MARTIN LUTHER

THE MOST momentous encounter in the long history of sacred music in America took place on a transatlantic sea voyage between religious pilgrims who couldn't even speak the same language. One group consisted of twenty-six Moravian emigrants on their way from Germany to Georgia under the leadership of Bishop David Nitschmann. The other group comprised four young clergymen from Oxford, members of the university's Holy Club, sent by the Church of England to proselytize among Amerindians for the Society for the Propagation of the Gospel. Of them two were conscientious and pious brothers: John and Charles Wesley, aged thirty-three and twenty-eight, respectively. Their goal was simple enough. "Our end in leaving our native country," wrote John, "was not to avoid want, (God having given us plenty of temporal blessings,) nor to gain the dung or dross of riches or honour; but singly this,—to save our souls; to live wholly to the glory of God." The Wesleys had undertaken their mission at the request of General James Oglethorpe, governor of the colony of Georgia and a trustee of the Society for Propagation of the Gospel, who also helped the Moravian colonists arrange their first land allotment in Georgia. The ship, the *Simmonds,* raised its anchor on 21 October 1735 and landed on 6 February 1736. What transpired onboard during those three and a half months would profoundly affect American religious music, mainly Christian but to a surprising degree non-Christian as well, from that time to the present.

Evidently there were curiosity and mutual admiration between the English missionaries and Moravian pioneers from the beginning. John Wesley was extremely well educated, fluent in Hebrew, Latin, and Greek, but not German. Even before the *Simmonds* set sail, John, in his industrious way, took steps to change that. On 17 October, at 10:10 A.M., "I began to learn German, in order to converse with the Moravians," he announced, "men who have left all for their Master, and who have indeed learned of Him, being meek and lowly, dead to the world, full of faith and of the Holy Ghost." Throughout the voyage Wesley worked on his German daily, usually for three hours in the morning. The day before the ship sailed, three of the Moravians, including their bishop, David Nitschmann, began studying English. "The English clergyman began to teach us English in lessons an hour long," wrote Nitschmann on 21 October. On 2 November: "I spent the best part of the day studying English."[1]

The German text Wesley studied from was a hymnbook published just that year with the title, *Das Gesang-Buch der Gemeine in Herrnhut*. It was written by Count Nicholaus Ludwig von Zinzendorf, a German nobleman who for over a decade had provided a sanctuary from persecution to Moravians on his estate in Saxony. During the voyage Wesley worked his way systematically through the book. In November he began on another Moravian hymnal, this one by J. Anastasius Freylinghausen. Wesley was powerfully drawn to the German singing from the very beginning. The Moravians held their regular *Singstunde* in the evenings, according to Nitschmann, "at the same time as the English held their divine service." On Sunday, 19 October, Wesley wrote: "8 o'clock, singing with the Germans." Two days later: "At seven I joined with the Germans in their public service." The sessions quickly led to broader discussions. "During the singing session several subjects were discussed with the English clergyman, among others the decline and loss of power," wrote Nitschmann, less than two weeks after setting sail. (Both he and Wesley had recourse to Latin when they reached an impasse in their mother tongues.) "The English parson, John Wesley, misses no opportunity to attend our singing sessions," he observed on 4 December. "We wish we could converse easily so that we could show him more clearly the way to God."[2]

Wesley seems to have regarded the Moravians with a kind of awe, not simply for their music but for their spiritual gifts more generally. Devout as he was, Wesley was striving for a deeper level of piety, and felt stymied. A particularly memorable object lesson took place amid a storm that blew up as Wesley was worshipping with the Moravians at their evening service.

> In the midst of the psalm wherewith their service began, wherein we were mentioning the power of God, the sea broke over, split the mainsail in pieces, covered the ship, and poured in between the decks, as if the great deep had already swallowed us up. A terrible screaming began among the English. The Germans looked up, and without intermission calmly sang on. I asked one of

them afterwards, "Was you not afraid?" He answered, "I thank God, no." I asked, "But were not your women and children afraid?" He replied mildly, "No; our women and children are not afraid to die."[3]

Wesley's exposure to decent hymn-singing came not from the established church, where singing was not a priority, but from prayer meetings at home led by his mother for children and servants (though neighbors "begged to be allowed to attend").[4]

In contrast, the Moravians, more properly known as the Unitas Fratrum, or Unity of Brethren, had a rich tradition of congregational song, favoring deeply personal and emotive hymns. Their founder, Jan Hus, had initiated this emphasis on congregational hymn-singing and in fact had died singing as he was burned at the stake for heresy in 1415. The Brethren began publishing collected hymns in 1501, with Polish and German translations appearing in the 1550s and 1560s. After enduring periods of persecution and near-annihilation during the Thirty Years' War, they found sanctuary in 1722 on the estate of Count Zinzendorf. Moravian hymns were impassioned, full of vivid imagery of Christ's atoning blood and a nearly erotic emphasis on communion with Christ, and their gripping emotional power appealed strongly to John. During his two years with the Moravians in America, John translated thirty-three of Zinzendorf's hymns with which he had commenced his German study, and he did so brilliantly, bringing them squarely into an English idiom, as in the first Moravian hymn he translated.

O Gott, du tieffe sonder grund!	O God, Thou bottomless abyss,
wie kan ich dich zur gnüge kennen?	Thee to perfection who can know?
du grosz höh, wie soll mein mund	O height immense! What words suffice,
dich nach den eigenschafften nennen?	Thy countless attributes to show?
du bist ein unbegreifflich meer:	Unfathomable depths Thou art!
ich sencke mich in dein erbarmen.	O, plunge me in Thy mercy's sea;
Mein hertz ist rechter weisheit leer:	Void of true wisdom is my heart,
umfasse mich mit deinen armen.	With love embrace and cover me.
Ich stellte dich zwar mir	While Thee, all-infinite I set,
Und andern gerne für;	By faith before my ravish'd eye,
doch werd ich meiner schwachheit innen:	My weakness bends beneath the weight;
weil alles, was du bist,	O'erpower'd I sink, I faint, I die.
nur end und anfang ist,	
verlier ich drüber alle sinnen.[5]	

It captures exactly the sense of absolute surrender to the divine, dying to be reborn in a new relation to God, that Wesley was arduously attempting to enact in his own experience.

On landing, the two Englishmen lived with the Moravians while their own vicarage was being built, and John Wesley's amateur ethnography continued. "We had now an opportunity, day by day, of observing their whole behavior," he wrote. "For we were in one room with them from morning to night, unless for the little time I spent in walking." He marveled at their industry, cheerfulness, and good humor; it seemed "they had put away all anger, and strife, and wrath, and bitterness, and clamour, and evil-speaking." Wesley continued his study of German grammar with Bishop August Gottlieb Spangenberg, then preparing to go to Pennsylvania, with whom he was able to converse in Latin. One conversation took place two days after landing in America. "I asked his advice with regard to my own conduct. He said, 'My brother, I must first ask you one or two questions. Have you the witness within yourself? Does the Spirit of God bear witness with your spirit, that you are child of god?' I was surprised and knew not what to answer. He observed it, and asked, 'Do you know Jesus Christ?' I paused and said, I know he is the Saviour of the world. 'True;' replied he 'but do you know he has saved you?' I answered, I hope he has died to save me. He only added, 'Do you know yourself?' I said, I do. But I fear they were vain words." The Wesleys were welcomed by friendly Amerindians, including Tomo-chachi, a Creek chief who had earlier been brought by Oglethorpe to meet George II in England. The chief spoke of his desire to have the Christian gospel brought to his people, but complained of the confusion wrought by competing French and Spanish colonists apparently bent on war. "The English traders, too, put us into confusion, and have set our people against hearing the Great Word," he told John Wesley. "For they speak with a double tongue; some say one thing of it and some another. Yet I am glad you are come. I will go up and speak to the wise men of our nation; and I hope they will hear."[6]

Meanwhile John Wesley continued to improve his German. In May he began translating one of his favorite books, William Law's *Christian Perfection,* into German. But mainly he lived and breathed hymns—singing, translating, composing. His diary reveals "the grip which hymns took upon his mind and heart, when once he had caught the fervor of Moravian Hymnody."[7] He sang constantly as he walked and traveled by boat between Savannah and Frederica, working the hymns into pastoral visits, bedside vigils, devotional meetings. He memorized the unfamiliar German hymns on his flute so that he would remember the melodies after his time with the Moravians was over. Intoxicated by these hymns, Wesley lived a kind of double life in Georgia, half English Anglican, half German Moravian. Five of the Moravian hymns he translated appeared in a *Collection of Hymns and Psalms* published in Charleston in 1737, which was the first hymnbook (not psalmbook) published in America.

The Wesleys' new home, Georgia, was not congenial to the life of the mind. The Georgia that they encountered was the roughest sort of colonial outpost, literally, it seemed, at the edge of nowhere, a difficult place for refined Oxford graduates whose idea of recreation was reading the New Testament in Greek and translating theological tomes. But in its own way Savannah was a strikingly cosmopolitan place and, so it seemed, a fertile ground for the Wesleys' energetic evangelism. Its population of just over 500 included French, Spanish, and Jews in addition to English and German; fewer than one-third belonged to the Church of England. England had encouraged missionary work and settlement by the Moravians partly as a Protestant bulwark against Spaniards and French colonists. The Wesleys' potential sheep were in every sense a "motley crew"; many of the British colonists had been repatriated from debtor prisons, and Savannah had a population of Irish felons. Having learned German, Wesley went on to learn Spanish, Italian, and conversational French, and included his translations of a French and a Spanish hymn in the Charleston *Collection.* "I began learning Spanish, in order to converse with my Jewish parishioners," he wrote in April 1737, "some of whom seem nearer the mind that was in Christ than many of those who call Him Lord."[8]

Hymns provided an invaluable spiritual lubricant, as journal entries from October 1736 reveal. "Finding there were several Germans at Frederica who, not understanding the English tongue, could not join in our public service, I desired them to meet me at my house; which they did every day at noon from thence forward," Wesley wrote. "We first sung a German hymn; then I read a chapter in the New Testament; then explained it to them as well as my little skill in the tongue would allow." A few French from Savannah begged for a service to be held in their language, as large numbers of people there did not understand English.

> Sun. 30.—I began to do so; and now I had full employment for that holy-day. The first English prayers lasted from five till half an hour past six. The Italian, which I read to a few Vaudois, began at nine. The second service for the English, including the sermon and the Holy Communion, continued from half an hour past ten, till about half an hour past twelve. The French service began at one. At two I catechized the children. About three began the English service. After this was ended, I had the happiness of joining with as many as my largest room would hold, in reading, prayer, and singing praise. And about six, the service of the Moravians, so called, began, at which I was glad to be present, not as a teacher, but a learner.[9]

Among the English and French settlers Wesley might exercise his authority as a clergyman of standing, but with the Moravians he remained always subservient, in awe of their manifest piety.

During their American mission, the Wesley brothers were appalled by the treatment of enslaved Africans there. Charles's journal reveals him to be particularly shocked by slavery. "It were endless to recount all the shocking instances of diabolical cruelty these men (as they call themselves) daily practice upon their fellow-creatures; and that on the most trivial occasions," he wrote as he prepared to leave the colony. "These horrid cruelties are the less to be wondered at, because the government itself countenances and allows them to kill their slaves, by the ridiculous penalty appointed for it, of about eleven pounds sterling, half of which is usually saved by the criminal's informing on himself. This I can look upon as no other than a public act to indemnify murder."[10] With General Oglethorpe, both Wesleys stood resolutely against introducing chattel slavery to Georgia, where it was still illegal. John's trips to South Carolina beginning in July 1736 brought him into contact with several enslaved Africans who profoundly affected Wesley's views and strategies as a missionary. One conversation in particular, a lengthy exchange about Christian faith with Nanny, a receptive bondwoman from Barbados he met on a plantation at St. Bartholomew's, stimulated Wesley enormously. "In the last months of his American ministry, and in his vehement denunciation of chattel slavery thereafter, giving the gospel to slaves was a constant, recurrent goal he seemed scarcely able to get out of his mind." As it turned out, the Wesleys' stay in Georgia coincided with a period of agitation among enslaved Africans and other bondpeople in that colony and in South Carolina. Insurrections broke out in Charleston in 1737, 1738, 1740, and most famously in the Stono Rebellion of 1739, when absconding slaves burned houses en route to freedom in Spanish Florida. For its part, Savannah in 1736 barely averted an uprising by transported Irish felons who organized a "Red String Conspiracy" to burn the city before escaping. The religious revivals of the 1730s and 1740s were part of the incendiary mix that resulted in a wave of leveling uprisings across the Atlantic World.[11]

Despite their good intentions, enthusiasm, and formidable intellectual training, the Wesleys seem to have been notably ill-starred in their American sojourn. Things went quickly awry, particularly for Charles, whose bouts of dysentery were compounded with the depression he suffered even before landing in Georgia. Both Wesleys had hoped to evangelize Indians, but found themselves ministering to contentious Europeans instead. The brothers made enemies among those English colonists who resented their ceaseless preaching, praying, and exhorting. John was a temperance man whose first act on landing in Georgia was to stave casks of rum. The fact that he eschewed meat didn't add to his popularity. Both brothers ran afoul of a volatile woman named Hawkins, wife of a surgeon, who successfully stirred tension between Oglethorpe and Charles, who served as the governor's secretary. "The gossip ran rife; to the general she whispered of Wesley's traitorous attitudes, and to the pastor she revealed the general's reputed adulteries. After less than three weeks in the country Charles's parishioners avoided him on the town's only street, and the servants returned his linen unwashed." Both brothers seem to have been unsuited to the task of evangelizing among polyglot settlers struggling to win a toehold in primitive conditions. "I was not only a member of the Church of England in my youth but bigottedly devoted to her and I believed that none save members of it could be saved," John Wesley would later write. "Whilst I was abroad, in Georgia, I observed every article of Church doctrine, even at the risk of endangering my life." Colonists regarded John as "almost a fanatic." He was suspected of harboring Roman Catholic sympathies on account of his refusal to admit dissenting Protestants to communion. He also accepted Roman Catholic saints and pressed for the introduction of rites. To top it off, John awkwardly mishandled a relationship with the niece of the chief magistrate of Savannah. Having passed up marriage while at Oxford, he found himself romantically entangled with the eighteen-year-old. "God commanded me to tear out my right eye," John explained later, "which I decided to do but, as I hesitated, my lady friend did what I could not." She abruptly married another man and left Georgia.[12]

In August 1737 John was presented with a list of grievances by the Grand Jury for Savannah. The first item complained about his alteration of metrical psalms; the second charged him with "introducing into the church and service at the Altar composition of psalms and hymns not inspected or authorized by any proper judicature." In desperation, Wesley wrote to his friend George Whitefield. "Only Mr. Delamotte is with me, till God shall stir up the hearts of some of His servants, who, putting their lives in His hands, shall come over and help us, where the harvest is so great and the labourers are so few," he wrote. "What if thou art the man, Mr. Whitefield?"[13] In February 1738 John rejoined his brother in England. Neither would set foot in America again.

John Wesley considered the mission to America a failure. "I went to America, to convert the Indians," he reflected on the voyage home; "but oh, who shall convert me? Who, what is he that will deliver me from this evil heart of unbelief? I have a fair summer religion. I can talk well; nay, and believe myself, while no danger is near. But let death look me in the face, and my spirit is troubled. Nor can I say, 'To die is gain'!" Others took a more sanguine view of the experiment. George Whitefield, an enormously successful evangelist in both Britain and North America, departed England on his first tour of the colonies on the same day that John Wesley returned, and his first stop was Georgia. "The good Mr. John Wesley has done in America, under God, is inexpressible," he wrote in his journal. "His name is very precious among the people, and he has laid such a foundation that I hope neither men nor devils will ever be able to shake." By this he meant the establishment of the small devotional societies served by itinerant ministers that proved so effective in reaching rural America's far-flung parishioners. They evolved ultimately into the circuit system, a key ingredient in Methodism's success toward the end of the eighteenth century and after. "In less than two years he had made considerable progress toward the development of the Methodist system—the circuit, the society, the itinerant ministry, and lay leadership—that was destined to play a crucial part in the journey of African Americans to a new faith and, in general, in the making of Methodism."[14] Picking up where Wesley left off, Whitefield developed some close associations with Moravians, took up Wesley's ministry among enslaved Africans, and went on to be a key figure, along with Jonathan Edwards, in the Christian awakening that swept through the American colonies during the 1740s.

The Wesleys continued their association with Moravians on their return to England. They met and conversed extensively with Peter Böhler, a young missionary on his way to South Carolina to evangelize among enslaved Africans. During the summer they traveled through Germany to the Moravian headquarters at Herrnhut. Within a few months both underwent long-awaited and famous conversion experiences. On 24 May, John Wesley was at a religious meeting in Aldersgate Street where an English Moravian was reading a text by Martin Luther: "About a quarter to nine, while he was describing the change which God works in the heart through faith in Christ, I felt my heart strangely warmed. I felt I did trust in Christ, Christ alone for salvation; and an assurance was given me that He had taken away *my* sins, even *mine,* and saved *me* from the law of sin and death." With the conversions came a dramatic about-face in the roles of the two brothers. "For John, the experience marked the end of his translation work; for Charles, the beginning of his hymn writing," observes Nuelsen. "It seems as if Charles' poetic urge had slumbered till then . . . John on the other hand translated no more after his own remarkable experience. All his poetic work on German, French and Spanish hymns date from before his conversion." Charles went on to become one of the most prolific of all Protestant hymn writers, authoring some 6,500 hymn texts (some estimates range as high as 9,000). They include some of the most frequently collected in the American Protestant tradition.[15]

One source of appeal of Charles Wesley's hymns is their ability to mediate between individual and collective experience. The "we" and "our" is reunited with the "I" and "my." This was something learned from the Moravians. "The Gospel hymn changes in his hands to the hymn of Wit-

ness, of Wooing, of Praise for the universal salvation wrought by Christ,"
Nuelsen explains. "Through the 'We' he is forced to the 'Me,' and 'Me'
forces him back to 'We.'" Wesley considered himself a kind of musical
warrior for Christ. One famous story has Charles preaching in London
and being shouted down by a gang of drunken sailors singing a scabrous
music-hall ditty about the exploits of a Nancy Dawson. Liking the tune
(probably a variation of "Pop! Goes the Weasel"), Wesley challenged the
sailors to come back later to hear his sacralized version. Expecting further
mirth, according to legend, the sailors found themselves unexpectedly won
to the faith. The hymn includes a rationale for hymn-writing that recurs
throughout the history of evangelical Christian music in America: Why
should the devil have all the good music?

Listed into the Cause of Sin,
Why should a Good be Evil?
Musick, alas! Too long has been
Prest to obey the Devil:
Drunken, or lewd, or light the Lay
Flow'd to the Soul's Undoing,
Widen'd, and strew'd with Flowers
  the Way
Down to Eternal Ruin

Come let us try if Jesus's Love
Will not as well inspire us:
This is the Theme of Those above,
This upon Earth shall fire us.
Say, if your Hearts are tun'd to sing,
Is there a Subject greater?
Harmony as its Strains may bring,
Jesus's Name is sweeter.[16]

Despite his relinquishment of hymn-writing to his brother, John continued
to wield influence over Methodist hymnody. He came to dislike what he
considered the almost sickly sensualism of many of Zinzendorf's hymns—
"so erotic that they are more suitable to the mouth of a lover than in that
of a sinner standing in the presence of Almighty God," he thought. John
reined in similar tendencies in his brother's hymns. In 1741 he would
break with the Unitas Fratrum on theological grounds. But he continued
to be a firm proponent of congregational song. "Sing all . . . Sing lustily . . .
Sing modestly . . . sing in time . . . sing spiritually," he exhorted. As Methodism became the dominant force in American religion in the next century,
so did hymns: "an aid to edification, a powerful means of propaganda,
but much more than this," Nuelson writes. "From the hymn Methodists
acquired theological knowledge and gained their acquaintance with the
Scriptures. It served them as prayer-book, as school-book, as catechism . . .
The Hymn book was the catechism of the Methodist Revival."[17]

THE Methodist revival would not arrive until late in the century, however.
Not until two generations after the Wesleys returned to England would
their hymns have any appreciable impact on the religious lives of Ameri-

cans. The legal trouble John Wesley had encountered in Georgia, where he was charged with altering psalms and introducing unauthorized hymns, was symptomatic of some of the tensions generated by the evangelical enthusiasms of the 1740s and 1750s, revivals that Whitefield credited the Wesleys with helping initiate. But the roots of those conflicts in turn extended back to the earliest English immigration to North America, and before that to the confessional schisms that convulsed Europe during the sixteenth and seventeenth centuries. Anglo-American church song was for the first two centuries embroiled in three distinct but interlocking controversies. The first was over the appropriateness of singing hymns, as opposed to "Psalms of David," in regular congregational worship. The second concerned the question of faithfulness to literal translation of sacred texts over and against aesthetic and practical considerations of singability. The third centered on the desirability of establishing stricter musical guidelines for congregational singing by rooting out loose, idiosyncratic unison singing in favor of a more refined and regulated approach. Because sacred song was at the experiential core of worship for a majority of American Christians, these controversies took several generations to emerge, evolve, and be resolved.

The apparently mundane but contentious question—which version of metrical psalms to use in worship—was only one manifestation of a fundamental divide in the Protestant world, between those who followed the German theologian Martin Luther and those who descended from his Swiss counterpart John Calvin. Luther loved German folk songs and Latin hymns, and he enjoyed singing in the family and church; he saw the potential of sacred music for elevating the experience of worship and tended to be tolerant, even encouraging, of innovation in liturgical music. Calvin was less charmed by the French folk songs he knew, more skeptical about encouraging people to express their piety through song and music. The Reformed tradition he inspired might be called strict constructionist on the issues of interpreting scriptural injunctions about music in worship; anything not specifically endorsed in the Bible was to be avoided. As in most cases, the Bible could send mixed messages (something Jewish musicians and cantors had been contending with for more than a millennium). Scripture made plenty of salutary references to joyful singing and music-making, but offered discouraging subtexts as well. "Let the word of Christ dwell in you richly in all wisdom; teaching and admonishing one another in psalms and hymns and spiritual songs, singing with grace in your hearts to the Lord," Paul had urged in Colossians 3:16. Yet to the followers of Calvin, even such apparently enthusiastic encouragement of singing did not provide carte blanche to perform all manner of ostensibly spiritual songs; some interpreted the passage to be advocating only silent song. And so within the Reformed tradition that shaped the Protestant liturgy in England and Scotland and eventually British North America, there arose a continuum, pitting those inclined to favor certain flexibility with the singing of scripture against those who felt that any form of congregational singing constituted a "set form" that "quenched the Spirit," and the less human tinkering with the divine word, the better. For the great majority the domain of the possible was defined by metrical psalms—the Old Testament Psalms of David, that is, translated and arranged into regular lines and stanzas—performed in church without instrumental accompaniment. The debate over church music effectively turned on how much poetic license was to be granted in translating the canon of David's psalms.[18]

Those western European immigrants trickling into North America during the seventeenth century had a variety of translations to draw upon. The first English volume to appear was the *Book of Psalms, Englished both in prose and metre,* published in 1612 by Henry Ainsworth, an English Puritan living in the Netherlands, and brought with the Pilgrims aboard the *Mayflower* to Plymouth. "Wee refreshed ourselves after our eares with singing of Psalmes . . . there being many of the Congregation very expert in music," remembered one Pilgrim of their departure from Leyden. The Ainsworth collection was relatively artful from both a literary and a musical standpoint; the translations were graceful, and the book contained fifteen meters and thirty-nine tunes, a substantial number. The Boston Puritans desired greater simplicity. In 1636, only six years after establishing their "City upon a hill," they founded Harvard College and commissioned a new psalmbook reducing the number of meters to six, bringing a corresponding reduction in tune possibilities. They also sought a higher standard of literalness. Its editors described it as "a plaine and familiar translation of the Psalmes . . . [we] have not soe much as presumed to paraphrase to give the sense of his meaning in other words; we have therefore attended heerin as our chief guide the originall, shunning all additions." Appearing in 1640, the *Bay Psalm Book* was the first English book published in America, and it dominated congregational worship in New England for several generations; by 1744 a twenty-sixth edition had been printed. "The Churches of New-England admit not into their Publick Services, any other than the Psalms, Hymns and Spiritual Songs, of the Old and New Testament, faithfully translated into English Metre," Cotton Mather could declare in 1726. "No, not so much as the Te Deum," which, he pointed out, had not entered the monkish canon until the mid-sixth century.[19]

This was the conservative context into which the innovative psalm col-

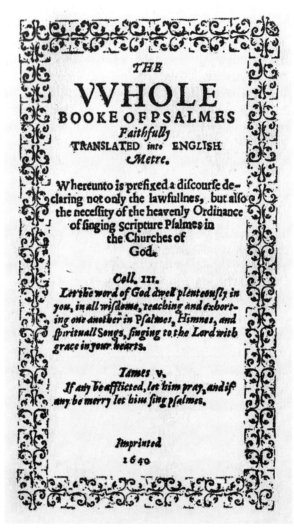

THE

VVHOLE
BOOKE OF PSALMES

Faithfully
TRANSLATED *into* ENGLISH
Metre.

Whereunto is prefixed a difcourfe declaring not only the lawfullnes, but alfo
the neceffity of the heavenly Ordinance
of finging Scripture Pfalmes in
the Churches of
God.

Coll. III.
*Let the word of God dwell plenteoufly in
you, in all wifdome, teaching and exhorting one another in Pfalmes, Himnes, and
fpirituall Songs, finging to the Lord with
grace in your hearts.*

Iames v.
*If any be afflicted, let him pray, and if
any be merry let him fing pfalmes.*

Imprinted
1640

1. Published at newly founded Harvard, the *Bay Psalm Book* was the first English-language book printed in America and went through dozens of editions over the ensuing century. Courtesy of Fine Arts Library, Michigan State University.

lection by a young English dissenter named Isaac Watts entered early in the eighteenth century. Born in 1674, Watts was a brilliant poet and philosopher, a distinguished pastor, and one of the most popular writers of the eighteenth century. As one historian of music puts it, "The poetry of Watts took the religious world of dissent by storm." Though he never visited America, he would become the single most important figure in the history of Protestant church music. During the eighteenth century he was the most widely read author in America, with his two major works, *Psalms of David Imitated* and *Hymns and Spiritual Songs,* going through seventy-four and thirty-four editions, respectively. These songs would dominate American Protestant worship for a century and a half. Of the most frequently published evangelical hymns between 1737 and 1860, eight of the top twenty were by Watts; the next closest, Charles Wesley, had two. Of the seventy-one most-published hymns, Watts wrote twenty-six—more than a third.[20] But this success would come later. As a young man at the turn of the eighteenth century, Watts was disturbed by the indifference to psalm-singing he observed during worship in England. Rather than blaming the worshippers, he held the psalms themselves partially responsible. "Some of 'em are almost opposite to the Spirit of the Gospel: Many of them foreign to the State of the New-Testament, and widely different from the present Circumstances of Christians," he wrote in the preface to an innovative collection of songs for worship he published in 1719. "Hence it comes to pass that when spiritual Affections are excited within us, and our Souls are raised a little above this Earth in the beginning of a Psalm, we are check'd on a sudden in our Ascent toward Heaven by some Expressions that are more suited to the Days of *Carnel Ordinances,* and fit only to be sung in the *Worldly Sanctuary* . . . Thus by keeping too close to *David* in the House of God, the Vail of *Moses* is thrown over our Hearts."[21] While psalms ought to be read and heard as God's word to human beings, they should be sung as the thoughts and language of Christians to God. In order to "accommodate" psalms to Christian worship, Watts insisted, "'tis necessary to divest *David and Asaph,* etc. of every other character but that of a *Psalmist and a Saint, and to make them always speak the common sense and language of a Christian.*"[22] The result was a path-marking volume titled *Psalms of David Imitated in the Language of the New Testament.*

Watts's liberties generated resistance on various grounds, both in Great Britain and the American colonies. Among older psalm collections, the *Bay Psalm Book* loomed as a formidable rival for the loyalty of English colonists. It took Watts's collection decades to penetrate the colonies. Though Watts had an eye on the New England market and corresponded with influential Puritans like Cotton Mather, the first reprint, published in 1729 by Benjamin Franklin, failed to sell. (Though no churchgoer, Franklin as a printer would play a role in several important developments in eighteenth-century religious music.) The first Boston reprint appeared in 1741, followed by one in New York in 1754. But his innovations in psalmody, while radical, were not unprecedented, at least in generating tension between tradition and reform. Because they responded to a widely perceived problem and displayed an undeniable rugged art, they were accepted quickly in England. Watts's bolder and more controversial innovation actually came a decade before *Psalms of David Imitated,* in the collection *Hymns and Spiritual Songs* (1707). Here Watts's challenge to Reformed tradition was more direct, for "man-made" hymns were exactly what Calvin had sought to eliminate from worship. Both *psalm* and *hymn* are derived from Greek (*psalmos* and *hymnos*) and generally are virtually synonymous. But following Calvin, psalms had come to stand for a particular type of biblical hymn. (Interestingly, *psalmos* derives from the Greek verb *psallein,* to play the harp, giving the word associations with instrumental music that were anathema to those who followed the strict Calvinist line on church music.) Hymns might be inspired by scripture, but they were composed by mortals, and this fact disqualified them from the meetinghouse.

Fortunately hymns had other uses besides congregational worship; they were, after all, pious poetry and might be profitably enjoyed as literature, even by liturgical conservatives. "By the gracious Providence of God, it is come to pass, that the religious, ingenious and sweet-spirited *Isaac Watts,* hath sent me the new Edition of his *Hymns;* wherein the Interest of Piety are most admirably suited," wrote Cotton Mather in 1711. "I receive them as a Recruit and a Supply sent from Heaven for the Devotions of my Family. There will I sing them, and endeavour to bring my Family in love with them."[23] For an orthodox Puritan, the family hearth, or perhaps devotional gatherings outside of formal worship, were appropriate places for such departures from the psalms. But the distinction was not simply one between sacred space—where the strict line inherited from Calvin held sway—and domestic space, where a more inclusive musical repertory could be tolerated, part-singing rather than unison singing practiced, and instruments played. Even special meetings of the church, such as the revival meetings that were beginning to energize worship in the colonies, could appropriate settings for hymns. The issue was not simply where, but when.

Singing was a key ingredient in the spiritual outpouring of the Great Awakening's revivals, specifically the singing of Watts and the traditional metrical psalms. Though Wesley's *Collection of Psalms and Hymns* appeared in 1737, it was in no way a Methodist hymnal; nearly half of its seventy-eight hymns were authored by Watts. The volume included seven translations by John, and not a single text by Charles. Whitefield, who more than anyone else set the tone and style of the revivals, incorporated congregational singing into his dramatic performances. Whitefield, however, "was no singing evangelist, and never a propagandist of the Methodist Hymnody: he preferred a sober strain of song, and greatly admired Watts' *Psalms and Hymns.*" As did Jonathan Edwards, the leading American evangelist of the period. Reflecting on the revivals at Northampton, Massachusetts, before 1740, Edwards wrote:

> Our public praises were then greatly enlivened: God was then served in our psalmody, in some measure in the beauty of Holiness. It has been observable, that there has been scarcely any part of divine worship, wherein good men amongst us have had grace so drawn forth, and their hearts so uplifted in the ways of God, as in singing his praises. Our congregation excelled all that I ever knew in the external part of the duty before, generally carrying regularly and well, three parts of music, and the women a part by themselves. But now they were evidently wont to sing with unusual elevation of heart and voice, which made the duty pleasant indeed.[24]

Hymn-singing did become embroiled in the sectarian schisms of the revival, with ministers like Charles Chauncy of Boston, an influential opponent of the revivals, decrying what he considered the rowdy and unseemly recreational singing of hymns outside of church. Though Edwards, after "long consideration," found no objection to such spiritual street-singing, he did balk at the abandonment of psalms in worship. For his church in Northampton he arranged a compromise whereby the ratio of psalms to hymns was fixed: of the three Sabbath services, worshippers were limited to singing "an Hymn, or part of a Hymn of Dr. Watts', the last time, *viz:* at the conclusion of afternoon exercise."

The process by which hymns came to be incorporated in regular worship services was a long and uneven one, varying by region and denomination in both Great Britain and New England. Throughout most of the eighteenth century, the singing of hymns was allowed in most churches only during revivals or for holidays or special services. Watts's hymns were nearly always the first to be adopted and often remained the only acceptable alternative to metric psalms. While evidence of congregational practice (as opposed to hymnbook inclusion) is scant, it appears that hymn-singing during regular worship occurred first among Methodists and Baptists, spreading later to Congregationalists, Presbyterians, and Dissenters, and finally, at around the beginning of the nineteenth century, to the Church of England and the Episcopal Church.[25]

THERE was the question of what was to be sung, and when and where it was to be sung. But there was yet another pressing issue: How was it to be sung? Beginning around 1720 reports began surfacing in the Boston area about the quality of singing in the churches. Primarily the work of Congregational ministers, these reports were laden with a hyperbole that now makes for amusing reading. Psalm tunes, wrote the Reverend Thomas Walter,

> are now miserably tortured, and twisted, and quavered, in some Churches, into a horrid Medly of confused and disorderly Noises . . . Our Tunes are . . . left to the Mercy of every unskilful Throat to chop and alter, twist and change, according to their infinitely divers and no less odd Humours and Fancies . . . much time is taken up in shaking out these Turns and Quavers; and besides, no two men in the Congregation quaver alike, or together; which sounds in the Ears of a good Judge, like Five Hundred different Tunes roared out at the same time, whose perpetual interferings with one another, perplexed Jars, and unmeasured Periods, would make a Man wonder at the false Pleasure which they conceive.[26]

What had produced this hideous disfiguring of the psalms? Psalm tunes had been a relatively uncontroversial area of practice. After two centuries of gimlet-eyed attention to the language of psalm texts, this controversy centered instead on melody, or the lack thereof. In terms of matching text to tune, Protestant psalmody can be understood as a system of interchangeable parts. Scripture was set to any of a number of metric patterns determined by the number of feet or syllables per line, and lines per stanza. Hence "common meter" included four-line stanzas with alternating eight- and six-foot lines:

> I love the Lord, because he doth
>   my voice & prayer heare.
> And in my dayes will call, because
>   he bow'd to mee his eare.   (Psalm 116)

"Short meter" stanzas were four lines: six, six, eight, and six feet long.

> The heavens doe declare
>   the majesty of God
> Also the firmament shews forth
>   his handy-work abroad.   (Psalm 19)

"Long meter" denoted four lines with an even eight feet in each line.

> Lord in thy wrath rebuke me not,
>   nor in thy hot wrath chasten me.
> Pitty me Lord, for I am weak.
>   Lord heale me, for my bones vext be.   (Psalm 6)[27]

Any psalm arranged in common meter, then, could be set to any tune that followed that pattern of lines and feet. Psalm imitators like Watts did not write tunes; they relied on preexisting melodies, often with lengthy lineages and traceable to distinguished composers and arrangers: Richard Allison, Louis Bourgeois, Thomas Ravenscroft, William Damon. Psalmbooks generally included text only; in America, the *Ainsworth Psalter* (1612) had included tunes, but the *Bay Psalm Book* contained no musical notation until 1698. Congregations (or their worship leaders) had the opportunity to choose among different tunes, which had proper names like "York," "Windsor," or "Martyr's." Only over long periods would specific psalms became associated with particular tunes.

The authors of psalters from John Calvin to Isaac Watts had intended their songs to be sung in unison by literate congregations with at least a rudimentary knowledge of music. But few congregants in New England possessed even this minimal knowledge after the first generation; in many communities psalmbooks, and the musical literacy required to follow the tunes, were rare. A common solution was a practice known as "lining-out," which by a slow process of historical accretion had resulted in a new musical practice by the eighteenth century that became known as "Usual Way" singing. In the majority of churches, as the supply of psalmbooks dwindled or the ability to read music faded, a new technique was adopted. A line or two of the psalm would be sung or, more often, spoken by a deacon, after which the congregation would sing back the passage in unison. That was the hope. But without a strong musical leader or instrument to set the tune, the psalm lines would become highly stylized. People would sing different notes, sometimes placing the words on different beats. Parishioners might sing the same words at the same time, but to different psalm tunes. Tempos slowed dramatically, such that a singer might expect to take a breath or even two in the course of singing a single word. Institutional memory confronted the vagaries of oral culture.

At the Westminster Assembly of 1644, English Puritans had authorized the practice of "deaconing," or lining-out. The following year the Dutch Reformed church in New York ordered that the church precentor line out the hymn, a procedure recommended in a treatise written by Puritan divine John Cotton in 1647. From the perspective of the more cultivated proponents of what came to be called "Regular Singing," this practice had become a disgrace. The problem was not merely aesthetic; the parroting of psalms too often led worshippers to perform them in such a way that their meaning was lost or even subverted. Reformers such as Thomas Symmes called for a campaign in musical literacy, training in both how to read music and how to produce more pleasingly the intended words of praise and to blend with other voices.[28]

In 1721 two important guides to Regular Singing appeared in Boston: Thomas Walter's *Grounds and Rules of Musick, Explained,* and John Tuft's *Introduction to the Singing of Psalm-Tunes.* These works, and the singing schools that sprang up to implement their musical reforms, generated heated controversies among Calvinist New Englanders through the Revolution. Debates over the use of hymns and psalms, and over performance practices of Usual Way lining-out and Regular Singing, anticipated and rehearsed social, cultural, and theological tensions that would come to a head in the revivals of the 1740s. Regular Singing effectively democratized congregational singing, empowering both younger church members and women, who were more likely to have the requisite training, and it was more likely to be adopted in churches located in more cosmopolitan, often urban communities. Its adherents tended to be wildly enthusiastic about Watts. Usual Way singing, with its elder-led lining-out, maintained a stronghold in more traditional rural churches (which were also, it turned out, the hotbeds of New Light revivals).[29] The singing school movement and the resistance to it inspired considerable public debate and acrimony, but within a couple of generations it had reshaped the terrain of Protestant sacred music in New England. From the gradual increase in musical literacy came the seeds of the choir, and the slow transformation of sacred music from ritual to performance in many churches. Lining-out largely disappeared from New England after 1800, although it continued to the south and west for generations. But long before that, the hymns and psalms of Watts had found their way to a new constituency that would preserve Usual Way singing longer than any other.

Virtually since their first arrival in North America, enslaved Africans had received religious instruction and participated in psalm-singing. A 1648 Massachusetts law stipulated that "children and servants" be instructed in "the grounds and principles of Religion." Toward the end of the century, Cotton Mather and John Eliot, the latter known for his evangelism among Native Americans, organized programs of religious instruction for bondpeople that included psalmody. Similar efforts were under way in New Amsterdam in the Dutch Reformed Church, which petitioned for schoolmasters to provide religious education for "both Dutch and blacks" and included in teachers' contracts this stipulation: "School shall begin with the Lord's prayer, and close by singing a Psalm." The Society for the Propagation of the Gospel, the English agency that sent John and Charles Wesley to Georgia, included psalm-singing in their work in New York, particularly at Trinity Church. "I have got our Clark to raise a Psalm when their instruction is over, and I can scarce express the satisfaction I have in seeing 200 Negroes and White Persons with heart and voice glorifying their Maker," wrote the Reverend Richard Charlton in 1745. The missionary society was also active in southern colonies. "The Negroes . . . have an Ear for Musick, and a kind of extatic Delight in *Psalmody;* and there are no Books they learn so soon or take so much pleasure in, as those used in that heavenly Part of divine Worship," reported Presbyterian missionary evangelist (and future president of the College of New Jersey) Samuel Davies in 1755. "My landlord tells me, when he waited on the colonel at his county seat two or three days, they heard the Slaves at worship in their lodge, singing Psalms and Hymns in the evening, and again in the morning, long before break of day," commented another missionary. "They are excellent singers, and long to get some of Dr. Watts' Psalms and Hymns, which I encouraged them to hope for."[30]

Though African-American psalm-singing was under way long before Watts was widely available in the colonies, his hymns quickly became favorites of slaves. Missionaries placed orders for Watts along with Bibles to Society headquarters in London. A Reverend Hutson in 1758 offered thanks to the Society for a shipment of books, "especially the Bibles, Dr. Watts' Psalms and Hymns, and the Compassionate Address." Two years later a different missionary reported being "obliged to turn sundry empty away who have come to me for Watts Psalms and Hymns."[31] Psalms were sung in New England meetinghouses, of course, where slaves and servants were seated separately from free whites, often in an attic. But they were sung outside of church as well: at public occasions like Election Day, at weddings and funerals, at private social gatherings, and within the family. In the South, where African-American slaves were frequently prohibited from practicing Christianity, or at the least segregated from white worshippers, "Dr. Watts" became a crucial part of the clandestine worship services often conducted in secret "hush harbors" (or "bush arbors") where spirituals took shape. The influence of Watts was probable in "another set of hymns, the words of which the plantation negro himself composed entirely at the beginning. They are usually short-metred, poetical descriptions of familiar Bible incidents, some of them of incredible length, and bristling with anachronisms," wrote Fredric Louis Ritter in 1884. "The blacks call this class of hymns 'figurated' from the Bible; and I have heard one which was descriptive of the battle of Christian and Apollyon, and consequently 'figurated' from Bunyan."[32]

The lining-out that had so exercised reformers and had been eradicated from New England by the nineteenth century—the long, slow, highly ornamented versions in which each syllable was drained for every ounce of musical value before singers moved to the next one—has continued among African-American congregations, even to the present. Consider the Blue Spring Missionary Baptist Association, which includes ten rural Baptist churches from southwest Georgia and is featured in the popular gospel music anthology *Wade in the Water*. Of their four performances, one is introduced as a "Dr. Watts" hymn. "But we know now this sermon will not be completed unless we can hear from Dr. Watts," the deacon intones, before leading a rendition of "A Charge to Keep I Have." The short-meter hymn (6.6.8.6) is raised by the deacon two lines at a time: the congregation, following in a hard-edged bluesy, melismatic, embellished style, with moans and handclapping, takes nearly a minute to complete each installment.

> A charge to keep I have, A God to glorify
> Who gave his Son my soul to save, And fit it for the sky.
> To serve the present age, My calling to fulfill,
> O may it all my pow'rs engage, To do my Master's will.

The entire hymn spans four minutes. It is somehow fitting that the hymn raised by the Blue Spring Association was actually composed not by Isaac Watts but by Charles Wesley, who along with John was violently affected by his brief encounter with chattel slavery in South Carolina, and whose obscure 1737 hymn collection foreshadowed the profound impact of the beloved Dr. Watts on African-American worship.

WHEN Timothy Dwight—poet, pastor, "Connecticut Wit," and president of Yale College—prepared a revision of Isaac Watts's psalmbook in 1799, he was therefore entering a long-standing and contentious transatlantic conversation. Watts's venerable *Psalms of David Imitated* was by then nearly a century old, and deficient in two regards, according to the Connecticut clergymen who commissioned Dwight's work: Watts had chosen to exclude certain psalms from his 1709 collection, and "in some of Dr. Watts's translation of the Psalms, there are expressions confined to particular places or countries." There was ample precedent for this project. Similar concerns had been addressed in North America by John Wesley in the 1737 Charleston *Collection;* in a revised edition published by a Massachusetts printer named John Mycall in the midst of the American Revolution; and in a revision published in Hartford by Joel Barlow in 1785. Each psalm collection was marked by the historical events of the years in which it appeared. "In making such alterations in Doctor Watts's version as respected objects merely local, I have in some instances applied the Psalm or the passage, to the Church at large, or to Christian nations generally; and in others, particularly to our own country," Dwight acknowledged on the front of his collection. "The latter I have done because every nation, like every individual, feeling his own concerns more than any other, will find various occasions of adapting its praise peculiarly to them."[33] As Dwight offered his Watts to the new century, his own concerns were clear: a sense of national pride tempered by apprehension of new secular ideas, and a deep commitment to reassert the authority of the established church at a time when constitutionally decreed separation of church and state seemed to threaten the Puritan ideals on which Connecticut had been founded and its culture maintained.

What did it mean to revise Doctor Watts, himself a reviser of David? Each of these revisions was, strictly speaking, an "imitation" rather than a retranslation. The imitation was a popular literary genre in the eighteenth century, allowing an author to pay homage to a respected literary ancestor, usually classical, while at the same time expressing individual creativity. Just as British writers Alexander Pope and Dr. Johnson had imitated the Roman poets Horace and Juvenal, respectively, Watts imitated the Hebrew psalmists. Since the singing of psalms required them to be set to regular meters in order to correlate with a small set of familiar tunes, a certain artistic license was allowed if not required. So Dwight was, in effect, imitating an imitation, as others had done. But the issues raised at the turn of the century were very different from even a generation earlier. A grandson of Jonathan Edwards, Dwight fashioned himself as a defender of the Puritan tradition in New England, particularly strong among Connecticut's "Standing Order." He looked on the decline in religious enthusiasm of the post-Revolutionary period with horror, and was appalled by the influence of deism among the new nation's elites. The most direct challenge posed by Enlightenment thought was the successful effort to separate church and state undertaken by America's most famous deist, Thomas Jefferson, who won his first term as president while Dwight was at work on his revision of Watts. In particular, the Yale president was attempting to displace a revision of Watts's psalms produced by Joel Barlow, another Connecticut clergyman (and "Wit") whose religious thinking had drifted in what struck Dwight and other keepers of the Puritan flame as a dangerously deist direction. Dwight's challenge was to honor the spirit of making psalms contemporary and appropriate to their American setting while avoiding the tendency to make them too contemporary, too local. He had to walk a fine line between nationalism and Christian universalism, America as a Christian nation and Christianity as an American institution.[34]

Watts himself had struggled with these challenges as a young man in the first decades of the eighteenth century. His solution to divesting David of outmoded idioms in order to make him "always speak the common sense and language of a Christian" was to replace the voice of the Jewish patriarch with the voice of a patriotic Englishman of the day. "Judah and Israel may be called England and Scotland," Watts proposed, "and the land of Canaan may be translated into Great Britain." The popularity of Watts's *Psalms of David Imitated* had received a boost from the Great Awakening. But within a generation the colonies were waging armed revolution against England; paeans to Great Britain as the land of Canaan no longer made sense. The first American nationalizer of the Psalms, John Mycall, who produced his version in 1781, was the most direct in his revisions. For lines that Watts had rendered as "Ye British Lands rejoice" (Psalm 19) and "The British islands are the Lord's" (Psalm 47), Mycall substituted "America rejoice" and "These random'd States are all the Lord's." Watts's "O Britain, trust the Lord: thy foes in vain, / And Britain blest the Lord that built the skies" became "Columbia trust the Lord; thy foes in vain, / Columbia bless the God who built the skies."[35]

Both Barlow (1785) and Dwight (1801) opted for less particular and more universalizing language. Where Watts had referenced "British lands" and Mycall "America," Barlow chose "Christian lands," and Dwight "Western lands." Frequently both opted to replace the name of a particular nation, whether Britain or America, with the word *Zion,* both a return to the original language of Psalms in the Bible and a familiar term for Americans used to thinking of their country as the fulfillment of their yearning for a millennial Promised Land. By looking at a particular stanza from Psalm 100, we get a sense of how psalms were "imitated," and how those imitations evolved to reflect particular circumstances.

Make a joyful noise unto the Lord, all ye lands. Serve the Lord with gladness: come before his presence with singing. (King James Bible, 1611)	Sing to the Lord with joyful voice; Let every land his name adore; The British Isles shall send the Noise Across the Ocean to the Shore. (Watts, 1719)
All people that on earth do dwell Sing to the Lord with cheerful voice Him serve with fear, his praise forth tell Come ye before him and rejoice. (Sternhold and Hopkins, 1618)	Sing to the Lord with joyful voice Let every land his name adore; America shall send the noise Across the ocean to the shore. (Mycall, 1781)
Make ye a joyful sounding noise unto Jehovah, all the earth: Serve ye Jehovah with gladness: Before his presence come with mirth. (*Bay Psalm Book*, 1640)	Ye sons of men in God rejoice; From land to land his name adore; Let earth with one united voice, Resound his praise from every shore. (Dwight, 1801)[36]

Deep tensions emerged between Barlow and Dwight, despite Yale ties and their friendship in earlier years. While Barlow traveled widely in Europe and developed a reputation as a cosmopolitan man of letters, Dwight increasingly came to support an idealized notion of the Puritan Connecticut past. In the view of Dwight and Connecticut's Standing Order, Barlow was a dangerous French-infected rationalist, a symptom of what seemed to be in the 1790s an effort to dismantle the central role of the church in the public life of Americans. Dwight took the position that the church was threatened by the secular energies of the new nation. The United States as it was developing would not serve as a city upon a hill; it was necessary to strengthen the church in order to save the new nation for its appointed role. In sermons and writings, he championed the Federalist party against the republican ideas articulated most persuasively by Thomas Jefferson. His greatest fear was of the French Revolution, an event in which Barlow was complicit by association. So Barlow's *Psalms,* despite their manifest poetical art, were deeply suspect by Connecticut's Standing Order. For this crucial part of congregation worship to be in the hands of a suspected infidel was unacceptable. In his own revisions of Watts, then, Dwight went out of his way to eliminate Barlow's changes, sometimes substituting his own formulations, in other cases reinstating the language of Watts, without the most obvious Briticisms. The warning that Mycall and Barlow had delivered to British tyrants, Dwight offered to America's leaders. Nicknamed the "Pope of Connecticut" by his opponents, Dwight used his influence as president of Yale to promote religious renewal, setting in motion some of the earliest activities of what would come to be known as the Second Great Awakening.[37]

The schisms generated by rival psalm and hymn collections during the eighteenth century were the earliest skirmishes of a ferment over church music that has continued to the present. Each major innovation in hymnody—whether involving texts, melodies, or canons of appropriate material—has brought pitched battles between those loyal to the traditional church music of their younger years and those eager to place their chosen religious creed into new musical settings. The dispute between Dwight and Barlow in particular has the features of what has come to be called a "culture war": a struggle for authority between those acting in the name of traditional values and those acting in the name of progress and innovation, in which both sides seek to enlist the powers of the state on behalf of their respective goals. Culture wars then and now are concerned with issues of nationalism, of competing notions of what constitutes the American way, of what should be shunned and what can be learned from ideas originating outside national borders. The American Revolution and its aftermath provided a fertile ground for testing ideas of religious and national solidarity as expressed in religious music. But throughout, Isaac Watts maintained a dominant position in American hymnody, "the liturgist for a new nation."[38] In imitating the psalms of David, Watts may have had in mind Britain as the New Israel, but his American audience thought differently. For many in the new nation, Britain had proved to be not Israel but Babylon.

CHAPTER TWO

Singing Independence

By the Rivers of Watertown we sat down & wept
when we remember'd thee O Boston.
— WILLIAM BILLINGS

ON 4 July 1783 a group of German-speaking Christian communists
in North Carolina staged the new nation's very first celebration of
American independence. General Cornwallis had surrendered at York-
town in 1781; a new treaty, signed in Paris in January, had codified the
new status quo. Now, in the small Moravian settlement of Salem nestled in
the wilds of Carolina, a musical celebration was to take place: a Day of
Solemn Thanksgiving to Almighty God, as the occasion was called. Not a
line of Watts, Wesley, or any other Anglophone hymnwriter was sounded;
in fact not a word of English was heard.

The day began dramatically. "The congregation was wakened with
trombones," wrote the congregational diarist, "and at the beginning of the
Preaching Service, the Te Deum was sung with the joyous pealing of the
trombones."[1] The afternoon was given over to the customary *Liebesmahl,*
or "love feast," comprising twenty-seven separate musical pieces—chorales, anthems, recitatives, a duet—carefully selected and arranged for balance and unity. Following custom, at the midpoint of the *Liebesmahl* a
hearty snack of sweet cakes, coffee, tea, and blended wine was served
to approximately 180 worshippers as the music continued around them.
The Day of Solemn Thanksgiving was concluded in the evening with a
Singstunde, a hymn festival of the kind that had so impressed John Wesley,
featuring a procession through the streets of Salem with singing, music,
and torches. Considered as a whole, the music, with its anthems and cho-

rales, arranged for voices, orchestra, and brass choirs, achieved a level of musical sophistication that would have been difficult to match in Boston or Philadelphia. Yet the repertoire had been selected and composed, dozens of parts copied, rehearsals conducted, in all of four days. Salem itself had been established only twelve years earlier.

The call for a Day of Thanksgiving, which came directly from Governor Alexander Martin, took the Moravians, like other North Carolinians, by surprise. But in a sense they were prepared. The task of planning the festivities was placed under the direction of Johann Friedrich Peter, one of the most celebrated of all Moravian musicians and composers. Born in Holland, educated in Germany, Peter had emigrated to America in 1770. He brought with him a vast library of European sacred music, including numerous works by Johann Sebastian Bach. After serving as musical director in several communities, Peter was assigned to Salem in 1780. For an annual salary of forty pounds, he took on a daunting variety of pastoral, clerical and administrative tasks, in addition to supervising musical activity and education. Within months he had "organized a weekly singing school, assumed responsibility for collecting donations to the music fund, was ordained a deacon, preached his first sermon in Salem, and served Holy Communion for the first time." The following year, Peter was asked to keep the official diary of the congregation. Before long he was placed in charge of the church archives and the boys' school. When Salem's head minister, Bishop Graff, died in 1782, Peter was asked to succeed him as preacher.[2]

Meanwhile there were the challenges of procuring and maintaining musical instruments in what was, after all, an isolated wilderness outpost. Some instruments were easier to obtain than others. Just months after the first settlers arrived in Bethabara, a neighboring community, the following was recorded: "Lovefeast was announced with our new trumpet, which we made from a hollow tree, and no trumpet in Bethlehem has a better tone." But high Moravian musical standards brought demands more difficult to fulfill. Violin strings of suitable quality were occasionally needed. The handmade organ was particularly temperamental. Minutes from an April 1781 board meeting contained a complaint: "The musicians wish that a better tone could be given to the organ which shrieks aloud when facing the congregation." And in July: "The swell mechanism on the organ should be fixed so that its creaking will not interfere with the congregation's devotions."[3]

In July 1783, though, questions of squeaky organs were dwarfed by a far greater challenge: a repertoire to commemorate such a momentous occasion. Fortunately Peter had, in addition to his own remarkable energies,

significant precedent and resources to draw upon. Moravians were invet-
erate archivists, and Peter had access to an extensive institutional memory
and to his own as well. Twenty years earlier, as a seventeen-year-old student in Germany, he had taken part in Moravian festivals to celebrate the
end of the Seven Years' War that had roiled both Europe and North America. Peter referred to detailed records of the 1763 Moravian peace festivals
held in Herrnhut and Gnadenfrey in Germany and in Moravian settlements in America. With no time to compose original musical settings, the
project was one of revising and adapting, a custom well accepted among
the Moravians. Much of the music was composed by Christian Gregor,
one of the most celebrated Moravian composers, whose corpus included
more than a thousand works contained in American collections. For example, "Das ist ein Tag," a short anthem based on Psalm 118 and selected
for the Salem *Liebesmahl,* was part of a larger work composed by Gregor
in 1761 and performed at the 1763 peace festival in Herrnhut.

Das ist ein Tag,	This is a day,
Das ist ein Tag,	this is a day
Den der Herr gemacht hat;	which the Lord our God made;
Lasset uns freuen	Let us be joyful
und fröhlich darinnen seyn.	and rejoice in it.[4]

Salem's Day of Thanksgiving opened with another piece used twenty years
earlier at German peace festivals, "Das Te Deum Laudamus," which featured trombone accompaniment.

Herr Gott, dich lober wir,	Lord God, Thy praise we sing,
Herr Gott, wir danken dir:	To Thee our thanks we bring;
Dich, Gott Vater in Ewigkeit,	Thou Father of eternity
Ehret die Welt weit und breit.	Both heavens and earth do worship Thee.
All' Engel und Himmels heer	To Thee all angels loudly cry,
Und was dienet deiner Ehr;	The heavens and all the powers on high
Auch Cherubim und Seraphim	Cherubim and seraphim all rejoice
Singen immer mit hoher Stimm:	singing with ever louder voice:
Heilig ist unser Gott!	Holy is our Lord God!
Der Herre Zebaoth!	The Lord of Sabaoth
(and on for more than 40 lines.)[5]	

The mood of the anthems and chorales alternated between ecstatic
praise and thanksgiving, and lamenting the violence and destruction that
had just ended. If the Solemn Day had one dominant musical theme, it was

this, from the opening chorale for both the morning's preaching service and the *Liebesmahl*:

Es ist Friede! es ist Friede!	Peace is with us! Peace is with us!
Freu dich, Volk des Herrn!	People of the Lord!
Es ist Friede! Es ist Friede!	Peace is with us! Peace is with us!
Ey das hört man gern!	Hear the joyful Word![6]

None of the chorales or anthems refers to local conditions or to the new nation. The message is rather one of general praise and thanksgiving. There are references to the trials of wartime, but these could as easily have been to the Seven Years' War as to the American Revolution, as in this chorale of unknown origin:

Freuden voll lasst uns nun singen,	Full of joy our hearts are singing,
Und unserm Gott Dankopfer bringen	And to our God thank off'rings bringing
Für Seine grosse Wunderthat!	For His great miracle of peace!
Schrecken voll auf allen Seiten	Far and wide the war was spreading,
Sah man die Kriegswut sich ausbreiten,	And terror by its sided was treading,
Die unser Land er schüttert hat.	To daunt us and our woe increase.
Es ward fast nichts gehört,	And little else was heard,
Als Feind und Feur und Schwerdt,	Than foe and fire and sword,
Noth und Jammer.	Need and sorrow.
Wie oft rief ich ganz ängstiglich:	How often I cried anxiously:
"Sieh drein, o Gott! erbarme Dich!"	"Look down, o God! and pity me!"[7]

The bass recitative that follows is heavy with yearning for an end to armed conflict:

> Das Land ist allenthalben jämmerlich verwüstet,
> und die Häuser sind zerrissen;
> weil nun die Elenden verstöret werden,
> und die Armen seufzen, will ich auf, spricht der Herr:
> Alle Krieger müssen die Hände lassen sinken.
> denn ich will auf, spricht der Herr,
> sie mussen die Hände lassen sinken.

> The land now lies in waste, pillaged and ravaged,
> and the dwellings torn asunder.
> For now the needy who endure oppression,
> and the poor who sorrow, shall I rise, saith the Lord:
> On the battlefields let all soldiers drop their weapons,
> for I shall rise, saith the Lord,
> all soldiers now must drop their weapons.[8]

After evoking the horrors of war, the service linked the preservation of the community through the coming of peace with the salvation brought by Jesus Christ. An anthem toward the end of the afternoon service draws from Psalm 150 in calling for a festive musical celebration:

Sie sollen loben Seinen Namen, im Reigen	Let them with dancing praise His Name,
mit Pauken und Harfen sollen sie Ihm spielen.	with timbrel and harps they shall play and praise him
Lobet Ihn in Seinen Thaten;	Praise Him for His mighty actions;
lolet Ihn in Seiner grossen Herrlichkeit;	glorify Him for his excellent greatness;
lobet Ihn mit Posaunen und Psalter und Reigen;	praise Him with brasses and psalt'ry and dancing;
lobet Ihn mit Saiten und Pfeiffen;	praise Him now with strings and with piping;
lobet Ihn mit hellen Cymbeln,	praise Him on the highest cymbals,
lobet Ihn mit wohlklingenden Cymbeln.	praise Him with the sound of loud cymbals.[9]

As the Wesleys had discovered, Moravians placed music at the center of worship, with none of the nervous scruples about musical instruments and part-singing that bedeviled the Puritans and other spiritual descendents of Calvin. In this they were conspicuously Lutheran. Brasses, horns, flutes, strings, and organs were used in worship on a regular basis. For no American sect was music more of a communal language, in a quite literal way. Historians have begun to explore the social meaning of soundscapes, the lost aural worlds of the past where, for example, rural church bells might convey an astonishing amount of information. In North America, the soundscape of the Unitas Fratrum was unique. The chorales played from the top of the tower by trombone choirs served as coded announcements of births, deaths, and weddings; on the basis of what was played, and how, a close listener might be able to determine not just what event had taken place, but who was involved. Music was a community responsibility; everyone was expected to learn the basics, and those showing talent were cultivated from an early age. "We are beginning to be short of men who can play the French Horn, and will try to secure two boys who will learn," read a typical board-meeting minute.[10] Moravians took their music very seriously and were, one senses, proud of their accomplishments. Yet they took pains never to lose sight of the fact that music was inspired by and directed to God; its purpose was praise and thanksgiving, not the entertainment of mortals, whether Brethren or not.

The inhabitants of Salem were of course spiritual kin to the same German settlers who had so impressed John and Charles Wesley during their 1735 transatlantic voyage to Georgia. They had lasted in Georgia longer than the ill-starred Wesleys, but not by much. Hammered by illness during the summer, and threatened by a Spanish invasion of Georgia from Florida, the few remaining Moravians decided in 1739 to relocate, eventually establishing a settlement in William Penn's colony, at a place they called Bethlehem, in 1741. Within a decade Prime Minister Lord Granville offered the Moravians an option on 100,000 acres of land in North Carolina, a region called Wachovia. The Unitas Fratrum moved decisively. By October 1753 a surveying expedition had been completed and the purchase of land finalized, and the town of Bethabara was promptly hewed out of the wilderness. It was constructed as a kind of beachhead, a staging post from which the more ambitious center of Salem would be established. Salem was built from scratch between 1766 and 1771, when its *Gemeinhaus*, or community center, was consecrated.

Beginning in the 1730s, the Unitas Fratrum did pioneering missionary work among African Americans in the Caribbean and Native Americans to the north. Inspired by a plea for missionary work from an African bondwoman named Anna on the Danish island of St. Thomas, the Moravians in 1732 sent two single brethren to proselytize there. One was David Nitschmann, who would later sail to Georgia with the Wesleys aboard the *Simmonds*. Enslaved Africans responded well to the egalitarian piety practiced by the Moravians, who in the 1750s extended their mission to Jamaica and Antigua, and the following decade to Barbados. The same brand of evangelical piety would succeed for Methodist missionaries in the southern colonies toward the end of the eighteenth century.[11] Meanwhile, Moravian missionaries pursued missionary work among Amerindians with equal zeal, establishing cordial relations with the Six Nations, the great Iroquois confederation. The Unity enjoyed some success in proselytyzing, along with a reputation for decency, during most of the century, though relations between whites and Amerindians turned increasingly bitter during the Seven Years' War and the Revolution, culminating in a brutal massacre of Moravian Indians by Pennsylvania militiamen in 1782.[12]

For Moravians, like most other North Americans, the most immediate cause for thanksgiving in 1783 was not national independence but the simple cessation of war and its infinite hardships. The war had created suffering for all inhabitants of the former colonies, but was particularly onerous for the Unitas Fratrum. As a German-speaking commune nestled among primarily Scotch-Irish settlers of the Piedmont, they were not fully trusted by either Tories or "liberty men." The Moravian church was officially recognized by the Church of England as "an ancient Protestant Episcopal

Church," and thus entitled to its privileges and immunities. This standing raised the suspicions of the primarily Presbyterian and Baptist neighbors, who had no fondness for the Anglican Church, and made it more difficult for the Moravians to break cleanly with George III. If perceived as disloyal, their Brethren in England might pay the consequences. Though they willingly paid a threefold tax for military exemption, nursed wounded and sick soldiers, and provided shelter and provisions to troops when asked, their refusal to bear arms was a sticking point for both parties in the war. Not until 1779 was this right statutorily protected by North Carolina's General Assembly. Beyond this, Moravian homes and storehouses were regularly plundered throughout the conflict by both loyalists and liberty men, and the Brethren were pressured to accept nearly worthless paper currency in their general store. Moreover, the legal standing of their claim to the 100,000 acres in Wachovia was challenged during and after the conflict.

At the most ordinary level of daily life, orderly Moravian settlements were continually invaded by a variety of disruptive influences, from British troops to backwoods outlaws. By the early summer of 1783, basic order seemed to be breaking down in Salem. Gossip was provoked by documented cases of "unauthorized meeting of unmarried members of the opposite sex in some of the family dwellings." Townspeople were consulting "conjurers and wise women"; they were engaging in "slander and backbiting," flouting congregational regulations, skipping worship services in favor of social gatherings. The evening *Singstunden* were particularly threatened by no-shows who chatted in front of their houses in the summer, waylaying members who might otherwise have made it to the services. In response the Elders took the grave step of withholding Holy Communion from offenders. In ordinary times the Moravian community was remarkably well organized and disciplined. Theirs was *Gemeinschaft* at its thickest. Patterns of socialization were established at the community level, with all Brothers and Sisters organized into peer groups by sex, age, and marital status. These were the categories within which people would learn how to be Moravian and do Moravian things: Children, Older Boys, Older Girls, Single Brothers, Single Sisters, Married People, Widows, and Widowers. Music-making was one important function of the peer groups. Submission to authority was a cardinal virtue. Like the Methodists they had influenced so decisively, the Moravians had an effective system of centralized, bureaucratic decision-making. Elders made careful decisions about exactly who was to do what, when, and where—from decisions of the greatest import, like when and where to establish new settlements, to what prices and wages would be paid and marriages approved.[13]

Ever since their arrival in North America the Brethren had considered their settlements as cities upon a hill; their attractive villages, hospitality, high-quality crafts, and music all played a role in the attempt to represent themselves favorably to the world. An officer in Pennsylvania during the Seven Years' War, Benjamin Franklin had "inquir'd a little into the practice of the Moravians" at Bethlehem: "some of them had accompanied me, and all were very kind to me. I found they work'd for a common stock, eat at common tables, and slept in common dormitories, great numbers together . . . I was at their church, where I was entertain'd with good musick, the organ being accompanied with violin, hautboys, flutes, clarinets, etc."[14] During wartime, the Moravian survival strategy was to practice even-tempered, faithful forbearance, turning the other cheek to avoid being clubbed on the head by a rifle butt. A particularly important challenge was staying on the good side of colonial politicians. Moravians generally succeeded regardless of who controlled the governorship or assembly. Their prowess in music provided a ready-made terrain of diplomacy, a sort of lingua franca that occasionally warranted some adjustment of the language in use. When North Carolina's Governor William Tryon visited Bethabara in 1767 he was welcomed with trumpets and French horns, and served dinner to the accompaniment of music. On Sunday, after a morning service conducted in English, "The Governor's Lady went alone into our *Saal,* and played a little on the organ, our girls came in and began to sing, which pleased the Lady so much that Br. Graff must play for them; then the Governor also came, and they entertaind themselves in this way most happily for a whole hour, the Lady being particularly pleased. She visited the girls in their own room, then had them come again to the *Saal* to sing for her, this time in German—she had the English Hymn Book and wanted the verses they were singing pointed out to her." Later all the guests attended a special *Singstunde,* whose responsive singing especially pleased the governor. "At bedtime the musicians played softly before the house." Governor Tryon returned four years later during a military campaign against backwoods "Regulators" and specifically requested singing by the Single Sisters. At a dinner celebrating the king's birthday, "several Healths were drunk, each being answered with a loud *Hurra* and the playing of a verse on the trombones by our musicians."[15]

Ten years later it was Salem's turn to host dignitaries. During the War of Independence, Traugot Bagge, a merchant and one of Salem's leading men, completed an English translation of the latest Moravian hymnbook for the benefit of non-German-speaking visitors. "There is something agreeable in the singing in the Brethren's meetings," he observed, "because it is very distant from the otherwise customary loud bawling of the hymns, &

thereby becomes the more devout & harmonious." Bagge pointed out that some of the hymns sung earlier by Moravians, which had struck even sympathetic outsiders like John Wesley as inordinately sensual, and "mixed with all sorts of play of words bordering upon dandling, are put out of all use long since." Those who wrote hymns, Bagge asserted, aimed at purity and simplicity, striving "to word them in such language that a devoutly considering heart . . . need not stop short or perhaps be silenced quite at the question: Understandest thou what thou singest?" Thus had the Brethren been preparing when they learned in July 1781 that the North Carolina assembly had decided to meet in Salem that November. The date happened to coincide with the tenth anniversary of the opening of the community *Gemeinhaus,* for which a commemorative sequence of preaching and musical services was being planned.[16]

The Moravians faced the prospect of hosting colonial politicians with trepidation but characteristic resolve: "This will make many changes in our ordinary programs," the record shows, "but if with all modesty we hold to our chief purpose, if our conduct shows all people that we are children of God, and if we treat them in an orderly manner and with courtesy, then the Saviour will turn to good the evil that was intended us." The acting governor, Alexander Martin, advised them on preparations for lodging and accommodations. Salem's Elders announced: "Musicians are to be reminded that they are not to play for the Assemblymen in private homes, saying that this is not our custom . . . Violins are to be kept locked up in order not to be used for unfitting purposes; also the mouthpieces of the wind instruments . . . In our Congregation music, however, we will not be disturbed. As long as there is no unusual disturbance, our week-day services shall be held in their usual order." In fact the assemblymen attended all services, demonstrating "respect and reverence," and so many flocked to the evening *Singstunde* that many had to listen outside the *Saal.* "Our music and singing had a great effect on them, and they listened with wonder and respect," wrote a distinguished Moravian. "An old, gray-haired gentleman came to me expressly before leaving and said that he had always heard that we were a religious people, which was largely the reason that he had made the long trip to come here, but it had far surpassed his expectations. He was convinced that God was in our midst, and if he could do anything for us in the Assembly, personally or by his influence, he would do it gladly."[17] So successful was the hospitality that the assembly decided to hold its next meeting in Salem.

The Salem Brethren learned that the United States had won its war of independence on Saturday, 19 April 1783. That same day, which happened to be the day before Easter, Governor Martin had announced the news to the North Carolina assembly. "We found it remarkable that, on this day commemorating the Rest of Our Lord in the Tomb, we learned that peace shall be restored to this land by the treaty drawn in Paris on January 20th of this year," Peter recorded in the official diary. The legislature immediately passed a resolution calling for a Day of Solemn Thanksgiving for sustaining the states through the war, restoring peace, "raising up a distressed and Injured People to rank among independent nations and sovereign Powers of the world," and assorted "other divine favors." On 18 June Martin issued a proclamation that read:

> In conformity to the pious intentions of the Legislature I have thought proper to issue this my Proclamation directing that the said 4th Day of July next be observed as above, hereby strictly commanding and enjoining all the Good Citizens of this State to set apart the said Day from bodily labour, and employ the same in devout and religious exercises. And I do require all Ministers of the Gospel of every Denomination to convene their congregations at the same time, and deliver to them Discourses suitable to the important occasion recommending in general the practice of Virtue and true Religion as the great foundation of private blessing as well as National happiness and prosperity.[18]

Private blessing and national prosperity through virtue and "true religion": this was American civil religion in its purest form. Apparently this proclamation only reached Salem on 30 June, when the governor was passing through Salem on his way to Salisbury (and attended the Moravian *Singstunde*). Just four days later, the celebration was on.

WHILE Moravians celebrated independence in the isolation of central North Carolina, some 700 miles northeast, William Billings, a Boston tanner and composer, had produced his own musical celebration of American victory. Actually, he produced not one but two: "Independence" and "Peace." Of any American musician of the day, Billings was the obvious choice for such an occasion. In April, when the cessation of hostilities was announced, it was to Billings that the town of Newburgh, New York, turned for musical inspiration. "At noon, the Proclamation of Congress for a cessation of hostilities was published at the door of the New Building, followed by three huzzas," recorded a witness; "after which a prayer was made by Rev. Mr. Gano, and an anthem (Independence, from Billings) was performed by vocal and instrumental music." This is the triumphant anthem sung at Newburgh:

> The States, O Lord, with Songs of Praise
> Shall in thy Strength rejoice,

And best with thy Salvation raise
To Heav'n their chearful voice.
To the King they shall sing Halleluiah.
Thy Goodness and thy tender care have all our fears destroy'd.
A covenant of Peace thou mad'st with us confirmed by thy word,
A covenant thou mad'st with us and seal'd it with thy Blood.
To the King they shall sing Halleluiah.
And all the Continent shall sing: Down with this earthly King,
   No King but God . . .
May his Blessing descend, World without end, On ev'ry part of the Continent.
May Harmony and Peace begin and never cease
and may the Strength increase of the Continent.
May American Wilds be fill'd with his Smiles and may the Natives bow to our
   Royal King.
May Rome, France and Spain and all the World proclaim the Glory and the
   Fame of our Royal King . . .
May his reign be Glorious, America victorious and may the earth acknowledge
   God is the King. Amen, Amen, Amen.[19]

No doubt there were many other towns where music by the Boston composer was heard. Billings was by 1783 easily the best-known and most prolific composer in British North America. He was also the most outspoken in promoting his own work and in commenting on the actual and proper state of sacred music more generally. But ironically, in contrast to the exhaustively documented preparations for the Moravian celebration, very little is known about the circumstances in which Billing's second commemorative anthem, "Peace," was composed or premiered. Only one copy survives, with a handwritten inscription: "Ladd's. Newport. August 1783." Though we do not know with certainty, it seems likely that the anthem was performed in Rhode Island, perhaps within a month of Salem's Day of Thanksgiving.[20]

Though its context remains blurry, the anthem itself presents a rich historical artifact. It is a long piece, running twelve minutes, and stands out among Billings' work in containing sections written solely for instruments. "Symphony is sounds without words intended for instruments," Billings explained, and "Peace" begins and ends with these short "symphonies." The introit consists of some twenty-nine measures of two-bar phrases (sounding at times vaguely reminiscent of "We Wish You a Merry Christmas"). Billings' original text, drawn from "sundry Scriptures and elsewhere," begins:

God is the King, God is the King, God is the King of all the Earth,
and let all the People say Amen, Amen, Amen, Amen, Amen;

let the Nations rejoice, rejoice, rejoice and be glad,
and the Multitude of Isles be glad, for God is the King of all the Earth.

A mortal king has been replaced by a divine one. The line "The Kingdoms of this World are become the Kingdoms of our Lord and of his Christ" is reiterated in the anthem.

> Rejoice, ye Americans in the Lord,
> Lift up your Voice and Sing,
> Deep in your hearts these Blessings record,
> that Christ is your Saviour and God is your king.
> For Kings shall be thy nursing Fathers,
> and Queens, and Queens, thy nursing Mothers.

A familiar image of the millennium appears toward the anthem's end:

> The Wolf shall dwell with the Lamb,
> and the Leopard shall lie down with the Kid,
> And the Calf, and the young Lion and the Fatling together,
> And a little Child shall lead them, shall lead them.
> The Cow and the Bear shall Feed; their young ones shall lie down together,
> and the Lion shall eat Straw like the Ox.
> Glory to God, Glory to God, Glory to God in the Highest.
> The sucking Child shall play on the Hole of the Asp.
> And the weaned Child shall put his Hand on the Cockatrice' Den.
> They shall not hurt nor destroy, saith the Lord,
> for the Earth shall be fill'd with the Knowledge of the Lord,
> as the Waters fill the Sea.[21]

The references to America stand out. And there is the powerful millennial image, drawn nearly word for word from Isaiah 11:6–9. After the image of the Earth filled with knowledge, Isaiah continues with a description of Israel restored:

> And it shall come to pass in that day, that the Lord shall set his hand again the second time to recover the remnant of his people, which shall be left, from Assyria, and from Egypt, and from Pathros, and from Cush, and from Elam, and from Shinar, and from Hamath, and from the islands of the sea.
>   And he shall set up an ensign for the nations, and shall assemble the outcasts of Israel, and gather together the dispersed of Judah from the four corners of the earth.

This image of America as the fulfillment of prophecy about the millennium resonated with many partisans of the new nation. For Billings and kindred souls, the Revolution could be squarely placed in a biblical typology. Loyal British subjects until the 1760s, patriots like Billings retooled the old Puritan notions of America as the New Israel to fit the conditions of this colonial uprising. The Revolution was understood by Protestant patriots as a sacred allegory; legends surrounding Boston's Liberty Tree and others like it had all the marks of sacred origin stories. They symbolized a rekindling of the Puritan drive to create a city on a hill, a shining beacon of Christian purpose for the example of the rest of the world. The British troops were Satan's minions, figurative Egyptian oppressors against whom the American Israel could wage its righteous struggle. George Washington was the American Moses, its righteous Joshua. Alexander Campbell, a Scottish immigrant and revivalist who founded the Disciples of Christ, proclaimed 4 July 1776 "a day to be remembered as was the Jewish Passover . . . This revolution, taken in all its influences, will make men free indeed." No wonder Franklin's proposed design for the Great Seal of the United States was a scene of Moses dividing the Red Sea, while Jefferson proposed an image of the children of Israel marching in the wilderness. The American Revolution, and the millennial rhetoric that surrounded it, had many of the trappings of a Protestant revival movement.[22]

Billings' text for "Peace" may strike modern readers as a generic, psalm-like paraphrase of scripture not recognizably distinct from what the Moravian composer Johann Friedrich Peter pulled together for Salem's Day of Thanksgiving. But in significant ways it stood apart. Peter's program drew on a centuries-long tradition of Moravian hymnody, more specifically on particular programs composed to celebrate earlier cessations of war. The texts and settings were essentially European, simply transplanted to American soil. Billings' "Peace" was created fresh for the occasion out of notably vernacular materials. Peter's settings were grounded in long-established traditions of German chorale, while Billings' melodies were essentially without precedent. There simply had been no previous British American composers. Billings had over the previous decade created a new musical idiom, nurtured to be sure by the sacred soundscape of psalmody and singing schools of eighteenth-century Massachusetts, but fundamentally divergent.

Beyond any doubt, Billings was a patriot. Where the Moravians were scrupulously neutral during the war, Billings was flamboyantly partisan. During the 1770s he paraphrased psalms and wrote patriotic anthems lambasting the British in plain language. He inhabited the Boston of Paul Revere, who engraved the frontispiece for his first tunebook, and Samuel Adams, who sang next to Billings in church choirs and concerts. His mother and father had been married by Charles Chauncy, the leading Boston minister who inveighed against the spiritual revivals of mid-century and opposed the promiscuous singing of psalms and hymns. This was the world painted by the great Boston portraitist John Singleton Copley, who must have known the composer. "Blind with one eye, one leg shorter

2. Engraved by Paul Revere, the frontispiece for William Billings' *New-England Psalm-Singer* (1770) shows an ensemble of singers performing a sacred song. Courtesy of Fine Arts Library, Michigan State University.

than the other," Billings emerges as the quaintly uncouth hero of Nathaniel D. Gould's *Church Music in America* (1853), where he is described as grabbing handfuls of snuff from his coat pocket and snorting it by the fistful. "We might infer, from this circumstance," Gould writes, "that his voice could not have been very pleasant and delicate." But "stentorian" it was, according to Billings' friend, the Reverend Dr. Edward Pierce, who when he happened to be singing next to Billings "could not hear his own voice."[23]

What little is known about Billings' childhood and youth reveals him to be a pure product of Boston's urban working class. For some reason, Billings' father effectively disinherited his widow, brothers, and only surviving son; when he died, in 1760, he bequeathed William exactly one shilling. Not quite fourteen, William took up tanning, opening a shop on Frog Lane. Even at the height of his fame it seems Billings kept his day job, which out of necessity grew increasingly varied as he grew older. He opened his first singing school around 1769, when he was twenty-three. During the 1770s and 1780s he taught at various singing schools in

Boston, Weymouth, Stoughton, and Providence, among other places. As late as 1798, two years before his death, he was listed as a "singing master." Billings' own education, musical or otherwise, had been minimal. He may have developed his taste for psalms, hymns, and anthems while attending Boston's New South Church. His chief musical influence seems to have been William Tans'ur (1706–1783), an eighteenth-century English composer of psalm tunes whose *Royal Melody Complete* reached the American colonies in the 1760s, and whose concepts and phrases about music composition turn up in several of Billings' own published writings.[24]

Beginning in 1770, without apparent preliminaries, Billings brought out a series of tunebooks. The first, *The New-England Psalm-Singer,* published the year of the Boston Massacre, included 126 original compositions. *The Singing-Master's Assistant,* published at the peak of wartime, in 1778, comprised 71 pieces, including the anthem "Independence." These were followed the next year by *Music in Miniature*, with 74 compositions, and, two years later, *The Psalm-Singer's Amusement*, with 24. *Suffolk Harmony*, containing 32 compositions, appeared in 1786, while Billings' last collection, *Continental Harmony*, was brought out by a committee in 1794 to support the then-destitute composer. In all but one of these tunebooks, *Suffolk Harmony*, Billings wrote many of the texts as well as composing the music. While each of Billings' collections is remarkable in its own way, perhaps the most astonishing is *The New-England Psalm-Singer,* appearing as it did without warning (but not without fanfare, thanks to the composer himself). Billings himself later referred to the tunebook as "my Reuben, my first born."[25] The title page announces the appearance of a distinctly new, and proudly American, product: "The New-England Psalm-Singer: or, American Chorister. Containing a number of Psalm-tunes, Anthems and Canons. In four and five parts. Never before published. Composed by William Billings, a native of Boston, in New-England."

Billings' tunebook ranks with Walt Whitman's 1855 *Leaves of Grass* as one of the great debut performances in American art. Both were remarkable displays of self-creation—and promotion—of a peculiarly individual, autodidactic sort of genius. Just as Whitman later set forth his poems with a striking prefatory manifesto, his own jacket design, typeface, and a paragraph of praise solicited from Emerson, so the twenty-four-year-old Billings wrote text, composed tunes (thereby increasing tenfold the number of original musical compositions published up to that point in America), solicited an engraved frontispiece from Paul Revere and an introductory hymn by the well-known Boston poet the Reverend Dr. Mather Byles, and assembled a lengthy introductory tutorial laying out some basic ideas and principles of music. In it Billings asserts that regarding musical composition, "*Nature is the best Dictator*, for all the hard dry studied Rules that ever was prescribed, will not enable any Person to form an Air any more than the bare Knowledge of the four and twenty Letters, and strict Grammatical Rules will qualify a Scholar for composing a piece of Poetry, or properly adjusting a Tragedy, without a Genius . . . So in fact, I think it is best for every *Composer* to be his own *Carver*. Therefore, upon this Consideration, for me to dictate or pretend to prescribe Rules of this Nature for others, would not only be very unnecessary, but also a great Piece of Vanity."[26]

Billings' entire performance is remarkable for its assurance, its sweeping sense of authority. And it was sui generis, "the first published compilation of entirely American music; moreover, it was the first tunebook produced by a single American composer."[27] Of the collection's 126 pieces, 118 were tunes for psalms and hymns, to be used in conjunction with a psalmbook like the *Bay Psalm Book* or Watts's *Psalms of David Imitated*. The remaining compositions included four anthems, three canons, and one set-piece. Most of the pieces are scored for four voices, the melody being assigned to the tenor. Several of the psalm tunes became part of the core repertoire for the next couple of generations: "Amherst," "Brookfield," "Chester," "Lebanon," "Africa," "Hingham," and "Suffolk." Of these, "Brookfield," a one-stanza plain-tune, and "Chester," which was later to acquire incendiary anti-British stanzas, were Billings' most famous and widely reprinted. The intriguingly named "Africa," with its startling melodic leaps in the sixth measure, has become a favorite of contemporary Billings performers. The first two stanzas proclaim:

> Now shall my inward Joys arise,
> And burst into a Song;
> Almighty Love inspires my Heart,
> And Pleasure tunes my Tongue.
>
> God on his thirsty Sion-Hill
> Some Mercy Drops has thrown,
> And Solemn Oaths have bound his Love
> To show'r Salvation down.[28]

Toward the end of his career Billings would write that "blacks who are brought here from Africa, are in general better constituted for music, than the natives of North America; indeed nature seems to have lavishly bestowed on them, all the mechanical powers requisite to constitu[t]e musical performers": strong lungs, good ears, melodious voices. But American-born black voices, he judged, "are but indifferent."[29]

Billings was more than an original and pathbreaking composer of tunes and musical texts. He was also a prose stylist of remarkable exuberance, which he applied in a running commentary on musical controversies generally and his own compositional techniques in particular. His second tunebook, though visually not as striking as *New-England Psalm-Singer,* opened with a flourish worthy of Henry Fielding, and is worth quoting at length.

> No doubt you (do, or ought to) remember, that about eight years ago, I published a Book entitled, The New England Psalm Singer, &c. And truly a most masterly inimitable Performance, I then thought it to be. Oh! how did my foolish heart throb & beat with tumultuous joy! With what impatience did I wait on the Book-Binder, while stitching the sheets and puting on the covers, with what extacy, did I snatch the yet unfinished Book out of his hands, and pressing it to my bosom, with rapturous delight, how lavish was I, in encomiums on this infant production of my own Numb-Skull? Welcome; thrice welcome; thou legitimate offspring of my brain, go forth my little Book, go forth and immortalize the name of your Author; may your sale be rapid and may you speedily run through ten thousand Editions, may you be a welcoming guest in all companies and what will add tenfold to thy dignity, may you find your way into the Libraries of the Learned.[30]

The young Whitman couldn't have sung his own praises more ecstatically. And Billings had a few scores to settle. His verbal ingenuity reaches a peak in "To the Goddess of Discord," a satirical allegory addressed to those who had criticized his first tunebook for emphasizing thirds, fifths, and octaves to the neglect of more sophisticated harmonic intervals. "Let an ass bray the Bass, let the fileing of a saw carry the Tenor, let a hog who is extream hungry squeal the Counter, and let a cart-wheel, which is heavy loaded, and that has long been without grease, squeek the Treble," Billings concludes defiantly; "and if the Concert should appear to be too feeble you may add the cracking of a crow, the howling of a dog, the squalling of a cat, and what would grace the Concert yet more would be the rubbing of a wet finger upon a window glass."[31]

Nothing unleashed Billings' prose energies more than the attacks on his musical preferences. As late as 1794, with his musical career in steep decline, he mustered this defense of the fuging tune, a musical form he had not created but with which he was associated, against those who thought it disruptive of the proper piety induced by straightforward homophonic psalms and hymns.

> It is an old maxim, and I think a very just one, viz. that variety is always pleasing, and it is well known that there is more variety in one piece of fuging music, than in twenty pieces of plain song, for while the tones do most sweetly coincide and agree, the words are seemingly engaged in musical warfare; and excuse the paradox if I further add, that each part seems determined by dint

of harmony and strength of accent, to drown his competitor in an ocean of harmony, and while each part is thus mutually striving for mastery, and sweetly contending for victory, the audience are most luxuriously entertained, and exceeding delighted; in the mean time, their minds are surprisingly agitated, and extremely fluctuated; sometimes declaring in favour of one part, and sometimes another.—Now the solemn bass demands their attention, now the manly tenor, now the lofty counter, now the volatile treble, now here, now there, now here again.—Oh inchanting! O ecstatic! Push on, push on ye sons of harmony, and

> Discharge your deep mouth'd canon, full fraught with Diaspasons;
> May you with Maestoso, rush on to Choro-Grando,
> And then with Vigoroso, let fly your Diapentes
> About our nervous system.[32]

In these passages a kind of synesthesia is taking place, by which musical tones and patterns take on personality and material form. Billings clearly imagines music in dramatic, even theatric terms, personifying tones and musical properties, imagining conflict, combat and resolution. His spirited endorsement of fuging tunes evokes what the Russian critic Mikhail Bahktin termed heteroglossia, the intermingling of different voices in literary texts. Also unmistakable is Billings' sense of the music as erotic, with musical performance of the fuging tune as an aural orgasm.

With his excitable persona, dramatic flair, and gift for stirring rhetoric, it's no wonder Billings became an effective musical propagandist for the American patriots. He wrote several nationalistic hymns and anthems during the 1770s; "Chester," which first appeared in the *New-England Psalm-Singer,* was the best known:

> Let tyrants shake their iron rod,
> And slav'ry Clank her galling Chains
> We fear them not we trust in God
> New englands God for ever reigns.
>
> Howe and Burgoyne and Clinton too,
> With Prescot and Cornwallis join'd,
> Together plot our overthrow,
> In one Infernal league combin'd.
>
> . . .
>
> The Foe comes on with haughty Stride;
> Our troops advance with martial noise,
> Their Vet'rans flee before our Youth,
> And Gen'rals yield to beardless Boys.[33]

Billings could be full of surprises, however, and the politics of his music were not unequivocal. The title page of *Psalm-Singer* contained the injunction: "O praise the Lord with one consent, and in this grand design, Let Britain and the Colonies, unanimously join." That was in 1770. But even his most militant collection, *The Singing-Master's Assistant*, published in 1778, contains two equivocal hymns, "Liberty" and "Europe," respectively:

God bless our gracious King	Let whig & torie all subside
& all his royal race	And politicks be dumb;
Preserve the queen & grant that they	A nobler theme inspires our Muse
may live before thy face.[34]	and trills upon our tongue.
	O praise the Lord with one content
	& in this grand design,
	let briton & her Colinies
	unanimously join.[35]

The first tunebook to appear in America since the outbreak of war, *The Singing-Master's Assistant* also included Billings' famous paraphrase of Psalm 137:

> By the Rivers of Watertown we sat down & wept
>   when we remember'd thee O Boston.
> As for our Friends Lord God of Heaven
>   preserve them, defend them,
>   deliver and restore them unto us again;
> For they that held them in Bondage
> Requir'd of them to take up Arms against their Brethren.
> Forbid it Lord God that those who have sucked Bostonian Breasts

Psalm 137:

> By the rivers of Babylon, there we sat down, yea, we wept,
> when we remembered Zion.
> We hanged our harps upon the willows in the midst thereof.
> For there they that carried us away captive required of us a song;
> and they that wasted us required of us mirth, saying,
> Sing us one of the songs of Zion.
> How shall we sing the Lord's song in a strange land?

Just how widely and commonly Billings' works were performed is difficult to know. The nineteenth-century historian Nathaniel Gould suggests they were ubiquitous, without providing much evidence. "These words, and the tune attached to them, were learned by every choir, and in every family, and by every child, and sung in the house and by the way, like popular songs at the present day," he wrote in 1853, "and perhaps did more to inspire a spirit of freedom than any one thing that occurred at this critical moment." (He adds, less confidently: "Not only this tune and these words, but many others of like character, were used, that breathed the spirit of the day, some of which S. Adams probably had, to say the least, *seen* before they were published.") These sentiments and solidarities must have helped Billings publish and sell his tunebooks, at least in the first part of his career as a composer. But there is some indication that they may have hurt his career as well. Three times in his first decade as a publishing composer Billings sought copyright protection for his works, ultimately without success. A petition to the General Court of Massachusetts was filed in 1770 but rejected. Less than two years later the petition was accepted by the colony's General Court, and the "William Billings Copyright Act" gained quick approval by the Massachusetts legislature, probably with the enthusiastic support of Speaker Samuel Adams. This endorsement unfortunately carried no truck with Governor Thomas Hutchinson, a bitter enemy of Adams; the governor refused to sign. A third attempt by Billings, in 1778, went nowhere, and thereafter he abandoned his attempts to secure copyright. As a result his work was widely reprinted in colonial tunebooks without remuneration.[36]

Though an inability to protect his compositions undoubtedly played a part, no single factor accounts for Billings' long financial decline, which began in the mid-1780s. In 1774, at the beginning of his fame and success, Billings had married Lucy Swan, a student at his singing school in Stoughton. In 1780 he was able to buy a house on Newbury Street, near the center of Boston. *The Suffolk Harmony* (1786) continued some of Billings' most popular and widely used compositions, including the innovative psalm tune "Jordan," in common meter double (8.6.8.6.8.6.8.6), usually paired with the famous Watts hymn whose wistful imaginings of New Canaan dovetailed with a classic American conception of itself as the Promised Land:

> There is a Land of pure Delight,
> Where Saints immortal reign;
> Infinite Day excludes the Night,
> And Pleasures banish Pain.
> Sweet Fields beyond the swelling Flood,
> Stand dress'd in living Green:
> So to the Jews old Canaan stood,
> While Jordan roll'd between.
> . . .
> Those gloomy Doubts that rise—
> And see the Canaan, which we love,
> With unbeclouded Eyes
> Could we but climb where Moses stood,
> And view the Landscape o'er;
> Not Jordan's streams, nor Death's cold Flood,
> Should fright us from the Shore.

Beginning in 1785, though, Billings was forced to take the first in a succession of part-time municipal jobs in order to support his growing family: trade inspector, hog catcher, leather inspector, even "scavenger" (street cleaner). In 1790 a concert of sacred music was organized at Stone Chapel as a benefit for Billings. Still, he was forced to mortgage his house, for forty pounds. In 1792 a subscription notice went out for what would be Billings' last tunebook, *Continental Harmony,* which was selected by a "large committee" drawn from Boston's musical societies. The notice was addressed "to the Benevolent of every Denomination: The distressed situation of Mr. Billings' family has so sensibly operated on the minds of the committee as to induce their assistance in the intended publication. The Inspection and Revision of the whole is submitted by Mr. Billings to the aforesaid committee, many of whom are deemed of approved knowledge in the science of Musick, and nothing will be offered to the publick but what they recommend and approve of."[37] The sweeping authority of the earlier Billings had vanished; decisions about repertoire were now in the hands of a committee. When his wife Lucy died in 1795 at the age of forty-two, Billings had six children to care for, ranging from ages two to seventeen.

A DIFFERENT kind of explanation for Billings' decline would place his work within a broad cultural shift taking placing at the end of the eighteenth century. In 1783, the year independence was celebrated and "Peace" composed, Billings, at the peak of his fame and always eager to display his literary talents, assumed editorship of *Boston Magazine.* "Every thing that has a tendency to improve the mind or reform the manners, or that is entertaining, and instructive, will be thankfully received," is how the new publication defined its editorial mission. One of the stories printed in the first issue, thought to be the work of Billings, is titled "The Life of Sawney Beane." It recounts the fantastic tale of a large Scottish clan from Galaway. The Beane family happen to be troglodytes who rob passersby, dismembering and pickling their victims for food. After decades of this savagery, a near-victim escapes (after seeing his wife butchered before his eyes) and returns with a small army of the king's men. In the cave they find hoards of treasure, along with "Legs, arms, thighs, hands, and feet, of men, women and children . . . hung up in rows, like dried beef." The entire clan—Sawney and his wife along with fourteen children and thirty-four grandchildren—are marched off to Edinburgh, where they are tortured and executed, their deaths being described in gruesome detail. Entertaining as the story must have been to some readers, its potential to "improve the mind or reform the manners" struck Boston's cultural elite, mainly Harvard-educated ministers, as dubious. The magazine was hastily reorganized with a new editorial committee, which ran a notice pledging that future issues would be "more respectable." Hoping to begin with a clean slate, the publishers specifically requested "that the defects of their first publication may not hurt their original design; and that the Magazine for November may be considered as the first number."[38] Thus ended Billings' ambitious foray into Boston's world of letters.

An analogous erasure would affect Billings' standing in the world of American music over the decades ahead, as his once-popular tunes were dropped from tunebooks and his own compilations struggled to find publishers and buyers. Billings himself remained remarkably consistent over his career in terms of his approach to music and text, if anything growing more sophisticated in the craft of musical composition. But the cultural terrain on which he was operating began a dramatic shift in the post-Revolutionary years. Billings found himself on the wrong side of a cultural divide that equated taste with cultivated respectability, and associated the indigenous and the vernacular with a lack of taste. Art might strive for the sublime but should at all times remain respectable. Religious songs and their singing should edify both performers and audience: expressing praise wasn't enough. Billings seemed uncouth and barbarous to the upholders of a new generation of musical orthodoxy, like Andrew Law, author of *The Musical Primer* (1793), and John Hubbard, who published his reform manifesto, *Essay on Music*, in 1808. The fuging song, with its impression of sensory abandonment seeming to come at the expense of a proper piety, was a particular target of the reformers, and Billings, an outspoken champion of fuging, seemed a kind of poster child for all that had gone wrong with American psalmody during the eighteenth century. Lowell Mason, America's leading musical entrepreneur of the antebellum years, would develop this goal of refined and proper church music into a lucrative commercial empire.

There was an irony in this. Billings' career, his livelihood as a singing-school teacher, and hence his composing career were made possible by the singing reform movement of the early 1700s, which had targeted the slow, loose, embroidered singing that developed among a populace with powerful piety but few tunebooks and no time for learning musical rudiments. The Calvinist distrust of music had come full circle. Singing schools had been established not to heighten the aesthetic pleasure of singing or listening—even if for many pupils this was the point—but to make that singing more pleasing to God. As a teacher, Billings himself subscribed to these ideals. But to the second wave of reformers that developed at the turn of the century, a composer musician like Billings had abused this opportunity in a way that was both impious and uncouth. Rather than looking ahead

to the possibilities of musical cultivation in American soil, the cultural orthodoxy looked back to the standard British psalmody that had existed before the beginning of American experimentation in the 1760s.[39] The campaign linked up with the efforts of a Protestant conservative like Timothy
Dwight to replace earlier, more vernacular versions of Watts's psalms with
a more theologically reliable one. The reformers may have had a point.
Nothing in the sources on Billings gives us access to his inner life. His ecstatic self-representation effectively screens his piety. Billings clearly knew
the Bible cold, and composed effectively in the sacred idiom, but we have
no way of knowing whether his genius was inspired more by Christian
piety or by the wellsprings of sonic intoxication. Would Billings have
worked in psalmody and sacred anthems if there had been alternative idioms of musical expression available to someone of Billings' ambitions, in
his time and place?

More clear is the fact that Billings' achievements in creating a new musical language for American church music would shape the future of
Protestant song in the United States more decisively than would the reformers who tried to excise him from the record. The raw beauty of his
open harmonies and unpredictable rhythmic energies would inflect the
shape-note songs and evangelical revival tunes that developed in the early
decades of the nineteenth century south and west of New England. Tunes
by Billings would turn up in the important antebellum shape-note compilations of the mid-nineteenth century. Shape notes were quite literally a
different language for representing music on the page, but this different
language made possible, even inevitable, a change in the sound of the music itself. In the case of the Shakers, a utopian sect establishing itself in
North America at the time of Billings' peak musical productivity, the quest
for a new music adequate to the experiential piety of the community
would lead to yet more innovations in writing music. Meanwhile, the refined sacred music of the Moravians would be overlooked by both the vernacular and elevated reformed musical streams. They were outside the
commercial marketplace that made, and eventually undid, Billings. Their
close-knit *Gemeinschaft* would set a different kind of example for utopian
sects like the Shakers. But their musical influence would continue to resonate through the hymns of their illustrious students, the Wesleys, whose
Methodist hymnody would become the most influential force in American
religious music in the coming century.

CHAPTER THREE

Marching to Zion

The day was kept as a general Holyday, but there was no music nor singing. Awaking some time in the morning I heard a sound and thought some were singing, but on listening attentively I found it was Pigs that was squealing, and I felt disappointed.

—JOSEPH BEECROFT

As William Billings labored on his second tunebook, *The Singing-Master's Assistant,* a group of nine religious pilgrims from the north of England were en route across the Atlantic. This was a much smaller group of dissidents than the Pilgrims and Puritans who had embarked for Massachusetts, bringing their psalmbooks with them, or even the Moravian contingent that had journeyed to Georgia with John and Charles Wesley. They sailed into New York Harbor on 6 August 1774. Most of the group headed up to a tract of unsettled land near Albany, where they proceeded to establish a community in a town later known as Watervliet. The leader of the pilgrims, a woman named Ann Lee, had been drawn about 1758 to a group of dissident "Shaking Quakers" in Manchester, England. Imprisoned for her beliefs in 1772, she was afterward known as Mother Ann Lee. The religious group she inspired, the United Society of Believers in Christ's Second Appearing but commonly known as the Shakers, had among its bedrock principles the rules of celibacy and of equality (but separation) of the sexes. Though the United Society fled England to avoid harassment, their lot in New York was difficult, especially in the first decade, when the Shakers poured themselves into evangelism. Her brother William died in July 1784; Mother Ann herself died two months later. One of the original nine, known as Father James Whitaker, led the group for only three years before he himself died. After 1787 the Shakers were under the direction of the American-born.[1]

Ann Lee was the daughter of a Manchester blacksmith, and married another. One of eight children, she was sent to work in a Manchester cotton mill at a young age. None of her own four children lived past age six. Her husband left her for another woman not long after their arrival in New York City. "Day and night she brooded over the nature of sin until her health, both mental and physical, was seriously undermined," according to Edward D. Andrews, author of the first modern history of Shaker music. "She became subject to wild outbursts of emotion, to visions, dark forebodings and vague messianic delusions." A life of vicissitudes had endowed Ann Lee with tangible spiritual power and singular gifts. One of the capacities that people observed was her power of musical expression. A man named Joseph Main recalled seeing her "sitting in a chair, and singing very melodiously, with her hands in motion; and her whole soul and body seemed to be in exercise. I felt, as it were, a stream of divine power and love flow into my soul, and was convinced at once that it came from Heaven, the source and fountain of all good. I immediately acknowledged my faith, and went and confessed my sins." Elizabeth Johnson recorded a similar experience. Ann Lee "came singing into the room where I was sitting, and I felt an inward evidence that her singing was in the gift and power of God. She came and sat down by my side, and put her hand upon my arm. Instantly I felt the power of God flow from her and run through my whole body."[2]

The songs that have come down through oral tradition use vocables instead of words, like this one:

Ve-um vum ve-um ve-um vum vum ve-um ve-um vum vum ve-um ve-um vum
Ve-um ve-um ve-um ve-um vum ve-um ve-um ve-um ve-um vum

No one knows exactly what these songs sounded like, and the cultivation of music was never a high priority among the Believers during Lee's lifetime. Little is known about her musical preferences, though like virtually all other pious Anglo-Americans she revered Isaac Watts. "Dr. Watts is now in heaven!" she is said to have remarked at one point. But about the body of Shaker song that succeeded Ann after her death in 1784, more is known than about any other nineteenth-century American sect. At the highwater mark of their range and extent they numbered somewhere around 5,000, spread across eighteen communities from Maine to Indiana. Estimates of the number of songs left behind range from 8,000 to 10,000. Unlike the usual Protestant diet of psalms and hymns (which after the Civil War would be augmented with so-called gospel songs), Shakers had a number of distinct genres of sacred song. There were hymns, to be sure, usually modeled after Watts and Wesley. But more significant were the "laboring songs" to accompany dances and marches; "gift songs" bestowed by spirits; the often-wordless "solemn songs"; and "extra" and "occasional" songs to be used for special occasions.[3]

It would be difficult to find a religious sect in America for which song played a more crucial role both in the ordinary tasks of daily life and worship and as a vehicle for the most extraordinary sorts of visions and divine communications. As one Shaker insisted, "We must remember that these were not just songs, but deep feelings from the soul." Daniel Patterson has identified several paradoxes inherent in the Shaker experience of music:

> Believers sang by ear and scarcely permitted a hymnal into the meetinghouse, yet they themselves preserved their oral tradition in voluminous transcriptions. Virtually no one was born a Shaker, and the membership was highly diverse—the converts came into the Society as children and as adults; they came educated and illiterate, native born and immigrant, New Englander and Southerner, Scotch-Irish and German, black and white and Indian—nevertheless, the Shakers developed a distinctive and remarkably unified song repertory. Many of their tunes were new and shaped to fit highly specific functions; they were at the same time firmly grounded in inherited melodic conventions. The United Society was one of the smaller religious bodies, but its songs far outnumber all the ballads and all the other spirituals known to have originated in American tradition.[4]

Song both heightened the individual encounter with the divine and knit together the community of Believers. Shakers sang to express joy and thanksgiving, to voice their dedication to the often difficult path they had chosen, to petition God for even greater spiritual devotion. And often they sang because they were "instruments" of spirits who chose them to relay a message to the earthly realm.

Sacred song had long been important to most Christians for many of the same purposes. What made Shakers unique was their commitment to and innovation of sacred dance. For Believers, dance was as inseparable from sacred song and collective worship as it was for non-European people from Native America or Africa. Father James, a founding English Shaker, regarded dancing as "the greatest gift of God that ever was made known to man for the purification of the soul." It could express joy, humility, communal solidarity. It fostered spiritual focus, unity, and harmony, "emblematical of the one spirit by which the people of God are led." Physical movement, from hand gestures to accompany songs to dizzyingly intricate patterns suggestive of a modern-day marching band on steroids, was loaded with symbolic meaning and spiritual significance. Shakers referred to their dominant form of collective movement not as dance but as "laboring." It was a fitting label, given the extreme self-discipline they required,

3. Shakers referred to their synchronized group movements not as dance but as "laboring," and created dozens of intricate patterns set to song in the decades after 1780. Courtesy of Shaker Museum and Library, Old Chatham, New York.

the important spiritual and communal gifts their conscientious execution was thought to bring, and the incredible elaboration they underwent. Over the decades after 1780, new dances entered the repertoire as others fell into disuse. Shaker dance was done with erect posture, using variations on two basic steps, shuffles and skips. Of course women and men didn't mix. A simple listing of some of the dances gives an indication of the sort of exhaustive elaboration and innovation they generated: "Back Manner," "Holy Order," "Step Manner," "Step and Shuffle," "Skipping Manner," "Turning Shuffle," "Drumming Manner," "Quick Dance," "Square Step," "Hollow Square," "Circular March," "Changeable March," "Heavenly March," "Square Check," "Antediluvian Square Shuffle."[5]

Very much a part of the social landscape of intense religious revivals that characterized the early decades of the nineteenth century, the Shakers maintained a position at the extremes. Their communities were essentially Protestant monasteries. But the practices and belief system captured by their songs share much with a variety of other sects, including the Mormons. Like most American Protestant sects and churches that followed the Puritans, Shakers understood themselves as a kind of new Israel, a fulfillment of biblical prophecy augmented by special revelation. North America was their Zion, although they originated in the old world of Europe. This circumstance required them to think carefully about other peoples they encountered in the New Zion, in particular American Indians. They were eagerly open to Pentecostal experiences of ecstatic visions and speaking (and singing) in tongues. Yet they worked carefully to refine and standardize those musical inspirations. And while they prided themselves on their apartness from "the World," their songs inevitably participated in a larger musical conversation that captures something important about the place of sacred song in America. A sect founded by a woman and committed to sexual equality, the Believers reveal the importance of sacred song as a domain where women were relatively safe from biblical proscriptions: against interpreting scripture, preaching, praying publicly, serving as an elder or deacon. But even among Shakers, gender considerations affected what sort of musical role a woman could play.

THE SONG usually known as "The People Called Christians" (Believers didn't title their songs) provides one useful window into the Shaker musical world. It is one of a very few Shaker songs to have "crossed over" into the realm of those they called "Worldlings." (Its better-known cousin, "'Tis a Gift to Be Simple," has become even more famous with the public as a result of Aaron Copland's borrowing of its musical theme for his ballet *Appalachian Spring*.) "The People Called Christians" appeared in the first Shaker songbook ever published, *Millennial Praises* (1811). The tune, in Dorian mode, as the majority of Shaker tunes tend to be, has a mournful but muscular sound; it resembles the English seafaring shanties "You Gentlemen of England" and "When the Stormy Winds Do Blow." Verses 1, 3, 4, and 6 capture crucial aspects of the Shaker self-understanding:

> A people called Christians Have many things to tell
> About the land of Canaan, Where saints and angels dwell;
> But here a dismal ocean, Enclosing them around,
> With its tides, still divides Them from Canaan's happy ground.

> The everlasting gospel Has launch'd the deep at last;
> Behold the sails expanded, Around the tow'ring mast!
> Along the deck in order The joyful sailors stand,
> Crying "Ho!—here we go To Immanuel's happy land."

> We're now on the wide ocean; We bid the world farewell!
> And though where we shall anchor No human tongue can tell;
> About our future destiny There need be no debate,
> While we ride on the tide, With our Captain and his Mate.

> The passengers united In order peace and love;—
> The wind all in our favor, How sweetly do we move!

Though tempests may assail us, And raging billows roar
We will sweep thro' the deep, Till we reach fair Canaan's shore.[6]

The allegorical voyage to a New Canaan is both a geographic and a meta-phoric reality: across the Atlantic, as the Believers and so many other religious pilgrims traversed, as well as through the "dreadful Ocean" of sin. The emphasis is on the Canaan to be reached, not the land of bondage from which the pilgrim has just escaped. Significantly, the song turns up almost verbatim in the 1835 *Southern Harmony,* an important early shape-note collection, and became a shape-note staple, reprinted in editions of the *Sacred Harp* tunebook throughout the twentieth century. William Walker, the compiler of *Southern Harmony,* apparently borrowed the text from the earlier *Dover Collection,* where it was attributed to an "I. Neighbors." But the song was already being sung at the Shaker society in Enfield, Connecticut, by 1810, most likely the work of a charismatic Believer named Richard McNemar.[7]

McNemar cut a particularly striking figure among the early Believers. A kind of Shaker apostle of the church, he contributed a number of songs to the Shaker repertoire, and turns up frequently in the documentary record of the early Believers (and also of the Second Great Awakening, in which he played an important role). Susan C. Liddil, the Believer who credited him with "A People Called Christians," remembered seeing him speak when she was a girl of ten: "his magnetic eloquence swayed and animated the audiences by its power as I could see while I trembled under its *greatness,* as it felt to me. And I looked with wonder on his tall erect form, his hair black and strong as an Indians, forehead high and white, a raised vein along the center brought to the surface of the skin by the warming force of his testimony, large full eyes 'blue as a Southern sky,' which seemed to draw . . . the electric currents from the very heavens above."[8] McNemar came to the Believers in his mid-thirties, having already lived a full life, spiritually and otherwise. Born in the Pennsylvania mountains in 1770, McNemar taught school at age fifteen and studied Hebrew, Greek, and Latin after joining the Methodists at age twenty-one. Later he joined the Presbyterians and was involved in a sectarian schism triggered by the camp-meeting revivals that broke out in Kentucky in 1800.

The revivals were triggered in part by disillusionment with Christianity in the aftermath of the Revolution, which led some westward-moving settlers to turn to deism while others sought out a more visceral faith based on direct experience: to know God's will not by reason but "by an inward light which shone into the heart." When Shaker missionaries passed through in 1805, McNemar was ready. "For upwards of 15 years my soul has been on the wheel, forming into union with professed followers of the

Lamb, but never did I find my mate, until I found the spirit from New Lebanon," he would write. "Now I can say with the prophet, 'This is my God, I have waited for him!'" McNemar's family clinched the conversion. His nine-year-old son had been subject to "very violent fits" after "being charmed by a large snake" near a spring. Feeling the onset of symptoms, the boy rushed into the house, where his father was arguing with three missionaries. In a "taunting ridiculing tone of voice" McNemar challenged the Believers to produce a miracle cure. At the insistence of his wife, Jenny, all prayed together. The son never suffered another fit; the entire family joined the United Society.[9] McNemar took the spiritual name Eleazer Wright.

Western Shakers encountered many of the same tribulations experienced by their eastern predecessors, and McNemar figured prominently in some notable adventures. In August 1810 a mob of 500 armed men marched on Union Village to demand the release of children they believed to have been kidnapped by Shakers. According to a witness, McNemar "quelled a furious wicked mob of three or four hundred men, by preaching poetry to them for two hours, from the house top of the old centre house, where he and a young brother were painting the eave troughs of the house." He continued his performance "until the whole mob were seated in the dooryard listening to him and were so charmed and surprised at his genius, that they all became good humored and returned home peaceably." Union Village was used as a staging ground to assist in the establishment of societies farther West. To shore up a new community in Indiana, which was being threatened by the depredations of religious opponents, including a Methodist minister named Peter Cartwright, McNemar and two others from Ohio made a 235-mile trek across the largely flooded lowland of southern Indiana to confer with the fledgling settlement. In their sixteen-day journey the group saw only a few isolated cabins and Indian camps. Challenges within the societies could be surprisingly hard-edged, complete with ritual humiliation. At Union Village, two Shaker zealots mocked McNemar and rolled him in the dust, accusing him of misinterpreting scripture. In each of these incidents McNemar had recently produced or was inspired to compose a sacred song: in the case of the siege of Union Village, a hymn on the clash between Christ and Herod; after the Indiana voyage, a sixteen-verse ballad.[10]

McNemar may have been a rawboned frontiersman, but he had a mystic's soul, and his accounts of visions and gift songs are among the most vivid recorded by Believers. Susan Liddil described him in action at Union Village during the time after dances and marches when Believers shared spontaneous gifts. McNemar spoke at length, then launched into his favorite song, with "clear voice, muscle, and the sweetest of all singers." He would stride up and down the aisle with his coat hanging open, keeping time with his hands and feet, his face "in rapturous glow, his eyes upward raised . . . it verily seemed the heavens were opened to his survey." McNemar was frequently transported by Shaker rituals. When a new dance form was introduced in 1823, McNemar became ecstatic, calling it "more heavenly than I ever saw before" and comparing it to "that which the children of Israel danced after their three days march out of Egypt. To me," he wrote, in language describing a Pentecostal experience, "it felt both awful & glorious to see such a vast body of well trained believers in a solid body of brethren & sisters alternately move round, like the rushing of a mighty wind." He wrote a hymn celebrating the dance in the language of Ezekiel. His most dramatic vision came another night in a workroom where he would sometimes retire during his leisure time to weave cloth. When it had become too dark to see his work, McNemar "heard singing off in the room in the sweetest voice that he had ever listened to in song. The singing continued for three quarters of an hour, song after song. The singer stepped forth as through a parting veil. And there stood Sarah Coulter in the aspect of early womanhood—her face 'like the face of an angel' and a signal light in the perfect form revealing 'All glorious within'—then vanished out of sight." To McNemar, this vision was "one of the greatest lessons of his life: considering the lowliness and humble, quiet and retiring manner of Sarah Coulter as a sojourner in life, seldom spoken of and little thought about."[11]

McNemar continued receiving gift songs until 1838. In his final years he endured a run-in with the new leadership of Union Village that led to his expulsion, a journey east to plead his case, and his eventual reinstatement and return to Ohio. Then, in 1839, he died. The Believers had just entered a decade of particularly intense revival fervor that they would call "Mother's Work." It was a kind of Shaker Great Awakening. Over the next decade and a half the Shakers would achieve their largest membership, and would generate an unprecedented outpouring of sacred song. On 16 August 1837, at the Watervliet society near Albany, a fourteen-year-old named Ann Maria Goff went into a trance, shook and whirled, and began singing: "Where the pretty angels dwell, Heaven! / Where the pretty angels dwell forever." Other girls in the community followed suit, going into a trance, recording conversations with spirits and celestial journeys. By 1838 Believers in all communities were reporting becoming "instruments" of gift songs bequeathed by an astonishing array of historical figures, from early Shaker leaders and recently departed members to Alexander the Great, Napoleon, and President Harrison to Mother Ann, Mohammed, and Jesus Christ. One of many gift sings attributed to Mother Ann, in 1844, features the vocables characteristic of her own songs: "Vum vi-ve vum vi-ve vum vum vo, Ve vum vi-ve vum vi-ve vum vum vo," etc. America's "founding fathers" were found to be particularly generous with song. "Washington was supposed to have influenced thousands of spirits to join the eternal Shaker church and to have first conducted the Indians to meetings of the sect," according to Andrews. "Being a Quaker and also a friend of the Indians on earth, Penn was likewise a favorite figure among the Believers; they admired Jefferson greatly, and for some reason included Columbus in their calendar of saints." These new gift songs tended to be different from earlier genres. The songs were melodically loose, often sequences of notes rather than crafted melodies. Verses and stanzas were less structured than the typical Shaker song. And the sheer volume of songs being generated put enormous strains on the abilities of communities to record them, let alone learn them.[12]

Why a revival of this sort just then? The year Mother's Work began, 1837, also featured the arrival in the United States of Frenchman Charles Poyen, whose lectures on animal magnetism fed a keen public fascination with mesmerism, clairvoyance, and somnambulism. These were mental states that described the mainly youthful Shaker sisters who received gift songs as well as spiritual impulses that would produce Spiritualism, Christian Science, and New Thought. The gift-song phenomenon may also have been a response to fears of a decline in piety and commitment, as the generation of adult converts like McNemar was dying off and the younger generation was thought to lack some of the fervent fire that came along with trials of the sort faced by earlier Believers. At stake was the distinctive Shaker notion of a dual masculine-feminine godhead. Believers were thought to have three distinct sets of parents: Christ and Mother Ann ("Heavenly Parents"); Father Meacham, Mother Lucy, and other founding members ("Spiritual Parents"); God the Father and Holy Mother Wisdom ("Eternal Parents"). Shaker theology, and the sacred song that gave communal expression to it, both articulated and celebrated this complex genealogy in ways that positioned the Believers among other communities of the faithful:

> Like other Christians, the Shakers had songs of prayer and praise to God, or admonition to the sinner and exhortation to the faltering saint. Like others with a millennial faith, they had songs of Jubilee, but of Jubilee arrived, not longed for. They sang not of Christ's atonement but of themselves taking up a full cross against the World, the Flesh, and the Devil. Their imaginations turned not to the Calvinist God, the fearsome regal Father, nor to the redeeming Son, whose sacrifice set other revivalists a-shouting, but instead

to the maternal principle in the Godhead, now newly revealed in and through Mother Ann.[13]

Given the gender conventions of the nineteenth century, this was a difficult undertaking. Though Believers professed and practiced equality of the sexes, it was the equality of "separate but equal." Women's responsibilities ran more to the intuitive and practical—transcribing music, receiving gift songs, exhorting Believers to good works—while men theorized about music, composed hymns, and wrote theology. Judging from hundreds of songs passed down during the decade of Mother's Work, the revival was in part a reassertion of the maternal power that was always threatened by the male principle. Unlike earlier Puritans moved by a conception of God the Father, or orthodox evangelicals focused on the redeeming son, Shakers preferred the image of godhead as nurturing Mother; the revival and musical outpouring that began in 1837 was the reassertion of the symbolic power of Mother Ann.[14]

Lyrically, many of the gift songs contain what strikes the modern reader as powerfully gendered language, with an emphasis on angels, flowers, and childlike purity.

> Oh what pretty souls! All joind, heart and hand,
> Singing on their way. Angels guard the band.
> These are virgin souls, Innocent and pure;
> Standing in holiness; Unto the end endure.
>
> I have an assortment of beautiful flowers;
> And now of my choicest take some.
> I dwell in Mother's garden, among her green bowers;
> And with her sweet songsters I've come.
> O here are some roses, O here are some lilies,
> And here are some sweet pinks too.

Many gift songs were bequeathed by or evoked birds, often doves.

> I am Mother's pretty little dove
> I sit upon a branch of union and love.
> She sent me to you to help you along,
> So now I will sing you a pretty little song.
> Hohoho la venvenvo, hohoho la venvenvo.[15]

If a reassertion of gender was crucial to Mother's Work, it came to be expressed largely through ethnic voices. Beginning in the Lebanon society in 1842 but quickly spreading to other Shaker settlements came "strange visitations" by large numbers of anonymous but clearly identifiable ethnic spirits: "Mexicans, Peruvians, Patagonians, Hottentots, Grecians, Persians, Turks, Moors, Chinese, Loo-choo Islanders, Jews and persons or families of Scotch, Irish, French and Spanish descent." (This was a kind of foreshadowing of the World Parliament of Religions and Columbian Exposition of 1893, with its polyethnic Midway Plaisance, where representatives of culture from around the world were brought in for the entertainment of fairgoers.) For Shakers as for more orthodox Christians, most of these groups were heathen, in need of saving evangelism. Shakers themselves were astonished by this "taking in" of Native spirits, who behaved so differently from ordinary Shakers. It was "inexpressible," wrote one, "to see so many persons possessed of Indian spirits acting out all the barbarian gestures, & speaking the Indian language with the utmost fluency." Ethnic performances could be quite stylized: "When the Eskimo spirits took possession of the bodies of brethren and sisters, the latter would perform the actions of driving dog-sledges: 'they would move about the floor, give a whistle, and accompany it with a motion of the hand, as though they were flourishing a whip.' 'Laplanders' and 'Greenlanders' exercised themselves by 'skating' about the floor; 'melancholy Siberians' walked about with folded arms; 'Arabs' sometimes seized and tried to hide various articles which they could lay their hands on; and 'Abyssinians' jumped about boisteriously [*sic*] with loud frantic shouts."[16] The missionary impulse may have had something to do with these performances, the sense that the Shaker faith had a universal reach across cultures; they were not far removed from the Pentecostal gifts of tongue-speaking practiced in the early church. The visitations also may have expressed the need of a marginalized sect to align itself with a broad range of spiritual ancestors. Shakers put a premium on ritualized humility, and "it was regarded as even more mortifying to take in an Indian or Eskimo or Hottentot spirit and be compelled to perform uncouth actions than it was to execute some of the earlier gifts."[17] It was a duty required from above, not a lighthearted or frolicsome release.

The Mother's Work revival and accompanying gift songs from spirits began to taper off after 1850, but Shakers continued to receive songs from Native spirits as late as 1893. These were the most radical of all the gift songs, partly because of their emphasis on the individual "instrument" who channeled them. "Instead of beholding the natives in visions, the inspired were led to dance as the bodily instruments of the Indian spirits, who were not concerned to provide a gift in which all could unite," historian Patterson notes. "Those Believers who were not themselves possessed stood apart observing the solo dancers." The most detailed account of a "taking in" of a Native spirit comes from Pleasant Hill, Kentucky, in 1857, where a Native spirit known as Red Hawk always took possession of a Shaker named John Bunnel:

he offered as an apology for his not attending meeting until it was half out, was that he had not confess'd all of his sins . . . he was verry glad to unite with us, he was verry anxious to lern how to dance our way, he appear'd to understand the Indian dance verry well; he would not go home for sometime after meeting was dismiss'd, he was all the time begging us to sing some of our prety songs, and lern him how to dance; finally by begging him with fare promises that we would sing for him this evening in our singing meeting he would go home, and done so; This same Chief has been here frequently before in his savage state; he was verry noisy and boisters with savage yells; today he was verry mild and gentle he says he has been dead 75 years and was kill'd in battle our meeting continued 2½ hours.[18]

From one perspective, the Believers were projecting a certain image of the pliant heathen. "The visits of the natives exhibited one significant pattern," observes Patterson: "when the Indians first came they showed 'some awkwardness & ignorance of the ways of white people,' but they were 'soon & easily tamed & brot into a degree of order & conformity' to Shaker customs. After one tribe had received gospel instruction, it withdrew and another came." One text was modeled after the then-popular genre of the dramatic farewell of the "vanishing Indian" called "Arkumsha's Farewell":

> Me tanke de white man who for me did fess
> Me tank de good Elder whom he did address
> Me feel poor and needy me want me soul save
> And now lest me weary de white man me leave.[19]

A sense of spiritual yearning is palpable in this Native song:

> Me cannot wear de great long face, And be de very sober,
> It makes me feel all out of place And de pretty time's all over.
> Me want de joy to fill me soul And love what be de mercy
> Come holy power and thro' me roll, Old bondage me will bury.
> Now me happy feel Dancing in de whites zeal,
> Me can step de tune complete
> De gospel shoes be on me feet
> Woo ne wip a wa Hal an e na hal an aw
> Woo ne wip a waw Hal an e na haw haw.[20]

This was "playing Indian," and usually not skillfully. Verisimilitude was not a criterion that held much relevance to Believers. But when Elizabeth West channeled a Wyandott "squaw" at Union Village, the elders tested her comprehension with a glossary and found her state of possession to be authentic.[21]

Believers seem to have performed ethnicity with as much gusto (and accuracy) as the blackface minstrels then ascendant in American popular culture. They actually had had more experience with flesh-and-blood African Americans, whose spirits also frequently took possession of Believers during Mother's Work, than they did with American Indians. Societies both east and west included a scattering of blacks. One was Patsy Williamson, a Believer at Pleasant Hill, a slave whose owners became Shakers in 1809. When her owners "turned away," the Society bought Williamson's freedom so she could remain at Pleasant Hill. In manuscript, African-American Shaker gift songs are indistinguishable from those of European Americans, without apparent African stylization, but we have no way of knowing how they were performed. Believers could remember details of gift songs with remarkable precision. When an elder named Abraham Perkins was serenaded by fiddlers and dancers during a visit to Pleasant Hill in 1873, he witnessed an African American who "beat the time with his hands by striking his body, exactly as the negro spirits did in our meeting room in 1843." A recent recording includes "Negro" gift songs that simulate the sounds of instruments like a banjo, and a song attributed to Williamson that has some African-American stylizations:

> O my pretty Mother's [Father's] [Savior's] home,
> Sweeter than the honey in the comb
> Come love pretty love, come, come, come,
> Come love pretty love, I want some.[22]

Nothing could have been further from Shaker intentions than minstrelsy. Some of the language used by "Worldlings" to describe Shaker song uses vocabulary that would be regularly applied to the spirituals sung by enslaved Africans. "Early national Shakers, for example, produced 'a kind of wild plaintive tune' and sang 'doleful melodies,' and even though they were considered 'a sober, honest and industrious people,' their singing 'not disagreeable,' the sound of their religion was 'wild and something like that of our American savages.'"[23] Believers had become grudgingly resigned to the presence of "Worldlings" at their open meetings, drawn by what seemed to many the comic appearance of the synchronized dances. During the sensational developments of Mother's Work, elders decided to close worship to the public for a time. But to their mortification, Believers found themselves the object of minstrel performers eager to capitalize on the exotic reputation of the sect. Worst of all, the minstrels were former Believers, as this 1846 message from Enfield made clear:

> The Apostates from Canterbury, have joined together, and are exhibiting themselves for money, in Shaker attire: in dances, songs, speaking in unknown tongues &c. &c. They are now in Boston . . . How many more we do not know but we expect there are some from other Societies. We have seen

their great glaring show Bills and enclose two slips from a Boston Paper to
you.

GREAT MORAL CURIOSITY
SHAKER CONCERT,
THE CELEBRATED AND FAR-FLUNG
CHASE FAMILY,
FROM CANTERBURY, N.H.

Who have performed for seven consecutive weeks,
to overflowing houses, at the

AMERICAN MUSEUM,

New York, and have received the unqualified commendation and patronage
of the people of Boston and other cities of New England, beg leave to an-
nounce most respectfully to the ladies and Gentlemen of this vicinity, that
they intend giving A Grand Levee.

So read playbills distributed by the apostate troupe even through the
Shaker community at Union Village. Featured as "the miraculous Shaker
tetotum" was Lydia Chase: "This young lady, whose long experience as a
Shaker, united with unheard of bodily powers, renders her a general wonder, will execute Astonishing Shaker Gyrations, eclipsing in Agility, Grace,
Muscular Ability and Wonder, the divine Fanny herself. Through a force
of long habit, and being peculiarly endowed, she can, without dizziness
or cessation, WHIRL ROUND LIKE A TOP, FIFTEEN HUNDRED
TIMES!" The concert was billed as "an intellectual and agreeable mode
to throw light upon a subject of interest and amusement to all."[24]

IN 1837, the year Mother's Work began, a twenty-three-year-old Englishman named William Clayton was baptized and began missionary work in
Manchester, England, the birthplace of Mother Ann and the United Society. Three years later he moved to Illinois, where he became secretary to a
local religious leader. In 1846, after a series of sometimes violent alterca-
tions with orthodox Protestants, Clayton joined a band of saints intent on
establishing a New Israel further west. That April, in an encampment
known as Winter Quarters, near the Iowa-Missouri border, he wrote a
hymn that became known by its first line, "Come, Come Ye Saints":

Come, come, ye Saints, no toil, nor labor fear, But with joy wend your way;
Though hard to you this journey may appear, Grace shall be as your day.
'Tis better far for us to strive, Our useless cares from us to drive:
Do this, and joy your hearts will swell—All is well! all is well! . . .

We'll find the place which God for us prepared, Far away in the West,
Where none shall come to hurt, nor make afraid: There the Saints will be blest.
We'll make the air with music ring,—Shout praises to our God and King:
Above the rest these words we'll tell—All is well! all is well![25]

Clayton's text could take a place alongside one of Richard McNemar's ballads of courage in the face of physical and social adversity. It voiced the familiar yearning to establish a New Israel where God's chosen people could live and worship in peace, free from the persecutions of a hostile and unwitting world. Like McNemar's great hymn of the ocean crossing to Canaan, "Come Ye Saints" became fixed with a shape-note tune published in *The Sacred Harp*. But Clayton was not a member of the United Society of Believers in Christ's Second Appearing but rather of a community that called itself the Church of Jesus Christ of Latter-day Saints. His prophet was not Mother Ann but a visionary named Joseph Smith. He was a Mormon, not a Shaker.

The two Christian sects had some notable differences. Unlike the Shakers, who found themselves the butt of apostate minstrels, Latter-day Saints were "tantalized" by the popular culture around them: minstrel shows conveyed by Mississippi riverboats, black sailors, immigrants of several ethnic backgrounds, even the rare enslaved African Americans living among the Mormons. A *New York Times* article from 1857 pointed out that Mormons "do not confine themselves to sacred music. All the popular songs of the day—English glees, negro melodies, and even sentimental ballads—they bring into their service. Their hymns are for the most part sung to familiar 'profane' airs." And there were far more substantial differences. Shakers took their cue from a woman and elevated the female principle in their understanding of the godhead; Mormons did not. Shakers upheld a code of celibacy; Mormons, for most of the nineteenth century, claimed a divine mandate for polygamy. Both believed that human history was unfolding in divinely ordained dispensations according to biblical prophecy, but the final timeline was not the same. For Shakers, the millennium had arrived with the coming of Mother Ann, and they were living in it, an archipelago of small villages. Most Mormons believed the millennium to be in the future, and their own role was to bring that millennium to fruition by building a New Israel in the Great Basin of Utah.

These different ends called for different means. While Shakers eschewed the ballot and refused military service, Mormons did not hesitate to embroil themselves in politics and statecraft. Writing about American Pentecostals, historian Grant Wacker shows how these Christians flourished by ingeniously harmonizing the primitive—the more primal, elemental aspects of their beliefs and practices—with a pragmatic sense of the art of the possible that would allow the church and its members to survive and prosper.[26] Shakers and Mormons clearly demonstrated both primitive and pragmatic instincts, but Saints have been far more effective than Believers in their pragmatism. Most obviously, the United Society has faded since the mid-nineteenth century to a handful of Believers, while Latter-day Saints are one of the fastest-growing religions in the United States and throughout the world.

Despite these differences, similarities between the groups are equally revealing. Sects are voluntary societies of people separated from the world and bound by a shared religious experience of new life and expectation of the coming kingdom of God. They emphasize the need to commit to habits of right living, total personal morality, and salvation through works. If mainstream Protestants, following Calvin and Luther, emphasize the Word, radical American sectarians emphasize the deed. Their rituals tend to render the ordinary extraordinary rather than to reduce the extraordinary to the ordinary.[27] The United Society and Latter-day Saints followed this pattern closely. Both began their American phases in upstate New York. The Shakers had of course originated in England but moved quickly to the United States, while the Mormons had established successful missions to England within the first decade, initiating the migration that included Clayton. Both were founded on revelations granted to inspired visionaries, Mother Ann Lee and Prophet Joseph Smith, who saw themselves as completing rather than supplanting Christianity. And these revelations continued, at times through Pentecostal modes of speaking and singing in tongues. Central to both Shaker and Mormon identity was the divinely ordained drive to establish settlements, a New Zion sanctuary beyond the reach of the corrosive disbelief of "Worldlings" and "gentiles." Coupled with this was a missionary zeal that compelled outreach to Babylon. Like the Shakers, Mormons paid considerable attention to Amerindians, but their sacred texts and historical experience brought Mormons much more closely into contact with Native America than Shakers ever ventured, despite a profusion of Native gift songs among the latter. And both sects placed high value on the ability of music to express joy, praise, and thanksgiving, to console and steel the spirit, to knit people more closely together as a community.

The first accounts of singing in the Mormon church mention the ecstatic tongue-singing of Lyman Wright, who assumed charge of the newly established church in Kirtland, Ohio, where he was reported to produce "a song which no one ever heard before, and which they said was the most melodious that they ever listened to. It was sung in another tongue." A new convert named Brigham Young showed the Pentecostal gift, and presently Smith did as well. The Kirtland singing was thought remarkable for its beauty and precision, one duet unfolding "simultaneously . . . beginning and ending each verse in perfect unison, without varying a word . . . as though we had sung it together a thousand times." Joseph Smith seems to have loved this singing (though he came to resent Pentecostal challenges to his own revelations). Like Ann Lee, Joseph Smith came of age in an era of revivals, with Methodists, Presbyterians, and Baptists in competition for souls in the district of western New York State known as the "burned-over" region because of its fervent piety. The sort of visions and revelations Smith had, beginning at age fourteen and increasingly at age seventeen, only gradually came to stand out from the general high pitch of Christian experience. In 1830 many threads of this story converged. In that year the Book of Mormon, based on revelations about hieroglyphic golden plates buried near Manchester, New York, was published; the Church of Christ (not yet Latter-day Saints) was organized in Fayette, New York; the first missionaries to Indians were sent west to Ohio and Missouri; and Joseph Smith had a revelation about hymns for the new church. This last was useful; while the Book of Mormon itself included some scattered references to hymn-singing, none provided much guidance beyond what the Bible had stated. In Smith's own upbringing, local Baptists rejected singing while Smith was drawn to the musical ebullience of Methodist worship.[28]

Smith's 1830 revelation, addressed to his wife, Emma, was much more formal and specific: "And it shall be given thee, also, to make a selection of sacred hymns, as it shall be given thee, which is pleasing unto me, to be had in my church," Smith intoned. "For my soul delighteth in the song of the heart; yea, the song of the righteous is a prayer unto me, and it shall be answered with a blessing upon their heads. Wherefore, lift up thy heart and rejoice, and cleave unto the covenants which thou hast made." Emma Smith received assistance in this project from the energetic convert William Wines Phelps, a newspaper editor from Ontario County who began publishing his new and adapted hymns in 1832 in the newspaper he had just founded. Work was delayed when a Missouri mob enraged by Mormon overtures to free blacks rioted and destroyed the press, but by the beginning of 1836 the long-awaited collection was released, listing Emma Smith as compiler. The volume contained ninety hymn texts (no tunes), more than half borrowed mainly from English hymn writers like Watts, Wesley, and Newton and rewritten to emphasize the Mormon drive to create a new Zion. But the roughly forty hymns by Phelps included some of the longest-lasting of all Mormon hymns.

However, music remained a point of contention. Among the many hardships faced by Saints during the pivotal decade of the 1840s were disputes over hymnbooks. Again pursuing the revelation to her husband of 1830, Emma compiled a second collection in Nauvoo in 1841 that seemed to back away from the triumphalist Zionism that was beginning to color

Mormon thinking. She included for the first time several Protestant classics, including "Am I a Soldier of the Cross," "When I Survey the Wondrous Cross," and "Amazing Grace." The timing was unfortunate, as Mormon theology was rapidly distinguishing itself even more dramatically from the Protestant mainstream. When the exodus to Utah began in February 1846, it included many British converts who maintained a fierce loyalty to the more militant hymns of the Manchester collection. Emma Smith's hymns were already obsolete, whereas the Manchester hymnal was reprinted many times over the succeeding decades.[29]

Early Mormon hymnbooks were notable for their use of and interest in Amerindians, both as represented in popular songs and as important figures in Mormon theology. Sometimes Mormon hymn writers borrowed tunes from popular songs about Indians as settings for hymns that addressed specifically Mormon issues. Phelps used a song called "The Indian Hunter" as the model for one hymn:

("The Indian Hunter")	(Phelps)
Let me go to my home	Come to me, will ye come
In the far distant west,	To the saints that have died,
To the scenes of my childhood	To the next better world, where
That I love the best,	The righteous reside,
Where the tall cedars are and	Where the angels and spirits
The bright waters flow	In harmony be,
Where my parents will greet me,	In the joys of a vast Paradise,
White man, let me go.	Come to me.

Some well-known hymns did more than just borrow settings. They expressed the uniquely conflicted role of Native Americans in Mormon theology and historical experience. Unlike Shaker gift songs, which ostensibly presented themselves from a native point of view, the Mormon hymns tended to address Indians as the inscrutable Other. One early favorite, "The Red Man," was modeled on an anonymous revival song called "Wandering Singer," which begins:

> Come tell me, wandering sinner,
> Say whither do you roam?
> O'er this wide world a stranger,
> Have you no Savior known?

Working from this model, Phelps wrote this eight-stanza hymn in 7.6.7.6:

> O, stop and tell me, Red Man, Who are you, why you roam,
> And how you get your living; Have you no God—no home?

With stature straight and portly, And decked in native pride,
With feathers, paints and brooches; He willingly replied,—

I once was pleasant Ephraim, When Jacob for me prayed;
But oh, how blessings vanish, When man from God has strayed!

Before your nation knew us, Some thousand moons ago,
Our fathers fell in darkness, And wandered to-and-fro.

And long they've lived by hunting Instead of work and arts,
And so our race has dwindled To idle Indian hearts.

Yet hope within us lingers, As if the Spirit spoke—
He'll come for your redemption, And break your gentile yoke.

And all your captive brothers From every clime shall come,
And quit their savage customs, To live with God at home.

Then joy will fill our bosoms, And blessings crown our days,
To live in pure religion, And sing our Maker's praise.[30]

Phelps's opening questions are clearly rhetorical, as the interrogator's well-informed reply reveals. In fact, Amerindians play a crucial role in the Book of Mormon (and appeared as early as 1823 in Smith's revelations from Moroni). Again, Smith was drawing upon a long tradition that sought to trace Native America to roots in the Eastern Hemisphere.

The Book of Mormon chronicles the experiences over a millennium and a half of three groups of Middle Easterners who migrate to the New World. The righteous are the Nephites, after the early prophet Nephi, while the fallen people are called Lamanites, breakers of the covenant cursed with "a skin of blackness." The book ends after the beginning of the fifth century C.E. with the wicked Lamanites "wandering the land seeking the lives of the few good survivors, including a prophet, Moroni, who has the final responsibility after his father, Mormon, to record what he has witnessed and hide the records in the hope that the account will help convert the descendants of those who are hunting him." Early Mormons often referred to present-day Indians as Lamanites, with all the pejorative associations, but some regarded Indians as descendents of the righteous Nephi rather than of Laman. Smith himself referred to American Indians as "literal descendents of Abraham." According to Smith's mother, his knowledge of the history of the natives was extraordinarily detailed; Joseph discussed "their dress, mode of travelling, and the animals upon which they rode; their cities, their buildings, with every particular; their mode of warfare; and also their religious worship. This he would do with as much ease, seemingly as if he has spent his whole life with them." In 1833 he described the Book of Mormon as a chronicle of the ancestors of "our western tribes of Indians . . . By it we learn that our western tribes . . . are descendants from that Joseph which was sold in Egypt." Though he hinted that the battles that end the book took place in Illinois, other early literature reflects the view that Central America may have been the setting of the book.[31]

In any event, Indians would prove to be a crucial ingredient in the Mormon project of building the new earthly Zion—what Smith called "the gathering of the elect of the Lord out of every nation on earth, and bringing them to the place of the Lord of Hosts, when the city of righteousness shall be built." According to Smith's *History*, "one of the most important points in the faith of the Church . . . is the gathering of Israel (of whom Lamanites constitute a part)." With this in mind Smith sent the first band of missionaries to the western border of Missouri in 1830 with this revelation: "For it is my will that in time, ye should take unto you wives of the Lamanites and Nephites that their posterity may become white, delightsome and just, for even now their females are more virtuous than the gentiles." (Since some of the missionaries were already married, this revelation may have been the origin of Mormon plural marriage.) The mission backfired, with non-Mormon Anglos accusing the missionaries of conspiring with Indians against other settlers, a charge that would hound Mormons for decades. One of the missionaries, Parley P. Pratt, attempted to clarify the church's relation to Native peoples in a proclamation. "The 'Indians' (so called) of North and South America are a remnant of the tribes of Israel; as is now made manifest by the discovery and revelation of their ancient oracles and records," Pratt wrote the year after Smith's murder in Nauvoo. "And that they are about to be gathered, civilized and made *one nation* in this glorious land."[32]

The question remained, which glorious land? As hatred of Mormons mounted in Missouri and Illinois during the 1840s, Saints found themselves with little choice but to head west—much farther west, to the Great Basin. This trek, which inspired William Clayton to pen "Come, Come Ye Saints," was the Mormon Exodus; it further galvanized the young church's already strong sense of identity with the chosen people of the Hebrew Bible. "Just as the original designation of the Saints as chosen was a repetition of God's paradigmatic act in choosing Abraham's seed, so the Mormon trek renewed the force of God's election of the Mormons in precisely the same way that the miraculous departure from Egypt and journey through the wilderness and into the promised Land renewed the identity of the Hebraic tribes as the citizens of His elect nation," writes historian Jan Shipps. "When Brigham Young led the Saints across the plains, he led them not only out of the hands of their midwestern persecutors but backward into a primordial sacred time."[33] The exodus of 1846 was more than a forced migration that began with a river crossing and ended with the entry into a valley surrounded by peaks, an American Kingdom of Zion. The Mississippi River had been covered with ice, and the band was able to cross from Nauvoo across the ice bridge. Like the Israelites escaping from Egypt, the Latter-day Saints organized themselves into a Camp of Israel commanded by a hierarchy of captains, and staved off starvation by subsisting on a miraculous mannalike substance and quail.

Hymns helped keep alive memories and visions, both the push and pull behind their migration. "Remember the wrongs of Missouri; Forget not the fate of Nauvoo," went part of one hymn: "When the God-hating foe is before ye, Stand firm, and be faithful and true." Just as important was the great millennial vision beckoning west:

> Israel, awake from thy long silent slumber,
> Shake off the fetters that bound thee so long;—
> Chains of oppression! we'll break them asunder,
> And join with the ransomed in victory's song!
> Arise! for the time has come, Israel must gather home,
> High on the mountains the Ensign we see;
> Fall'n is the Gentile power, Soon will their reign be o'er,
> Tyrants must rule no more, Israel is free![34]

"Like the children of Israel," Shipps writes, "the Saints made their way through the wilderness to claim their 'inheritances,' and in so doing conjoined experience and scripture to take possession of that special relationship to God which once had been the sole property of the Jews."[35] Of course, they drew on Christian beliefs and symbols as well, believing that the revealed truth of the Book of Mormon and of several direct revelations to Joseph Smith showed the Latter-day Saints to be the completion and fulfillment of the Christian church in the same way the early Christians saw themselves as completing and fulfilling Judaism.

While Mormons had engaged with Indians in Missouri since the earliest days of the church, a different set of Indians and issues awaited the Latter-day Saints of the western exodus. A basic church policy toward Amerindians emerged during the early 1850s under the leadership of Brigham Young. "I have uniformly pursued a friendly course of policy towards them [the Indians]," Young wrote in 1854, "feeling convinced that independent of the question of exercising humanity towards so degraded and ignorant a race of people, it was manifestly more economical and less expensive, to feed and clothe, than to fight them." This sort of Mormon pragmatism began to flourish in the land they called Deseret under Young's leadership.

Mormon leaders beginning with Smith pursued a strategy of what historian Richard White has called "the Middle Ground," exploiting an ethnic triad to differentiate themselves from other Anglos when it served their interests to ally with Indians, and differentiating themselves from Indians when they needed to make common cause with other whites. "An ambivalent theology of the Lamanite allowed Mormon and Indian interests to be distinguished so that Mormons could practice a flexible 'politics of the Indian,'" Stanley Kimball points out. But the Middle Ground of Deseret was decidedly dangerous, with Mormons regularly straying into the crossfire of federal policies of confining Indians to reservations and Indian resistance. They intervened in the Amerindian slave trade in the Great Basin, and they faced the challenge of hostile raiding parties. An 1865 treaty signed by Utah leaders transferring territory to the U.S. government provided only a brief respite. By the 1880s Mormons found themselves facing much the same threat of federal power. In 1887 Congress passed both the Edmunds-Tucker Act, which disincorporated the church, and the General Allotment Act, which established a new system for Indian reservations. "Both acts grew out of the same determination to force the Mormon Church and Indians to abandon their corporate, communal lives," argues David Whitaker. "Where Mormonism was forced to abandon plural marriage and ecclesiastical control of Utah society, the Indians were forced to abandon their communal life by forsaking their tribal leaders for programs that promised allotments in fee simple and citizenship to those Indians who adopted farming on individualized plots like 'good' Americans." Ironically, by that decade many missionaries to the Indians were Mormon apostles gone into hiding to avoid prosecution on polygamy charges.[36]

THE epochal migration from the Middle East to America was perhaps the crucial narrative undergirding Mormon sacred history, and it presaged the symbolic significance of the exodus to Deseret. But a more recent transatlantic migration played a major role in shaping Mormon attitudes toward music and repertoire. William Clayton, author of "Come, Come Ye Saints," was only one of several important early British converts. In 1840 a missionary contingent that included Brigham Young was sent to England and quickly compiled a new hymnbook in Manchester specifically for British converts; it would be reprinted dozens of times over the nineteenth century. As with evangelism of Amerindians, the mission to Britain was understood as fulfilling prophecies about gathering the chosen people to a New Israel; fittingly, a prevailing theme in the new hymnbook was an exhortation to leave the spiritual Babylon of England for the United States.

Not surprisingly, the sea and its crossing contributed one of the themes of Mormon song. American missionaries often composed hymns while crossing the ocean. A popular song called "The Sea":

> The sea! The sea! The open sea!
> The blue, the fresh, the ever free! . . .
> I'm on the sea! I'm on the sea!
> I am where I would ever be . . .
> I've lived since then in calm and strife
> Full fifty summers a sailor's life.

was easily adapted by John Taylor in his posthumous tribute to Joseph Smith, "The Seer":

> The Seer, the Seer, Joseph the Seer!
> I'll sing of the prophet ever dear . . .
> He's free! he's free! the Prophet's free!
> He is where he will ever be;
> Beyond the reach of mobs and strife
> He rests unharmed in endless life.[37]

By the end of 1841 at least 500 British converts had made their way to Nauvoo. The Mormon missionaries in England apparently had particular appeal for British musicians, who converted and migrated to Nauvoo, creating an active subculture of musicians. Into the 1870s more than half of the adult population of Utah was foreign born, mainly British and Scandinavian. "Many villages in Utah became outposts of old-world culture and many of the best musicians in Mormondom in the mid-nineteenth century were European emigrants."[38]

These transatlantic exchanges had the effect both of shaping the repertoire of Mormon hymns and songs, and of raising the musical quality. Joseph Smith had a notable penchant for martial pomp and circumstance, including military bands, and in 1843 personally selected the site for the Nauvoo Music Hall, completed after his death, in 1845. Growing up amid the musical activity created "one continual holiday for us children, who had very little idea of the meaning of it," recalled one Mormon. Much of the music played at concerts was secular in origin. A band concert might include two overtures, two grand marches, a number with the choir titled "God Save the Band," and a finale. There would also be vocal performances of popular songs by soloists, duos, and glee clubs. "The Mormon bands all seem to have considered their work a religious duty," according to Michael Hicks; "they were to spread music through the nation of Zion, elevate the people's tastes, stir their hearts with hymns and martial airs, and provide a social pastime for Saints."

For the first generation in Deseret, the boundary between the sacred and the nonsacred was particularly porous, because they understood themselves to be living already in sacred time. Formal worship was almost beside the point, when music and dance were always already sacralized by virtue of being the spontaneous expression of a chosen people already living in their promised land. But as church leaders saw it, if Latter-day Saints were to be ready for the Second Coming, the fruits of culture needed to be cultivated, not through asceticism as the Shakers had, but through education and refinement. "Taking the golden age of David's Jerusalem as a model, Smith and Young both believed they could transform their diverse followers into a cohesive society whose glory would gradually fill the earth." Whatever the merits of rough-and-ready congregational singing, as singing reformers in New England had decided over a century earlier, only trained voices could properly glorify God. As early as 1836, Latter-day Saints in Kirtland had organized a choir, which in turn necessitated singing schools to train choir members. A man named Gustavus Mills had served as the first Mormon music "professor" until implicated in a sex scandal. But the movement to establish choirs and singing schools continued both in larger communities and in small settlements, in the Great Salt Lake Valley and overseas. As with instrumental bands, these choirs received infusions of musical talent from Great Britain; hundreds of Welsh converts fabled for their singing abilities arrived in Deseret in 1849. Hence Joseph Beecroft's disappointment on waking up on his first Christmas Day in Deseret to what he thought was singing; the recent émigré had every reason to expect more than the squealing of pigs.[39]

Ever the pragmatist, Brigham Young saw more than spiritual and aesthetic rewards from the proliferation of singing schools and choirs. Better health, particularly protection against "lung fever," was touted by Mormon leaders as an additional benefit of active singing. Healthy lungs were thus part of the rationale for an ambitious singing school established in 1860 under the direction of a Scottish-born assistant to Young. The Mormon leader's pragmatism carried over to another practice of some ambivalence to Mormons: dancing. As antebellum American Christians, many Latter-day Saints instinctively felt trepidation at the potential licentiousness of social dancing; at the same time, the rank and file enjoyed it, and the leaders were not hesitant to put some distance between their church and the Protestant churches they had left behind. Young and others made the argument that a proper attitude and approach could consecrate what might otherwise be a wicked pastime; dancing schools were established. Leaders also noticed that the kind of vigorous physical dancing favored by Mormons was an effective way of keeping warm during the long journeys across the plains and mountains to Deseret, and worthy of encouragement on this basis. But Young himself remained cautious, not wanting sacred dance to occupy the same importance in Mormon sacred life that it had come to occupy for the Shakers. "When we come to the things of God, I had rather not have them mixed up with amusement like a dish of suc-cotash," he said. Later on, when the church came under direct fire for countenancing plural marriage, its leaders took a stronger line against so-cial dance. "At the same time the church leaders heatedly defended plural marriage and went into hiding to escape prosecution, they also allied themselves with non-Mormons in the national outrage against the waltz, mazurka, and polka."[40] The federal antipolygamy law passed in 1882 wreaked havoc among the Mormon musical community as well as its lead-ership ranks, compelling many musicians to flee the country or to go into hiding to avoid prosecution.

Out of this experience of federal prosecution would come one of the key developments in the remarkable Mormon evolution over the twentieth century into a position of mainstream cultural acceptance. That same year, 1882, saw the arrival in Salt Lake City of Evan Stephens, a Welsh bachelor who more than any other figure would bring Mormon music to a national and world audience. During the first years in Deseret, a large choir com-posed of the remnants of the choir that had been established in Nauvoo, as well as newly arrived Welsh immigrants, began performing in a new, vaguely arklike structure called the Tabernacle. During the 1870s the en-semble, which had begun referring to itself as the Tabernacle Choir, grew in size and ambition under the leadership of George Careless, a British vio-linist who had trained at the Royal Academy of Music and performed un-der notable European conductors before being converted and convinced to lend his talent to Deseret. A performance of Handel's *Messiah* in 1876 in Salt Lake City was a milestone. When Stephens arrived six years later he began building a Sunday-school choir whose numbers exceeded those of the Tabernacle choir, and whose performances were well attended and widely praised. These were the years when lively, rhythmically infectious "gospel songs" were sweeping through evangelical Protestant churches, and they made inroads among Latter-day Saints as well. Stephens was ambivalent about the popularity of these Sunday school–derived songs, es-pecially if they threatened to supplant traditional hymns from formal wor-ship, but he was not above borrowing some gospel conventions for musi-cal settings that he contributed to Mormon hymnbooks.[41]

Eighteen-ninety was a watershed year for the Latter-day Saints. Bowing to federal pressure, the newly installed Mormon president issued a docu-ment disavowing plural marriage, and the church's political party was disbanded. The vision of a New Jerusalem in the Great Basin in which Latter-day Saints would exist apart from the secular world was over. No longer living in sacred time, Mormons would find the need to establish a more clearly marked boundary between sacred and secular. The same year, Stephens was called to direct the Tabernacle Choir, which under his leadership would begin its long ascent to a position as an American musical icon. In 1893 the choir was invited by Welsh entrepreneurs to participate in a choral competition at the World Columbian Exposition in Chicago, and placed second. The Exposition would prove to be a crucial nexus in the development of several strains of sacred music in the United States. In this case, it helped establish a national audience for the Tabernacle Choir. In 1910 the choir began recording for the Columbia record label. Still under the direction of Stephens, in 1911 it undertook a successful tour of the East Coast that included a performance at the White House. In 1929 the choir began a weekly radio program for National Broadcasting Company, which would evolve into the longest-running of all American radio shows. Since then, the choir has become an American institution, praised by U.S. presidents, honored by postal stamps, anthologized by *Reader's Digest*, and serving, Hick points out, as "the butt of thousands of media jokes and parodies . . . regularly referred to in situation comedies and comic monologues."[42] The choir functions as a visible symbol of the mainstreaming of Latter-day Saints at the same time that it has helped to secure wide social acceptance for the church. Even the repertoire receives an imprimatur of respectability. We might call the Tabernacle Choir the anointed voice of America's civil religion, endorsing through their performances everything from hymns by Luther and Watts to show tunes by Rodgers and Hammerstein and medleys from classic Disney animations.

Even in this most pragmatically middlebrow of Mormon institutions linger the now-faint echoes of the primitive. "In the Mormons' song there is a magnificent note of religious frenzy, a diapason of devotion, an echo of deeds of fanaticism and of grappling with the desert, to make it blossom like a rose," wrote a critic in 1911. "Their song has the note of triumph over difficulties, and dangers overcome. It is the note of the pioneer, the roadbreaker into the wilderness; and, indeed, they do not in looks belie their ancestry. There is fire in their eyes, and thunder in their throats."[43] Sacred songs, especially those grounded in the experience of exodus and deliverance, are always available to dissenting voices who find in them what Kenneth Burke called equipment for living, a usable past adaptable to political struggles of the present.

A gay Mormon struggling for recognition among fellow Latter-day Saints invoked the story of a western pioneer who took ill on the trail.

Singing "Come, Come Ye Saints" was his last act. He sang in a "very faint but plaintive and sweet voice," according to a contemporary account; no one joined him, and when he finished, there wasn't "a single dry eye in the camp." The next morning his body was discovered in his wagon. "When I first read this story, it occurred to me how similar the emotions it evoked were to those I felt when my first partner Mark died," wrote a Latter-day Saint in 1997. "Whereas the early Mormons were literally driven from their homes through physical violence or threat of it, we gay and lesbian people more often are driven away from our families or friends through a conspiracy of silence, a refusal to face or deal with the fact of our homosexuality." Through the resonance of the most traditional of Mormon songs comes the will to struggle for a place in the community, the analogy completed by a new verse:

Come, come, ye Saints, no toil, nor labor fear,	Come, come ye gays and lesbians rejoice!
But with joy wend your way;	Join in song; hearts will tell.
Though hard to you this journey may appear,	We stand as one and raise a mighty voice!
Grace shall be as your day.	In the light we shall dwell.
'Tis better far for us to strive,	As we share with pride this message true:
Our useless cares from us to drive:	We're God's gay children and we're loved too!
Do this, and joy your hearts will swell—	Affirm this truth and spirits swell—
All is well! all is well!	All is well! All is well![44]

Like the first generation of Latter-day Saints, no less than for Mother Ann's followers, sexual identity—whether gay, lesbian, polygamous, or celibate—has been central to religious identity. And sacred song has been a key means of establishing and marking that identity both within the community and to the outside world.

CHAPTER FOUR

Holding the Fort

The mass of "gospel" hymns which has swept through American churches and well-nigh ruined our sense of song consists largely of debased imitations of Negro melodies made by ears that caught the jingle but not the music, the body but not the soul, of the Jubilee songs.

— W. E. B. Du Bois

IN 1875, as the American evangelist Dwight Moody and his musical partner Ira Sankey were completing their two-year revival mission through Great Britain, they were feted at a farewell dinner hosted by their key patron, the Earl of Shaftesbury. Paying tribute to their exertions over the previous two years, which saw Moody and Sankey conducting revivals that reached millions, the leading British philanthropist of his age singled out a particular musical contribution: "If Mr. Sankey has done no more than teach the people to sing 'Hold the Fort,' he has conferred an inestimable blessing on the British Empire."[1]

A generation before American popular music like ragtime—let alone jazz, blues, or rock and roll—entered public awareness, music from the United States had established itself as a vibrant transnational phenomenon. Unlike secular genres that more readily come to mind as American musical exports, the first wave of American music to generate enthusiasm on foreign shores was distinctively Protestant and evangelical. The year 1873 saw two musical harbingers from the United States cross paths in Britain: the Jubilee Singers, recently formed to raise money for a new college for freed slaves, called Fisk, and nearly disbanded before achieving a remarkable turnaround in the United States; and the evangelical partnership between Chicago revivalist Dwight Moody and his stalwart musical sidekick, Ira Sankey.

These two tours, the Jubilee Singers and Moody-Sankey, had much in common. Both were conspicuously Christian in motivation and musical content, products and engines of the leading edge of a major wave of evangelical Protestant revivalism in the United States. Both had the support of Lord Shaftesbury and other key British figures pursuing middle-class reform and stability. Both found an enthusiastic response to what seemed to be distinctively American musical idioms. There were some notable differences in the aims of each group, as well, apart from the visibly racial one. For Moody and Sankey, the goal was to save souls through their gut-level appeals to the emotions and sensibilities of the crowds that flocked to hear them. The Jubilee Singers, in contrast, were sent to England not so much to save souls as to raise funds for their struggling college. To W. E. B. Du Bois's ear, there was a world of difference between the haunting slave spirituals performed by the Jubilee Singers and the alternately muscular and sentimental white gospel hymns popularized by Sankey. But different ears hear things differently, or are attuned to pick up traces and associations that elude other listeners. At some underlying level, the gospel songs of Sankey and his gospel-writing cohorts had something in common with the spirituals. And it took a European backdrop to make these associations audible. Listeners related both sets of music to European folk musics. African-American worshippers clearly used hymns by Watts and Wesley, musically converted though they may have been, but some listeners heard strains of Scottish ballads as well, just as they heard Scottish resonances in what seemed quintessential musical products of American evangelical Christianity. Both gospel songs and slave spirituals were produced by transnational migrations of people and ideas, and took on new meanings through being heard in transnational contexts.

JOHN BROWN'S Body" was one of the Jubilee Singers' most celebrated songs, and like so many secular movement songs in the United States, it began as a hymn. But even before it was a hymn, it was a lowly popular ditty, written by a musician from Philadelphia, titled "Say, bummers, will you meet us?" As in so many other cases, it was Methodists who sacralized it, changing the line to "Say, Brothers, will you meet us?" The better-known lyrics about John Brown were created in 1861 by the Second Massachusetts Infantry, known as the Tiger Battalion, while stationed at Fort Warren in Boston Harbor. Among the Tigers was a Scotsman named John Brown who became the butt of jokes playing on the name of the famous abolitionist. The verses proved infinitely adaptable and became wildly popular in the North. "One can hardly walk on the street for five minutes without hearing it whistled or hummed," a contemporary observed. The song was quickly learned by other regiments at Fort Warren, some of whom were transferred to Washington, D.C. It was there that President Lincoln heard the song, as did Julia Ward Howe, who composed the verses that became "The Battle Hymn of the Republic." More than Howe's gentrified version, "John Brown's Body" was a popular Union marching song that lent itself to infinite customizing on the part of soldiers who sang it. The line "We'll hang Jeff Davis from a—"could be adapted to any tree in the vicinity, for example. Names of other casualties could be substituted for John Brown's body "a-mouldering in the grave." There were even nonabolitionist versions for Yankees opposed to emancipation. Immediately after the Civil War, the song was played by regimental bands and sung by processions of black schoolchildren at Decoration Day celebrations held in places like Charleston, South Carolina, to mark the defeat of the Confederacy.[2]

Exactly when "John Brown's Body" entered the Fisk repertoire is unclear. The group had been founded in October 1871, five years after the Fisk Free Colored School was founded in Nashville under the aegis of the American Missionary Association (AMA) to educate newly emancipated African Americans. Like other "freedmen's schools," Fisk faced dire financial and social hardships. The school's treasurer, a lanky, driven Union veteran named George L. White, assembled a choral group of nine singers and a pianist to raise funds for the institution (and the AMA). The group struggled through months of poorly attended concerts staged along the route of the Underground Railroad before reaching an enthusiastic audience of clergy at Oberlin College in Ohio, where it quickly won the support of one of the nation's most prominent ministers, Henry Ward Beecher. After playing concerts on the East Coast the Singers returned to Tennessee with $25,000. An invitation to sing at the second World Peace Jubilee in Boston followed shortly, then a performance at the White House for Ulysses S. Grant. Early in 1873 White and the Singers' new manager, Gustavus Pike, decided to heed the advice of supporters like Beecher and Mark Twain to take the group on an unprecedented fundraising tour of Britain. Despite difficulty finding a steamship that would transport African Americans, the Jubilees boarded a British Cunard steamer for Liverpool in April 1873.

The British response to "John Brown" was "really astonishing," according to Jubilee member Benjamin Holmes. Twain, one of the troupe's staunchest American admirers, saw them in London during his own tour of England. "Their 'John Brown's Body' took a decorous, aristocratic English audience by surprise and threw them into a volcanic eruption of applause before they knew what they were about," he wrote. "I never saw anything finer than their enthusiasm." The song was a particular favorite of William Gladstone, founder of the Liberal party and four-time prime minister. At their second performance for the Gladstones, he told the Jubilee Singers: "'No song can equal that one' & Mrs. [Gladstone] said 'I have prayed God to spare me long enough to hear that song again and now my prayer is answered. I do so thank you.'" The song seems to have had special appeal to European royalty. At a diamond-studded dinner party hosted by Gladstone and attended by the Swedish celebrity vocalist Jenny Lind, the Prince of Wales specially requested "No more auction-block for me," which he enjoyed. "Nothing, however, awakened such enthusiasm as 'John Brown,'" recalled manager Gustavus Pike, "and Mr. Gladstone asked me if it could not be repeated as a special favour to the Grand Duchess Czarevna, whose father-in-law had emancipated the serfs in Russia."[3] Less august audiences were equally moved. At a dinner of the Congregational Union attended by ministers and delegates, Pike reported, "Nothing bore them up on loftier wings than the singing of the 'John Brown' song." In Londonderry, their Presbyterian sponsors originally stipulated that the Jubilees omit "John Brown" and other secular songs but relented in the face of audience pressure. The song made a powerful impact at a private performance for a group of London Quakers who had once profited from Caribbean slavery but had become leading supporters of the British abolitionist movement. At the same time, writes historian Andrew Ward, "'John Brown' would become such a favorite of the British military that the Forty-second Highlanders would sing it with dubious congruity as they vanquished the ferocious Ashanti of West Africa."[4]

The context of British imperialism in Africa is crucial to understanding the reception of the Jubilee Singers in England. The group performed at the annual meeting of the Freedmen's Mission Aid Society, a British counterpart to the AMA that promoted cooperation between the two nations on the evangelization of Africa. The meeting was attended by Lord Shaftesbury and featured a rousing address by the Reverend J. S. Moffatt, brother-in-law of David Livingston. Afterward, "when the cheering subsided, and the singers arose and gave the famous 'John Brown' song, the sight was such as we have not witnessed in London for many years. As the refrain rang out, 'John Brown died, that the slave might be free,' the dense audience could suppress their feelings no longer; they rose from their seats, and their applause was deafening, hats and handkerchiefs were waved, and the excitement continued until 'God save the Queen' was sung."[5]

What meaning could a militant marching song performed by trained singers of African descent have had for British missionaries and other imperialists? State-sponsored imperialism, Christian mission, and the development of anthropology were deeply interlinked with the British reception. "The emergence of anthropology did not come about in the nineteenth century by accident," Virginia Dominguez has written. "The expansion of European colonialism, the growth of an almost unbending faith in science, the combined condescension and universalization inherent in global, all-encompassing theories of biological and social evolution, and the successful domination of much of the world's political economy by nineteenth-century European and American capitalism made the emergence of academic anthropology not only possible but highly likely." Charles Darwin had published *The Descent of Man* in 1871, and Herbert Spencer's *Study of Sociology* appeared in 1873. The following year saw publication of Edward Burnett Tylor's *Primitive Cultures,* which introduced the notion of cultural survival within evolutionary stages of development; ethnography could assist in the process of eliminating from modern civilization those vestiges of less civilized cultures. "It is a harsher, and at times even painful, office of ethnography to expose the remains of crude old cultures which have passed into harmful superstition, and to mark these out for destruction," he wrote. "Yet this work, if less genial, is not less urgently needed for the good of mankind. Thus, active at once in aiding progress and in removing hindrance, the science of culture is essentially a reformer's science."[6]

In the United States, the interest in and study of slave spirituals played a crucial role in the formation of a sensibility of concern for "culture on the margins." Slave narratives such as Frederick Douglass' first focused attention on "sorrow songs" as providing access to the interior lives of enslaved subjects and their culture. "Go Down, Moses," the first spiritual printed in its entirety, was transcribed at Fortress Monroe, on the Chesapeake, by a Young Men's Christian Association (YMCA) minister from New York, and was published in the New York *Tribune* in the following standardized English:

> When Israel was in Egypt's land, O let my people go!
> Oppressed so hard they could not stand, O let my people go!
> CHORUS—O go down, Moses, Away down to Egypt's land,
> And tell King Pharaoh To let my people go![7]

Building on the writing of Douglass, radical abolitionist Thomas Wentworth Higginson, who commanded the first regiment of freed slaves against the Confederacy, carefully collected examples of spirituals he encountered among members of the South Carolina Volunteers he commanded at Port Royal, an island off the coast of South Carolina. Higginson published his findings first in the *Atlantic Monthly* in 1867, and three years later in *Army Life in a Black Regiment and Other Writings.*

Trained at Harvard Divinity School, Higginson was forced out of the ministry in 1850 by businessmen in his congregation who objected to his radical political affiliations. Higginson was involved in workingmen's associations, ran for Congress in 1848 on the Free Soil ticket, and was involved in the early days of the women's rights movement at Seneca Falls, supporting the participation of women at the 1853 World's Temperance Conference in New York. A great admirer of Theodore Parker, who had also been trained in the ministry, Higginson served as Parker's "principal lieutenant" in forcibly resisting enforcement of the Fugitive Slave Act in Boston. He traveled to Kansas in 1856 to militate against the expansion of slavery to the territory, and supported John Brown's attack on Harper's Ferry.[8]

In 1861 Higginson was invited to command the first all-black Union regiment. In addition to his fiery politics, he had a romantic literary sensibility. Introducing readers of the *Atlantic* to slave spirituals, Higginson wrote:

> Often in the starlit evening I have returned from some lonely ride by the swift river, or on the plover-haunted barrens, and, entering the camp, have silently approached some glimmering fire, round which the dusky figures moved in the rhythmical barbaric dance the negroes call a "shout," chanting, often harshly, but always in the most perfect time, some monotonous refrain. Writing down in the darkness, as I best could,—perhaps with my hand in the safe covert of my pocket,—the words of the song, I have afterwards carried it to my tent, like some captured bird or insect, and then, after examination, put it by. Or, summoning one of the men at some period of leisure . . . I have completed the new specimen by supplying the absent parts.[9]

Conducting this sort of protoethnography, Higginson transcribed thirty-seven spirituals for his *Atlantic* article, including the famous "Many Thousand Go":

> No more peck o'corn for me,
> No more, no more,—
> No more peck o'corn for me,
> Many tousand go.
> No more driver's lash for me, (*Twice.*)
> No more, &c.

The songs, Higginson concluded, were "more than a source of relaxation, they were a stimulus to courage and a tie to heaven." Although not all the spirituals were obviously religious, he never heard soldiers singing profane or vulgar songs. The few "Ethiopian Minstrel" ditties introduced by some of the soldiers failed to catch on. But, he went on, the former slaves under his command "sang reluctantly, even on Sunday, the long and short metres of the hymnbooks, always gladly yielding to the more potent excitement of their own 'spirituals.' By these they could sing themselves, as had their fathers before them, out of the contemplation of their own low estate, into the sublime scenery of the Apocalypse. I remember that this minor-keyed pathos used to seem to me almost too sad to dwell upon, while slavery seemed destined to last for generations; but now that their patience has had its perfect work, history cannot afford to lose this portion of its record. There is no parallel instance of an oppressed race thus sustained by the religious sentiment alone. These songs are but the vocal expression of the simplicity of their faith and the sublimity of their long resignation."[10] Writing in 1867, after the war but long before the failure of Reconstruction to achieve anything approaching basic political or economic rights for southern blacks, Higginson implies that something of value will be lost with the end of slavery: not only the songs themselves, but a kind of nobility of fortitude in the face of unendurable suffering, of which the music is a sublime trace. It is something of this "imperialist nostalgia" that must have played through the minds of the European aristocrats and reformers who listened so raptly to the Fisk Jubilee Singers.[11]

By the time Dwight Moody and Ira Sankey began their British revival tour in July 1873 the Jubilees had been in England for two months and had already entertained the Queen and the prime minister. Moody and Sankey's itinerary took them from York and Sunderland, through Scotland and Ireland, and to large cities in the north of England before winding up in London in early 1875. An estimated 1.5 million came to the London rallies alone. As a leading historian of American revivalism writes, "Charles Finney made revivalism a profession, but Dwight Moody made it a big business." Music played a major role in Moody's success in both the United States and Britain. Over the course of a revival meeting, music took many forms. Most distinctive were Sankey's solos, but meetings also featured performances by large mixed-voice choirs recruited in advance from local churches and hastily rehearsed by Sankey, and, of course, congregational singing by all present. "Mr. Moody breaks up the fallow ground, and Mr. Sankey's music is like an angel's song at the pearly gates, to invite the troubled sinner in from the troubles of a perishing world." The two had met as thirty-somethings in 1870 at a YMCA convention in Indianapolis. Sankey so impressed Moody with his rendition of "There Is a Fountain Filled with Blood" that the Chicago evangelist asked him to join his revival efforts. "An immense, bilious man, with black hair, and eyes surrounded by flaccid, pendent, baggy wrinkles, who came forward with an unctuous gesture," was how one observer described Sankey. Another compared him to "the honest proprietor of a meat-market."[12]

Sankey's repertoire struck some critics as a trifle redolent of the music hall, melding unlikely combinations of "a circus quickstep, a negro minstrel sentimental ballad, a college chorus, and a hymn." The songs raised eyebrows especially among Anglican traditionalists. "Some of the melodies of Moody and Sankey are popular enough, but it is quite another question whether they are worthy of association with God's worship," sniffed one. "Are they and the hymns they accompany not rather the exponents of a somewhat unwholesome and sentimental feeling, too personal and effeminate for worship?" In Presbyterian Scotland even organs and hymns were proscribed. Yet the American gospel songs, inspired by and composed in the most particular American circumstances, struck a popular nerve. Their songs would exert an enormous influence on the musical worship of evangelical Protestants in Britain and America, reaching "vast numbers hitherto unacquainted with hymns and unused to public worship," according to hymnologist Louis Benson. "The new melodies penetrated even the music halls and were whistled by the man on the street. Some of the new hymns became household words; notably "ho! My comrades, see the signal" and others by Bliss and Crosby. Revival meetings were only one means by which the influence of gospel songs like "Hold the Fort!" was spread. In 1873 Sankey began bringing out gospel songbooks, first as small booklets and swelling to large volumes of some 1,200 songs by 1903. In 1875 the collection was titled *Sacred Songs and Solos,* which went through six editions. "Hold the Fort!" took the lead position throughout. Sankey's various gospel-song compilations, with their distinctive Gothic typeface, were tightly controlled through copyright and aggressively distributed by publishers like Biglow and Main and John Church and Company, earning sizable royalties for their authors. The Jubilee Singers likewise compiled and sold collections of their songs at venues in which they performed.[13]

Hold the Fort!" was probably the most successful song of the Moody-Sankey tour, if one is to judge from audience reaction. Musically, it typified the predictable yet animated tunes that characterized much of period gospel song, its bouncy rhythms and rousing refrains giving it away as neither a psalm nor a hymn but a kind of evangelical marching song. "It was a pleasure never to be forgotten, to hear ten thousand Londoners singing heartily 'Hold the Fort,' and other familiar songs," wrote one observer. "Everybody seemed to know them; and in the cars, the homes of the people, as well as in the churches, they were heard. It was almost impossible to get out of the reach of these holy, heavenly melodies." In Dublin the congregation joined in singing "with one mighty voice . . . The words have a martial, inspiriting sound, and as the verse rolled forth, filling the great hall with a mighty and musical noise, one could see the eyes of strong men fill with tears." When the evangelists were gently skewered by a circus clown ("I am rather Moody tonight; how do you feel?" "I feel rather Sankey-monious.") the audience hissed, then, according to Sankey, "arose and joined with tremendous effect in singing . . . 'Hold the fort, for I am coming.'" The reaction was the same in Scotland. "In the remote Highland glen you may hear the sound of hymn-singing; shepherds on the steep hillsides sing Mr. Sankey's hymns while tending their sheep," wrote an observer; "errand boys whistle the tunes as they walk along the streets of the Highland towns; while in not a few of the lordly castles of the north they express genuine feeling." As Moody and Sankey sailed out of Liverpool to return to the United States in 1875, crowds sang them off with "Hold the Fort!" First appearing as sheet music in 1870, the song was internationally known within a few years. It was translated into most European languages as well as Chinese and several languages of India, becoming "popular beyond any other Sabbath School song of the age."[14]

Like "John Brown's Body," "Hold the Fort!" originated in the U.S. Civil War. It was inspired by a Signal Corps message flagged from Kennesaw Mountain near Atlanta by General William T. Sherman as part of the Battle of Altoona. On 4 October 1864, the story goes, Sherman's subordinate, Brigadier General William Vandever, dispatched two messages: "Sherman is moving in force. Hold out." And "General Sherman says hold fast. We are coming." The Confederates retreated the next day, and the encounter was judged a Union victory. Sherman would later praise Altoona as a model defense of a fortification, sealing its reputation as the most famous Civil War signaling episode. Over the next decade the episode inspired both poems and dramas. Philip P. Bliss was a thirty-two-year-old singer and choirmaster in 1870 when he heard the story related at the Winnebago County Sunday school convention in Rockford, Illinois. The guest speaker was Daniel Webster Whittle, a decorated Union veteran wounded at Vicksburg who was probably near Kennesaw as a staff officer. At the Rockford convention, Whittle offered the incident as "an illustration of the inspiration derived by the Christian from the thoughts of Christ as our commander and of His coming to our relief." Bliss was moved to write the song while staying at Whittle's home in Chicago. Later the two men formed an evangelical partnership, Whittle preaching and Bliss singing.[15]

As in the United States, the revivals through which the gospel songs gained fame in England coincided with periods of social and economic stress, and succeeded by reducing complex political issues to more easily graspable moral problems. But the success of gospel songs must also be attributed to their affinities with British popular music, the secular songs of the music hall. The song drew on melodic conventions as familiar in the

British Isles as in Anglo America. A commentator in Glasgow wrote of Sankey's music: "Much of it is so Scottish and Irish in its construction that to our people familiar with such music, it is sometimes difficult to realize that what we hear is sacred song. Usually short turns and strains remind us irresistibly of something we know, but cannot recall. In some of the melodies the effect is more marked. Who does not feel the sweetness of Irish melody in 'Sweet by-and-by' . . . and the thorough Scottish ring in such songs as 'Hold the Fort' . . . and many others. It takes us by surprise to hear gospel truth wafted in the strains of our national music; but is it not possible that this may be the true though unexpected reason why these simple songs have found such a direct and wonderful entrance to the Scottish heart?"[16]

Musically, both "Hold the Fort!" and "John Brown's Body" share features of nineteenth-century popular music. Both are comprised of a series of eight-bar verses followed by an eight-bar chorus. Both feature propulsive march rhythms based on dotted eighth-note rhythms and simple harmonic alternations between tonic, dominant, and subdominant. The songs present more of a contrast in their texts. "John Brown" consists of a series of loosely related declamations, which could be extended indefinitely as circumstances and creativity permitted. It somewhat resembles an AAB blues, with the A line repeated not twice but three times. Rather than conveying a linear narrative, "John Brown" achieves its meaning by an accretion of loosely related images and lines. In contrast, "Hold the Fort!" is Christian allegory. Its breathless account of shifting momentum in the hard-fought cosmic battle follows a more linear narrative. In the first verse, reinforcements are suggested, and victory seems "nigh." In the second, "mighty men" fall as courage fades under the onslaught of Satan's "mighty host." The third verse suggests a counterattack under "glorious banner" and bugle, while the final celebrates the sighting of the "Great Commander," whose assistance has been anticipated throughout.

"John Brown's Body"	"Hold the Fort!"
John Brown's body lies a-mold'ring in the grave	Ho! my comrades, see the signal
John Brown's body lies a-mold'ring in the grave	Waving in the sky!
John Brown's body lies a-mold'ring in the grave	Reinforcements now appearing,
His soul goes marching on	Victory is nigh!
Glory, Glory! Hallelujah!	"Hold the fort, for I am coming,"
Glory, Glory! Hallelujah!	Jesus signals still,

Glory, Glory! Hallelujah!
His soul is marching on.

He captured Harper's Ferry
  with his nineteen men so true
He frightened old Virginia
  till she trembled through and
  through
They hung him for a traitor,
  themselves the traitor crew
His soul is marching on.
Glory, Glory! Hallelujah! etc.

John Brown died that the slave
  might be free,
John Brown died that the slave
  might be free,
John Brown died that the slave
  might be free,
But his soul is marching on!
Glory, Glory! Hallelujah! etc.

The stars above in Heaven are
  looking kindly down
The stars above in Heaven are
  looking kindly down
The stars above in Heaven are
  looking . . .
On the grave of old John Brown
Glory, Glory! Hallelujah! etc.

Wave the answer back to heaven,—
"By thy grace, we will."

See the mighty host advancing,

Satan leading on;

Might men around us falling,

Courage almost gone:
"Hold the fort, for I am coming," etc.

See the glorious banner waving,

Hear the bugle blow;

In our Leader's name we'll triumph

Over every foe.
"Hold the fort, for I am coming," etc.

Fierce and long the battle rages,

But our help is near;

Onward comes our Great Commander,

Cheer my comrades, cheer!
"Hold the fort, for I am coming," etc.

"John Brown" is unmistakably historical and partisan. The Jubilee Singers performed it defiantly as their ship neared New York Harbor after a long tour of Europe, raising the hackles of southern passengers on board. "Hold the Fort!" on the other hand relativizes the Civil War, reducing its significance in comparison to the ongoing universal struggle between Christ and Satan. The song, which continued to resonate with American audiences as the Moody-Sankey revivals continued through the 1870s, functioned to displace the regional animosity stoked by the Civil War by idealizing and sacralizing that most traumatic of conflicts. It stands as an early example of the outpouring of the postwar decades, when so much popular culture served to reconcile and unify North and South. "Americans now had their Homeric tales of great war to tell," writes historian David Blight: "Within five years of the conflict, speakers gave the Union veterans their place in a direct line from Thermopylae to Gettysburg, from the 'storied Wallace' and the Scottish tribes to 'Sheridan's ride' and 'Sherman's march to the sea.' Americans now had a defining past of mythic battles, as the 1869 orator in Hornellsville, New York, put it, that would 'stir the heart of the Irishman at home or abroad.'"[17] Though Moody eventually tired of the song, "Hold the Fort!" enjoyed resurgence under evangelist Billy Sunday. (Billy Graham's Cold War crusade never warmed to it, reportedly spooked by the presence of the word "comrade.") Perhaps the song's more interesting legacy is as an object of parody adapted to partisan use in presidential campaigns of the 1870s and 1880s. It shed its bourgeois origins to become a working-class anthem used by the Knights of Labor, the Wobblies, and the AFL-CIO, as well as by prohibitionists and suffragettes. Another measure of the song's range is that by 1877 it had penetrated even the insular musical world of the Shakers, where visitors to Canterbury, New Hampshire, would hear the Sisters singing "The Ninety and Nine" and "Hold the Fort!" By the late nineteenth century, even Shaker hymn-writers were taking their musical cues from Moody and Sankey.[18]

With its theme of Manichean combat against Satan's "mighty host," "Hold the Fort!" was emblematic of a reaction against the feminized sentimental gospel songs ascendant during the Victorian period. The trope of righteous armies was well established and particularly evident in slave spirituals, but was challenged after the Civil War by domestic themes explored by women gospel hymnists whose songs were crafted for use in Sunday schools but which quickly found favor in revivals, prayer meetings, and eventually congregational worship. Many gospel songs of the period enacted a struggle for cultural authority between feminine and masculine models and voices within evangelical Christianity. The hymns were part of the well-documented move among American Protestants away from the stern, judging, patriarchal God of Calvinism toward a more humanized, loving Jesus-as-friend, or even lover. "If the scenario of the older hymns was that of a criminal pleading before God with Christ as his advocate," writes historian Sandra S. Sizer, "that of the gospel hymn is one of Jesus on trial before a huge, anonymous and largely hostile jury, with happy Christians appearing on the witness stand on his behalf."[19]

Not coincidentally, gospel hymnody allowed women a forum for praying and interpreting scripture, activities that were often proscribed by a literal reading of 1 Corinthians 14:34: "Let your women keep silence in the churches: for it is not permitted unto them to speak." Women like Anna B. Warner, Phoebe Palmer Knapp, Clara H. Scott, and the preternaturally prolific Fanny Crosby wrote thousands of gospel hymns during the second half of the nineteenth century. Their songs tended to emphasize the value of the domestic sphere as a crucial space for spiritual development, to valorize women's work and experiences of time as cyclical rather than linear, to offer the home as an allegory for heaven, to value oral culture over literacy, and to see spiritual autobiography as a sign not of triviality but of spiritual authority. Between about 1870 and 1920, writes Jane Hadden Hobbs, "female hymnists created texts that undermined patriarchal religion by centering power in the home rather than in the church, by locating God within themselves, by separating physical intimacy from sexual submission, and by emphasizing service rather than conquest." Like many lyricists of the day, Crosby was exploited by copyright conventions that assigned rights not to the lyricist but to the composer of the music; working under more than 200 pseudonymns, Crosby was paid a flat fee of one or two dollars per hymn.[20]

This sensibility also affected male hymn composers like Sankey, many of whose songs similarly idealize the domestic sphere. A particularly well-known example is Sankey's signature solo number, "The Ninety and Nine," which he performed widely in the British revivals, evidently generating as much enthusiasm as did "Hold the Fort!" It is an elaborate retelling of the parable of Matthew 18:12, concerning the shepherd who takes more delight over saving the one lost sheep than in the ninety-nine who never strayed from the hillside: "Even so," scripture intones, "it is not the will of your Father which is in heaven, that one of these little ones should perish." Rhetorically, the text is quite complex for a hymn, featuring third-person narration interspersed with dialogue between the Good Shepherd and an interlocutor who moves the parable forward by asking leading questions: "Lord, Thou has here The ninety and nine; Are they not enough for Thee?" and in the second verse: "Lord, whence are those blood-drops all the way that mark out the mountain's track?" and "Lord, whence are Thy hands so rent and torn?" in the fourth.

Gospel hymn-writers' narratives of song creation follow a distinct pattern. In all cases hymnists downplay their own creative contribution, emphasizing instead their role as human transcribing machines for the word of God. Among nineteenth-century white evangelicals the oral "mother tongue" was seen as having more spiritual worth than the literate "father tongue"; texts apparently received from God with minimal mediation carried more authority than those composed through human genius. Among evangelicals, then, gospel hymns "transcend categorization as mere poetry; they are sacred texts, transcribed in response to divine dictation rather than composed." Crosby (1820–1915) began writing poetry when

4. Dwight Moody and Ira Sankey began publishing gospel songs in 1873, earning substantial royalties for their authors. This sheet music was published the year after the evangelists returned from Great Britain. Courtesy of The Lester S. Levy Collection of Sheet Music, Special Collections, The Milton S. Eisenhower Library of The Johns Hopkins University.

still a girl, and was encouraged by no less than William Cullen Bryant. During a Methodist revival service in New York City, she was converted to Christianity during the singing of Isaac Watts's "Here, Lord, I Give Myself Away." Crosby, who wrote texts to gospel perennials such as "Blessed Assurance," "Every Day and Hour, Jesus Keep Me near the Cross," "Rescue the Perishing," and "Pass Me Not, O Gentle Savior," recalled writing many of her hymns "all at once, almost in a twinkling, the words came stanza by stanza as fast as I could memorize them."[21]

Sankey's account of writing "The Ninety and Nine" conforms to this pattern. He discovered the text, by Elizabeth Clephane, in Scotland, but had no musical setting until Moody unexpectedly asked him for a song appropriate for a sermon on the Good Shepherd.

> The impression came upon me, "Sing the hymn and make the tune as you go along." It was almost as if I heard a voice, so vivid was the sensation. I yielded to it, and, taking the little newspaper slip and laying it upon the organ before me, with a silent prayer to God for help, I commenced to sing. Note by note, the music was given to me clear through the end of the tune. After the first verse, I was very glad I had got through, but overwhelmed with fear that the tune for the next verse would be greatly different from the first. But again looking up to the Lord for help in this most trying moment, He gave me again the same tune for all the remaining verses, note for note. The impression made upon the audience was very deep; hundreds were in tears.[22]

Emotional abandon was one of the earmarks of evangelical revivals, but unlike earlier revivals led by George Whitefield or Charles Finney, the Moody-Sankey meetings struck notably sentimental chords. The theme of the prodigal male—the wayward or tippling husband or father, the wild-oats-sowing son—was particularly resonant. While "The Ninety and Nine" was figurative, several of Sankey's signature numbers evoked the fallen male more directly. Ideally they became interwoven with Moody's sermons and spontaneous dramas that emerged out of the audience. "One day Mr. Moody had been preaching on the return of the prodigal son, and at the close of the sermon had asked Mr. Sankey to sing, 'O prodigal, come home, come home!' A young man who had been in a backslidden state, came up the aisle to his father and mother, who were godly people; he first put his arm around his father's neck and kissed him, and asked his forgiveness with many tears; then kissing his mother, he asked her forgiveness also. The audience was so overcome that they were obliged to retire to the vestry."[23] These prodigal narratives dovetailed well with the restricted female roles prescribed by the nineteenth-century cult of domesticity. Middle-class white women, a major constituency of Moody's, were assigned as guardians of the home and hearth, nurturers of children, and helpmeets of beleaguered breadwinners, while men were delegated to deal with the harsh realities of an increasingly market-driven and temptation-strewn society.[24]

The theme of overcoming the spiritual/spatial separation from God through the saving grace of a personal savior also appears in what was probably the Jubilee Singers' most renowned song, "Steal Away to Jesus." But the old spiritual offers a radically different perspective. Rather than taking the view of the concerned mother/Good Shepherd worrying and ultimately rescuing her wandering boy/lost sheep, "Steal Away" highlights the oppressed person forced to flee his or her circumstances to reunite with a saving Christ. In "The Ninety and Nine," the narrative voice is identified with the Good Shepherd, the selfless rescuer in search of the lost creature. The straying sheep is never depicted or described in any way. Likewise, in "The Prodigal Child" the point of view is of the domestic circle, the faithful parent remembering the beloved, strayed child. The prodigal is unknown and unmarked; the "sorrow and shame," "sin and blame," are left unspecified, as is the smiling "tempter." The domestic hearth beckons, with its warmth, its bread, and the opportunity to reconcile with old friends. Both Sankey favorites concern the rescue and recovery back to a nurturing community.

The perspective of "Steal Away" emphasizes not recovery of a lost community but freedom through escape. Wholeness—reunion with God—can come only by leaving. Stealing away is not a problem but a solution—the means to salvation, not an action that produces a crisis that must be solved through the intercession of a savior. The song famously evokes the doubled meanings of the slave spirituals. "In the lips of some, [spirituals like 'Steal Away'] meant the expectation of a speedy summons to a world of spirits," wrote Frederick Douglass; "but, in the lips of our company, it simply meant, a speedy pilgrimage toward a free state, and deliverance from all the evils and dangers of slavery." Or as Wash Wilson, eighteen years old when the Civil War began, told an interviewer in Texas in 1937, "W'en you hear de sarbants er singin' 'Steal Away ter Jesus' dat's de signification dat dars gwine be a 'ligious meetin' somewhar dat night. De plantation owners 'fore an' atter Freedom dey don' lak dem 'ligious meetin's, so de sarbants jes' nacherley gwine slip off."[25] We can imagine the singer stealing away to worship in a covert "hush harbor," stealing away to freedom in the North, or from earthly existence to a heavenly realm. But in no version is there a human community to be restored, a home or family to provide sustenance. And there is no role at all for an earthly master. The two songs encapsulate the profound existential difference between the experience of Christianity for free and enslaved persons, who exist in completely different relation to family, community, society, and the law.

"The Prodigal Child"	"Steal Away"
Come home! Come home!	Steal away, steal away,
You are weary at heart,	steal away to Jesus,
For the way has been dark,	Steal away, steal away home,
And so lonely and wild;	I ain't got long to stay here.
O prodigal child!	My Lord calls me,

Come home! Oh, come home!
  Come home!
Come, oh, come home!

Come home! Come home!
For we watch and we wait,
And we stand at the gate,
While the shadows are piled;
  O prodigal child!
Come home! Oh!, come home!
  Come home!
Come, oh, come home, come home!

Come home! Come home!
From the sorrow and blame,
From the sin and the shame,
And the tempter that smiled,
  O prodigal child!
Come home, oh, come home! etc.

Come home! Come home!
There is bread and to spare,
And a warm welcome there;
Then, to friends reconciled,
  O prodigal child!
Come home, oh, come home! etc.

He calls me by the thunder,
The trumpet sounds it in my soul,
I ain't got long to stay here.

Steal away, steal away,
steal away to Jesus
Steal away, steal away home,
I ain't got long to stay here.
Green trees are bending,
Poor sinners stand trembling,
The trumpet sounds within my soul:
I ain't got long to stay here.

Steal away, steal away, etc.
My Lord calls me,
He calls me by the lightning;
The trumpet sounds it in my soul:
I ain't got long to stay here.

Steal away, steal away, etc.
Tombstones are bursting,
Poor sinners are trembling,
The trumpet sounds within my soul:
I ain't got long to stay here,
Steal away, steal away, etc.

In contrast to the formal Victorian address of Sankey's songs, there is a vernacular directness to "Steal Away." As in "John Brown," the text consists of a series of related declamations rather than a sequential narrative. In the first and third verses, divine power is naturalized through the totemic forces of thunder and lightning. The alternating verses feature apocalyptic imagery of green trees bending, tombstones bursting, sinners trembling. There is the suggestion of the magic and spirit possession we find later in a Delta blues like Robert Johnson's "Hellhound on My Trail" (1937):

> I got to keep movin', blues fallin' down like hail
> I can't keep no money with a hellhound on my trail. . . .
> I can tell the wind is risin', leaves tremblin' on the tree
> All I need's my little sweet woman to keep my company.

Musically, too, "Steal Away" presents many features of what would later be called the blues, particularly the melody's structure as a ladder of thirds.[26]

"Steal Away" seems to have galvanized as wide a range of nineteenth-century audiences as can be imagined, even beyond Europe and North America. Dwight Moody recounted that when he first heard the Jubilee Singers perform in England, "they stole his heart and led him at once to appreciate the power of their music for good"; Sankey occasionally performed his own rendition of "Steal Away," to which he added the verse "Our God is calling / the nations are awakening." They performed it to great effect for the former vice president of the Confederacy, Alexander Hamilton Stephens. "O, it is wonderful!" he said afterward. "I never heard anything like it." Queen Victoria specifically requested the song during a command performance at a garden party. A tour of India brought the Jubilee Singers to the Taj Mahal: "We gather round the sarcophagi and soon the great lofty dome echoes the first Christian song it has ever caught up, and that song the cry of a race akin to those whose dust sleeps in the crypt beneath. As the tones of that beautiful slave song, 'Steal Away to Jesus,' which we had sung before emperors, presidents, kings, and queens, awoke the stillness of that most wonderful of temples, we were so much overcome by the unique circumstances that it was with the utmost difficulty that we could sing at all."[27] In Australia, the singers found themselves at a mission station singing before an audience of aborigines. An initially cool response was turned around by "the tones of the old slave song ['Steal Away']." "First, wonder . . . then joy, as the full volume of the melody filled the humble little church," director Frederick Loudin recalled. "When we had finished they gathered about us, and, with tears still flowing, they clasped our hands and in broken accents exclaimed, 'Oh! God bless you! we have never heard anything like that before!'"[28]

The origins of "Steal Away" are obscure. It is said to have originated with Nat Turner, leader of the famous Virginia rebellion in 1831, but evidence is scant.[29] The Jubilee Singers performed relatively few slave spirituals during their first concerts, emphasizing instead light classics and popular songs. When "Steal Away" entered their repertoire is not known, although they definitely performed it at their November 1871 appearance at Oberlin, which marked the beginning of their ascent. A retired missionary named Alexander Reid claimed to have taught the Jubilee Singers a version based on a song from an old slave named Uncle Wallace who lived nearby in Texas, and who in turn had learned it from local slaves who sneaked off their plantation by canoe to worship at Reid's Choctaw mission. With the permission of George White, Reid met the Jubilee Singers in Brooklyn. "I gave the jubilee troop six songs in writing, spent a whole day in practicing them on the tunes, until they got them perfectly," Reid recalled. "I sometimes feel as if I must have been inspired for that special occasion. Though fond of music, I don't know one note from another, and never could master courage to start a tune in meeting. Yet on that day I stood up before Professor White and his trained 'Jubilees' (eleven of them) and sang my six songs over and over again until I had anchored the tunes firmly deep down in their hearts."[30]

Technically the song was daunting to perform. "The singers had to hit the opening syllable in perfect balance, without hesitation," Andrew Ward writes. "If one voice stuttered out of sync, the entire effect could be lost."[31] Different lines had to be sung at slightly different tempos, with subtle rhythmic pliancy, creating rubatos in the phrases "steal away home" and "I ain't got long to stay here." A description of a Jubilee performance by a London critic gives a sense of the precision and concentration required:

> They arranged themselves in front of the platform in a phalanx three deep. They stand with head erect and somewhat thrown back, and looking upwards, or with eyes nearly closed. It is evident the audience is nothing to them, they are going to make music and listen to one another. The first song was, "Steal away to Jesus." It was sung slowly; the first chords came floating on our senses like gentle fairy music, and they were followed by the unison of phrase, "Steal away—to Jesus," delivered with exquisite precision of time and accent; then came the soft chords, and bold unison again, followed by the touching, throbbing cadence, "I hain't got long to stay here"; next follows the loud, lofty trumpet call in unison, "My Lord calls me, the trumpet sounds it in my soul; I hain't got long to stay here." But it seems as though the angels also were speaking to the sufferer, for we hear again those beautiful chords delivered with double pianissimo, whispering to the soul, "Steal away to Jesus."[32]

In describing the melodies of the spirituals, the words "wild" and "weird" were used repeatedly. "The wild melodies of these emancipated slaves touched the fount of tears, and gray-haired men wept like little children," reported a leading Presbyterian minister in a representative description. An Ohio newspaper wrote of "the characteristic style and weird cadence of their nation"; the Hartford *Courant* marveled at their "strange and plaintive melodies." "They sing the most touching of Christian melodies, full of Jesus, and of Heaven; the most wild of plantation melodies, full of sorrow and aspirations for freedom," observed a clergyman present at a concert at Lincoln Hall attended by President Grant and other Washington dignitaries. These comments echo Henry Wadsworth Longfellow's famous poem about a slave singing at midnight:

> And the voice of his devotion
> Filled my soul with strange emotion;
> For its tones by turns were glad,
> Sweetly solemn, wildly sad.[33]

Some of this language echoes Higginson's, and it is likely that some in the audience would have read his accounts. "Almost all their songs were thoroughly religious in their tone, however quaint their expression, and were in a minor key, both as to words and music," he wrote in the *Atlantic Monthly*. "The attitude is always the same, and as a commentary on the life of the race, is infinitely pathetic. Nothing but patience for this life,— nothing but triumph in the next." Higginson noted an interesting theological pattern underlying the songs he recorded at Port Royal. Writing about a spiritual, "Down in the Valley," full of language of conflict and "lurid imagery of the Apocalypse," he observed: "This book [Revelations], with the books of Moses, constituted their Bible; all that lay between, even the narratives of the life of Jesus, they hardly cared to read or to hear." The theology of the slaves, like Lincoln's, was grounded in the Old Testament, particularly Exodus, and often more Hebraic than Christian.

But there was an even more obvious source of ideas and language for thinking about slave spirituals: *Uncle Tom's Cabin* (1852). The novel literally begins and ends with sacred song, and several of the crucial scenes feature hymn-singing. In the very first scene, Master Shelby explains to a slave trader that Tom "got religion at a camp-meeting, four years ago; and I believe he really *did* get it." Shortly afterward we meet Tom's family as they prepare their cabin for weekly prayer meeting, and in this episode we encounter much of the language later used to describe the spirituals.

> After a while the singing commenced, to the evident delight of all present. Not even all the disadvantage of nasal intonation could prevent the effect of the naturally fine voices, in airs at once wild and spirited. The words were sometimes the well-known and common hymns sung in the churches about, and sometimes of a wilder, more indefinite character, picked up at camp-meetings.
>
> The chorus of one of them, which ran as follows, was sung with great energy and unction:
>
> > "Die on the field of battle,
> > Die on the field of battle,
> > Glory in my soul."
>
> Another special favorite had oft repeated the words—
>
> > "O, I'm going to glory,—won't you come along with me?
> > Don't you see the angels beck'ning, and a calling me away?
> > Don't you see the golden city and the everlasting days?"
>
> There were others, which made incessant mention of "Jordan's banks," and "Canaan's fields," and the "New Jerusalem"; for the negro mind, impassioned and imaginative, always attaches itself to hymns and expressions of a vivid and pictorial nature; and, as they sung, some laughed, and some cried,

and some clapped hands, or shook hands rejoicingly with each other, as if they had fairly gained the other side of the river.[34]

As a mother and daughter await sale and separation at a slave warehouse, we hear them "singing together a wild and melancholy dirge, common as a funeral hymn among the slaves:

> O, where is weeping Mary?
> O, where is weeping Mary?
> 'Rived in the goodly land . . .

"These words," Stowe continues, "sung by voices of a peculiar and melancholy sweetness, in an air which seemed like the sighing of earthly despair after heavenly hope, floated through the dark prison rooms with a pathetic cadence, as verse after verse was breathed out."[35] The symbolic charge of hymns reaches a climax during the final chapters, when Tom is being brutalized at the hands of Simon Legree. As Tom and others first trudge onto Legree's plantation, Legree orders them to strike up a song. Uncertain what to do, Tom begins a hymn:

> "Jerusalem, my happy home,
> Name ever dear to me!
> When shall my sorrows have an end,
> Thy joys when shall—"

"Shut up, you black cuss!" roared Legree; "did ye think I wanted any o'yer infernal old Methodism? I say, tune up, now, something real rowdy,— quick!"

The other slaves then break into a minstrel song, which Stowe describes in terms nearly identical with Frederick Douglass' account of the meaning of slave songs: "It was sung very boisterously, and with a forced attempt at merriment; but no wail of despair, no words of impassioned prayer, could have had such a depth of woe in them as the wild notes of the chorus. As if the poor, dumb heart, threatened,—prisoned,—took refuge in that inarticulate sanctuary of music, and found there a language in which to breathe its prayer to God! There was prayer in it, which Simon could not hear. He only heard the boys singing noisily, and was well pleased; he was making them 'keep up their spirits.'"[36]

Hymns begin to turn the tide. Legree is haunted by a "wild, pathetic voice" chanting ominous spirituals from the attic: "O there'll be mourning, at the judgment-seat of Christ." He struggles to control Tom, whom he hears singing an Isaac Watts hymn:

> "When I can read my title clear
> To mansions in the skies,

> I'll bid farewell to every fear,
> And wipe my weeping eyes. . . ."

"So ho!" said Legree to himself, "he thinks so, does he? How I hate these cursed, Methodist hymns! Here, you nigger," said he, coming suddenly out upon Tom, and raising his riding-whip, "how dare you be gettin' up this yer row, when you ought to be in bed? Shut her old black gash, and get along in with you!"

Though Tom submits, Legree realizes he has lost his power over him. Though Tom is murdered, his family and the others on the Kentucky plantation are freed by the son of the man who sold them:

An aged, patriarchal negro, who had grown gray and blind on the estate, now rose, and, lifting his trembling hand said, "Let us give thanks unto the Lord!" As all kneeled by one consent, a more touching and hearty Te Deum never ascended to heaven, though borne on the peal of organ, bell and cannon, than came from that honest old heart.

On rising, another struck up a Methodist hymn [by Charles Wesley], of which the burden was,

> "The year of Jubilee is come,—
> Return, ye ransomed singers, home."[37]

Subsequent students and proponents of spirituals, like Higginson and William Francis Allen, who along with Charles Pickard Ware and Lucy McKim Garrison published the important collection *Slave Songs of the United States* (1867), which for the first time included musical transcriptions, were less interested in "Methodist hymns," however adapted, than in ostensibly autochthonous spirituals. But there are clear continuities in language and conception from Douglass through Stowe, Higginson and Allen to Du Bois, who famously celebrated "sorrow songs" in the romantic language of racial pluralism that characterized his thinking at the turn of the twentieth century. Douglass admired Stowe's novel, and tried to exploit its strategic value for the abolitionist cause; likewise, Du Bois knew of and respected the work done by Higginson in bringing slave spirituals to a broad audience, while pointing out that "the world listened only half credulously until the Fisk Jubilee Singers sang the slave songs so deeply into the world's heart that it can never wholly forget them again." Du Bois perceived the religious song of southern African Americans from a respectful distance, acknowledging that it was not part of his cultural heritage growing up in New England. "The Music of Negro religion is that plaintive rhythmic melody, with its touching minor cadences, which, despite caricature and defilement, still remains the most original and beautiful expression of human life and longing yet born on American soil," Du Bois wrote in 1903. "Sprung from the African forests, where its counterpart can still be heard, it was adapted, changed, and intensified by the tragic soul-life of the slave, until, under the stress of law and whip, it became the one true expression of a people's sorrow, despair, and hope."[38]

While the Jubilee melodies may have remained distinct from standard hymnody and the music-hall sound of gospel songs, they occupied a space where older European musical forms converged with African song patterns. "It is a coincidence worthy of note that more than half the melodies in [the Jubilee] collection are in the same scale as that in which Scottish music is written; that is, with the fourth and seventh tones omitted," pointed out Theodore F. Seward, who directed the Jubilee singers for a time. "The fact that the music of the ancient Greeks is also said to have been written in this scale, suggests an interesting inquiry as to whether it may not be a peculiar language of nature, or a simpler alphabet than the ordinary diatonic scale, in which the uncultivated mind finds its easiest expression." Higginson himself alluded to this startling affinity, though his interest was more in lyrics than music. He explained that long before the war, he "had been a faithful student of the Scottish ballads, and had always envied Sir Walter the delight of tracing them out amid their own heather, and of writing them down piecemeal from the lips of aged crones. It was a strange enjoyment, therefore," he continued, "to be suddenly brought into the midst of a kindred world of unwritten songs, as simple and indigenous as the Border Minstrelsy, more uniformly plaintive, almost always more quaint, and often as essentially poetic."[39]

The deep structural affinities between African and European folk musics extend to harmonic, melodic, and rhythmic features. "Weird" or "wild" as they may have struck many ears, the Jubilee Singers' spirituals shared some fundamental features with more familiar European-derived musics, including gospel songs like "Hold the Fort!" Musicologist Peter Van der Merwe speculates that most of the characteristics of the modern blues-tinged "popular style" originated in Near Eastern music, which was extended to northern Europe by the Roman Empire. The later rise of Islam brought Arab musical instruments and styles to both Europe and Africa, peaking during the mid to late Middle Ages. Though displaced by European musical traditions, these Arab elements lingered on in the folk music of remote regions like Scotland and Ireland, whence they were transplanted to Appalachia and the rural South. Following the work of John Storm Roberts, Van der Merwe speculates that musical elements common to both British folk musics and West African musics—harsh nasal singing with abundant melisma—reinforced each other in America. This created the distinctive hybrid that by the late nineteenth century was producing ragtime, blues, and white parlor music. These musics shared a number of melodic, harmonic, and rhythmic features: a blurring of the distinction between major and minor, part of an increased importance of modality in organizing melody; weakening opposition between tonic and dominant; decreased importance of harmonic cadences; supplanting of the dominant chord by the subdominant; and increased use of polyrhythms, producing syncopation.[40]

However much musicians were struck by musical affinities between spirituals and European folk music, a concern with foreign missions was crucial to the favorable reception of the Jubilee Singers, especially in Britain. Whether or not their songs reminded listeners of European folk musics, the Singers were representatives of a "race" very few of which had had the opportunity for receiving Christian evangelism of the kind provided at Fisk. In Ireland, the Jubilee Singers were considered "in a sense a reward to Irish people, for their interest in the African race." To Londonderry Presbyterians, the Jubilee Singers symbolized perseverance in the face of oppression and intolerance (in this case, oppression by the Catholic Stuarts). According to Pike, "our Irish friends justly claimed a goodly part in those triumphs which were incidentally celebrated by the Jubilee band . . . What is more gratifying than to be a yoke-fellow, a joint-heir, a judge upon the throne with the King of kings?"[41] But more often, their performances triggered visions of evangelizing Africa. The troupe provided an object lesson in the salutary effects of Christianity on members of the "African" race, heightened by a lingering sense of guilt for British complicity in slavery.

"Having made a great effort in America for the benefit of their own people," Lord Shaftesbury announced on one occasion, "these Jubilee Singers have come here to see whether they can excite a like sympathy, and stir the hearts of the English people to join with them in elevating the negro race to the position to which they are entitled by the laws of God and the great capacities with which he has endowed them." In London, the brother-in-law of David Livingston spoke of how from his mission station he could see the Atlantic on one side, the Indian Ocean on the other and far to the north. "When he stood there, with heathenism on every side, no wonder perhaps he sometimes felt cast down; but, looking at the Jubilee Singers, he could see where light and hope were to come," Pike observed. "It was utterly useless, humanly speaking, for us, alone, to seek to evangelize Africa, but in the trained members of the African race we might look for glorious fruits." At a farewell concert in London at the end of their British tour, Jubilee member Benjamin Holmes spoke of the mission of Fisk University, for which the entire campaign had been conducted: "We hope that

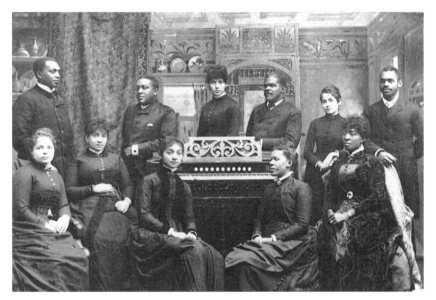

5. The Fisk Jubilee Singers followed their astonishing debut tour of the British Isles with a grueling three-year European tour beginning in 1875 and a six-year world tour beginning in 1884. Courtesy of Photographs and Prints Division, Schomburg Center for Research in Black Culture, The New York Public Library, Astor, Lenox, and Tilden Foundations.

men and women will be educated there who shall go to Africa—that country which has so long been in bondage and sin—and carry the glad tidings, and tell the Africans that there is a God for them . . . By the assistance of the good people of England and America, and by our own efforts, we hope by the blessing of God to get, before many years, even Africa to praise God and serve Him as you do. (Applause.)"[42]

These were early stirrings of what would come to be called Ethiopianism, a new variation on the Judaic notion of a chosen people, which would mobilize movements as disparate as Garveyism, the Nation of Islam, and Jamaican Rastafarianism. "The unification or redemption of African people was to be accomplished through the sustained labors of New World blacks, who would return to the motherland as preachers and teachers, carrying with them the elevating power of Christianity," explains Yvonne Chireau. "Ethiopianism thereby provided the theological rationale for the endeavors of numerous African American churches and missionary associations in the latter part of the nineteenth century, and it undergirded the ideology of secular black nationalism in the century to come."[43]

Embedded in the apparently homegrown American songs of the Jubilee Singers and Moody-Sankey, then, were myriad transatlantic accents. The

European success of the Jubilee spirituals and the Sankey gospel songs can be attributed to both novelty and familiarity. The texts, with their emotional directness and alternately tear-jerking and heart-pumping drama, were fresh to Europeans, and American evangelical ideas about the use of music in worship differed markedly from European conventions. Most startling to Europeans, initially, was the notion that such songs could be performed in sacred space. The new repertoires overcame initial resistance, however, and became wildly successful because they were heard by European audiences as addressing their own concerns about spiritual vitality, social dislocation, and the British duty to Christianize Africa. And they addressed those concerns in musical idioms that resonated powerfully in non-American ears. Deep musical affinities between the new American hymns and the popular songs of Europe made the former intriguingly recognizable. Rather than "debased imitations of Negro melodies," as Du Bois thought, the new gospel hymns drew more on the secular song of the popular music halls, which turned out to have its own formal similarities to African-American song—simultaneously inward looking, drawing on the legacy of slavery, and outward looking, as the United States felt its way into a new imperial role that would be suddenly clarified by 1898. Through music we see the pattern that others have noted, that much of the thinking and rhetoric about foreign peoples was developed on the domestic front, in the context of subduing the Indians and alternately containing and occasionally emancipating the aspirations of African Americans.

CHAPTER FIVE

Dances with Ghosts

And when the race lies crushed and groaning beneath an alien
yoke, how natural is the dream of a redeemer, an Arthur, who
shall return from exile or awake from some long sleep to drive
out the usurper and win back for his people what they have lost
. . . The doctrines of the Hindu avatar, the Hebrew Messiah, the
Christian millennium, and the Hesûnanin of the Indian Ghost
dance are essentially the same, and have their origin in a hope and
longing common to all humanity.

—JAMES MOONEY

FROM the very earliest encounters between Europeans and the Native
peoples of the Americas, Christian hymns have served as a medium of
cultural exchange, a currency through which incompatibilities of language
and custom could apparently melt away. Bringing Christian religion to the
heathen aborigines had motivated Europeans in North America from the
very beginning. A papal bull granted to Ferdinand and Isabella of Spain
had authorized Columbus' voyage. "Come over and save me" pleaded the
Indian figure on the official seal of the Massachusetts Bay Colony more
than a century and a half later. From initial contact onward, intriguing theories began to circulate among European intellectuals that Amerindians
were in fact remnants of the Lost Tribes of Israel whose conversion was
a prerequisite to the conversion of the European Jews that would usher
in the second coming of Christ and the millennium. Converting Native
Americans was not only about saving their souls; it was part of the fulfillment of biblical prophecy that would finally end history.[1]

Beginning in the sixteenth century, Spanish, French, and English missionaries used their sacred songs strategically to capture the attention and
loyalty of those they hoped to win to the gospel of Christ. The experience
of the chaplain to Sir Francis Drake is typical. "In the time of . . . prayers,
singing of Psalmes, and reading of certaine Chapters in the Bible, they sate
very attentively; and observing the end at every pause, with one voice still
cried, Oh, as greatly rejoycing in our exercises," he wrote in 1579. "Yea

they took such pleasure in our singing of Psalmes, that whensoever they resorted to us, their first request was commonly this, *Gnaáh,* by which they intreated that we would sing."[2] At the same time, European explorers, traders, and clergy found themselves encountering very different sorts of musical performances among Native peoples. Their songs, invariably embedded in dances and rituals, were perceived with distaste and incomprehension, as part and parcel of heathen behavior that justified the various forms of exploitation and suppression that marked Euro-Indian contacts from the very beginning. In order to be Christian subjects, the thinking went, the Natives first needed to be civilized. With few exceptions, this process involved changes in dress, labor, custom, and family and communal life, all of which drew resistance. Music was one of the exceptions. It was an area, like trade, in which Native Americans could justifiably feel they received something of value for all they surrendered. In the endless dialectic of Amerindian accommodation and resistance, music often greased the wheels of accommodation.

Over the centuries, music could seem to serve the interest of colonizers and missionaries as a kind of sonic opium, placating the objects of their attentions. Of course, Indians often deployed the music for their own strategic purposes. The Ghost Dance phenomenon, which reached a tragic climax on the Great Plains in 1890, was an instance in which sacred song functioned not as a sign of irenism but as an expression of resistance. Instead of defusing the political tensions that were building in the final years of Indian resistance to federal Indian policy, Ghost Dance songs helped ignite tensions that led to a slaughter at Wounded Knee Creek and the end of Native resistance to full U.S. authority over Indian sovereignty.

The Ghost Dance was a classic instance of the mutual incomprehension that often afflicted the interactions of Europeans and Native Americans. The frames of meaning for Lakota Ghost Dancers and government Indian agents and military personnel were wildly divergent. What Lakota dancers undertook as a religious ritual to salvage a traditional way of life struck most Anglo-Americans closest to the ground as a threatening war dance. The Lakota hope for reunion with ancestors appeared to them an expression of almost suicidal fatalism. But the Ghost Dance and its songs were rooted in traditional Lakota beliefs and ritual practices.[3] At the same time, the ceremony was freighted with non-Indian symbols and ideas. An Oglala Sioux named George Sword offered this description of the ceremony:

> The persons in the ghost dancing are all joined hands. A man stands and then a woman, so in that way forming a very large circle. They dance around in the circle in a continuous time until some of them become so tired and overtired that they became crazy and finally drop as though dead, with foams in mouth

all wet by perspiration. All the men and women made holy shirts and dresses they wear in dance. The persons dropped in dance would all lie in great dust [made by] the dancing . . . When they come from ghosts or after recovery from craziness, they brought meat from the ghosts or from the supposed messiah. They also brought water, fire, and wind with which to kill all the whites or Indians who will help the chief of the whites. They made sweat house and made holes in the middle of the sweat house where they say the water will come out of these holes. Before they begin to dance they all raise their hands toward the northwest and cry in supplication to the messiah and then begin the dance with the song, *"Ate misunkala ceya omani-ye,"* etc.[4]

Like the other cases we have encountered so far, the Ghost Dance religion featured some distinctively Judaic ideas: the dream of a messiah, a covenant, a millennium. It echoed the Pentecostal practices of Shakers and Mormons. It participated in the same spiritual energies that were beginning to find expression among the earliest American Pentecostals across the American Midwest, and that became unmistakable in the Los Angeles Azusa Street revivals of 1906. The notion of a messiah who would lead Indians to a triumphant recovery of a purified world was of course an age-old notion among a variety of Christian sects over history, but it had a parallel among Indians as well, in earlier prophet-leaders like Neolin and Tenskwatawa. The Ghost Dance religion was the culmination of more than a century of Amerindian spiritual ferment, but it was not the end. It provided a spiritual basis for cultural resistance expressed through the selective use of beliefs and music borrowed and "converted" from their Judeo-Christian origins.

OUR understanding of Indian religion, music, and history is deeply marked by an inescapable source bias: what historians have to work with to make sense of the Indian past is, with the exception of archaeological evidence, filtered through the perception and prose of non-Natives, who often lacked sympathy or basic comprehension of what they were observing. Thus we must be reconciled to the impossibility of knowing *anything* definitive about what Indian music may have sounded like before a European presence on the continent. The technique of ethnographic upstreaming, whereby scholars use evidence from present-day or recent Indian practices as a way of extrapolating backward to a presumably stable past is essentially unreliable because musical practices tend to absorb "external" elements so discrete that peoples who make and use the music are themselves unconscious of those influences. Unlike bones, pottery, tools, or built structures, music leaves no material trace (though instruments may survive). We may have written accounts, but these invariably derive from

European pens; even when offering simple descriptions or ostensibly recording the words of Indians, they introduce the possibility of myriad biases. The same goes for musical transcriptions, which generally were produced in unnatural settings, and even field recordings, whose production required a kind of ritual performance in itself.

And so it is with Ghost Dance songs, among which are some of the very earliest sound recordings, dating back to 1893. The very act of recording or transcribing, which reifies the music, separating it from the setting that gives it meaning—the sights, smells, tactile impressions, memory associations—represents a profound if less tangible alteration of the musical text. But as historian Daniel Richter has demonstrated, it is possible for historians to proceed by "facing East from Indian country": to read—and hear—sources "against the grain," listening hard for those intrusions of the Indian voice and perspective.[5] The question is, why and where did the songs originate, and how were they transmitted to the broader Ghost Dance community? How did they relate to other songs, both Indian and non-Indian, and how did they help Indians to make sense of and respond to the continually changing material and spiritual conditions they confronted?

Answering these questions requires paying attention to the early ethnologists and ethnomusicologists on whose reports and studies we rely for documentary evidence. These reports seldom treat the music in isolation from other practices, but consider sound as part of a larger whole. Much of what we know of the Ghost Dance of 1890 derives from the efforts of a single individual. Born in rural Indiana to Irish-born parents in 1861, James Mooney was a kind of self-taught ethnologist, a member of the first generation of remarkable scholars who collected around the Bureau of American Ethnology, founded in 1879 as a division of the Smithsonian Institution by Major John Wesley Powell. Mooney dated his consuming interest in Indians to his twelfth year, when he became intrigued by an uprising on the West Coast and decided to master the name and location of all American tribes. He never attended college but graduated valedictorian from high school (giving a graduation address on U.S. Indian policy) before working briefly as a schoolteacher and newspaper reporter. Mooney lobbied unsuccessfully for a job at the bureau before finally traveling to Washington, D.C., where he wangled a meeting with Powell, who eventually offered him a position (initially as a volunteer). From 1885 until his death in 1921 Mooney worked for the Bureau of American Ethnology both in Washington and in the field. He was also a devoted Irish nationalist. From early childhood he developed a deep attachment to Irish literature and folkways, which he continued to research and publish on throughout his life. He also served as first president of the Washington

Gaelic Society and agitated for Irish home rule. This cultural heritage left Mooney with "an awareness of ancient glories, of a sense of wrong and deprivation, and a dream of a golden age returned."[6]

Mooney's great gifts were in indefatigable research, vivid and detailed writing, and an integrity that led him to speak truth to power even at risk to his career. In his first decade at the bureau he published works on the linguistic classification of North American Indians, and on the Cherokee and Sioux. As alarm about an "Indian Outbreak" triggered by the Ghost Dance circulated east to Washington, Mooney embarked in late 1890 for four months in "Indian Territory" (now Oklahoma), where he observed Arapaho, Cheyenne, Kiowa, Comanche, Apache, Caddo, and Wichita Indians. A year later he spent three months mainly among the Sioux and Paiute. In the summer of 1892 he returned again, this time spending time in Wyoming with Shoshone and Arapaho as well as Sioux. Mooney also traveled to the Southwest for fieldwork with Navajo and Hopi Indians. He participated in the dance, took photographs, and made field recordings among Arapaho and Cheyenne. All told, the fieldwork covered 32,000 miles during twenty-two months on location with twenty tribes.[7]

Mooney's most dramatic coup was tracking down Wovoka, the Paiute messiah/leader of the 1890 Ghost Dance movement. Playing all the cards he could assemble, Mooney located the elusive Wovoka in Mason Valley, Nevada, on New Year's Day 1892, nearly foundering in an unusually deep snowfall. By then Wounded Knee was infamous. On 15 December 1890, Sitting Bull had been shot and killed by Indian police while being arrested. On 28 December federal soldiers apprehended a band being led by Big Foot from Cheyenne River Reservation toward Wounded Knee Creek. The next morning, shooting rang out while troops were disarming Indians; 146 Sioux were killed, along with 25 troops. Mooney quickly learned that press accounts had failed to get even the most basic elements of the story correct, at least concerning Wovoka. "Different writers have made him a Paiute, a half-blood, and a Mormon white man," Mooney wrote in his 1896 study. "He has been denounced as an imposter, ridiculed as a lunatic, and laughed at as a pretended Christ, while by the Indians he is revered as a direct messenger from the Other World, and among many of the remote tribes he is believed to be omniscient, to speak all languages, and to be invisible to a white man."[8]

Mooney pieced together a different story. Wovoka, which means "The Cutter" in Paiute, grew up in—and rarely left—Mason Valley, Nevada. Many Paiute worked as day laborers for whites in the vicinity. Wovoka was informally attached to a local rancher named David Wilson, who gave him the name Jack and taught him some English and "a confused idea of the white men's theology." Mooney recounted what the spiritual leader told him on the first day of 1892. "The sun died," Wovoka said, referring to an eclipse, and he was taken up to the other world—"a pleasant land and full game of game"—where he saw God with all the ancestors going about their ordinary activities. "God told him he must go back and tell his people they must be good and love one another, have no quarreling, and live in peace with the whites," Wovoka told Mooney; "that they must work, and not lie or steal; that they must put away all the old practices that savored of war; that if they faithfully obeyed his instructions they would at last be reunited with their friends in this other world, where there would be no more death or sickness of old age." Wovoka was given a dance, with specific instructions for performance, and control over the elements. He then returned to earth and began his mission. The Wovoka that comes into focus through Mooney's interviews was notably disarming. He denied any responsibility for Ghost Shirt wearers at Wounded Knee, who believed that special shirts would stop federal bullets. When asked directly, Wovoka allowed that it was better for Indians to adopt white civilization. "He makes no claim to be Christ, the Son of God, as has been so often asserted in print," Mooney reported (although Wovoka was regarded as such by many of his non-Paiute followers). "He does claim to be a prophet who has received a divine revelation," which other sources linked to a serious fever he had experienced during a solar eclipse in 1889.[9]

For once there was actual physical evidence to support Mooney's account. He persuaded Wovoka to let him examine a document he had prepared for a delegation of Cheyenne and Arapaho who had visited Mason Valley the previous summer. In the rough "Carlisle English" of the Indian who recorded them, Wovoka delivered these instructions:

What you get home you make dance, and will give you the same. When you dance four days and in night one day, dance day time, five days and then fifth, will wash five for every body. He likes you flock you give him good many things, he heart been satting feel good. After you get home, will give good cloud, and give you chance to make you feel good. And he give you good spirit. And he give you all a good paint.

You folks want you to come in three [months] here, any tribes from there. There will be good bit snow this year. Sometimes rain's, in fall, this year some rain, never give you any thing like that. Grandfather said when he die never no cry. No hurt anybody. No fight, good behave always, it will give you satisfaction, this young man, he is a good Father and mother don't tell no white man. Jesus was on ground, he just like cloud. Every body is alive again, I don't know when they will [be] here, may be this fall or in spring.

Every body never get sick, be young again,—(if young fellow no sick any more,) work for white men never trouble with him until you leave, when it shake the earth don't be afraid no harm any body.

You make dance for six weeks night, and put you foot [food?] in dance to eat for every body and wash in the water. that is all to tell, I am in to you. and you will received a good words from him some time, Don't tell lie.[10]

The key elements are laid out with economy: the requisite ritual dancing and washing; the ethical injunctions to behave well, to avoid violence and lying, and to maintain peaceful relations with whites (who are not to be taken into confidence, however); the promises of health, well-being, and youth; prophecies about weather; the allusion to the second coming of Christ. "The great underlying principle of the Ghost dance doctrine," wrote Mooney, "is that the time will come when the whole Indian race, living and dead, will be reunited upon a regenerated earth, to live a life of aboriginal happiness, forever free from death, disease, and misery."[11]

The Ghost Dance had spread quickly over a vast region through an intricate social network. As Mooney pieced it together, the first Ghost Dance had taken place on Walker Lake reservation in Nevada shortly after Wovoka's original vision, in January 1889. From there it spread immediately to Ute and Paiute scattered across Nevada and Oregon, and subsequently to many small adjacent tribes, including Bannock, Shoshone, and Gosiute. Through southern Arapaho enthusiasts the religion reached the Mojave and Walapai Indians. The crucial development was the crossing of the new religion to the eastern side of the Rockies and north of Oklahoma. The Shoshone and northern Arapaho became key players in this dispersion. They sent delegations from Wyoming to meet Wovoka, were persuaded, and carried news of the Ghost Dance to the plains. Those accepting the religion included Assiniboine, Gros Ventres, Cheyenne, Mandan, and Pawnee. For a host of reasons, many Indians failed to embrace the Ghost Dance: Blackfeet, Crow, Ojibwe, Omaha, Nez Percé, and most southwestern Amerindians, including Navajo. Even among Sioux, Mooney estimated that perhaps half embraced it. Still, he concluded, some thirty to thirty-five Indian nations were at least somewhat involved with the dance, representing a population of some 60,000. This made it the largest Indian movement since the Shawnee prophet Tenskwatawa had with his brother Tecumseh organized armed resistance among Shawnees, Kickapoos, Potawatamis, Winnebagos, and Creeks against Anglo-American encroachment in the trans-Appalachian West in the first decade of the nineteenth century.[12]

Aiding the dispersion was the fact that a previous Ghost Dance movement had developed among the Paiute as recently as 1870, under the leadership of a prophet named Wodziwob; Wovoka's own father had been caught up in it. Experiencing a vision in 1869, Wodziwob had predicted the reincarnation of Paiute dead and urged ritual body painting, bathing, and performance of the traditional Paiute Round Dance. The Great Basin Round Dance, later grafted onto their own local religious practices by plains Indians, was embedded in a five-day festival that was both religious and social, a time for courting. Holding hands, men and women would shuffle clockwise in a circle, sometimes around a center pole, while a male dance leader would walk around the circle, sometimes speaking. Dancers accompanied themselves with songs taught to them by song leaders who received them in dreams. With regularly repeated phrases, the songs were melodic and seemed to resolve to a tonic; they had an almost European sound to them, one that would be exported in the 1890 Ghost Dance to Native peoples with very different-sounding music cultures. No instruments were used in either Ghost Dance, an absence that was exceptional for dance music. Wodziwob's Ghost Dance was last performed in 1871; followers became disillusioned when the prophecy failed to materialize. And it never escaped the Great Basin, as did the second Ghost Dance. Alphabetic literacy was crucial to the success of the latter, Ronald Niezen has argued. "The Ghost Dance could never have become so widespread, and would probably have died out within a year of its inception, had it not been for the efficient aid it received from the returned pupils of various eastern government schools, who conducted the sacred correspondence for their friends at the different agencies, acted as interpreters for the delegates to the messiah, and in various ways assumed the leadership and conduct of the dance."[13]

Each of the dozens of tribes that adopted the Ghost Dance modified the ritual to fit its traditional practices. "The differences of interpretation are precisely such as we find in Christianity," Mooney wrote, "with its hundreds of sects and innumerable shades of individual opinion." Music was an aspect of the Ghost Dance religion that varied according to group (although the Great Basin idiom of the Paiute provided the musical foundation for most worshippers). "The Ghost-dance songs are of the utmost importance in connection with the study of the messiah religion," he insisted, "as we find embodied in them much of the doctrine itself, with more of the special tribal mythologies, together with such innumerable references to old-time customs, ceremonies, and modes of life long since obsolete as to make up a regular symposium of aboriginal thought and practice." He described the process of song-creation with some care.

> There is no limit to the number of these songs, as every trance at every dance produces a new one, the trance subject after regaining consciousness embodying his experience in the spirit world in the form of a song, which is sung at the next dance and succeeding performances until superseded by other songs originating in the same way. Thus, a single dance may easily result in twenty

or thirty new songs. While songs are thus born and die, certain ones which appeal especially to the Indian heart, on account of their mythology, pathos, or peculiar sweetness, live and are perpetuated. There are also with each tribe certain songs which are a regular part of the ceremonial, as the opening song and the closing song, which are repeated at every dance. Of these the closing song is the most important and permanent. In some cases certain songs constitute a regular series, detailing the experiences of the same person in successive trance visions.

As during the 1871 Ghost Dance, no drums or rattles were used, "excepting sometimes by an individual dancer in imitation of a trance vision." This feature set the songs apart from every other form of Indian dance music with which Mooney was familiar.[14] His 1896 report for the Bureau of American Ethnology included an extensive section on the songs, providing transliterations, English translations, and brief annotations for each song, and in many cases musical settings. Included were seventy-three Arapaho Ghost Dance songs, nineteen Cheyenne, four Comanche, nine Paiute, twenty-six Sioux, fifteen Kiowa, and fifteen Caddo.

Mooney's admiration for the songs is evident. He praised a Lakota song for the way it "summarizes the whole hope of the Ghost dance—the return of the buffalo and the departed dead, the message being brought to the people by the sacred birds, the Eagle and the Crow":

> The whole world is coming,
> A nation is coming, a nation is coming,
> The Eagle has brought the message to the tribe.
> The father says so, the father says so.
> Over the whole earth they are coming.
> The buffalo are coming, the buffalo are coming,
> The crow has brought the message to the tribe,
> The father says so, the father says so.

His favorites were the Arapaho songs, which he praised as "first in importance, for number, richness of reference, beauty of sentiment, and rhythm of language." Perhaps the careful preparations of the Arapaho singers produced what struck Mooney as their high quality. "As with church choirs," he observed, "the leaders, both men and women, frequently assembled privately in a tipi to rehearse the new or old songs for the next dance." The songs are a transcriber's dream, especially in comparison to the challenges posed by the bulk of American Indian music, with its unwillingness to conform to European notation. The story of their transcription, let alone their field recording, is something of a mystery. Mooney's biographer, L. G. Moses, dates his foray into recording to late 1893, on the Caddo and Wichita reservation, where he used a new Edison Graphaphone purchased by the bureau. He adds that Mooney had the assistance of no less than John Philip Sousa in making musical notations, but that the ethnologist actually felt less certain of the accuracy of the texts.[15] In any event here are two Arapaho songs apparently recorded by Mooney, probably late in 1893.

> Hey! When I met him approaching
> My children, my children
> I then saw the multitude plainly.

This song was brought from the north to the southern Arapaho by Sitting Bull. It refers to the trance vision of a dancer, who saw the messiah advancing at the head of all the spirit army. It is an old favorite, and is sung with vigor and animation.

In both performances, the texts are as carefully metered and timed as Protestant psalms: measured, but with a smoothly tripping rhythmic delivery. Each line is repeated precisely. The melodies fall comfortably within the diatonic scale, without microtones. The words are delivered firmly and evenly, without apparent affect or overt emotional quality. Without the translations, the listener would have no way to tell which was a song of impending millennial triumph, and which was the song of desperate hunger and thirst.

Characteristically, Mooney perceived the Arapaho's songs in relation to the religion he knew best. "The hope held out [by the Ghost Dance] is the same that has inspired the Christian for nineteen centuries," he states at one point: "a happy immortality in perpetual youth." It was this impulse to relativize Ghost Dancers and Christians that made Mooney's superiors worry about public reaction to his study. If the "messiah religion" had so many common features with Christianity, maybe Christian belief wasn't so far removed from the benighted sensibilities of savages. Mooney's study situated Wovoka's Ghost Dance in a tradition of Native prophets extending back to earliest contact with Europeans. He narrated a series of Indian movements led by religious leaders: the Pueblo Revolt of 1680, coordinated by Popé, a Tewa; the revolt led by Condorcanqui against the Spanish in Peru, in 1781; Pontiac's anticolonialist confederacy, inspired by Neolin, "the Delaware Prophet"; the resistance to American expansionism led by Tenskwatawa and Tecumseh in the years before and during the War of 1812; struggles against Indian removal led by the Kickapoo prophet Kanakuk in the 1820s and 1830s; and opposition to Anglo usurpation in the Pacific Northwest after the Civil War led by religious visionaries Smoholla and Squ-sacht-un (also known as John Slocum). Many of these North American new religions included ceremonial dances and moral codes that proscribed consumption of alcohol and other behaviors associated with Europeans.[16]

MOONEY]   SONGS OF THE ARAPAHO   977

28. ANI'QU NE'CHAWU'NANI'

Moderato.

A - ni'- qu ne'- cha - wu' - na - ni',   a - ni' - qu ne'-cha - wu' - na - ni';

a - wa' - wa bi'-qă - na' - ka - ye' - na,   a - wa' - wa bi'-qă - na' - ka - ye' - na;

i - ya - hu'h ni' - bi - thi' - ti,   i - ya - hu'h ni' - bi - thi' - ti,

Ani'qu ne'chawu'nani',
Ani'qu ne'chawu'nani';
Awa'wa biqăna'kaye'na,
Awa'wa biqăna'kaye'na;
Iyahu'h ni'bithi'ti,
Iyahu'h ni'bithi'ti.

Translation

Father, have pity on me,
Father, have pity on me;
I am crying for thirst,
I am crying for thirst;
All is gone—I have nothing to eat,
All is gone—I have nothing to eat.

This is the most pathetic of the Ghost-dance songs. It is sung to a plaintive tune, sometimes with tears rolling down the cheeks of the dancers as the words would bring up thoughts of their present miserable and dependent condition. It may be considered the Indian paraphrase of the Lord's prayer.

6. Source: James Mooney, *The Ghost-Dance Religion and the Sioux Outbreak*, Part 2, 14th Annual Report of the Bureau of Ethnology (Washington, D.C.: Government Printing Office, 1896), 977.

Mooney's chapter titled "Parallels in Other Systems" contained a more daring assertion. Here he demonstrated that the sorts of beliefs and practices of the Ghost Dance had been constituent of each of the Abrahamic religions, not to mention a host of greater or lesser-known sects and cults. "The systems of our highest modern civilizations have their counterparts among all the nations, and their chain of parallels stretches backward link by link until we find their origin and interpretation in the customs and rites of our own barbarian ancestors, or of our still existing aboriginal tribes," Mooney proposed. "There is nothing new under the sun." He spun out detailed analogies between Indian prophets like Wovoka and biblical figures like Jacob, Abraham, Moses, Paul, Mohammed, Joan of Arc, George Fox, John Wesley, Mother Ann Lee, the Kentucky revivalists of the Second Great Awakening, William Miller, and numerous other sects. "The Indian messiah religion is the inspiration of a dream. Its ritual is the dance, the ecstasy and the trance. Its priests are hypnotics and cataleptics. All these have formed a part of every great religious development of which we have knowledge from the beginning of history."[17]

Common to all organized religions, Mooney proposed, were systems of ethics, of mythology, and of ritual. "In this message from the high priest of the Ghost dance [Wovoka] we have a synopsis of all three," he argued. Mooney was particularly impressed by Ghost Dance ethics:

> The moral code inculcated is as pure and comprehensive in its simplicity as anything found in religious systems from the days of Gautama Buddha to the time of Jesus Christ. *"Do no harm to any one. Do right always."* Could anything be more simple, and yet more exact and exacting? It inculcates honesty—*"Do not tell lies."* It preaches good will—*"Do no harm to any one."* It forbids the extravagant mourning customs formerly common among the tribes—*"When your friends die, you must not cry,"* which is interpreted by the prairie tribes as forbidding the killing of horses, the burning of tipis and destruction of property, the cutting off of the hair and the gashing of the body with knives, all of which were formerly the sickening rule at every death until forbidden by the new doctrine . . . It preaches peace with the whites and obedience to authority until the day of deliverance shall come. Above all, it forbids war—*"You must not fight."* It is hardly possible for us to realize the tremendous and radical change which this doctrine works in the whole spirit of savage life.[18]

To Mooney, then, the Ghost Dance religion was not an ominous spiritual mutation that threatened a future of armed insurrection. It was, in fundamental ways, a *better* religion than the traditional beliefs it subsumed, conducive to assimilation and Christianization. The militant, apparently antiwhite form it took at Pine Ridge was anomalous, a response to local conditions. "The Ghost dance itself, in the form which it assumed among the Sioux, was only a symptom and expression of the real causes of dissatisfaction," primarily inadequate food rations and a variety of broken promises and bureaucratic afflictions. "The Sioux outbreak of 1890 was due entirely to local grievances, recent or long standing." And Mooney had his own explanation for the extraordinary behaviors associated with the ceremony. "The most important feature of the Ghost dance, and the secret of the trances, is hypnotism," he concluded. "It can not be said that the Indian priests understand the phenomenon, for they ascribe it to a supernatural cause, but they know how to produce the effect, as I have witnessed hundreds of times."[19]

There was an additional ingredient in the religious mix. Mooney was one of many contemporaries who perceived uncanny, perhaps sinister connections between the Ghost Dance and the Latter-day Saints. Most prominent among them was General Nelson A. Miles, a major figure in the Civil War as well as in major campaigns against Indians, including the command at Wounded Knee. "I am inclined to believe that there is more than one person impersonating this Messiah," Miles said, offering as evidence the fact that the messiah was able to address various tribes in their respective languages. "I cannot say positively, but it is my belief the Mormons are the prime movers in all this," he told reporters a few weeks before the Wounded Knee massacre, in which he was involved. "It will [probably not] lead to an outbreak, but when an ignorant race of people become religious fanatics it is hard to tell just what they will do." In an article published shortly after the massacre, Miles elaborated this hypothesis, holding what he called a "religious sect of people living on the western slopes of the rocky Mountains" responsible for making "these superstitious savages believe that all who had faith in this 'new religion' would occupy the earth, and all who did not would be destroyed." His conclusions were based on reports that flowed in from a diverse group of informants, including Indian agents, army officers, Indian interpreters, and concerned citizens. Allegations of Mormon involvement in fomenting the Ghost Dance continued to circulate for years after Wounded Knee, and have been largely accepted by most subsequent historians.[20]

Mooney himself included speculations along these lines, phrased less judgmentally, in his 1896 report. In an appendix titled "The Mormons and the Indians" he quoted extensively from a pamphlet apparently reflecting the views of Mormon fundamentalists. The centerpiece was an exegesis of scripture suggesting that Wounded Knee fulfilled the last of seven signs portending the end of time and restoration of the Mormon millennium. The pamphleteer drew from Isaiah 5:7 for the metaphor of the Lord's vineyard as the house of Israel: "In the part of the vineyard the American Indians, descendants of the righteous branch of Joseph, who were led to the Western Continent or hemisphere—Zion—we find the vine, the stone-power of the Latter Days," a reference to Psalm 80. The slaughter at Wounded Knee indicated that biblical prophecy was continuing to unfold, with the federal government in the role of the chief priests and Pharisees to which Christ's stern parable was addressed: "The husbandmen upon this land began the last pruning of the vineyard in 1891. Prominent among which stands our government in fulfilling Matt. 21:33–41, saying, let us kill the heirs and hold the inheritance, as shown in the massacre of Wounded Knee; the butchery of Sitting Bull; the imprisonment of Short Bull and others; the breaking up of reservations, and the attempts to destroy the treaty stipulations above mentioned by forcing the mark of the Beast, citizenship and statehood, upon the American Indians, which will ultimately terminate in a war of extermination. Isa. 10:24–27; Dan. 2:34; Isa. 14:21."[21]

This was no doubt a fringe interpretation of the meaning of Wounded Knee, but a well-known hymn from this period provides a more accessible version of the place of Indians in the unfolding of the destiny of Latter-day Saints in the American West. "Great Spirit! Listen to the red man's wail!" it begins. "Great Chieftain! Save him from the pale-faced foe." The hymn goes on to document the loss of hunting and fishing grounds, prairies "fast departing to the Christian's sway." Thanks to "cursed firewater's stultifying flame," Indians are vulnerable to "the cheating pale-face," while European diseases prove beyond the ken of "grey-haired med'cine men." Following this desperate petition, "A dazzling vision burst upon his sight—A glorious angel from the Holy One!"

"Your prayer is heard" he said, "and I am here
To tell you what will shortly come to pass:
A day of joy for all your tribes is near;
Your foes shall perish like the sun-scorched grass.

"The Holy Book your fathers hid is found,
Your 'Mormon' brothers will the truth reveal;
Though troubles press, and all seems black around,
Obey their words—your soul's deep wounds will heal.

"Not many moons shall pass away, before
The curse of darkness from your skin shall flee;
Your ancient beauty will the Lord restore,
And all your tribes shall dwell in unity . . ."

The angel left, and darkness came again,
But light and joy dwelt in the Indian's soul.
Oh! may the day soon dawn for Ephraim's reign,
When all the "glorious land" he shall control.[22]

Although Mormons had actively proselytized among Indians in the Great Basin, and won significant numbers of converts among tribes that later took up the Ghost Dance, there is little indication that Mormon Indians had any direct involvement with Wovoka's movement. Rather, Mormon leaders tried to discourage the Ghost Dance, partly out of fears that they would be accused. Accounts stressing Mormon influence were often based on hearsay and rumors filtered through the pervasive anti-Mormon attitudes of the late nineteenth century. However, even if a direct causal relationship cannot be proved, the Ghost Dance–Mormon nexus stands as an intriguing case of religious convergence, of twin-culture reinforcement. For religions to reciprocally influence each other is more the rule than the exception; the practices of certain Ghost Dance adherents were most likely Mormonized just as Mormonism absorbed some influence from Amerindian beliefs and practices.[23]

MOONEY brought a powerful historical imagination to bear on the Ghost Dance movement, and his achievements in observation and narration are extraordinary by any standards, all the more so given the prevailing racism of fin-de-siècle American anthropology. Like the work on black spirituals a generation earlier by Higginson and Allen, Mooney's project marked a watershed in the development of an interest in understanding marginalized peoples or ethnic groups through the careful interpretation and cataloging of their musics. Initiated by radical Unitarians and transcendentalist romantics like Emerson and Thoreau, then taken up by abolitionists, this budding ethnographic impulse was advanced and altered in the final decades of the nineteenth century by professional ethnologists and folklore collectors.[24] Mooney was not alone in his attempt to take Indian religion, particularly its musical forms, seriously. Three other pioneering ethnologists, two women and the third Amerindian, were making equally pathbreaking investigations of Indian culture, bringing to the study of Native musics a technical sophistication that was beyond Mooney's means. In doing so they played a significant part of the foundation of the field of ethnomusicology.

The first, Alice Cunningham Fletcher, was a protégé of Frederic W. Putnam, who directed the Peabody Museum of American Archaeology and Ethnology in Cambridge and instituted Harvard's graduate program in anthropology. She divided her time between Boston, where she was a fellow of the Peabody Museum, and Washington, D.C. In 1895 she was the first woman elected vice-president (presiding officer) of a section of the American Association for the Advancement of Science, the leading organization for anthropologists in the United States.[25] Fletcher began her association with Omaha Indians in 1881, when they requested assistance in securing land titles. Her first encounters with Indian music were not auspicious. "I think I may safely say that I heard little or nothing of Indian music the first three or four times that I attended dances or festivals, beyond a screaming downward movement that was gashed and torn by the vehemently beaten drum," she later recalled. A change occurred when she was convalescing from a serious illness on the reservation. "They sang softly because I was weak, and there was no drum, and then it was that the distraction of noise and confusion of theory were dispelled, and the sweetness, the beauty and meaning of these songs were revealed to me."[26]

Fletcher's innovative work on Omaha music, eventually published in 1893, was made possible by collaboration with an informant named Francis La Flesche. Of mixed Omaha, Ponca, and French ancestry (his father was an Omaha headman), La Flesche had been raised Christian and educated at a missionary boarding school. Like William Apess, George Copway, and Ely Samuel Parker, he was a bicultural mediator and autoethnographer of the sort so important in the early anthropology of American Indians. He recalled a visit by a group of government inspectors who requested the performance of an Indian song: "There was some hesitancy, but suddenly a loud clear voice close to me broke into a Victory song; before a bar was sung another voice took up the song from the beginning, as is the custom among the Indians, then the whole school fell in, and we made the room ring. We understood the song, and knew the emotion of which it was the expression. We felt, as we sang, the patriotic thrill of a victorious people who had vanquished their enemies; but the men shook their heads, and one of them said, 'That's savage, that's savage! They must be taught music.'"[27] Like his classmates La Flesche studied western music, but he retained his knowledge of traditional songs. Born nearly twenty years after Fletcher, he became her lifelong companion and adopted son, inheriting her estate when she died in 1923. During the years before publication of *A Study of Omaha Indian Music,* a Peabody Museum publication for which Fletcher made certain La Flesche received credit on the title page, La Flesche worked patiently with Fletcher and her collaborator, John Comfort Fillmore, repeating songs until they were satisfactorily transcribed. Thinking her own training in musical analysis inadequate to a reliable study of the music, Fletcher had enlisted the assistance of Fillmore, a European-trained pianist and composer, who proceeded to run a series of experiments demonstrating, to his satisfaction, that Indians possessed the same harmonic sense as European Americans.

This kind of intellectual division of labor was not uncommon among early ethnomusicologists. Precisely at the time that Fletcher, La Flesche, and Fillmore were refining their work in the mid-1880s, a Boston philanthropist named Mary Hemenway had established an ambitious archaeological expedition initially under the direction of pioneering anthro-

7. Beginning in the 1890s, James Mooney, Alice Fletcher, Frances Densmore, and other folklorists used Edison's newly invented gramophone to make numerous field recordings of Amerindian music. Courtesy of Nebraska State Historical Society Photograph Collections, Lincoln.

pologist Frank Hamilton Cushing. By 1890 the Hemenway Southwestern Archeological Expedition, now under the direction of Jesse Walter Fewkes, began a scientific study of Indian music. Fewkes was the first to use Edison's newly invented phonograph in the field, recording the Passamaquoddy Indians of Maine, and he turned next to Zunis of New Mexico. For musical expertise Hemenway enlisted Benjamin Ives Gilman, a lecturer in psychology at Harvard. Gilman brought all the rigor of scientific positivism to his analysis of the music, developing a new forty-five-line staff that made possible the notation of quarter tones. Using Fewkes's recordings, he made notes on details like the condition of the batteries and the speed of the cylinder machine that affected the pitch of the music when played back. His article on Zuni melodies, published in the Hemenway Expedition's journal in 1891, concluded that the Indian songs he had studied demonstrated no evidence of fixed scales, keys, or harmonies.[28]

Fillmore drew very different conclusions in his "Report on the Structural Peculiarities of the Music," which accompanied Fletcher's 1893 Peabody publication. He had developed his own scientific methodology, a kind of ethnographic focus group. After isolating the melodies, he played back different versions—varying the harmonies, playing deliberately off-key—to Omahas to ascertain which sounded best to them. He was testing for "a latent harmonic sense which might, unconsciously on their part, be a determining factor in their choice of melody tones." Fillmore found the results of his experiments "entirely successful. Whatever chords were natural and satisfactory to me were equally so to them, from which it seems proper to draw the conclusion that the sense of harmony is an innate endowment of human nature, that it is the same for the trained musician and for the untrained primitive man, the difference being purely one of development."[29] Because his results were so conclusive, Fillmore felt justified in publishing the Omaha songs in four-part harmony, often with the instruction *"Flowingly, with feeling."*

Fillmore's study provides a textbook example of "social evolutionism," the notion that human cultures are not essentially different, simply positioned temporarily at different points on the evolutionary continuum. The music made by Indians in 1890 was what Europeans had produced at some earlier stage in their development, and Indians, with proper assistance, would progress to the stage currently enjoyed by whites. "Indian song is an absolutely spontaneously natural product," he judged. His condescension was manifest in the titles of his articles, such as "What Do Indians Mean to Do When They Sing, and How Far Do They Succeed?" Fillmore allowed that to the non-Indian ear, Omaha music might sound (as it did to Fletcher) "mere barbaric noise; 'all sound and fury, signifying nothing.'" The harsh vocal timbre and questionable intonation of Indian singers, he asserted, reflected the circumstances in which their music was made: fighting to be heard for distances above a strong wind, sometimes competing with loud drumming. Nevertheless Fillmore was clearly impressed by what he heard. "The Wawan ceremony is profoundly religious, its symbols are treated with as great reverence as any priest treats the crucifix or the Sacred Host; all phases of religious emotion are embodied in its songs," he wrote. "He who knows, feels and appreciates this, who penetrates so far into the Indian feeling as to be partly oblivious of non-essential accessories, can begin to appreciate the feeling Miss Fletcher expressed to me when she told me that she had never been so powerfully impressed or so profoundly stirred by any music as by the Wawan songs, except by some of the great Wagnerian music dramas." Of a piece titled "Choral. Wa-Wan Wa-an. After Pipes Are Raised," taken from a Calumet ceremony that Fletcher was fortunate to observe, he wrote: "The whole choral impresses me with its beauty, nobility and dignity. Indeed, I know not where to look for a finer musical expression of noble, dignified religious feeling within the limits of the choral." He was particularly struck by the Omahas' use of harmonic thirds and sixths. "Practice of this sort is to be found in Beethoven and in Schubert; more of it in Schumann and in Chopin; most of all in Liszt and Wagner," he wrote. "That some of these primitive melodies, created by a people who never use harmony and who have no musical theory of any kind nor even a musical notation should be explicable by referring them to a latent perception of these relationships and explicable in no other way, is certainly a surprising fact."[30]

Fletcher herself wrote eloquently of the religious significance of the Omaha music, which she attributed to its unalienated nature, its origin in a social system that refused the separation of work and nature:

> Among the Indians, music envelopes like an atmosphere every religious, tribal and social ceremony as well as every personal experience. There is not a phase of life that does not find expression in song. Religious rituals are embedded in it, the reverent recognition of the recognition of the creation of the corn, of the food-giving animals, of the powers of the air, of the fructifying sun, is passed from one generation to another in melodious measures; song nerves the warrior to deeds of heroism and robs death of its terrors; it speeds the spirit to the land of the hereafter and solaces those who live to mourn; children compose ditties for their games, and young men by music give zest to their sports; the lover sings his way to the maiden's heart, and the old man tunefully evokes those agencies which can avert death. Music is also the medium through which man holds communion with his soul, and with the unseen powers which control his destiny.[31]

Whereas Fillmore focused on the structural elements of harmony and rhythm, Fletcher paid special attention to the texts, noting that they showed a latent sense of metrical form in the same way that the melodies showed latent harmony. She was reminded not of European classics but of music of a different body of Indians. "Taking a broad outlook over the two, one finds much in common in Indian and Aryan songs," she wrote. "Wherever one man yearns toward the mysterious unseen powers that environ him, whenever he seeks expression of his personal loves, hopes, fears and griefs, his song will answer in its fundamental directive emotion to that of every other man; this is particularly true of our folk music, which embraced in the past the Mystery songs, like the Ragas which controlled the elements, and other religious songs of our ancestors."[32] In her own way, Fletcher shared Fillmore's notion of a universal musical sense; but whereas he was concerned to analyze it in musicological terms, Fletcher perceived commonality at the level of broad emotional import, of the most deep-seated spiritual yearnings, of motivation and purpose. In this she had much in common with Mooney.

Fletcher's study of Omaha music, which won praise from Franz Boas, appeared in the same year as the World Columbian Exposition in Chicago. Organized by a cabal of the city's leading businessmen, the fair was conceived as a salute to the glories of Western civilization. The Exposition cost an estimated $46 million and attracted more than 21 million paying customers. At the fair, not within White City but on a mile-long mall called the Midway Plaisance, was a massive smorgasbord of exhibits, restaurants, and theaters showcasing the exotic riches of the world's diverse cultures: "Egyptian swordsmen and jugglers, Dahomean drummers, Sudanese sheiks, Javanese carpenters, Hungarian gypsies, Eskimos, Chinese, Laplanders, Swedes, Syrians, Samoans, Sioux . . . 'from the nightsome North and the splendid South, from the wasty West and the effete East, bringing their manners, customs, dress, religions, legends, amusements, that we might know them the better.'" Fletcher was involved in arranging exhibits for the North American Ethnology exhibit, a part of the World's Congress Auxiliary, as was Mooney, who took time off from his fieldwork on the Ghost Dance to assist the Bureau of Ethnology. Fletcher also presented a paper on "The Religion of the North American Indian" at the World Parliament of Religions, a first-time gathering organized as part of the World's Congress, where she was irritated to see no Amerindians included among representatives of other major world religions. She also delivered papers at the congresses devoted to music and anthropology. But it was Fletcher's collaborator Fillmore whose lectures attracted the larger audiences, and who found time to make recordings and conduct more of his focus-group experiments on Amerindians and other non-European peoples who were gathered at the Midway Plaisance.[33]

In attendance at Chicago was a young musician from Minnesota who would surpass both Fletcher and Mooney in documenting the musical lives of American Indians. As with Fletcher, it was not love at first hearing for Frances Densmore. "At the World's Fair in Chicago, in 1893, I heard Indians sing, saw them dance and heard them yell, and was scared almost to death," she later wrote. But Densmore became intrigued. She read Fletcher's study of the Omaha, struck up an acquaintance with Fillmore, whom she met in Milwaukee, "soaked my receptive mind in what army officers wrote about Indians, and what historians wrote about Indians" in the publications of the Bureau of American Ethnology. Unlike Mooney and Fletcher, Densmore had no need of a musicologist collaborator to make transcriptions or analyze them; she herself was a trained musician with a finely honed ear. She had received the most advanced training in music available in the United States, first at Oberlin Conservatory, a kind of multicultural outpost in nineteenth-century Ohio, and in Boston, where she studied piano and counterpoint and worked as a professional musician and choir director. At the same time, Densmore was indefatigable in her fieldwork, beginning in 1905 with her study of Minnesota Ojibwes. She made her first recordings at White Earth in 1907, and the following year was summoned to Washington, D.C., to begin work with the Bureau of American Ethnology. She could be quite ruthless in her pursuit of Indian song. At the St. Louis Exposition she succeeded in recording the song of an uncooperative Geronimo, then being held as a kind of celebrity prisoner of war. "He was humming to himself as he worked at an arrow, measuring it carefully by putting it in the crook of his elbow to see if it exactly reached to the tip of his middle finger," she recalled. "I slipped into ambush behind him where I would not attract his attention, and noted down his song. He sang it softly with a peculiar swing, beating the time with his foot." Usually Densmore paid her informants for the music according to a fixed fee scale.[34]

Densmore's training in ethnomusicology had begun informally years earlier, in Red Wing, Minnesota, where she grew up in a house overlooking the Mississippi River. "Opposite the town, on an island, was a camp of Sioux Indians and at night, when they were dancing, we could hear the sound of the drum and see the flicker of their camp-fire," Densmore recalled. "Instead of frightening me with stories of war dances and scalps, my wise mother said, 'Those Indians are interesting people with customs that are different from ours, but they will not hurt you. There is no reason to be afraid of them.'" As Densmore later recounted it, this experience was formative; of her years of formal musical training, "underneath it all was the call of an Indian drum, low and clear." She began lecturing on Indian music in 1895, two years after the Columbian Exposition. Her first article, published in 1903, was a journalistic digest of Mooney's Ghost Dance study. Densmore began lecturing on Indian music after her awakening in Chicago. At first she was under the sway of Fillmore's argument about the universal harmonic sense. "The Navajo Indian howls his song to the war god on the chord of C major, and Beethoven makes the first theme of his Eroica Symphony of precisely the same material." But as she continued her fieldwork through the first half of the twentieth century Densmore became increasingly skeptical of Fillmore's theory. "Indians have no musical system, no rules of composition, few musical composers, no teachers and no concerts," she wrote in her final lecture, delivered in 1954 at age eighty-seven. "Is it any wonder that their music is a foreign language to the white race?"[35]

Part of the problem with Fillmore, she came to realize, was his reliance on the piano for transcribing and playing back Indian songs to his Native informants. The author of a history of the pianoforte, Fillmore was incorrigibly keyboard-centric. But Indian music lost all its "native character" when played on a piano, Densmore discovered. The proper way to learn the songs from sheet music was to hum them repeatedly while tapping the rhythm as accompaniment, not to pick them out on a keyboard. The translation of song to keyboard probably explains why Fillmore's experiments on Indian preference for four-part harmonies were so unequivocal. "A line of melody played with single notes was weak and feeble," Joan Mark observes. "It sounded incomplete whether compared with the hymns and harmonized songs that were the staple of piano music or with the Indians' customary lusty outdoor singing, in unison but with a wide range of voices and the powerful accompanying beat of the drum." Densmore was struck by Indian music as oral culture preserved in memory. "I have heard of an Indian who can sing all night for three or four nights, singing each song only four times and not repeating a single song"; there were reports of some knowing as many as 400 songs. Three years after Fletcher's death Densmore was able to write: "It is to be regretted that Miss Fletcher, by endorsing the work of Prof. Fillmore, placed herself in a position where she could not speak independently on a subject which she, more than any other observer of that time, had an opportunity to study in the field."[36] Beginning with her study of Chippewa music, Densmore presented only transcribed melodies as her informants performed them, no harmonizations as Fletcher had allowed.

Like Fillmore and Gilman before her, Densmore developed a rigorous methodology for her studies, which she explicated in some depth. She developed a detailed typology for comparing Indian musics based on a set of tables of analysis, which she adjusted upward (at one time including as many as twenty-two tables) and then downward as she recognized that many of those variables were common to all the Indian musics she studied. For her analysis of Teton Sioux music, published by the Bureau of American Ethnology in 1918, Densmore pioneered a system for representing musical sound graphically, anticipating an important technique in ethnomusicology. Following Fillmore's lead, she conducted tests on Indians using specially contrived tuning forks to demonstrate that Indians were not tonally insensitive but were actually capable of recognizing minute pitch intervals. (Densmore herself was a board-certified listener, with a report conducted by a psychology laboratory at the University of Iowa in 1914 attesting to her own "superior natural musical organism" for discriminating between pitches, intervals, intensity, and time.)[37] She pursued her work over an extraordinarily long career that spanned two world wars and the Depression, when her activities were scaled back. As recently as three years before her death at age ninety, she had conducted research on Seminoles and lectured at the University of Florida.

Like Fletcher and earlier collectors of slave spirituals such as Higginson and Allen, Densmore was dedicated to preserving the remnants of a culture that seemed clearly poised on the brink of extinction. "The music which I bring you today is but an echo," she announced in 1899, near the beginning of her career. "The songs are the songs of yesterday. The winds of the prairie and the pines of the forest have heard many of them for the last time. In a few more years the songs and the singers will alike be forgotten . . . We have spared their lives, but the Fate which decrees that the weaker race shall always give place to the stronger has condemned the Indian to the slow torture of degeneracy and final extinction." Decades later she explained to a reluctant informant that she "was collecting the songs of the Indians for the benefit of their children and that voices would be preserved in Washington in a great building that would not burn down."[38]

What Indians made of ethnographers' experiments and interviews is difficult to recover. We get glimpses from a story Densmore told about her first venture into the field, when she tried to coax a "medicine man" into performing some music. "'When do you sing?' I asked most politely. Shingibis waved his hand in the direction of a white spire which pricked the distant green, and replied, 'White man goes to church over there. I don't go to church. Have Indian church at home. I sing when I have Indian church.'" This idea is echoed in the comment by a Comanche head man regarding the superiority of peyote religion to Christianity. "The white man," he said, "goes into his church house and talks about Jesus, but the Indian goes into his tipi and talks to Jesus." There is substantial documentary evidence that American Indians had been fascinated by European sacred song since earliest encounters, but the nature of that attraction is not always spelled out. Apparently the Omaha studied by Fletcher were as surprised by the amount of verbal content in Anglo singing as she was struck by the widespread use of vocables in Indian singing. "Words clearly enunciated in singing break the melody to the Indian ear and mar the music," she found. "They say of us that we 'talk a great deal as we sing.'"[39]

WE CAN trace two alternative musical paths out of the apparent debacle of the Ghost Dance: two rebuttals (out of many) of the "vanishing Indian" theme that motivated Fletcher and Densmore. One is the peyote ceremony, first "discovered" by Mooney in 1891; the other is Ojibwe hymn-singing, which developed alongside the presumably less hybrid Indian songs studied by Fletcher in her first major work. Both paths emerged directly out of the musical practices studied by the early ethnologists. Both practices emphasize healing as a primary goal and involve the addition of Christian elements to traditional practices, in differing ratios. Drums are not part of the practice of Ojibwe hymn-singing, for example, while they are central to the peyote ceremony. But while peyote religion is outward looking, deemphasizing tribal affiliation in favor of a broader pan-Indian identity based on the heightened spiritual consciousness facilitated by peyote, Ojibwe hymn-singing is intensely inward looking, using the ritualized performance of ancient hymns as a way of asserting community and personal survival in the face of extreme poverty and dislocation.

Mooney himself provided a fugitive glimpse of one future of Indian religious music in his annotation of a Comanche Ghost Dance song. "This song was probably sung at daylight, when the first rays of the sun shone in the east, after the dancers had been dancing all night," he wrote. "The introductory part is a suggestion from the songs of the mescal rite, to which the Comanche are so much attached. Although the words convey but little meaning, the tune is unique and one of the best of all the ghost songs on account of its sprightly measure."[40] By "mescal rite" Mooney meant what is more commonly known as the peyote ritual. His comments suggest that the religious use of peyote was already under way while the Ghost Dance was a live practice. (In fact the Ghost Dance was not extinguished during the 1890s; there is evidence of its persistence among Pawnee into the 1930s, among Dakota to around 1950, and into the 1980s among at least two elderly Wind River Shoshone.)[41] Peyote use for medicinal, prophetic, and communal purposes among Natives of the lower Rio Grande and northern Mexico evidently extends back millennia. With its resemblance to a sacrament, peyote use was targeted by Christian missionaries from the beginning of European settlement, first by the Spanish, who in 1620 mobilized the Inquisition against it, with little success. The practice survived the political turbulence that overtook Mexico, eventually taking root in Oklahoma. But as the United States swallowed northern Mexico in the first half of the nineteenth century, long-standing trade and migration networks were disrupted, and peyote supplies dried up. Ironically, this de facto embargo was eventually eased by the completion in 1881 of a Texas-Mexican railroad line that facilitated transportation of cactus.

A number of features recommended the peyote ceremony to Indian communities in the demoralizing aftermath of Wounded Knee. It promised healing and the restoration of a sense of collective spirit. Because it focused on the peyote ritual itself rather than on the particular tribal context in which it was practiced, it was easily adaptable, as inclusive as the Ghost

Dance had been. And it combined what struck many Indians as the palpable strengths of Christian belief and practice with unmistakably Native features in a way that reinforced rather than compromised both. In contrast to the Ghost Dance, where percussion was proscribed, the peyote ritual is accompanied by drums and rattle. The songs are a focal point of the ritual, always repeated four times, punctuating the purification, smoking, and eating performed as part of the rite. Because the peyote ritual has survived much longer than the Ghost Dance, its songs have become more indigenized according to specific Indian group and therefore more musically variegated than were Ghost Dance songs, which were heavily inflected by the musical style of the Great Basin. Some songs include references to Jesus, but according to Weston La Barre, an early ethnographic authority on the peyote religion, the impact of Christianity remains "very thin and superficial." Rather, peyotism "is an essentially aboriginal American religion, operating in terms of fundamental Indian concepts about powers, visions, and native modes of doctoring," he wrote. "The Christianity of many native Christians is precarious at best . . . when it comes into any very serious conflict with native culture."[42]

But the pattern that recurs regularly in American sacred music—establishing cultural legitimacy through Protestant signifiers—has held with the peyote ritual as well. Some Ute peyote leaders even offered to coordinate with Episcopal services. "We like church," wrote a Ute peyotist. "We want to meet every Sunday and have church and pray and be good . . . we want to rest on Sunday and then on Monday we want to work and farm."[43] This strategy was taken up in 1918 during House subcommittee hearings on federal legislation banning peyote use, where the ceremony was defended at length by two individuals with distinguished careers in Indian ethnography. The lead witness, James Mooney, characteristically played up the ceremony's affinities to Christianity, so that it sounded vaguely like an evangelical Protestant prayer meeting, complete with women and children. Also testifying was La Flesche, Fletcher's collaborator and by then a distinguished employee of the Bureau of American Ethnology, where he did authoritative work on the Osage, with whom he had attended an all-night worship service: "While I sat waiting to see fighting and some excitement the singing went on and on and I noticed that all gazed at the fire or beyond, at a little mound on top of which lay a single peyote. I said to the man sitting next to me, 'What do you expect to see?' He said, 'We expect to see the face of Jesus and the face of our dead relatives. We are worshiping God and Jesus, the same God that the white people worship.' All night long the singing went on and I sat watching the worshipers."[44] La Flesche himself had never used peyote but had a "feeling of gratitude" for the religion because of its salutary effect on the lives of people he knew, including his sister, a physician who worked mainly with Omaha people. "A strange thing has happened among the Omahas," she wrote to La Flesche in a letter he read at the hearing. "They have quit drinking, and they have taken to a new religion, and members of that new religion say that they will not drink; and the extraordinary part of the thing is that these people pray, and they pray intelligently, they pray to God, they pray to Jesus, and in their prayers they pray for the little ones, and they ask God to bring them up to live sober lives; they ask help of God."

The subcommittee also heard testimony from an Osage chief and peyotist named Fred Lookout:

> *Mr. Tillman:* Is this a Christian religion, or is it a mere worship of peyote, or the drug itself?
> *Chief Lookout:* We worship God Almighty; we worship to Him.
> *Mr. Tillman:* Then explain to this committee where you get any authority from the Bible for the use of this bean in worship?
> *Chief Lookout:* I do not understand about the Bible. If the Bible gives any authority for the use of this peyote, I am not familiar with it.
> *Mr. Tillman:* Then where do you get your authority for the use of it?
> *Chief Lookout:* All of my people use this peyote, and some other members of the tribe came to me and persuaded me to use it. That is how I came to use it . . .

To be sure, some Indian peyotists did cite scripture in defense of their ritual, especially Exodus 12:8, which stipulates the consumption of "bitter herbs" with the Passover feast.[45] In any event, legislation banning peyote was approved by the House but failed in the Senate. But the close call prompted a gathering in Oklahoma to legally incorporate a Protestant-sounding body called the Native American Church. It was incorporated in 1918, though legal difficulties have shadowed it ever since; peyotists have continued to be prosecuted under state law. In the *Oregon v. Smith* decision of 1990, for example, the U.S. Supreme Court found that two Native American Church members fired for using peyote were not entitled to state unemployment benefits denied to people discharged for "misconduct." In other words, the First Amendment's free exercise clause could not be construed as restraining states from prohibiting the sacramental use of peyote. A federal law passed in 1993 in response was ruled unconstitutional by the Supreme Court.

Farther north, in the Great Lakes, a very different postscript to the Ghost Dance was developing among the Indian nation that had been the object of Densmore's earliest fieldwork: the Minnesota Ojibwe, or Ashinaabeg, as they call themselves. While the peyote ritual drew on

Christian and traditional Native symbols and practices to create a religion distinct from both, Ojibwe hymn-singing suggests a different kind cultural reworking. The Ojibwe (*Chippewa* is the Anglicized term) were one of the groups specifically identified by Mooney as not embracing the Ghost Dance. By the time Densmore began her fieldwork at the turn of the century, Ojibwes had assimilated Christian music brought to them by Roman Catholic missionaries for centuries, and by a variety of Protestant missionaries for several generations. The establishment of the White Earth reservation in northwestern Minnesota in 1867 had brought with it the all-too-familiar patterns of disease, dislocation, poverty and colonial dependency. By the 1880s Ojibwe were experiencing the same poverty and dispossession as the plains-based practitioners of the Ghost Dance. In fact contemporary accounts mention the appearance of Sioux-style dancing in 1891. But the more significant Native response to dispossession was the development of a distinctive hymn-singing style undertaken by separate voluntary associations of young men and women, and centered on rituals for funerals and grieving.

Even as these rituals abandoned the drum and accompanying dance, and used translated texts faithful to the English-language originals, the Ojibwe sense of the freelance hymn-singing diverged from missionaries' expectations. "No music so blinds my eyes with tears as the songs of these Christian Indians," wrote an Episcopal bishop in northern Minnesota. "Indian voices are very sweet and you could not believe that they were the same voices you have heard in the wild heathen grand medicine or the horrid scalp dances. I am sure that in the charms of song which goes up to heaven from this world they sound as sweet to Jesus as any Christian song." But to missionaries' chagrin, interest among Ashinaabeg in singing far exceeded their interest in scripture and sermons. "Under the religious leadership of elders, in candle-lit shacks and wigwams far from the mission house, performances were ritualized to make room for the practice of alternative values," writes historian Michael McNally. "In these contexts, hymn-singing seemed less about the performance of other people's songs than about the way of life required of those who were entrusted by the community with the task of singing them. Hymn societies became primary social networks through which age-old values of reciprocity, subsistence, and the seasonal round were negotiated within the bounds of the new life on the reservation."[46]

All manner of hymnological bricolage was in order among Ojibwe hymn-singers. For example, a hymn recorded by Gertrude Kurath at the Isabella Reservation in 1954 borrows the most familiar setting of one famous hymn—Isaac Watts's "Alas, and Did My Savior Bleed"—as the setting for an Ojibwe translation of another universally known Protestant song, Charles Wesley's "O for a Thousand Tongues to Sing," written in 1739 to mark the first anniversary of his own conversion. The first verse was inspired by the Moravian Peter Böhler. The hymn was a favorite of John Wesley as well, to judge from the thumb-marks on the hymnbook that was his "constant companion" for fifteen years of itinerant evangelism. Analyzing the third stanza of this hymn, McNally shows how Ojibwe hymn texts translate alien concepts like original sin into a more familiar idiom. Wesley's

> He breaks the power of reigning sin,
> He sets the prisoner free;
> His blood can make the sinful clean,
> His blood availed for me

becomes, when retranslated from the Ojibwe:

> He is able to do it, throw it [all] away
> The sins/things done wrong
> It cleanses/purifies [people]
> That blood of Jesus.[47]

Among Ojibwe singers, these familiar hymns are performed ponderously, so slowly that the syllables lose their ordinary sense and become rather like vocables. In this way they resemble both the Usual Way lined hymns of Puritan New England and the "raised" hymns of the African-American church. And the contexts and manner in which they were performed had the effect of reinforcing ties of kinship, community, and reciprocity rather than inculcating values of Christian duty and humility. The indigenization of Protestant hymns served as ritual of survival and hope, somewhere between resistance and accommodation, not perceived as anything but authentically Ashinaabe, at least by participants. "When one Ojibwe man heard hymns at a ceremony honoring a new drum," McNally reports, "he whispered his opinion that such 'Christian' music was disrespectful to the drum . . . hymn singing stood in opposition to other music of Ojibwe tradition in that the hymns do not involve a drum."[48] But this seems to have been a minority view. After gradually dropping out of usage during most of the twentieth century, ritualized hymn-singing was resurrected by a group of White Earth elders in the 1980s, serving both as a way to preserve the Ojibwe language and as a form of cultural criticism. The same cultural work is done by hymns in other contemporary Indian communities, such as the Kiowa of southwestern Oklahoma.[49]

And so Indian sacred songs have refused to vanish, any more than the

Indians themselves. The sort of pristine, uncontaminated aboriginal music so prized by Fletcher and Densmore is gone, but then it never really existed, at least in the static, unchanging form early ethnologists imagined. Continuous social exchange long predated the arrival of Europeans to North America, and as always music expressed those contacts. The images, phrases, and even tunes of Ghost Dance songs, Ojibwe hymns, peyote songs, and other Amerindian musics bear faint traces of the Judaic heritage that has shaped other American sacred song, now combined and reworked in forms barely recognizable to the long stream of Catholic and Protestant missionaries who carried them to North America with such ambitious hopes. By origin, the ancestors of at least certain groups of Amerindians may have been the first Asian peoples to reach North America. By the nineteenth century, American missionaries, some of whom had cut their teeth evangelizing Native Americans, were casting a hopeful eye and sailing across the Pacific. During the decades of military subjugation that followed the Civil War, the depleted populations of American Indians were beginning to be reinforced by a new Asian diaspora. Immigrants from China and Japan would introduce new religious and musical practices that would quickly encounter the same familiar pressures to accommodate to Protestant forms that all religions have faced in America. In fact those influences had already begun subtly reshaping them in their homelands.

CHAPTER SIX

Onward Buddhist Soldiers

In order to build a Pureland, the Bodhisattvas make use of beautiful music to soften people's hearts. With their hearts softened, people's minds are more receptive, and thus easier to educate and transform through the teachings. For this reason, music has been established as one type of ceremonial offering to be made to the Buddha.

— *MAHAPRAJNAPARAMITA SASTRA*

IN 1993 a Jewish hip-hopper from Brooklyn fell under the spell of the Dalai Lama. "I happened to catch him when he was walking out of a room. It was wild," Adam Yauch recalled of their 1993 meeting in Arizona. "He grabbed both of my hands and looked at me for a second and I felt all this energy. I just walked to my room and it clicked in my head. I thought, I need to write a song about this."[1] The song that emerged was "Bodhisattva Vow," which appears on the Beastie Boys' 1994 album, *Ill Communication*. First comes "Shambala," which begins with preternaturally deep Tibetan chanting before shifting into a loose rhythm vamp, the drums laying down a three-over-two clave beat while bass, rhythm guitar, and keyboard add desultory chords to the mix. An undertone of chanting continues. "Shambala" segues into "Bodhisattva Vow," a fairly straightforward Buddhist sutra delivered as an electronically edged rap, with lots of echo. Three stanzas of sixteen lines each, interspersed with instrumental breaks featuring cymbals clashing over an ascending four-note melody (a simple whole-tone scale, which often serves in Western music as a musical signifier of "the Orient"), are played on a reedy-sounding horn. Underneath, the chanting continues:

> As I develop the wakening mind
> I praise the Buddhas as they shine
> I bow before you as I travel my path
> To join your ranks, I make my full time task

For the sake of all beings I seek
The enlightened mind that I know I'll reap . . .[2]

Exactly one hundred years earlier, a German-born intellectual named Paul Carus had an equally revelatory encounter with two Buddhist monks who had come to Chicago for the World Parliament of Religions. This was the same body to which Alice Fletcher had presented her paper on American Indian religion, and was disappointed to find no Native people alongside representatives of all the world's religions. The parliament was part of the famed World Columbian Exposition that Fletcher had helped plan, as had James Mooney, who cut short his fieldwork on the Ghost Dance to help organize exhibits on American Indians. Frances Densmore had attended also, and been "scared half to death" by the sound of Indian yells. The experience helped crystallize Densmore's decision to dedicate her life to the study of Indian music; the impact on Carus of the luminaries in Chicago was much the same.

A number of charismatic young spokesmen for world religions were present at the parliament. Perhaps the most celebrated was the Calcutta-born Swami Vivekenanda, the first Hindu missionary to America and founder of the Vedanta Society, which became the primary institution for American Hindus. But Carus was more intrigued by the Buddhist missionaries: Anagarika Dharmapala, from Ceylon, the first Therevada Buddhist missionary to America, who would found the Maja Bodhi Society in Chicago in 1897; and a Rinzai Zen abbot from Japan named Sōen Shaku. Both missionaries were well prepared to present a sympathetic account of their religion to a relatively open-minded but still culturally blinkered American audience. Dharmapala had met and worked alongside American Theosophists Helena Blavatsky and Henry Steel Olcott in Ceylon; with Olcott he collaborated in Asia on behalf of ecumenical Buddhism. Somewhere Dharmapala had picked up an Irish brogue, which he used to good effect at the World Parliament. Sōen had studied English and Western philosophy at Keio University in Tokyo, an institution that placed great value on Western-style modernization in late nineteenth-century Japan. Through the papers they read and the friendships that ensued, Carus realized that Buddhism, at least the version he heard presented at the World Parliament, provided what he had been looking for: a way of connecting his ideas about what he called the "Religion of Science" with a preexisting religious tradition that was both authentic and credible.[3] Before long Carus would find in music an important avenue for promoting what he considered an appropriate religious form for the age of modern science. His musical choices reveal a pattern often followed by world religions in the United

States: the adaptation of non-Christian beliefs to the Protestant hymn form in an effort to give them traction in a culture in which hymns serve as the common currency of religious practice.

Carus was an authentic nineteenth-century polymath, in the tradition of the maverick philosopher-mathematician Charles Peirce (whom Carus counted as a colleague). He knew something about everything and a great deal about most things. In person he was endlessly erudite and magnetic, and corresponded with thousands of individuals during his career. In the forty years that preceded his death in 1919 Carus wrote 74 books and approximately 1,500 articles on subjects ranging from philosophy and religion to poetry and mathematics. He also edited 732 issues of a periodical called the *Open Court,* and more than 100 issues of another journal, *The Monist.* Carus arrived in the United States in 1884 while in his early thirties. He had been born in Germany in 1852 to a family that took scholarship seriously. His father was a Lutheran pastor and church bureaucrat. Carus received a doctorate in classical philology—Friedrich Nietzsche's original field of study—from one of Germany's leading universities, Tübingen, before serving in the Prussian field artillery. For a time he taught at a military academy in Dresden, but resigned in 1881 after suffering a crisis of faith about orthodox Christianity. Carus made his way out of Germany, first to Belgium, then to England, before landing in the United States.[4]

Carus made a life-changing connection the very next year, when his monograph *Monism and Meliorism* caught the eye of a philosophically minded industrialist from La Salle, Illinois, named Edward C. Hegeler. In 1856 Hegeler had emigrated from Germany to the United States, where he eventually developed new technologies and amassed a fortune in the zinc business. Carus' exposition of "the unitary conception of the world," in which spirit and matter represented "two aspects of one and the same reality," appealed to the older industrialist.[5] Carus wasted no time in ingratiating himself to Hegeler during a visit to his home; within a short time he had married Hegeler's daughter Mary and by 1887 assumed the editorial reins at the Open Court Publishing Company. Funded by Hegeler, Open Court's books and journals functioned something like a university press in an era before they existed in the United States. One of the tasks Carus applied himself to was reconciling religion with modern science. He had lost his belief in Christian theism, but admired aspects of Christian ethics and retained an interest in spiritual experience. The 1893 parliament convinced Carus that Buddhism provided the perfect conceptual vehicle through which to achieve this reconciliation. Buddhism as he had come to understand it was compatible both with a Darwinian universe and with the most salutary forms of Christian ethics.

In seven years at Open Court before the World Parliament, Carus had mentioned Buddhism in print only twice, with no particular enthusiasm. In the five years after 1893 he wrote six books on Buddhism, one of which, *The Gospel of Buddha,* sold more than three million copies in thirteen editions, including Dutch, Russian, Czech, Chinese, Japanese, and Thai translations. But Carus never formally converted to Buddhism, choosing rather to keep his spiritual options open. "I have said repeatedly that I am a Buddhist, but you must not forget that I am at the same time a Christian in so far as I accept certain teachings of Christ," he wrote to Dharmapala: "I am even a Taoist, in so far as I accept certain doctrines of Lautsze. I am an Israelite, in so far as I sympathize with the aspirations of the Israelitic prophets. *In one word, I am, as it were, a religious parliament incarnate . . .* To say that I am a Buddhist and nothing else but a Buddhist would be a misstatement, and, indeed, it would be unBuddhistic, it would be against the teachings of Buddha himself . . . 'The beloved of the gods honors all forms of religious faith.'" Despite Carus' reluctance to commit, both Dharmapala and Sōen admired him and saw him as a useful ally, an intellectual beachhead in their efforts to win a favorable hearing for Buddhism in America. Sōen referred to Carus as a "Taoist sage" and as "a second Columbus who is endeavoring to discover the new world truth." He knew how to play to Carus' sense of historicism. "Buddha who lived three thousand years ago, being named Gautama, now lies bodily dead in India," he wrote Carus; "but Buddha in the twentieth century being named Truth, is just to be born at Chicago in the New World." For his part Dharmapala saw the importance of connecting Buddhism not just to modern science, but to Christianity as well. "Christ is the Buddha of a latter time."[6]

Carus understood well the multiple layers on which such a campaign would need to be waged in the United States. In 1899, after mulling over the issue for at least two years, he wrote to "Uncle" Daniel Carter Beard—a founder of the Boy Scouts, prolific illustrator of children's books, and then professor of the New York School of Applied Design for Women—urging Beard to create a visual rendering of an occidentalized Buddha, an image appropriate to the robust, energetic, and optimistic civilization of the United States. Carus had grown up in a family steeped in German art and culture, particularly music, and throughout his life was no less willing to experiment with musical forms than with other fields of intellectual endeavor. His first foray into hymn-writing was inspired by Admiral Dewey's 1898 victory in Manila. An unabashed patriot who defended American actions in the Philippines against European critics, Carus composed a patriotic anthem titled "Unfurl the Flag: A New National Hymn." The first musician he approached to provide a musical setting declined on the grounds that the text was "too closely reasoned" for an effective hymn.

Carus had better luck with Charles Crozat Converse, composer of the melody for the gospel song "What a Friend We Have in Jesus." He rushed the hymn into print through Open Court, hoping to have it sung on the Fourth of July, and proposed sending copies to U.S. sailors stationed in Manila.[7]

The following year Carus took an important step in developing his religio-musical ambitions: Open Court published his *Sacred Tunes for the Consecration of Life: Hymns of the Religion of Science*. The fifty-page collection was as much a manifesto as a musical work. The governing principle of *Sacred Tunes* was laid out on the title page in an epigraph from Isaiah 42:9–10: "Behold, the former things are come to pass, and new things do I declare: before they spring forth I tell you of them. Sing unto the Lord a new song." In the preface Carus explained that the rise of modern science required some fundamental adjustments in how religion was understood and practiced. The first step was to clarify the exact relation between the two: "Science and Religion are different, they form an antithesis, and are frequently supposed to exclude each other. But the antithesis of Religion and Science is a contrast, not a contradiction. Science and Religion do not exclude each other; they are complimentary . . . Science is thought, but religion is sentiment. Science affords insight; insight regulates sentiment; and sentiment determines conduct. Science is knowledge and the acquisition of knowledge; but religion is conviction, i.e., honesty of knowledge and faithfulness in its practical application."[8]

For Carus, the obvious response was to synthesize the two. Much work had already occurred on the "Science of Religion"—otherwise known as the "higher criticism"—but Carus' interest lay elsewhere. His "higher synthesis" was a "Religion of Science," which he contrasted with religion based on divine revelation. "Science is not a noisy thing; it is a still, small voice; but nothing equals its efficiency, nothing can suppress it, and no one can overcome it. Its authority is above all human authority; it is superhuman, it is divine," he wrote. "History has witnessed the storm of religious fanaticism and the devout fire on the altar of pious ritualism, but God was neither in the storm nor in the fire: God reveals himself in the still, small voice." Here Carus alluded to a well-known hymn by John Greenleaf Whittier, adapted from his poem "The Brewing of Soma," which drew an unflattering comparison between the emotional abandon of Protestant revivals and the ecstatic inebriated transports of primitive Hindu priests. In the final stanza of the poem, and in the hymn, "Dear Lord and Father of Mankind" (1872), Whittier beseeches God to move worshippers to reverent silence rather than noisy outbursts of the holy spirit:

> Breathe through the heats of our desire
> Thy coolness and Thy balm;
> Let sense be dumb, let flesh retire;

Speak through the earthquake, wind, and fire,
O still, small voice of calm!⁹

For his part, Whittier was quoting the Hebrew Bible, 1 Kings 19, in which the prophet Elijah flees to the wilderness of Beersheba, where he senses the presence of the Lord but actually hears God—not in a powerful wind, not in an earthquake, not in a fire, but in "a still small voice" that speaks to him after the fire.

Carus sought to align himself with the spirit of coolly rational reverence, but what musical forms should such a religion of science take? Should hymns speak in the "still, small voice" of a God of science? "These hymns of the Religion of Science exhibit a deliberate conservatism by the side of a sweeping radicalism," he maintained. "They represent the old religion spirit, i.e., man's aspiration after the truth, in its latest phase, as modified and modernised under the influence of the scientific methods of our age. This is not new wine in old bottles," Carus insisted, "but old wine in new bottles; it is a preservation of the old religious ideals in a new form; it is an adaptation of the most sacred endeavors of the past to the conditions of the present with its changed environment."¹⁰ Carus' *Sacred Tunes* provides a kind of musical Rorschach test of how a savvy European cosmopolitan intent on presenting "old wine in new wineskins" conceived his American audience—what sorts of sentiments and musical settings would appeal to the progressive and spiritually attuned people likely to be receptive to a faintly Buddhist "Religion of Science."

The fourteen hymns reveal an extremely eclectic musical imagination at work, well grounded in European art music. One hymn is actually titled "The Religion of Science." Carus revealed that it was modeled on a missionary hymn by Edgar Alfred Bowring—probably "Watchman, tell us of the night," usually set to a tune by the prolific American hymn composer Lowell Mason but set in this collection to an obscure tune by W. C. Filby. Revealing Carus' national origins, "Resist Evil" draws on the tune (and theme) of Martin Luther's "Ein' feste Burg," familiar in English as "A Mighty Fortress Is Our God." Two of the hymns—"Truth Our Home" and "Nirvâna"—use the same tune, by Gabriel Voigtländer, a German composer and poet who lived in the first half of the seventeenth century. The latter has some of the sentimental hyperbole of a nineteenth-century American Sunday school hymn:

Sweet Nirvâna,
Highest Jhâna!
Rapture sweeter than all pleasures,
Thou the measure of all measures,
Thou the treasure of all treasures,
O, immortal Buddhahood!

Fittingly, Carus set "Bridal Chorus" to Richard Wagner's "Lohengrin" (known to modern ears as "Here Comes the Bride." On the other hand, "The God of Iron" features an obscure tune but shows a sternly Nietzschean side to Carus: "We have discussed repeatedly the problem of ethics and the role which strength plays in ethics, and have denounced the idea which represents a sheep who patiently allows itself to be devoured by the wolf as the symbol of morality," he lectured. "While the wolf's conduct no doubt cannot be regarded as moral, we must at least grant that he possesses the virtue of courage."[11]

Several of the tune selections reveal a taste for the arcane. For "Eternity," Carus borrowed the tune "Wie schön leuchtet der Morgenstern," written during an outbreak of the plague by Philipp Nicolai, a sixteenth-century Lutheran theologian, poet, and composer, some of whose melodies were later harmonized by J. S. Bach. "The Goal" uses a setting by Demetrius Bortniansky (1751–1825), a Ukrainian composer who studied in Italy, wrote opera and sacred music, and directed the Russian imperial court chapel choir. Carus set "At the Grave" to a tune by the distinguished composer, conductor, and educator Karl Friedrich Zelter, a friend of Goethe and professor of music at the University of Berlin. The most intriguingly complex tune lineage, and perhaps the greatest dissonance between text and tune, is the case of "Allhood." Carus identified the tune as "twelfth century," but it is actually the Silesian folk melody known as "Schönster Herr Jesu." Sometimes referred to as the "Crusader's Hymn," this seventeenth-century German hymn would have been familiar to American Protestants as "Fairest Lord Jesus," as harmonized in 1850 by Richard Willis. Compare the stringent Kantian abstraction of Carus' text with the personalized romantic glow of the American version:

"Allhood" (verse 3)	"Fairest Lord Jesus"
Unity of Nature's laws,	Fairest Lord Jesus,
Cosmic order, without flaws,	Ruler of all nature,
In us all thy power stirs.	O thou of God and man the Son.
Norm etern of all design,	Thee will I cherish,
Radiant art thou and divine,	Thee will I honor,
O Glory of the Universe.	Thou, my soul's glory, joy, and crown.
Prototype of truth and right,	Fair is the sunshine,
Union where all things unite,	Fairer still the moonlight,
Principle of Love unfurled.	All the twinkling, starry host:
Thou condition'st rational thought,	Jesus shines brighter,
Standard of the moral ought,	Jesus shines purer,
O Spirit-motion of the world!	Than all the angels heaven can boast.

Only one hymn, "Immortality," features Carus' own melody (though he enlisted the help of several others, including the aforementioned gospel hymn-writer Converse, to provide a selection of voice arrangements for his hymn).

At least two of Carus' hymns would have had a familiar resonance with turn-of-the-century American churchgoers. The collection's opening hymn, "Higher," was one of the few to use an English tune: Samuel Sebastien Wesley's (grandson of the prolific Charles) "Aurelia," a familiar setting for "The Church's One Foundation," written in the nineteenth century by Samuel J. Stone:

> The Church's one foundation
> Is Jesus Christ her Lord;
> She is His new creation
> By water and the word:
> From heaven He came and sought her
> To be His holy bride;
> With His own blood he bought her,
> And for her life He died.

Compare Carus' second verse, which parses awkwardly and is starkly antifoundational in its theology:

> We reverence tradition,
> And heed inspired men's
> Prophetic intuition,
> But seek high'r evidence.
> There is but one foundation,
> But one sure ground, forsooth:
> It is the revelation
> Of science and its truth!

Carus' "Godward" was set to another beloved Lowell Mason hymn tune, "Bethany," the usual setting for "Nearer, my God, to Thee" (and still under copyright when *Sacred Tunes* was published). The tune provided an opportunity for Carus to reflect on continuity and change. "More than any other hymn it is expressive of the noblest and highest religious sentiment, and it seems that there could never have been a time when that beautiful melody did not exist!" he wrote; "We are in all things apt to think that our ancestors partook of all the revelations which we possess to-day, and it is natural that we read the history of the past in the light of the living present . . . But we know more to-day about God than our ancestors knew three, or four, or five centuries ago. We have learned that God is not a loving being, but, as Christ has it, he is love; he is not a spirit, or some spirit, but, as we read in the Gospel of Saint John, he is spirit [Carus provides the

Greek here]; he is not an individual, not a concrete personality in the human sense, but a superpersonal presence, being the condition of all personality and rationality."[12] Just as the most timeless hymn tunes are historically situated, so is human knowledge of the divine. Again, Carus' skepticism is driven home. Sarah F. Adams' "Nearer, my God" goes:

> Nearer, my God, to Thee, Nearer to Thee!
> E'en though it be a cross That raiseth me;
> Still all my song shall be, Nearer, my God, to Thee,
> Nearer, my God, to Thee, Nearer to Thee.
>
> Though like the wanderer, The sun gone down,
> Darkness be over me, My rest a stone;
> Yet in my dreams I'd be Nearer, my God, to Thee,
> Nearer, my God, to Thee, Nearer to Thee.

Carus counters:

> Nearer, my God, to thee, Nearer alway;
> E'en though thou other be Than prophets say;
> Other thou art, but higher, Bidding our souls aspire,
> Bidding our souls aspire, Godward alway.
>
> Doubt comes from God, in sooth, Though conquering creeds;
> Doubt prompts our search for truth And higher leads.
> Who on doubt's path ne'er trod, Ne'er saw the face of God
> Ne'er saw the face of God, Doubt truthward speeds.

Here thoroughgoing, nearly Cartesian doubt becomes a necessary precondition of meaningful revelation. Only those who, like Carus, have experienced what William James called "the religion of the twice-born" acquire credible faith in an era of modern science.

It is difficult to recover how *Sacred Tunes* was received, by whom, or even if the collection or its individual hymns were ever used in worship. But there are a few clues. Through Sōen, Carus was to build his most fertile Buddhist connection, with a Japanese epigone of Sōen's named Daisetz Teitaro Suzuki. Suzuki's first project with Carus was translating *The Gospel of Buddha* into Japanese, while he was still living in Japan. Then Suzuki came to La Salle, which he used as a base between 1897 and 1908, collaborating frequently with Carus. In 1903 Carus financed a trip by Suzuki to lecture at the newly established Buddhist mission in San Francisco. The mission had tried to use Carus' *Sacred Tunes* but found the hymns "too philosophical." *The Gospel of Buddha* was a different matter. "The 'Gospel of Buddha' takes here the place of the Bible and is read at every service," Suzuki wrote to Carus. "Especially among the Japanese Buddhists your name is very well known and I have had a cordial reception from them, as a shrub growing under a towering tree."[13] With these Japanese colleagues, Carus made effective use of his position at Open Court to spread the gospel. When Sōen returned to the United States in 1905 for a lecture tour, Suzuki interpreted for his old *sensei,* and Carus quickly published the translations under the title *Sermons of a Buddhist Abbot* (1906).

All this syncretism was quite consistent with the historical development of Buddhism, which along with Christianity has been perhaps the most culturally adaptive of all world religions. Since its origin in northern India some 2,500 years ago, Buddhism has moved gradually eastward, through China, Tibet, Thailand, Korea, and Japan, adapting to and blending with preexisting teachings and practices. Rather than supplanting older indigenous religions, Buddhism has found myriad ways to graft itself onto those preexisting forms, creating hybrids with cultures extremely different from those of the Indian subcontinent. "In most cases, the Indian-born teaching absorbed as much as it impacted," observes Martin Verhoeven. "Buddhism did not merely coexist with other religious systems, but radically transformed each country it entered. Simultaneously, each country transformed Buddhism into something of its own image and likeness." Chinese Buddhists found ways to harmonize Buddhism with the Confucian and Taoist ideas. In Tibet Buddhism developed a theocratic form as it blended with Lamaism and the sacrificial rites of the bon-po cult. Japan added a distinctive stamp to Buddhism (which had arrived there via China and Korea), developing a symbiotic relationship with the *kami,* or local deities, of Shintoism and developing a more worldly profile, symbolized in the abandonment of celibacy by priests. The process was bound to continue as Buddhism encountered Christianity, with ecumenical-minded Buddhists finding important overlaps in the realm of ethics, and their Christian counterparts seeing in Buddha an analogy to Jesus Christ, and in *bodhisattvas* the Buddhist equivalent of saints. Thus could Dharmapala declare in 1894, the year Carus published *The Gospel of Buddha:* "Christ is the Buddha of a latter time."[14]

It was no accident that Buddhism struck sympathetic Americans as compatible with their own conceptions. As Verhoeven writes, "long before the East came West, the West went East," the result of mainly European colonial rule and imperial ventures. "Ironically, then, the immense popularity that Oriental religions and philosophy enjoyed in the West can be attributed somewhat to the strange fact that the hybrid forms of Asian thought exported to the Occident were already customized for Western consumption." Thus, "The Buddhism that Americans such as Paul Carus encountered early on was something of a 'mirror in the shrine'—a looking glass that reflected back the image of the beholder." Though both Sōen and

Suzuki were adherents of Zen Buddhism, Carus was especially taken by the Jodo Shinshu sect. An extreme form of Mahayana Buddhism, which transformed Buddhism from an uncompromising exercise for elite monks to a religion more accessible to people living ordinary lives, Japanese Shin Buddhism minimizes the differences between priests and laypeople. Priests are allowed to eat meat, marry, and hold day jobs in addition to maintaining hereditary temples. Most important, Shin holds that salvation can be achieved by faith alone, through ritual devotion to Amida Buddha. The early Jesuit missionaries to Japan in the sixteenth century were astonished to find that the "Protestant heresy" they confronted in Christendom had already infected the "heathen" culture of Japan. But Carus was impressed by Jodo Shinshu's "progressive" brand of "Buddhistic Protestantism." "In my opinion," he announced, "Buddha's intention was nothing else than to establish what we call a Religion of Science."[15]

In 1889, six years after the World Parliament had brought a variety of non-Christian missionaries to America, Dr. Shuye Sonoda and the Reverend Kakuryo Nishijima arrived in San Francisco, the first Jodo Shinshu missionaries to the United States. Although their efforts were aimed at maintaining the faith among Japanese living in America rather than at winning European American converts, their arrival generated some resistance. In early decades Japanese Buddhists in America kept a low profile, reluctant to draw attention to their differences in an era of rampant nativism. Beginning as the Young Men's Buddhist Association (modeled after the Young Men's Christian Association), the group renamed itself the Buddhist Mission of North America in 1914. (Thirty years later, while incarcerated in Utah, ministers and church members voted to change the name to Buddhist Churches of America.) Most Japanese living in America during the early twentieth century had emigrated from the same region and were members of the Jodo Shinshu sect. The tendency to adopt the terminology and forms of Protestant Christianity was noticeable from the turn of the century: "*Socho* became 'bishop,' *gatha* 'hymn,' and *kaikyoshi* or *jushoku,* 'minister.' *Bukkyokai* and *otera* were translated as 'church' or 'temple,' *dana* as 'gift,' and *sangha* as 'brotherhood of Buddhists' . . . Terms associated with religious service—*shoko,* the offering of incense; *juzu* or *nenju,* rosarylike beads; and *koromo,* the robe worn by the priest—were retained."[16]

Japanese American ears had been adjusting to Christian church music for some time. Protestant missionaries from the United States had begun introducing gospel songs like "Jesus Loves Me" and "There Is a Happy Land" in Japan as early as 1872. A missionary conference held in Tokyo in 1878 laid down the following ground rules: "1st that all hymns should if possible be native productions. 2nd. That they should be in the metre of the native poetry. 3rd. That no attempt should be made at rhyme." These dicta were frequently ignored; one missionary observed about the early hymns: "These translations which Rev. Ballagh gave me must have had rhythm and metre enough to be sung, for we used them right away." In America, as in Japan, Christianity had particular appeal for pro-Western, reform-minded Japanese intellectuals, who were attracted to *fukuinkai,* Japanese gospel societies in which Christian hymns were sung. But Christianity was not the only religion in Japan affected by Western influence; European-style Buddhist music had been practiced at Ryukoko University, the leading seminary for training Jodo Shinshu priests, since the 1870s.[17]

The same tendency toward hymnody was evident in Hawaii, where, beginning with shipwrecked sailors, Japanese began arriving earlier and in greater numbers than on the mainland. Again, Jodo Shinshu was the dominant form of Buddhism. Built in 1918, the Honpa Hongwanji temple was reputed to be the only Buddhist temple in the world with a pipe organ and indirect lighting. At Hongwanji, Sunday schools were established. The celebration of Buddha's birth was called "Buddhistmas," while the anniversary of Gautama's enlightenment was commemorated with "pontifical" vespers and processions. Buddhist gathas were translated into English and set to familiar Protestant hymn tunes: "Onward Buddhist Soldiers," "Buddha, Savior, Pilot Me," and "Joy to the World, The Buddha Has Come." A Congregationalist minister who attended an English-language service in Hawaii in 1928 recorded these observations:

> I went into a Buddhist temple, which ministers to a Congregation of English-speaking young Oriental Americans. It is most tastefully appointed. Except for the altar equipment, which is, of course, pronouncedly Buddhistic in its symbolisms, you would almost have to be told you were in the courts of the "heathen." It looks much like a church. The Buddhists, physically, are made very much as we are, and, of course, have pews on which they sit—for all the world like Christians. They are very quiet—and come into their temple softly and silently . . . I purchased a little hymnal in the literature department of the temple. Much of the ritual is excellent, and with substitution of the name of Christ for that of Buddha could be heartily recommended to many of our churches in which worship has been neglected until it isn't even missed.[18]

The "little hymnal" was almost certainly *Vade Mecum*—Latin for "go with me"—compiled by Ernest and Dorothy Hunt, Buddhist converts of Anglican background ordained in Honolulu in 1924. It was published the same year under the auspices of the Honpa Hongwangi Mission, with music written by R. R. Bode, an organist who directed the first choir at Hongwangi. The volume, which included 114 untitled gathas, had an ecumenical thrust. "It is the fervent desire of the authors of this little volume that the heresy of separateness now prevailing among Buddhists of Honolulu may soon be abolished," the Hunts stated on the title page. "They have endeavored therefore to keep to the fundamental and ethical teaching hoping that all English-speaking Buddhists, whatever their affiliation, may be able to use it." The hymns reflected the themes of popular Protestant Christian hymns. Dorothy Hunt contributed one called "Buddha's Soldiers":

> Have you heard the sound of footsteps
> As of soldiers marching on?
> Have you seen their banners waving?
> Have you heard their battle song?
> Have you watch'd their blazing torches,
> Lighting up their columns long?[19]

The collection proved popular enough to generate five editions by 1932. Further revisions took place in 1939, 1962, and 1990 under the titles *Standard Gathas* and *Praises of the Buddha*. These new editions complicate the predicted pattern of religious and musical adaptation to America; sometimes "Americanization entails Japanization," as George J. Tanabe has argued. Despite the evident "Americanization" of Japanese American Buddhists in Hawaii over the twentieth century, the number of Japanese-language gathas actually increased after the original 1924 all-English edition, to approximately half. The very success of hymn-singing in Hawaii required that gathas be provided for Japanese-speaking worshippers. Congregational-style hymns had already penetrated Japan, and many of the Japanese-language hymns appearing in the 1939 *Standard Gathas* were actually imported from Japan. But nearly all the English-language gathas came from *Vade Mecum*. The 1949 edition substituted roman letters for Japanese *kanji*, preserving the sound of the Japanese language for congregations less literate in the Japanese syllabary.

VADE MECUM may have had a successful record of publication, but it was not the first collection of Buddhist hymns to be published in English in the United States. That distinction lies with Carus, who in 1911 had published his ponderously named *Buddhist Hymns: Versified Translations From the Dhammapada and Various Other Sources: Adapted to Modern Music*. As a result of his further research and decade-long collaboration with Suzuki, Carus' attraction to Buddhism had continued to increase after the 1890s, when he saw it as serving the religion of science. "Buddhism has constantly grown upon me and I have found more and more reason to justify my esteem for both this grand religion and its noble founder," he wrote in the preface to *Buddhist Hymns.* "I can repeat the words and make them my own which the venerable Professor Fausböll said after having spent a lifetime on the study of Pali literature, 'the more I know of Buddha the more I love him.'" The hymn collection grew out of his admiration for Buddhist literature, "which among all the religious literature on earth— and here not even the Bible can be said to make an exception—is distinguished by purity, profundity, and loftiness."[20]

Carus' goal was one of cultural translation: "to enter into the real spirit of the ancient religious poetry of Buddhism" by reducing it "to the same form of song into which religious sentiments have developed among us [Americans]." With customary erudition, Carus provided the original Pali texts, as well as page citations from the *Dhammapada.* Among other evidence, Carus related the story of Ashvaghosha, "the Neighing Horse," whom Carus compared to St. Ambrose (340–397 C.E.), predecessor to Pope Gregory I in regulating Catholic chants. For a "propaganda- tour" to Pataliputra, Ashvaghosha composed a tune designed to impress hearers with the core Buddhist conceptions of impermanence and emptiness. According to legend, the song was so successful that 500 royal princes renounced their worldly lives and became Buddhists; fearing for the future of the country, the king of Pataliputra forbade the performance of that music thereafter.[21]

Carus had the support of a Buddhist abbot from Sacramento who had received training from the Dalai Lama and credited "inspiring music and words" for his success in winning converts. "I am greatly rejoiced you have completed a hymn-book for Buddhist worship, for as you say music is a great help in edification," he wrote Carus. "True, Oriental nations are not musical in the western sense of the term, but for the life of me I cannot understand why they should not take kindly to your suggestion as to accepting the hymns, but we must overlook their weakness. Some probably have the idea that it savors too much of the Christian form of worship, but I do not see it in that light. Buddha taught when you are in Rome do as the Romans do, etc." Carus' own orientation was uncompromisingly highbrow. Early Buddhism might have prohibited novices from attending secular musical performances, he acknowledged, and contemporary priests in Burma, Siam, and Ceylon shunned music as profane and sensuous. "Yet there is a difference between the noble strains of Johann Sebastian Bach and foolish rag-time tunes, between the sonatas of Beethoven and the operettas of Offenbach; and we know that in the age when Buddhism flourished in India, when the prosperity of the country reached its highest mark, sacred music existed."[22]

THE THREE CHARACTERISTICS.

Sabbe sankhara anicca,
Sabbe sankhara dukkha,
Sabbe sankhara anatta.

Anguttara-Nikaya, III, 134.

L. VAN BEETHOVEN.

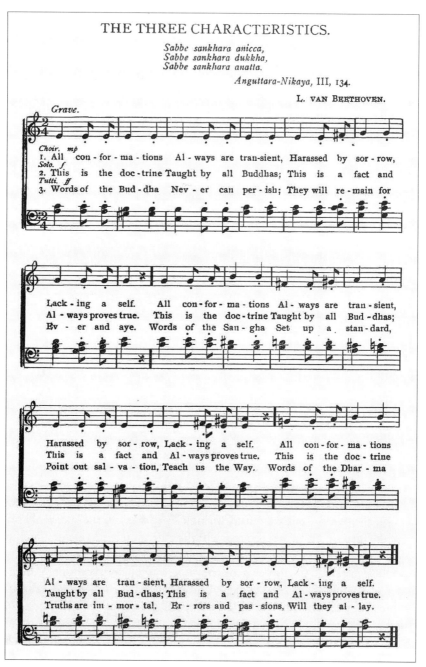

8. Source: Paul Carus, *Buddhist Hymns: Versified Translations from the Dhammapada and Various Other Sources Adapted to Modern Music* (Chicago: Open Court, 1911), 22.

Buddhist Hymns includes six hymns from the earlier collection, *Sacred Tunes,* including settings adapted from Bortniansky, Zelter, Voigtländer, and Wagner. But there are eight new works, for three of which Carus himself provided the tunes: "The Buddhist Doxology," "Self-Reliance," "The Religion of All Buddhas." An unnamed German chorale provided the tune for "The Buddha's Hymn of Victory," a German folksong for "Happiness." For the rest he turned to European composers. "The Essence of the Doctrine" was set to a tune by Hans Georg Nägeli, a Swiss composer and music publisher who was concerned with ethical considerations of music and wrote simple, straightforward songs for the people; the brief "An Ancient Rule," set to Mozart; "The Three Characteristics," reproduced in Figure 8, set to a theme from Beethoven's Seventh Symphony. For Carus, this blending of European art music and Buddhist scripture made perfect sense. "In the writer's opinion the classical music of Europe is pervaded by the deep religious spirit which may very well be regarded as Buddhistic," he wrote in the foreword, singling out Chopin's "Nocturne" as conveying a sense of "the irritation of Samsara resolved in the calm of Nirvana."[23]

Missing from *Buddhist Hymns* were the familiar gospel hymns of Lowell and Wesley that appeared in his earlier collection. But some of the evangelical Christian spirit remained. Carus' attempt to reconcile Buddhism with American Christian triumphalism shows clearly in "The Buddhist Doxology":

> Bright shineth the sun in his splendor by day,
> And bright the moon's radiance by night;
> Bright shineth the hero in battle array,
> And the sage in his thought shineth bright;
> But by day and by night, none so glorious, so bright
> As Lord Buddha, the source of all spiritual light (twice).

But this passage from "The Buddha's Hymn of Victory" is more typical:

> Through many births I sought in vain, The builder of this house of pain;
> Now, builder, thee I plainly see, This is the last abode for me.
> Thy gable's yoke, thy rafters broke, My heart has peace, all lust will cease.

Since Carus drew his texts mainly from the *Dhammapada* (which he translated as "Hymns of the Faith"), there were limits to how far he could adapt them to a familiar spiritual idiom. Musically there were no such constraints. Carus felt confident that European-derived music would eventually supplant indigenous Asian music as the setting for Buddhist texts. "In our opinion it is only a question of time when western music and western singing will be introduced in the religious institutions of the Flowery Country [Japan]," he predicted. "The first steps in this direction, consisting in the establishment of schools of music after Italian and German patterns, have been taken and some national songs have already been composed by native composers."[24]

Buddhism was not the only world religion undergoing this sort of musical identity transmutation during these decades. American Judaism was also experiencing similar pressure, generated from within, to bring its music into line with Christian norms. In 1908, for example, a cantor hired by a Reformed synagogue in Baltimore did exactly what Carus had done, transposing familiar classical pieces and operatic arias to serve as musical settings for Jewish liturgy. "Repertoire, then, had to be consistent with the respectability of the clergy and congregational decorum," writes ethnomusicologist Mark Slobin of the new turn among Reformed Jews, "and was based on contemporary European classical favorites, above all the music of the bourgeoisie, tastefully performed by the cantorial soloist while the worshippers sang hymns directly inspired by four-square, four-part Protestant standards." This musical impulse in time would be largely reversed, with a return to traditional forms. But Carus' hymns appear to have entered the canon of American Shin Buddhism. Of the seven English gathas published in Senshin Temple's service book, two texts are by Carus, and three by A. Raymond Zorn, who collaborated with the Hunts on *Vade Mecum*; there are twenty-one other gathas and four "dharma school" songs in Japanese. The *Shin Buddhist Service Book* begins with Carus' "The Teachings of All Buddhas":

> Commit no wrong but good deeds do,
> and let thy heart be pure
> All Buddhas teach this doctrine true
> Which will for aye endure.
> Hate is not overcome by hate,
> By love alone 'tis quelled
> This is the truth of ancient date
> Today still unexcelled.

The same hymn opens a 1994 recording of English gathas produced by the Buddhist Churches of America. In both cases the musical setting comes not from the European art-music tradition but from a composer named C. Iwanaga. Also included is "In Lumbini's Garden," with a gospel-sounding tune by R. R. Bode:

> Softly blew the breezes
> On that summer morn,
> In Lumbini's garden,
> Where the Lord was born.
> From the earth sprang flowers,

> Birds in warbles sang,
> While through earth and heaven,
> Strains of music rang.

Like other Bode compositions, this setting has the ring of post–Civil War gospel songs.[25]

These collections contain many gathas shaped by different musical traditions. But Protestant-style hymnody continues to have a place in worship. World religions scholar Diana Eck observed this of a Sunday morning service at Senshin Temple, a long-standing congregation of mainly Japanese American Shin Buddhists in south-central Los Angeles. Taking her seat in a pew, Eck noticed a hymnal and heard the sound of a church organ. "The ritual idiom reminded me of my hometown Methodist Church in Bozeman, Montana," she recalled. "We stood for a hymn, sat for a scripture reading, stood for a responsive reading, just as I had all my life. And yet the content was Buddhist, and the overall feeling I had as a worshipper was of a Methodist-Buddhist blend, the Methodism being supplied from my own religious background. The hymn we sang together seemed to be a direct adaptation of Protestant hymnody. We sang:

> Sweet hour of meditation, The quiet hour of peace,
> When from life's care and turmoil I find a blest release.
> In silent contemplation, New faith and hope I win.
> More light and deeper knowledge, New strength to conquer sin.[26]

Although Eck doesn't specify the melody, the metered stanzas would easily fit Wesley's "Aurelia," the usual setting for "The Church's One Foundation" (and one borrowed by Carus for *Sacred Tunes*)—or any number of other tunes in the commonly used 7.6.7.6.7.6.7.6 meter.

Other musical alternatives exist, of course, for Shin Buddhists in the United States. The temple where Eck observed Methodist-style hymnody, Senshin, was also the site for a different kind of musical adaptation. As part of the midsummer celebration of O-bon, a Buddhist holiday to commemorate the souls of ancestors, the temple has staged festival works composed by Noboku Miyamoto, a Los Angeles–born Sansei singer-songwriter and performance artist. One song she created for O-bon, "Tampopo Ondo," fuses English verses with Japanese choruses and uses a panoply of traditional Japanese instruments, including *shamisen* (lute), *shakuhachi* (flute), and *taiko* drums. "According to Jodoshinshû, Truth and Reality are ours for the receiving," a note explains. "We need do nothing but hear and receive the Truth. But to simply hear and receive is as difficult as it is to just dance. To 'just do' anything is extremely difficult, for it involves setting aside one's ego for a moment. Bon odori is an exercise in 'just dancing,' in 'just hearing and accepting,' in 'being a river forever flowing and changing instead of a riverbank forever watching.'" The image developed in the song is one of dandelion *(tampopo)* seeds being carried by the wind, a metaphor both for the dance and for the fluid, contingent nature of reality, the endless circle-of-life cycles of samsara.

> The seed of the dandelion, scatters in the sky—
> Tampopo Tampopo—Hi- Hi
> A windblown weed, a wildflower, watch it fly—
> Tampopo Tampopo—Hi- Hi . . .
> Dancing on the wind, spinning from a world it leaves behind,
> Dancing on wind, new life begins.

Okagesama de ("with your help")	On this special night—
Okagesama de	Past and present are one—
Okagesama de	On this night of O-bon—
Okagesama de	Dandelions return—

The song is a kind of stylized simulation of Japanese folk music, though its rhythms clearly mark it as a hybrid form. Miyamoto grew up in Los Angeles during the wartime internment crisis and was shaped by Black Power, anti–Vietnam War, and Asian American empowerment movements of the 1960s, all of which left traces in her eclectic musical stylings.[27]

BETWEEN Carus and Miyamoto came a major disruption and hardship in the lives of most Shin Buddhists: the wartime internment of Japanese Americans. In 1944, while incarcerated at the Topaz Relocation Center in Utah, priests and members of what had been the Buddhist Mission of North America changed their name to the Buddhist Churches of America. But various laws aimed at restricting immigration of Chinese and Japanese, culminating in the federal Asian Exclusion Act of 1924, had already put Shin Buddhists on the defensive. (Interestingly, despite a record of unabashed patriotism, Carus was subjected to anti-German harassment in his final years, which coincided with the "100 percent Americanism" campaigns aimed at German language and culture during World War I.)[28]

Compared to the decades following the World Parliament of Religions, the interwar and World War II years were a period of relative dormancy for the development of American Buddhism. As a result of the incarceration of Japanese Americans, the leadership of American Shin Buddhism was assumed by Julius Goldwater, born in 1908 in Los Angeles to German-American Jewish parents. Goldwater was a protégé of the Hunts who was converted in Hawaii in 1928 before being ordained in Kyoto. During wartime internment Goldwater traveled widely to all camps, distributing literature including his adaptation of the Hunts' *Vade Mecum*. The flavor of the liturgies distributed by Goldwater was strikingly Protestant, with gathas intermingled with responsive readings, collective affirmations, and a sermon to create an order of service that one might expect in a Presbyterian church.[29] When Buddhism reemerged as a force in American culture in the 1950s, its dominant strain was not Shin, but Zen. But despite the wartime rupture, a strong historical thread connected the American Buddhism of Carus' day with the postwar renascence. The single most significant figure for renewed interest in Buddhism in the postwar United States was the same Rinzai Zen scholar who had shaped popular notions of Buddhism early in the century through his long collaboration with Paul Carus at Open Court: Daisetz Teitaro Suzuki.

Shin Buddhism has the deepest institutional roots of any Buddhist community in the United States, and it is uniquely bound up with the historical experiences of Japanese Americans through exclusion and internment. But Zen has clearly been the more prominent form of Japanese Buddhism in terms of its public profile, especially in the arts. Both of Carus' mentors in Japanese Buddhism, Sōen and Suzuki, were Zen adherents. Whereas practitioners of Jodo Shinshu sought musical forms that accommodated with the European American mainstream, Zen made minimal changes in traditional ritual. Organs or Methodist-style hymns are nowhere to be found. Rather, chanting is the centerpiece of communal worship. "There is hardly a Zen temple or center where men and women do not assemble in the main hall at least once a day and chant sutras and the words of the masters who have realized the highest truth," writes Philip Kapleau, an influential Buddhist convert. "Chanting forms the focal ground on which every ritual, ceremony, and rite of passage is performed, setting a tone through which participants acquire a heightened awareness of and receptivity to what is being enacted."[30]

In practice, Zen chanting involves a leader, a congregation, and musicians. In traditional *zazen* (Zen practice), instruments are used only to demarcate timing of zazen. A *mukugyo* (woodblock) shot followed by four rings of a *kei* (hammered metal bowl-gong) initiate zazen; the meditation is ended by one bell ring followed by two staccato notes on the block. "The strong, clear voice of the lead chanter is heard alone to introduce the chants, evoking a response in the full 'chorus' of between fifty and three hundred chanters," Kapleau continues. "The pulselike throb of the wooden drum offers a counterpoint to the vibrant ring of the bowl-gong even as they mesh to contrast and harmonize with the drone of chanting." First, worshippers are summoned at dawn to the main *zendo,* or communal meditation space, by the resonant booming of a large taiko drum. The taiko player then produces a variety of percussive sounds: sweeping sticks, Latin *guiro*-like, along the ridged rim; an accelerating cadence ("clackety clack, clackety clack") on the rim; a concluding pattern played on the drumhead itself. "After the drum ends, with no gap the large *keisu* . . . or bowl-shaped gong, is struck, its deep resonance filling the zendo. The keisu player sits poised before it, deftly holding a large padded cylindrical striker in both hands to intone the introductions to the different chants and to punctuate the chanting after all have joined in . . . In Zen it is said, 'Don't strike the instrument; let it be struck.'" Each successive chant is joined by a wooden-fish drum. "It begins slowly, 'thump . . . thump . . . thump,' gradually building in speed, like a departing train, as the individual voices blend into a single sonorous drone." The percussionist guides the instrument, letting it "play itself" to the fullest extent possible. "The sound of this fish-shaped, hollowed-out drum is deep enough to ride underneath the vocal chanting, thus setting a cadence that can be followed by all."[31]

Like Carus, Kapleau was profoundly influenced by Suzuki, whom he met as a court reporter at the Tokyo war crimes trials. In the 1950s Kapleau attended Suzuki's lectures at Columbia before beginning eleven years of formal Zen training in Japan with a series of Zen masters, including Yasutani Rōshi, who allowed Kapleau to take notes on their private sessions. His resulting study, *The Three Pillars of Zen,* was the first book on Zen by a Westerner, and it made it possible, in theory, for people to learn zazen on their own. Kapleau also took steps to Americanize Zen at the Rochester Zen Center he founded in 1966, allowing Western clothing during meditation and English-language sutras. Two types of chants are performed at Rochester: sutras, the words of Buddha or revered teachers; and dharani—extended mantras consisting of vocables, "a rhythmic sequence of sounds that expresses, through its unique spiritual vibrations, the essential truth transcending all duality." Chanting is not to be confused with reciting. The sound is performed at each chanter's lowest natural pitch; it emanates from the lower belly and resonates in the head cavities. "The particular words of the chants emerge from one's basic pitch; thus the words flow together into a drone issuing from the hara (the lower abdomen)," Kapleau explains. "The pitch does not rise and fall in a sing-songy way. Zen chanting is a unique way of engaging the deepest level of mind. It circumvents the intellect to awaken understanding and energetically expresses feeling without emotionality."[32]

Despite its adherence to traditional forms, Zen has been adapted in the United States. According to Zen scholar G. Victor Sōgen Hori, "Americanization occurs under the guise of a sincere belief that one is following

Japanese Zen tradition." At the Rochester Center, sutras like the "Four Bodhisattvic Vows" and the "Heart of Perfect Wisdom" are chanted in English, carefully phrased in order to achieve the proper cadence and euphony. "The advantage of chanting these in one's own language is that when repeated regularly the truth of the words is hammered home to the subconscious mind, thereby instilling greater understanding and faith," Kapleau states. "No conscious effort need be made to grasp the meaning, for it is absorbed spontaneously, unchecked by the rational mind." But Kapleau's decision to translate sutras into English was controversial, and led to a break with Yasutani.[33] While Suzuki's influence on Kapleau may have been important, his larger impact on the culture came through the artists who studied with or read him. In the 1950s and 1960s Zen provided an important set of ideas to a group of artists ranging from novelist Jack Kerouac to poets Gary Snyder and Allen Ginzberg and composer John Cage. Suzuki himself reflected on the deep parallels between Zen and art. "The Zen-man is an artist to the extent that, as the sculptor chisels out a great figure deeply buried in a mass of inert matter, the Zen-man transforms his own life into a work of creation, which exists, as Christians might say, in the mind of God," he wrote in 1959. "What differentiates Zen from the arts is this: While the artists have to resort to the canvas and brush or mechanical instruments or some other mediums to express themselves, Zen has no need of things external, except 'the body' in which the Zen-man is so to speak embodied."[34]

John Cage was one of several influential artists and intellectuals to encounter Suzuki at Columbia University, where the latter taught for several years after his return to the United States in 1949 under the auspices of the Rockefeller Foundation. "I had read *The Gospel of Sri Ramakrishna*. I became interested, in other words, in Oriental thought," Cage recalled. "And I read also a short book by Aldous Huxley, called *The Perennial Philosophy*, and from that I got the idea that all the various religions were saying the same thing but had different flavors . . . So I browsed, as it were, and found a flavor I liked and it was that of Zen Buddhism. It was then that Suzuki came to New York, and I was able to go to Columbia once a week for two years to attend his classes." Cage recalled a free-form seminar with people standing near the door while others catnapped and jets from a nearby airport periodically drowned out discussion. "Suzuki was not very talkative," admitted Cage. "He would frequently say nothing that you could put your finger on. Now and then he would." It was Suzuki's teaching that led Cage to the compositional technique for which he is best known: chance operations. "I think that the idea of change, or the ego itself changing direction, is implicit in Suzuki's understanding of the effect of

Buddhism on the structure of the mind," according to Cage. "I use chance operations instead of operating according to my likes and dislikes. I use my work to change myself and I accept what the chance operations say. The *I Ching* says that if you don't accept the chance operations you have no right to use them. Which is very clear, so that's what I do."[35]

Cage's most famous work, 4′33″, is also his most Zen. The work was first performed on a warm, rainy evening in August 1952 in a ramshackle barn-like hall in the woods at the end of a dirt road near Woodstock, New York. The audience included a cross-section of the Manhattan music scene, including some vacationing members of the New York Philharmonic. It was the second piece performed by pianist David Tudor, a long-time Cage collaborator. Tudor started a stopwatch, sat down, closed the lid of the piano, and waited for thirty seconds. Then he restarted the watch, this time for two minutes twenty-three seconds. And again for one hundred seconds. All in silence—sort of. "In the Maverick that night," writes Will Hermes, "one could likely hear the sound of breeze in the trees, rain pattering lightly on the rooftop, the chirping of crickets, a dog barking aimlessly somewhere in the distance, the sound of bodies shifting their weight on creaky pine benches, the sound of breath being drawn and being expired." Audience reaction was mixed; one local artist stood up to propose that Cage and his cronies be driven out of town.[36]

Another way to explain 4′33″ is as a kind of formal answer to the famous koan attributed to an eighteenth-century Japanese Zen master: What is the sound of one hand clapping?[37] Because what the audience hears during a performance of Cage's piece is exactly the sound of one hand clapping. Or could hear, depending on the performance context, which is always different: a Zen monastery different from a barn near Woodstock different from Alice Tully Hall in New York. "The most important piece is my silent piece," Cage later wrote. "I always think of it before I write the next piece." It was his way of capturing "the is-ness of life." Cage's foregrounding of random ambient sound influenced the approach of artists ranging from Philip Glass and Steve Reich to The Who, Brian Eno, and hip-hop producers. Glass had begun studying yoga in 1962, and learned of the *I Ching* through an English painter friend who had joined the Native American Church and used peyote. But it was Cage who introduced Glass to Buddhism.

"I certainly did not learn about him [Cage] at music school," Glass recalled. "He was not considered a serious musical influence at that time. Certainly not by the people at Juilliard. Then in *Silence* there were all these references to Zen koans." For Glass, the influence was less formal than a means of inculcating a lived sensibility. "The real impact of Buddhist practice affects how you live your life on a daily basis, not how you do your art," he told an interviewer. "How you live day by day, moment by moment. The impact of Buddhism is not theoretical, as in how you paint or how you write a novel. That's hardly as interesting as how you live on a daily basis, don't you think?" Saxophonist Sonny Rollins speaks in much the same terms: "I retain elements of different kinds of Buddhism. Trying to draw specific lines to it doesn't work for me. I've studied some Zen and yoga. My music is my yoga. That's the way I practice. That's the way I meditate. That's the way I seek enlightenment during this lifetime. And I've found out that to play my instrument, to concentrate and get inside of myself, is my way of doing all of these spiritual things. I'm trying to get some understanding of life and how people interact with each other, to get beyond jealousies and hatreds and envies. This is my great work, and the instrument gives me a path to travel with."[38]

Adam Yauch of the Beastie Boys shares this eclectic sensibility. After a period of using marijuana and hallucinogens, he was drawn to the liberating consequences of meditation. "Buddhism is like a manual to achieve enlightenment—there are these five things and these six things within the first thing, and all these little subdivisions," he told an interviewer. "And despite all of that right-brain information, it's very heart centered. At least that's the feeling I get from the Tibetans." Yauch's own daily practice is desultory. "I meditate in the morning and before I go to sleep . . . I can get focused on what happened during the day, pull that into perspective, and that'll make my sleep a little more peaceful," he says. "Then I set up what's going on the next day or get centered for those activities in the morning. A lot of times on tour I don't get a chance to because it's so crazy running around." There was also a political dimension to Yauch's interest in Buddhism, originally piqued during a visit to Nepal, where he met a group of refugees who had just escaped by climbing over the Himalayas wearing sneakers and windbreakers. "They were talking about not going back home until Tibet was free and I think the idea of just leaving home struck me really strongly," Yauch said. "Then the more I learned about the nonviolence, that's what probably kept me interested and working on it, because I think that the lesson of nonviolence is something the rest of the world needs so badly."[39] In 1993 the Beastie Boys invited a group of Tibetan Namgyal monks to tour with them, performing purification rituals and sacred dances to open each performance before bands like Green Day, Boom Poetics, and the Beastie Boys took the stage. Beginning in 1996 the rappers organized the summer Tibetan Freedom Festivals and created the feature-length documentary *Free Tibet.*

What Yauch attempts in a song like "Bodhisattva Vow" (a percentage of whose earnings were donated to the Tibetan cause, according to the album's liner notes) is the same project that Carus undertook a century earlier—the translation of Buddhist ideas into a musical idiom that would give it resonance in American culture. In 1900 the comparable cultural medium was hymnody, which since before the founding of the nation had been a cultural dominant, the sole form of musical activity for large masses of Americans. In this way the Beastie Boys, with their mass-culture bona fides, had much more in common with Carus than did an avant-gardist like Cage, who courted artistic (not to say social) obscurity almost as a matter of religious principle. The "white Negro" Beat writers of the 1950s had found in Buddhism an inspiration for their lives and art; white rappers had enshrined it amid platinum record sales. As American Jews, Yauch and comrades also fit a different tradition of Buddhism in America, its embrace by Jewish converts. Liberal-minded Americans, whose culture is already a web of interlinking narratives of diaspora, could hardly resist the story of Tibet: ruthlessly occupied by China since 1950, led by one of the most charismatic religious leaders in the world, who had led his own mass exodus to India in 1959, accompanied by perhaps a million fellow Tibetans, and thirty years later won the Nobel Peace prize. The 1990s saw a new form of Buddhism achieve celebrity. The fascination and embrace of Tibetan Buddhism by figures from the entertainment world—Richard Gere, Martin Scorsese, Tina Turner, among others—has been widely noted.[40] "Boomer Buddhism" has been lauded for its potential to challenge rampant American materialism and individualism, denigrated by others for reducing Buddhism to orientalized self-help therapy. Beastie Buddhism is exemplary of the New Age embrace of Buddhism. But it also looks back to earlier figures like Thoreau, Olcott, and, musically speaking, Paul Carus.

CHAPTER SEVEN

Yossele, Yossele!

In every living soul, a spirit cries for expression—perhaps this plaintive, wailing song of Jazz is, after all, the misunderstood utterance of a prayer.

—FIRST INTERTITLE OF *THE JAZZ SINGER* (1927)

> Where are the Hebrew children?
> Where are the Hebrew children?
> Where are the Hebrew children?
> Safe in the promised land.
>
> —THE SACRED HARP

IN 1927 the famous cantor Yossele Rosenblatt was approached by agents from Warner Brothers hoping to persuade him to agree to appear in a film then in production. Knowing that religious scruples would stand in the way, the film company was prepared to offer $100,000. "Think of what it would mean for raising the prestige of the Jew and his faith if a man like you were to be held up as its representative to the non-Jewish public." Rosenblatt demurred. "But there isn't enough money in the world to make me profane my sacred calling by putting on an act anywhere, whether it be on the screen or the stage." Warner's agents persisted. "But how about just letting us have the use of your voice, without your being seen, in selections like let us say, *'Kol Nidre'* and *'Umipnei Chatoeinu'*?" Rosenblatt responded indignantly. "Did you say *'Kol Nidre,'* that hallowed prayer that is chanted by the cantor at the inauguration of the holiest day of the year? Under no circumstances would I permit that to pass my mouth anywhere except in a house of G-d."[1] But the cantor did travel to Hollywood, where he was lionized by no less a figure than Charlie Chaplin. And Rosenblatt did finally appear in *The Jazz Singer,* the film that brought Vitaphone sound technology to a mass audience for the first time. His name even appears on the sign outside the theater where he is shown singing *Yahrzeit,* a secular eulogy for the dead.

The story of the second-generation Jew who runs away from home to pursue his career in show business and returns to sing *Kol Nidre* for his dying father is recognized as a Hollywood milestone and over the last decade has inspired some brilliant analysis of racial thinking in early twentieth-century America. As Krin Gabbard has argued, *The Jazz Singer*'s Oedipal plot is perhaps the *Ur*-narrative of Hollywood; the film has inspired three direct remakes and lent its storyline to untold other films.[2] But the film also reminds us of how central Jewish themes and stories have been to American sacred music in all its diversity. The Hebrew Bible is the single crucial font of all the sacred music of the Americas: it has provided the stories, metaphors, images, particular song texts, and self-conceptions that have animated most religious folk of America. To paraphrase Alfred North Whitehead's comment about Plato, nearly all of America's religious music can be regarded as footnotes to the sacred music of the Jews. We have seen how the singing of paraphrased passages from the Old Testament have constituted the basis of musical worship for the great majority of European settlers in North America. Ancient Jewish melodies formed the musical basis for the Gregorian chants and plainsong brought by Spanish explorers and missionaries to Spanish America. These texts and songs were quickly transmitted to Native peoples, who adapted and adopted them in myriad forms. In New England, the *Bay Psalm Book* was the first book published in North America and remained a Protestant touchstone for a century. Even with the introduction of hymns beginning in the mid-1700s, psalmody remained the sacred music of choice for most congregations. In particular, the hymns of Isaac Watts were closely modeled on metrical psalms, and employed the familiar metrical tunes developed for psalm-singing. These "Dr. Watts" hymns were early favorites of African-American Christians and formed the foundation of black church music from the mid-eighteenth century through the twentieth century.

Jewish traditions were equally important at the level of theme and metaphor. The Puritans, at least the sector that left behind voluminous writings, understood themselves as conducting an errand into the wilderness, creating a New Jerusalem in the wilds of North America. Their sense of being a covenanted people escaping bondage was central to their self-understanding. Cotton Mather, the most formidable of all Puritan scholars and a clergyman deeply concerned about the proper use of music in worship, was so obsessed with understanding his co-religionists as successors to the biblical Jews that he donned a skullcap and took to calling himself a rabbi, at least in his study. The struggle for independence from Britain reinforced this self-image: the colonies claimed the role of a New Israel seeking freedom from British Egypt. At the time of his death George Washington was lionized as the American Moses (or, alternatively, Joshua.) When the Continental Congress debated a design for the Great Seal of the United States,

Benjamin Franklin proposed Moses parting the Red Sea while Thomas Jefferson offered an image of the Israelites marching into the Wilderness. As Sacvan Bercovitch has demonstrated, these biblical figures and tropes have proved remarkably durable in providing a metaphorical language for American national identity.[3]

A wide variety of religious communities have found comfort and justification in the same stories and metaphors. No narrative stakes a stronger claim to be the archetypal American narrative than does the Hebrew Exodus. English Puritans, African Americans, Mormons, Shakers all shared a consciousness of being a chosen people cast adrift in a hostile world, and found solace and musical equipment for living in the poems and narratives of the original diasporic people: the children of Israel. The Shaker communities founded their enormous body of sacred songs on biblical themes of dispersion and exile. So did Mormons, who moved progressively westward toward the Great Basin to escape religious persecution, finally establishing their own New Zion in the Salt Lake Valley, all the while perceiving the American landscape and peoples through lenses shaped by their reading of Jewish history. A series of American Indian prophets beginning with Tenskwatawa early in the nineteenth century borrowed language and theology from Jewish scripture. Shaped by a very different cultural milieu, composer John Cage once organized an "event" at Black Mountain College that featured painting by Robert Rauschenberg, dance by Merce Cunningham, poetry by Charles Olson and M. C. Richards, accompanied by a multimedia collage. "Later that summer, vacationing in New England," he recalled, "I visited America's first synagogue, to discover that the congregation was there seated precisely the way I had arranged the audience at Black Mountain."[4] Closer to the present, some Spanish-language Pentecostal churches in east Los Angeles have dropped the black gospel sound customary for worship, using instead the Psalms of David, sung in Hebrew to minor modes. "East Los Angeles was our Jerusalem and the birthplace for Victory Outreach," reads its mission statement. "Spiritually speaking, California is our Judea and the United States is our Samaria. The 'uttermost parts' is the rest of the world."[5]

For no American population has the Exodus story had more profound resonance than for African Americans. Enslaved Africans created a rich repertoire of spirituals using the inspiration of the escape from Egypt across the Red Sea to the Jordan River and finally into the land of Canaan. "The essence of slave religion cannot be fully grasped without understanding this Old Testament bias," asserts historian Lawrence Levine. "It is important that Daniel and David and Joshua and Jonah and Moses and Noah, all of whom fill the lines of the spirituals, were delivered in this world and delivered in ways which struck the imagination of the slaves. Over and over their songs dwelt upon the spectacle of the Red Sea opening to allow the Hebrew slaves past before inundating the mighty armies of the Pharaoh. They lingered delightedly upon the image of little David humbling the great Goliath with a stone—a pretechnological victory which postbellum Negroes were to expand upon in their songs of John Henry."[6] Likewise, upon Samson, Noah, Jonah, Jeremiah, Ezekiel, Amos, and Hosea. Through abolitionism, civil war, and emancipation, we have seen how spirituals provided a crucial (if ambivalent) means of African-American self-expression and point of access for white cultural curiosity.

In the twentieth century, the Rastafari religion developed in Kingston among Jamaicans who proclaimed Haile Selassie a new messiah and Ethiopia the true Zion, a promised land to which the African diaspora should return from its captivity in Babylon. This was part of a larger discourse of Ethiopianism founded on Psalm 68:31—"Princes shall come out of Egypt; Ethiopia shall soon stretch out her hands unto God"—whose currents reached the United States early in the twentieth century via immigrants from the West Indies and Latin America and led to the establishment of congregations of "Black Jews" in northern cities. One influential leader was Arnold Josiah Ford, an immigrant from Barbados who moved to New York City, worked as a jazz bassist, became a rabbi at Beth B'nai Abraham in Harlem, authored the *Universal Ethiopian Hymnal* for Marcus Garvey's Universal Negro Improvement Association, and traveled to Ethiopia to witness the coronation of Emperor Haile Selassie and to negotiate the establishment of a black Jewish homeland north of Lake Tana.[7]

To be sure, Jewish texts and metaphors have not been used at all consistently across time or religious group. The language and forms have been borrowed at times faithfully, at other times superficially, if these terms even make sense when referring to allegory. Sometimes the notion of a homeland has dropped away, calling into question whether such an identity can be considered diasporic. Related at one level, Egyptian bondage and Babylonian captivity have different implications when applied to America; depending on one's perspective, "Egypt" or "Babylon" can refer to Africa, Europe, North America, or some combination. The term *Jewish music* is ambiguous, because unlike apparently comparable genres (Buddhist music, Christian music), Jewish music refers not just to sacred or liturgical songs but to the music of a diverse people shaped by migration and cultural exchange over thousands of years. Important distinctions can be drawn between biblical Hebrews, children of Israel, Jews, and modern Israelis. Even taking a synchronic view, Jewish identity means different things to different people, or more accurately several things at once: an organized religion and an ethnic identity; a cultural legacy and a spiritual orientation; a set of ethical codes and a sense of nationhood. A music defined in terms of a people rather than a religion clearly will encompass a wider range of functions, and boundaries between the sacred and the secular will prove even more difficult than usual to establish. But regardless of the particular terms around which Jewish identity is defined, the language and themes of biblical Israel have been remarkably pervasive in the religious lives of a broad spectrum of Americans.

One undeniable legacy of the Hebrew Bible has been the deeply ambivalent attitude toward music held by many American religious people, from Puritans to present-day Muslims. Understanding this legacy is crucial for understanding the tensions present to varying degrees in American Jewish music and, more to the point, the conflict at the heart of *The Jazz Singer*. The Bible is peppered with contradictory dicta about the propriety of music in worship. Two concerns recur, one over technology, the other over sensuality, and both can be traced to Genesis 4:21. The passage has harp- and pipe-playing, and by extension music more generally, being invented by Jubal, one of the sons of Cain. (His brother, Tubal-cain, is credited with inventing brass and iron tools; between them they are credited with founding human culture.) This lineage raises the specter of moral degeneracy, and Jewish Midrashic literature develops an association between music and sexual corruption. One of the longest-standing Judaic proscriptions is the ban on women making music in the synagogue. Women's voices, like their hair, were thought to have the power to lead men astray, and as a result in many Jewish communities women were restricted to singing in front of their husbands and male kin (or in all-female settings). "He who stares even at a woman's little finger with the intention of deriving pleasure from it, is considered as though he had looked at her secret parts," opined Maimonides. A verse from Solomon's Song of Songs—"For your voice is sweet and your face beautiful"—has been cited by Talmudic scholars and rabbis as a warning to men to avoid the sexual attraction of women's song. "A woman's voice is indecency," goes one saying, while mixed singing is considered nearly pornographic: "Men singing and women answering is promiscuity; women singing and men answering is like fire set to chaff."[8]

A diametrically different position is sounded in the Psalms of David, which famously encourage instrumental music. Psalm 149 exhorts the people of Israel:

> Praise ye the Lord.
> Sing unto the Lord a new song,
>   and his praise in the congregation of saints.
> Let Israel rejoice in him that made him:

> let the children of Zion be joyful in their King.
> Let them praise his name in the dance:
> > let them sing praises unto him with the timbrel and harp.

And Psalm 150:

> Praise him with the sound of the trumpet:
> > praise him with the psaltery and harp.
> Praise him with the timbrel and dance:
> > praise him with stringed instruments and organs.
> Praise him upon the loud cymbals:
> > praise him upon the high sounding cymbals.
> Let every thing that hath breath praise the Lord.

But this ecstatic endorsement was muffled by the worry that the use of instruments, a kind of labor, would interfere with proper observance of the sabbath. It was the destruction of the Second Temple in 70 C.E. that chilled the possibilities for instrumental music so conspicuous in the Psalms. The conditions that made musical worship acceptable were altered. Psalm 137, so ubiquitous in the American sacred soundscape, is taken as definitive although it actually refers to the destruction of the First Temple in the sixth century B.C.E.:

> By the rivers of Babylon, there we sat down,
> > yea, we wept, when we remembered Zion.
> We hanged our harps upon the willows in the midst thereof.
> For there they carried us away captive required of us a song;
> > and they that wasted us required of us mirth, saying,
> Sing us one of the songs of Zion.
> How shall we sing the Lord's song in a strange land?

This theme recurs in Lamentations 5:14, also written to mourn the fall of Jerusalem to the Babylonians and the subsequent dispersion of the Israelites: "The elders have ceased from the gate, the young men from their musick. The joy of our heart is ceased; our dance is turned into mourning." The idea that music represents joy and is thus totally incompatible with the sorrow and collective mourning required by the destruction of Israel and banishment of the divine presence became part of rabbinic orthodoxy and has held sway among a majority of Jewish communities down to the present. "Joy and music are for the future, for the time of total redemption, as in the passage 'Then was our mouth filled with laughter and our tongue with singing.'" It was only proper that Israel's sorrow be shared by putting away the instruments that signify triumph, replacing them with the sounds of mourning.[9]

The mysticism that developed in sixteenth-century Palestine brought about a major revaluation of music in Jewish life. "The Kabbalists viewed music too as having fallen into the realm of evil, on account of human sin," writes musicologist Eliyahu Schleifer. "It was therefore necessary to find a *tikkun* [repairing] for music, so as to lift it up towards its divine source. The *tikkun* for music was to sing it in sacred circumstances, such as during the Sabbath meal or with the holy words of prayer."[10] The Hasidic culture in which Yossele Rosenblatt came of age followed the lead of Kabbalism in celebrating music, but only within careful guidelines; many ancient strictures still held, particularly regarding gender. Samuel Rosenblatt later wrote of his father the future cantor: "when none of the men were around, his mother would croon to him melancholy Russian folksongs, or lively *Chassidic* melodies. Only when she was alone with her child would she take this liberty, for Jewish religious law did not permit singing by women in the presence of men. 'It was different, of course,' so my father used to reminisce, 'when only *I* was there. *I* was not yet a man. And so my mother could sing to me to her heart's content. And until this very day her sweet singing rings in my ears."[11]

Within this intimate familial soundscape, the filmic world of *The Jazz Singer* and the diasporic experience of Cantor Rosenblatt begin to converge. The grueling dilemma that Jack Robin faces in the film—the choice between career and culture, individual self-realization versus filial piety—was taken up in a different register by Rosenblatt. Al Jolson, who transformed himself from a runaway cantor's son into one of the leading secular entertainers of the early twentieth century, achieves a satisfying resolution of the film's knife-edged Oedipal tension by singing *Kol Nidre* while his dying father listens from his sickbed.

Cantor Rosenblatt, as renowned and commercially successful as Jolson in his own musical realm, was confronted by the Warner brothers with much the same dilemma. His remarkable career was a long exercise in triangulating the boundary of the legitimate for a cantor. He spent his childhood in the Ukraine, where, his son wrote, "The enthusiasm and zeal of the *Chassidim* entered into the very marrow of his bones. Later on it expressed itself in the tempo and the animated nature of his musical compositions and in the distinctive flavor that he injected into the traditional motifs of the prayers as he chanted them." Rosenblatt served a series of synagogues in Hungary, Austria, Germany, then various congregations around New York City, and finally in Tel Aviv, where he died of a heart attack in 1933. He continually pushed at the boundary of the musically permissible while remaining scrupulous in his adherence to Jewish law regarding diet and sabbath observance. The balance was not always easy to strike. Rosenblatt broadened his repertoire to include opera that he performed in concert halls and, for a time, in vaudeville. His decision in 1918 to turn down an offer of $1,000 a night to perform the part of Eleazar in the Chicago Opera's production of *The Jewess* made headlines in the Jewish press around the world. "I never cared for monetary success," he told an interviewer, "and I have certainly no desire to obtain glory for myself at the hands of aristocratic non-Jews who might come to the opera to see for themselves how a Jew forsakes his God and forswears his religion and his people on account of money." Rosenblatt invoked the cautionary tale of a cantor from Vilna who agreed to perform *Kol Nidre* for a countess and subsequently lost his voice and his mind, "dying a stranger among strangers sans voice, sans honor, sans a congregation."[12]

Despite its deserved reputation as a watershed film, *The Jazz Singer* had both thematic and technological precursors. Jews had appeared in Edison one-reel documentaries like *Arabian Jewish Dance* and *A Jewish Dance at Jerusalem* as early as 1903. The films depicted Hasidic life in an exotic mode, with male dancers clad in striped coats rotating like dervishes across the screen. Most pre-1927 films portraying Jews were melodramas, literary adaptations, slapstick comedies, and biblical spectacles. Jews were often stereotyped beyond the point of recognition, even by Jewish filmmakers, usually as suffering victims, always clearly Other. *Humoresque* (1920), about a poor family whose mother is devoted to her musically talented son, began a vogue for films dealing with Jewish ghetto life. But *The Jazz Singer* was unprecedented in its popular success, both in the United States and abroad. It earned Warner Brothers three million dollars, establishing it as a major studio, and launched Jolson's career as a film star. And it ensured that sound technology was the future of film. Reviews were mixed, many of them praising the special effects while criticizing the story. A critic for *Film Spectator* wrote: "It is too Jewish, a fault that I would find in it if there were too much Catholic, Mason, or anything else." Samson Raphaelson, author of the short story "Day of Atonement" (1922) and a successful 1925 stage adaptation of *The Jazz Singer* starring George Jessel, was less than impressed by the film. "I had a simple, corny, well-felt little melodrama, and they made an ill-felt, silly, maudlin, badly timed thing of it," he complained. "There was absolutely no talent in the production at all, except the basic talent of the floating camera."[13]

Harry Warner had also tried to persuade Darryl Zanuck that *The Jazz Singer* was "too Jewish," but Zanuck reminded the Warners of the success of *Nanook of the North*, and the film got made.[14] Consequently, for great numbers of Americans, many of whom had never met Jews and certainly had no inkling of the appearance or sound of their religion, *The Jazz Singer* was the first popular window into some of Judaism's most sacred rituals, practices that gave even a cantor pause. The film made a spectacle of Jewish ritual, and incidentally provided a bit of movie-palace ethnography for unsuspecting audiences. Manhattan's Strand Theatre even distributed a program during the premier of the film that included a glossary of Yiddish terms: "*Kibitzer*—a busybody. *Shiksa*—a Non-Jewess. *Cantor*—chanter of sacred hymns. *Kol Nidre*—sacred hymn chanted only on eve of Yum [*sic*] Kippur (Day of Atonement)."[15]

Kol Nidre, performed twice in *The Jazz Singer,* is both the film's most penetrating ethnographic display and its most substantial musical performance. It's no coincidence that the film premiered on 6 October 1927, the night following Yom Kippur. Given its associations with atonement, filial piety, and ethnic solidarity in the face of pressures to assimilate, no more appropriate musical symbol of reconciliation between long-estranged father and son could be imagined. *Kol Nidre* means "All Vows." It registers the annulment of all unfulfilled promises made to God by individuals over the previous year. Its purpose is to alleviate anxiety through atoning for sins, to allow worshippers to begun the Day of Atonement without the baggage of forgotten vows. Before sunset on the eve of Yom Kippur, flanked by two distinguished members of the congregation holding Torah scrolls, the cantor chants three times in Aramaic:

> All vows, bonds, obligations, promises, engagements, pledges and oaths, which we have vowed, sworn to, assumed or bound ourselves with from this Day of Atonement unto the next Day of Atonement—may it come unto us for good; lo, of all these do we repent. They shall all be absolved, released, annulled, made void and of none effect; they shall not be binding nor shall they have any power. Our vows shall not be vows; nor shall our bonds be bonds; nor shall our oaths be oaths.[16]

The origins of ritual, text, and melody have never been definitely established. The ritual is thought to extend back at least a thousand years. It has generated disapproval among Jewish authorities from the beginning, surviving because of its popular appeal to the rank and file. The melody, which also defies precise attribution, is a pastiche of melodic elements compounded from various sources, requiring creative arrangement and embellishment on the part of the cantor. The Ashkenazic version of *Kol Nidre*—Sephardic and oriental Jews use tunes that sound very different—contains more ancient *misinai* tunes (said to be passed down from Mount Sinai) than any other prayer. The form is endlessly variable—no two published versions are the same, and every cantor follows a slightly different sequence. Because of the clear influence of medieval German melodies, it's likely that the familiar Ashkenazic tune was probably composed in south-

9. A real-life cantor's son, Al Jolson sang his own excerpts of *Kol Nidre*, in Aramaic, at the climax of *The Jazz Singer* (1927). Courtesy of Wisconsin Center for Film and Theater Research, Madison.

ern Germany near the turn of the fifteenth century. But no transcriptions of the tune predate the eighteenth century, by which time it had acquired a wealth of embellishments. The two versions performed in *The Jazz Singer*—the dubbed version and the climactic version actually sung by Jolson—are standard Ashkenazic renditions, slightly abridged to save time, and without the triple repeat.[17]

As the son of a cantor, Jack possesses *Kol Nidre* in his very marrow. At the climax of the film, Jack is confronted with a stark choice: he must choose between career and ethnic identity; between glamorous Jewish girlfriend or mother; between show business and synagogue; between theater music and sacred chant. And between blackface and Jewish face. Jack Robin is not just any popular stage singer; his fame, like Jolson's, is based on a particular genre of show business, minstrelsy, as contemporary filmgoers well knew. Jack appears to be white, but as a Jew he is not really white; in blackface he appears and performs songs associated with African Americans; but neither is he black. Ironically, it is only by blacking up and singing minstrel songs that Jack can separate himself from his nonwhite origins in the Jewish "race," and "pass" as a Caucasian American. But to invoke the blackface minstrel is to summon at least a fugitive memory of the flesh-and-blood people from whom the conventions of the minstrel stage are appropriated.[18]

The notion of a deep affinity between Jews and African Americans, whether by blood or blackface, was a commonplace of the time, not least among Jews. "Is there any incongruity in this Jewish boy [Jolson] with his face painted like a Southern Negro singing in the Negro dialect?" asked a writer for *The Forward.* "No, there is not. Indeed I detected again and again the minor key of Jewish music, the wail of the *Chazan,* the cry of anguish of a people who had suffered. The son of a line of rabbis well knows how to sing the songs of the most cruelly wronged people in the world's history." A rabbi at Jolson's funeral observed: "It is from Rabbi Yoelson that he [Jolson] received the form and content of his singing. When you listened to any of his songs, you noticed the half and quarter tones, the sigh and the sob, the sudden inflections of the voice and the unexpected twist— all these are elements that come out from the Cantorial singing of our people." No less a participant-observer than George Gershwin would declare that "the Hebrew chants possess a peculiarly plaintive wail which give them a universal appeal. Men like Al Jolson and Eddie Cantor . . . owe their great success to the intense Jewish feeling they possess for melody."[19]

This Jewish facility with "sorrow songs" was regarded as a kind of racial-cultural inheritance, grounded in a history of oppression: "wounds recognize wounds," in Cynthia Ozick's formulation. Historically and culturally, blacks and Jews struck observers as having a great deal in common. Both Jews and African Americans were evidently people of the diaspora, uprooted from their respective homelands. (In minstrelsy, it was African Americans' mythic longing for the familiar old South, rather than Africa, that was stressed.) Important lines between cantorial singing and jazz music became blurred in the early twentieth century. The talents of Jewish Tin Pan Alley composers and vaudeville artists were traced to their ethnic heritage, in particular the fact that several key figures were the sons of cantors. What historian Jeffrey Melnick calls the "sacralization" of Jewish popular music had the effect of sanctifying what would otherwise have been a slightly distasteful association with African Americans and their culture. It also obscured the deep influence of African Americans' expressive culture by identifying a kind of quasi-biological source for the jazz-inflected performance of American Jews. This attribution helped smooth the process by which musical collaborations generally worked to the financial advantage of white Jews rather than that of African Americans. Their shared sense of uprootedness took musical shape in the "melancholy" sound always attributed to Jewish music, a form of "imperialist nostalgia" for a vanishing way of life whose passing is regarded with ambivalence.[20]

Associating melancholy with minor modes had as much to do with the mind's conception as the ear's perception. Melodies that struck ears conditioned by western European musical conventions as mournful or melancholy could have very different connotations for ears conditioned in eastern Europe. "Many traditional Jewish melodies . . . are in major and the minor ones are not necessarily sad and wailing, as is commonly misunderstood," argued a Jewish hymn reformer in 1931. "Melodies in minor very often reflect the deep and subtle religious spirit of the traditional synagogue."[21] One distinctive feature of Jewish music was the use of a mode called *frigish,* a scale that includes an augmented (raised) interval between the second and third steps (sometimes between the third and fourth). Derived directly from the Arab *hijaz, frigish* was used extensively by Bulgarians, Ukrainians, and Rumanians, from whom it found its way into the music of eastern European Jews.[22]

The proverbial "tear in the voice" was another notable signifier of Jewish music. When Sara Rabinowitz hears her son Jack singing in blackface as his father lies close to death, she exclaims: "He sings like his Poppa, with a tear in his voice." The phrase turned up the same year in an article by Alexander Woolcott on Irving Berlin; he remarked on "the lugubrious melodies which, in the jargon of Tin Pan Alley, have a tear in them," a sound Woolcott associated with "generations of wailing cantors." Among klezmer musicians who also favor the sound, the term of art is *krekhts,* Yiddish for "sob." Ethnomusicologist Mark Slobin has compared sonograms of *krekhts* performed by different fiddlers in order to generate a kind of "family portrait" of the technique. The sonograms reveal that fiddlers of the 1920s produced the "sonic sigh" differently from contemporary artists, who have taught themselves to reproduce the sound from recordings. "These preliminary findings do suggest that the modern krekhts is a cousin to, not a twin of, the older sigh," he concludes. "The krekhts as perfected by modern masters . . . is a bridge across an abyss of memory, spanning the Holocaust and Americanization with the smallest, most delicate stopping of the string and flicking of the finger."[23]

There was no precise equivalent to *frigish* or *krekhts* among African-American musics, but there were comparable deviations from standard western European tonalities: the use of gapped and pentatonic scales, and vocal melisma. Blues singing had its own "tear in the voice." So the perception of musical affinities between Jewish and African-American musics wasn't the result of overheated racial-cultural imaginings. As a result of the migrations of musical idioms over many centuries, the African- and Arab-derived musics did share features both at the level of deep structure and at the level of "ornamentation," melisma being a particularly important technique. Through the early decades of the twentieth century, too, Jews shared a history with African Americans: a history of migration to urban centers of the United States in the years when both Jewish popular music and jazz were incubating. Between 1880 and 1920 the number of Jews in the United States rose from 250,000 to nearly 3.4 million. More than two-thirds were immigrants from Europe. This population boom represented an increase from 0.5 percent to more than 3 percent of the total population. New York City alone increased more than twentyfold in Jewish population, from 73,000 in 1877 to nearly 1.8 million in 1927, the year of *The Jazz Singer.* Meanwhile the African-American population was also rising sharply, from just under 92,000 in 1910 to 152,000 a decade later, to nearly 328,000 by 1930.[24]

During these decades New York City became a center of the mass-culture industries, and Tin Pan Alley established itself as the hub of popular music-writing, publishing, and distribution. Jews played central roles in creating and marketing these new forms of mass culture. Entertainers like Irving Berlin, George Gershwin, Eddie Cantor, and Al Jolson acted as mediators between the suppliers and consumers of mass culture as well as among various ethnic groups in New York, chiefly Jews and African Americans but Irish Americans as well. Clearly, jazz would have developed differently if it had not been for Berlin, Gershwin, Jerome Kern, Harold Arlen, and other masters of the thirty-two-bar standard. These songwriters saw themselves as mining African-American folk musics as raw material for a higher music of the American cosmopolitan melting pot. African-American jazz artists would later invert the terms of the equation and treat Tin Pan Alley standards as the raw material from which to fashion the art of jazz.[25] Cultural exchange was hastened through the emergence of African-American Judaism during the same period, when a figure like Arnold Josiah Ford could play jazz bass and write Ethiopianist hymns as well as serve as rabbi for his congregation. The pioneering soul singer Solomon Burke, for example, grew up in Philadelphia the son of a black Jewish father and a holiness Christian mother. As cultural consumers, Jews found their experience of American life shaped by their encounter with urban commercial culture in a way that no other American ethnic subcultures had been. Second-generation Jews like Jack Robin learned how to be American from watching movies like *The Jazz Singer* and listening to songs like Berlin's "Alexander's Ragtime Band."

All of this helps explain one striking implication of *The Jazz Singer:* the moral equivalence it asserts between Orthodox Judaism and the secular religion of show business. The point is made most bluntly during the fierce argument that erupts after Jack returns home for the first time as a young man on the make in show business. He shows up at the family home in high spirits and proceeds to charm his mother in an extended session of bantering whose very banality made it revolutionary: small-talk immortalized on film. But his father soon enters, appalled. Jack soon lets slip the news about his stage appearance.

> *Cantor:* A singer in a theatre—*you* from five generations of Cantors!
> *Jack:* You taught me that music is the voice of God! It is as honorable to sing in the theatre as in the synagogue!
> My songs mean as much to my audience as yours to your congregation!
> *Cantor:* Leave my house! I never want to see you again—you *jazz singer!*

Jack reiterates the point even more bluntly to his mother, who has come to his dressing room to plead. "Would you be the *first* Rabinowitz in five generations to fail your God?" she asks. Jack shoots back: "We in the show business have our religion, too—on every day—the show *must go on!*" But doubts remain, as Jack explains to Mary: "I'd love to sing for my people—but I belong here . . . but there's something, after all, in my heart—maybe it's the call of the ages—the cry of my race . . . The Day of Atonement is the most solemn of our holy days—and the songs of Israel are tearing at my heart."

Mary responds with a line out of Max Weber's analysis of the Protestant ethic. "Your career is the place God has put you," she insists. "Don't forget *that,* Jack." Not long afterward, having lost the (short-term) struggle for Jack's soul, she stands in awe listening to his *Kol Nidre.* "A jazz singer—singing to his God," she whispers reverently to the Broadway director at her side. This is crossover at its most palpable, the disruption of both sacred/secular and racial boundaries.

THAT music of the Judaic tradition could resonate so successfully with different sectors of Jazz Age America was nothing new; it was consistent with the adaptive tendencies of Jewish music over many centuries. The history of Jewish music is a history of cultural encounters stretching from Persia and Turkey in the East to Spain and, ultimately, the Americas. "The essence of the Jewish experience with history has been that Jews have moved like peddlers from community to community, carrying their musical merchandise with them," writes Shleifer. "Some rabbis and cantors traveled to distant places expressly intending to transplant their liturgical chants to the cultural soil of foreign Jewish communities." As the Jewish diaspora bifurcated into Ashkenazic (centered in Eastern Europe) and Sephardic (centered in Iberia) groupings, it came into contact with increasing numbers of host cultures, adapting musical idioms along the way. In the words of musicologist Amnon Shiloah, Jewish music came to resemble a "musical Tower of Babel." Women played an important role as musical brokers in this exchange despite their generally proscribed role. In Yemen and other Arab countries Jewish women adopted songs of non-Jewish women, or improvised Judeo-Arabic folk poems to rural Arabic tunes for use in women's life cycle ceremonies. After the expulsion of Sephardic Jews from Spain in 1492, both gentile and Jewish songs were preserved mainly by Jewish women in the various countries to which Sephardic Jews emigrated.[26]

One diasporic eddy took place in central Europe. Beginning in the twelfth century hundreds of Jewish communities in the German Rhineland were set upon by Christian Crusaders. These Ashkenazim began migrating east, eventually settling in Poland, Russia and the Balkans. They brought a rich cultural legacy with them, including a polyglot language composed of German and Hebrew, which over the succeeding centuries folded in Slavic elements, creating Yiddish. The Rhineland Jews also brought distinctive methods of chanting the Torah, which like the language, blended ancient Judean with medieval German elements. Their synagogue tunes sounded surprisingly familiar to Jews already settled in eastern Europe, partly because the songs had escaped the Germanizing influence, with its emphasis on harmonic complexity. These ancient *misinai* tunes thought to date back to Mosaic times made inroads into both synagogue songs and secular Yiddish folk music of the region. The repertoire eventually traveled to North America with Eastern Ashkenazim during the peak immigration of the late nineteenth and twentieth centuries (and, after 1948, to Israel.)[27]

Kabbalist and later Hasidic mysticism underwrote these exchanges through the notion of *tikkun*, which provided a theological rationale for musical borrowing. "A direct and immediate result of the new freedom to recast secular melodies as sacred entities were the *piyyutim* of Israel Najara, which were based on Arabic and Turkish sounds," observes Schleifer. "Najara used to sit in Arabic coffee houses in order to learn new tunes (and was severely criticized for this, even in Kabbalistic circles). The idea of *tikkun* also inspired European Jews to introduce baroque music into the synagogue, and the same idea inspired eastern European Hasidim to adopt foreign tunes and 'Judaize' them." As in Tin Pan Alley, certain figures played key roles as mediators in this exchange process. "Cantors have done more than anyone else to introduce alien tunes into music used in the synagogue—and outside of it as well."[28]

But the expanding role of the cantor among European Jews during the modern era met resistance. Rabbis generally opposed the encroachment of cantors for the same reasons that popes and archbishops resented the way composers had appropriated sacred texts for mere "sensual" enjoyment of the musical experience. As early as the ninth century, rabbis and religious leaders from a variety of Jewish settings expressed a distrust of music's power as a seductive siren song, even if a man was doing the chanting, and they resented the potential of overelaborated music to lead worshippers away from proper piety, to put sensuous enjoyment above spirituality. There was a different sort of resentment captured by the Yiddish proverb "Ale khazonim zanen naronim" (All cantors are fools), the popular disdain for the showy aesthete. Reformed Jews had their own reasons for resisting the ascendance of cantors. In Germany, beginning early in the nineteenth century, many Jews had responded to the secular currents of the Enlightenment in part by adjusting to Protestant patterns that seemed to reflect a more universalistic worldview.

Traditional worship could strike outsiders as terribly gauche. "At the end of each strain, the whole congregation set up such a kind of cry, as a pack of hounds when a fox breaks cover," wrote one visitor to an Ashkenazi synagogue in Amsterdam. "It was a confused clamour, and riotous noise, more than song or prayer . . . I shall only say, that it was very unlike what we Christians are used to in divine service." Modern Jews should sit in pews, listen to sermons, sing congregational hymns rather than traditional *piyyutim*. "Formerly, the cantor had led the service by chanting the Hebrew prayers in the *nusach* (melodic formulas determined by liturgical time and regional style), while the congregation responded in a prescribed, albeit apparently cacophonous, manner," explains Benjie-Ellen Schiller. "Now a rabbi, who was seen as functioning akin to a Protestant minister, read the service that centered on his sermon. A four-part choir rendered the newly notated music of the prayers, which themselves were often translated into German, while the congregation prayed silently." Long sabbath services were shortened, and even architecture and décor were simplified. *Kol Nidre* was one casualty of the Reform impulse. Fearing anti-Semitic charges that the ritual proved that Jewish oaths were meaningless, the German Reform movement of the mid-nineteenth century urged that the rite be jettisoned. Not until after World War II did it reappear consistently in Reform congregations.[29]

In the United States, this Reformed ethos dominated Judaism through the end of the nineteenth century, and its impact on the practice of worship was powerful. The result was a turn toward Protestant-style hymnody. American synagogues followed their Christian counterparts in proffering congregational governance rather than strong leadership by cantors or rabbis as was often the case in Europe. In fact, neither cantors nor rabbis were to be found in America before about 1840, when a large wave of German-Jewish immigration began. Organists and choir directors were installed in synagogues, but both remained subordinate to the figure of the highly educated rabbi, modeled on the Protestant minister. Jewish leaders made frequent (and envious) reference to Protestant church music, especially the way it encouraged congregational participation in services that stressed a passive response to the spoken word. Sermons could be properly balanced by hymns. But in practice, participation in worship was often less than spirited, raising the concern of rabbis. By the end of the century a Jewish Awakening was taking place even among Reformed Jews, argues historian Jonathan Sarna; this movement was "characterized not only by a revival of certain Jewish ceremonies, like Chanukah and the synagogue celebration of Sukkot, but also by a return to distinctive Jewish terminology, such as greater use of the word 'Jew' as opposed to 'Hebrew' and 'Israelite,' and the almost complete abandonment by the Second World War of such once commonly used terms, borrowed from Protestantism, as the Jewish 'church,' the Jewish 'minister,' and the Jewish 'Easter.'" Singing needed to be part of this renewal of Jewish forms. "Music is the language . . . of humanity and we have as yet been . . . too intellectual and too little emotional," argued Rabbi Isaac Mayer Wise, the leading architect of Reformed Judaism. "We need not become Methodists . . . but we should touch the soul, make people do what they seldom do in our synagogues, cry." Another popular speaker exhorted: "Give us congregational singing which comes direct from the heart and ascends as a tribute to God."[30]

The Jewish Awakening was quickened by the massive immigration of Ashkenazim after 1880. Jews from eastern Europe brought with them a strong attachment to the experience of worship provided by the *chazzan,* or cantor, whose role had become increasingly prominent during the nineteenth century, ultimately "reigning as the musical star of the sacred world—indeed, of the musical culture as a whole." The peak decades of Jewish immigration were also the era of superstar cantors, figures with the crossover appeal of opera singers, a vogue that began in Europe but continued in New York and other cities. The competition for talent generated bidding wars that drove salaries up to astonishing levels. Cantors acted as free agents, especially in New York, where they could sell their services to the highest-bidding synagogue rather than remain rooted. The biggest stars worked out lucrative arrangements for freelance earnings outside the home congregation. Some even hired managers. Yossele Rosenblatt was considered by many to be the "king of cantors." In 1917, when World War I cut off the supply of cantors from Europe, Rosenblatt was nearly lured away from his home synagogue in New York by an offer that would have paid him $6,000 to chant for three days on high holidays alone, leaving him to freelance the rest of the year. Located on 116th Street between Fifth and Lenox, the First Hungarian Congregation Ohab Zedek was perhaps the most prestigious synagogue in the city. The board members dispatched the rabbi to talk him out of it. "Suppose you will pocket the $6,000. Then what?" he asked the cantor. "You will be like certain other individuals who possess the ability to sing, a *chazan* without an *Amud* [pulpit], a sort of gypsy. People won't think of you anymore the way they used to." The congregation raised Rosenblatt's salary, reduced his service, and allowed him to officiate outside of Ohab Zedek. He stayed at the synagogue for another decade.[31]

Celebrity cantors like Gershon Sirota, Hershman, and Rosenblatt saw little harm in performing in concert halls and vaudeville theaters, which were sometimes pressed into use for sacred services. During his career in vaudeville, Rosenblatt appeared on bills with Al Jolson, Sophie Tucker, Eddie Cantor, Fanny Brice, George Jessel, Molly Picon, and the Marx Brothers. The most celebrated cantors received regular offers to appear in opera. Through concerts and recordings they enjoyed the same sort of financial rewards and mass popularity as opera singers, and were admired by figures like Caruso. The language of a London critic on a recital at Albert Hall gives a sense of the superlatives heaped on Rosenblatt:

> You cannot talk about Cantor Rosenblatt's wonderful voice. That would be misleading. He has a series of voices. The lowest sounds like the bass tones of the cello. The middle one is a clear oboe-like tenor; and out of that he breaks straight into sweet, thick falsetto—a couple of octaves of it—for all the world like the voice of a woman soprano heard on the gramophone . . . His agility—he has a perfect trill—might make the most accomplished soprano leggiero jealous. Sometimes he begins a series of florid passages in his bass cello voice, continues in his tenor, and finishes away among his octaves of head-tones . . . And it is all wonderfully done; so wonderfully . . . that you find it difficult to believe in him as a flesh and blood singer. Only a robot, you feel, brought to extra perfection, should be able to sing like that.[32]

Some figures like Moishe Oysher (1907–1958) began their career in theater but became celebrated cantors. Richard Tucker sang both opera and lucrative Sabbath services. "Finally, there was considerable overlap in 'audience' between the Yiddish theater and the synagogue. Except for the ultra-Orthodox and those too Americanized to straddle two languages and cultures, many listeners enjoyed and criticized performances on the stage and in the sanctuary every week." In short, argues Slobin, "If the dilemma of freedom versus inherited career choice really did hold true in America, the New World was more old-fashioned than the Old."[33]

THOUGH *Kol Nidre* is *The Jazz Singer*'s most conspicuous musical performance, it's not the only distinctively Jewish music featured in the film. It stands out partly because it works into the plot of the film rather than serving as background music. There is a great deal of nondiagetic music in the soundtrack of *The Jazz Singer,* mainly excerpts from Tchaikovsky. Less familiar to most viewers is the vaguely exotic eight-bar melody that accompanies the character Yudelson "the kibitzer," a faintly comical family friend of the Rabinowitzes, a stock character of Yiddish comedy. The melody is in the *frigish,* with an augmented second between the second and third note of the scale, a mode that signifies Jewishness at its most exotic. Slobin describes the tune as "mock–Hasidic," showing how it builds on musical conventions developed by Yiddish theater for half a century. Another such tune shows up, this one with more of a stage history: "Yosl, Yosl," a 1922 hit for Nellie Casman, described as "a robust, lusty singer whose persona was every bit as vital as her material."[34] Casman's stage song points us toward another domain of Jewish music where overlaps between sacred and secular are perhaps harder to detect but no less revealing.

The word *klezmer,* a Yiddish contraction of *kley* and *zemer* ("instrument" and "song"), referred to the subculture of professional Jewish musicians of eastern Europe. Beginning at least as early as the fifteenth century, *klezmorim* provided music for a variety of festive occasions, particularly weddings, where their repertoire expanded in order to accompany a variety of dances. Influenced by liturgical chants, the wordless songs of Hasidism, and unaccompanied peasant folksongs, these musicians defied the long-standing Jewish taboo against musical instruments and were consequently considered somewhat outside the bounds of the mainstream Ashkenazic community. But their instrumental technique was deeply influenced by the expressive chants of the *chazzan,* and their music was rarely notated and generally learned and taught by ear. "Commentators like to say that Hasidic or cantorial melodies 'influenced' klezmer," writes Slobin, "but I prefer to think of styles as strands of the same musical tapestry, woven by a shared aesthetic." *Klezmorim* instruments varied by location, including fiddles, hammered dulcimers, flutes, basses, drums, and cymbals. Clarinets and brass instruments became increasingly popular in the nineteenth century, decidedly non-Jewish instruments that may have been picked up (along with costumes) from czarist Russia's army surplus in the same way African-American musicians took up trumpets and horns discarded after the Civil War.[35]

Klezmer emerged from a particularly vibrant contact zone, where musics from Turkey, Greece, Ukraine, Rumania, and Moldavia met and cross-pollinated. Always itinerant, *klezmorim* became even more mobile in the late nineteenth century as czarist persecution and industrial dislocations caused large-scale emigrations from Russia. Cultural exchange occurred within diverse Jewish communities as well as outside. "The paraliturgical tunes heard around the dinner table on Friday night at the outset of the sabbath (songs called *zmires*), the melodies mothers used to rock children to sleep, the love songs of young women, the highly ornamented and powerful prayer settings of the cantor in the synagogue—these and other components of the music culture were interwoven, stitched into a fabric of feeling that included those threads, principally wedding music, that belonged to the klezmer."[36] These musicians occupied the classic liminal status of cultural mediators, viewed with suspicion by other Jews while facing the endemic anti-Semitism of the Slavic world. But they moved back and forth between Jewish and Christian circles relatively easily, forging close bonds with another group of itinerant outsiders. *Klezmorim* and Gypsy musicians played together and even, when circumstances required, passed for one another. "Klezmorim, in short, were city-minded musical ambassadors, carrying tunes and styles across a vast network of Jewish culture that stretched from the Ottoman borderlands to the bourgeois bulwarks of central Europe," writes Slobin. "They combined the restlessness and spiritual spark of a *dybbuk* (a displaced soul seeking a body) with the cozy, gossipy communality of traditional small-town and emerging big-city Jewish life."[37]

Versatility was crucial; *klezmorim* were expected to perform repertoires and dances for celebrations of diverse ethnic background, both Jews and non-Jews, and for people of various class backgrounds. (And few *klezmorim* could support themselves through music; most held day jobs as barbers or tailors.) In this way klezmer ensembles resembled territory jazz bands that played regional circuits in the American West. Dave Tarras, a clarinetist from Ukraine who later moved to the United States, recalled traveling hundreds of miles with his father's ten-man ensemble (three fiddles, flute, clarinet, trumpet, trombone, tuba, and percussion), playing mainly waltzes and mazurkas for weddings and banquets hosted by Polish landowners and aristocrats. Like audiences for African-American territory bands, *klezmorim* were sometimes insulated from the worst forms of discrimination. "They had for us the greatest respect: they used to come for us with a wagon with four big horses, and give us good seats, and take us,"

Tarras recalls of the Polish nobility who hired them. "After two or three days (at the wedding) they gave us along [*sic*] a sack of potatoes, and chickens, and bread, and brought us back to the door. Maybe they were anti-Semites, but it never came out. They had respect." Still, *klezmorim* were well represented in the mass migration of Jews from eastern Europe after 1880. Tarras arrived relatively late, after serving a stint in a czarist military band in World War I. He left the chaos of Bolshevik Russia for New York in 1921 and got his first break two years later. Noticed as a musician who "plays Jewish beautifully," Tarras was hired by a vaudeville orchestra called "The Oriental-American Syncopators." By the end of the decade, a crack sight-reader, he was in demand in New York for recording sessions and broadcasting. As in Europe, Tarras was sometimes required to pass as Polish or Greek at recording sessions.[38]

Tarras played an indirect role in the creation of the greatest of all Yiddish musical hits (and a song that demonstrates well the sort of mythology that innovative and successful songs tend to generate). In November 1937, three young sisters from Minnesota registered their first big hit with a Yiddish show tune called "Bei Mir Bist Du Schön." Recorded exactly ten years and a month after *The Jazz Singer* opened in Manhattan, the song would prove to be another triumph for nearly everyone involved, including singers, lyricist, publisher, and, once again, Warner Brothers. The song seemed to come out of nowhere. Maxene Andrews recalled their father awakening and dragging them out to the intersection of 45th and Broadway in Manhattan. "Around the corner was a little music store, and they had put up a speaker so that this song—'Bei Mir Bist Du Schoen'—was going out over the crowd," she wrote. "The police were trying to keep the traffic moving. And all we could hear was all these people chanting, 'Play it again! Play it again!'" The song saturated the airwaves over New Year's weekend in 1938. Warner Brothers rushed to throw together a film vehicle for their surprise hit. The song gave the Andrews Sisters a first gold record for a female vocal group. It won the ASCAP award for most popular song of 1938. It was a best-seller as sheet music. Retranslated into French, Russian, Swedish, and German, "Bei Mir Bist Du Schön" had by 1950 sold somewhere near 14 million copies, and would gross millions. "While the overall influence of Yiddish music on the American landscape was slight, the effect of 'Bei Mir Bist Du Schön' on the American Jewish community was huge," writes Henry Sapoznik. It "became the anthem of second-generation Jews who saw the song's acceptance as a symbol of their own."[39]

The song actually began with a Yiddish title, "Bay Mir Bistu Sheyn" (To Me You Are Beautiful). Yiddish theater composer Sholom Secunda composed it for a 1932 musical, *Men Ken Lebn Nor Men Lost Nisht*. Though the show closed after one season, the song, which featured a clarinet solo by Dave Tarras in the bridge, was a crowd pleaser. Described in the press as an old Jewish song, the song in fact followed a conventional standard thirty-two-bar AABA structure. (Like many such standards, it included a rarely performed sixteen-bar "verse" followed by the thirty-two-bar "chorus," actually the heart of the song.) Harmonically it remained in a sturdy A minor, eschewing the more exotically "Jewish" *frigish*. Rhythmically, unlike the Jazz Age klezmer of the Dave Tarras generation, which had a nervous sort of rhythmic energy, "Bei Mir"—as opposed to "Bay Mir"— swung hard. In 1937 Secunda headed to Hollywood in pursuit of crossover dreams but was turned down by Warner Brothers as "too Jewish" (this a decade after the studio's blockbuster success with *The Jazz Singer*). Meanwhile, the lyricist Sammy Cahn and Lou Levy had seen Secunda's song performed in Yiddish at the Apollo Theater in Harlem by a pair of African-American performers named Johnnie and George. This sort of musical borrowing was not unusual; a number of African-American artists, including Ethel Waters, Paul Robeson, Willie the Lion Smith, and Duke Ellington, were drawn to Yiddish music, in particular "Eli, Eli," which was a mainstay both for Yossele Rosenblatt and Al Jolson; both Cab Calloway and Slim Gaillard recorded Yiddish songs in the late 1930s. Cahn convinced Warner's publishing subsidiary to license the song from the Kammen Brothers, who with inexplicable prescience had paid Secunda thirty dollars for rights to the song. In a twist out of *The Jazz Singer,* Cahn later said he bought his mother a house with his earnings from the hit song, while Secunda's mother spent years praying for forgiveness, convinced that her son's poor luck was due to her own sin.[40]

But it was the Andrews Sisters who made the song a hit, just as—in symbiotic fashion—they became a marquee act by recording it. Sammy Cahn knew of the song, of course, as did Lou Levy, who later managed the Andrews Sisters and was a good friend of Jack and Dave Kapp of Decca, whose label first recorded it. Recollections vary, but it seems most likely that the Andrews spotted the song on the piano at Cahn's apartment and were intrigued. They quickly recorded a Yiddish version of the song that Kapp rejected because he didn't want a "race record." Cahn and Saul Chaplin were assigned to grind out lyrics in English, but the title remained. Or rather, what had been a Yiddish title ("Bay Mir Bistu Sheyn") was Germanized, stripped of its Jewish inflections through a kind of double linguistic crossover. "Bei Mir Bist Du Schön" was a hit in Germany until the Nazis discovered that it was actually Yiddish, not German, and composed by a Jew. Attempting to ride their wave of popularity, the Andrews Sisters began performing Yiddish numbers at Jewish women's clubs, fueling rumors that they were Jewish. (Their father was Greek-born.) In February the Andrews Sisters tried to repeat their luck with another Yiddish song with English lyrics by Cahn and Chaplin. This time it was "Yosl, Yosl" (Joseph! Joseph!), the same Casman tune that figured as background music in *The Jazz Singer*. The song did reasonably well, making the *Billboard* top thirty hits in March.[41]

In the meantime "Bei Mir Bist Du Schön" was recorded by the Benny Goodman Quartet, with Martha Tilton on vocals. Goodman chose a big-band arrangement for the band's historic Carnegie Hall concert in January 1938. The song remained one of Goodman's biggest hits during the peak years of the swing era. In one of those ironies that American popular music thrives on, Goodman's great fame as "King of Swing" cast a retrospective spotlight on Dave Tarras, who became known as the "Jewish Benny Goodman" (roughly akin to dubbing Ray Charles "the Negro Nat 'King' Cole"). But in fact Goodman himself lacked any penchant for Jewish or klezmer musical stylings; he was shaped by his classical training and the blues. While his parents were Russian-born immigrants—his father from Warsaw, his mother from Lithuania—Goodman was no cantor's son. His first musical training occurred at a Chicago synagogue, and he later joined the band at Hull House, the settlement house founded by Jane Addams.[42] Lacking the touch for klezmer, Goodman delegated Jewish-jazz duties to trumpeter Ziggy Elman (Harry Finkelman), whose trumpet was featured on the flip side of "Bei Mir Bist Du Schön." It was Elman who gave the Goodman band its occasional Jewish inflection. Beginning with the Blue-bird recording of a klezmer tune Elman titled "Freilach in Swing" (And the Angels Sing), Elman developed an ABA arranging formula through which klezmer was assimilated to big-band jazz: begin with straight-ahead swing, segue into up-tempo klezmer, than return to standard swing at the end.

BENNY GOODMAN provides one ending for this complex transnational story of cantors and jazz. Like many first- and second-generation American Jews, Goodman deployed his musical brilliance to accumulate cultural capital, eventually marrying into the blue-blooded Hammond family of Park Avenue (his brother-in-law was jazz producer John Hammond). *The Benny Goodman Story* (1955), one of the best of the jazz biopics, assimilates Goodman's own life to the story of *The Jazz Singer*. Like Jack Robin, Steve Allen's Goodman strives for acceptance and a Gentile woman through assimilation. Again he succeeds by demonstrating prowess in African-American culture, attained in this case not through face paint but through the tutelage of musicians Kid Ory and Fletcher Henderson. But this Goodman is an unconflicted Jack Robin; he brought African Ameri-

cans (and Jews) into his big band, and Yiddish music into the swing repertoire, without much apparent ambivalence. The film ends at Carnegie Hall
with Ziggy Elman featured playing a klezmer trumpet solo to "Freilach in
Swing."

But this story is complex enough to warrant some alternate endings.
One would take as its central figure not the real Benny Goodman but the
"Jewish Benny Goodman," Dave Tarras, and the klezmer revival he helped
stimulate. Inspired by the 1960s folk revival that drew mainly on Anglo-
American roots music, the renascence of klezmer since the 1970s show-
cases a familiar pattern of immigrant culture: grandchildren striving to recall what the children repressed. The children of swing's jitterbug generation reached back to the music of Tarras, acquiring the conviction that
klezmer was not just fun but authentic—more so than Yiddish music theater or even Hasidic *niggun.* The destruction of European Jewry, followed
by the creation of Israel in 1948, has further complicated the lines of musical descent. Despite its clear origins in eastern Europe, klezmer has come
to be perceived as a distinctive product of the American diaspora both
in Europe and in Israel. Meanwhile, in worship, "American Jews found
themselves singing Israeli music born not in the synagogue at all but in
song competitions and popular Israeli culture," especially after the Six-
Day War. The music of modern Israel, however, comes from elsewhere.
"One of the curious ironies of music history is that much of what passes
for a 'Jewish' sound in contemporary times, adapted from Palestinian
(later Israeli) Jewish music, is in fact derived from Eastern Europe due to
the stylistic affinity between the two adjacent regions," writes Slobin, who
cites "Hava Nagila" and the accompanying dance called *hora* as an eastern European import that has become a quintessential musical symbol of
international Judaism.[43]

Perhaps this chapter would end most fittingly the way it began, with a
Hollywood version of racial cross-dressing that inverts Jack Robin's transformation in *The Jazz Singer.* The film is *Bird,* Clint Eastwood's tribute to
jazz saxophonist Charlie Parker. One scene finds the young Jewish trumpet
player Red Rodney wandering into a bar where Parker and sidemen are in
search of musicians to play in Brooklyn that afternoon. The scene cuts to
the courtyard of an Orthodox synagogue, where a wedding party is under
way. Men and women are dancing in their respective rings. Wearing yar-
mulkes, the band is playing a klezmer-sounding wedding tune. The bride
and groom are hoisted up on their chairs. As Parker begins pouring a torrent of notes over the melody, the father of the bride studies the band in-
tently. Then, seeing his daughter laughing, he smiles and murmurs: "Fantastic." Delighted young girls gather around the musicians to watch the

intriguing music more closely. Afterward the father hands Rodney (whose real name turns out to be Chudnik) some bills as payment. "These are not Jewish boys," he tells Rodney, "but good."[44] They could have been black Jews, of course, but that's beside the point. In sixty years, *The Jazz Singer* had come full circle, reversing its poles from a Jew in blackface to blacks in Jewish-face.

CHAPTER EIGHT

Come Sunday

> There in my solitude, I began to browse over the keys like a gentle
> herd pasturing on tender turf. Something happened to me there. I
> had a strange feeling inside. A sudden calm—a quiet stillness. As
> my fingers began to manipulate over keys, words began to fall in
> place on the melody like drops of water falling from the crevices
> of a rock.
>
> —THOMAS A. DORSEY

LIKE many sacred songs, the gospel classic "Just a Closer Walk with
Thee" appeared with the kind of serendipity befitting a Shaker "gift
song." According to a widely told story, composer Kenneth Morris heard a
railroad porter singing the song during a stop at a train station. Morris
boarded the train but couldn't get the song out of his head; he got off at the
next station, where he switched to a train heading in the opposite direction, back toward the infectious song. He got off the train, found the porter, had him sing the song, and jotted down the words and music. Shortly
afterward Morris published a revised version of what he had heard, a song
that became both a favorite church song and a frequently covered jazz
standard.[1]

A striking number of hymns and gospel songs have this sort of story attached to them, but generally the circumstances are bleaker. Personal tragedy has been easily the leading incubator of Protestant evangelical music.
Poignant origin stories provide crucial endorsements of some of the most
long-lasting and beloved hymns and songs. The list of Christian hymns
that are said to have emerged directly out of crisis and tragedy—the death
of children, spouses, close friends; terminal illness, paralysis, depression,
mental collapse; debt, imprisonment, war horror—is remarkable. That a
song grows directly out of personal crisis or suffering authorizes it to
speak to the travails of others; it serves as a spiritual imprimatur. The song
can reach people in times of crisis and suffering because it has emerged out

of crisis and suffering, not out of the songwriting factories of Tin Pan Alley or Nashville. The list of famous gospel songs and hymns revered for the circumstances of their origin is long and distinguished: Charles Converse's "What a Friend We Have in Jesus," Joseph Scrivener's "All Is Well with the Lord," Robert Lowry's "Shall We Gather at the River," Kenneth Morris' "Just a Closer Walk with Thee." In recent years, volumes like *Songs in the Night: Inspiring Stories behind 100 Hymns Born in Trial and Suffering,* written by a colonel in the Salvation Army, and *Ev'ry Time I Feel the Spirit: 101 Best-Loved Psalms, Gospel Hymns, and Spiritual Songs of the African-American Church* have appeared.[2]

No song has been surrounded by a more dramatically charged set of tragic circumstances than "Take My Hand, Precious Lord." Written by Thomas A. Dorsey, a piano-playing bluesman from Chicago, the song may be the most celebrated of all in twentieth-century black gospel. Composed in the aftermath of the death of Dorsey's wife and infant son, "Precious Lord" is credited with launching the career of Dorsey as the foremost composer and impresario of African-American gospel music. All told, Dorsey would write some 500 gospel songs, not including his blues and jazz compositions. During the 1950s and 1960s he so dominated the world of black gospel that gospel songs were referred to simply as "Dorseys" (in the same way that all raised hymns were known as "Dr. Watts" in African-American congregations).[3] In composing "Precious Lord," the erstwhile bluesman Dorsey, torn for several years between his desire for worldly acclaim and his resolution to forsake worldly music in favor of a Christian calling, came down decisively on the side of the religious call. Or alternatively, "Precious Lord" revealed to Dorsey a recipe for church music that would allow him to combine worldly success—as father of gospel blues and longtime leader of the National Convention of Gospel Choirs and Choruses—with a sense of doing the Lord's work.

Duke Ellington told very different stories about the inspirations for his compositions. But decades later, the same dynamic revealed itself in his career. Unlike Dorsey, who was in his early thirties and little known outside Chicago when he developed the formula that was to define his career, Ellington had long been world famous by the time he crossed the musical line into the sacred. His greatest honors—the White House lionizing by Lyndon Johnson and Richard Nixon, the Ivy League honorary degrees, the infamous brush with the Pulitzer—were yet to come, but by 1958, when he recorded "Come Sunday," Ellington had amassed all the fame and name recognition (not to be confused with commercial success, of course) that it was possible for an African-American composer to obtain. As with Dorsey, the recording signaled a new direction for Ellington, a preoccupation with sacred music that was to dominate the last decade of his very active career. "Now I can say openly what I have been saying to myself on my knees," he would write later of his turn toward sacred music.[4] Both Dorsey and Ellington accomplished the resolution of their lifelong need to harmonize musical, worldly, and spiritual goals partly through collaboration with the same vocalist, Mahalia Jackson, who served as a kind of musical midwife and muse for the two composers.

The notion of crossover is crucial to understanding both the musical development of Dorsey and Ellington and the larger world of American popular music of the twentieth century. Most familiar is the phenomenon of racial crossing, whereby the music of one ethnic or racial group is adapted by another, typically flowing from African-American sources to European-American performers and audiences. This is the classic story of American "love and theft": Elvis Presley absorbing gospel and rhythm and blues, Mick Jagger the sounds of Chicago blues.[5] Somewhat less obvious is the crossing of the very porous boundary between sacred and nonsacred musics. If the history of American music is the history of whites blacking up—admiring, expropriating, co-opting, mimicking, celebrating black music—it is equally the story of singers and musicians learning from and then leaving the churches, taking techniques evolved for praising God in the sanctuary and adapting them to the nightclub, cabaret, dance hall, and concert stage. Closely related is the crossover between performance in a venue where tickets are sold to audience members and worship in a space where a congregation has gathered to participate as a community of faith.

The always-porous boundary between sacred and nonsacred can be crossed from both directions, though. While Dorsey, Ellington, and, to use a contemporary example, jazz composer Wynton Marsalis have crossed over to the sacred from the realms of blues and jazz, many artists have moved in the other direction—Ray Charles, for example—or have oscillated between sacred and secular throughout their careers, as have Rosetta Tharpe, Al Green, and Aretha Franklin. In all cases, the sacred-secular boundary is an extremely labile one, constructed and signaled by particular choices made about the space in which music is performed, the use of particular instruments, the dress worn by performers, the texts used, and the musical forms presented.

THERE are some uncanny parallels in the lives of Thomas Andrew Dorsey and Edward Kennedy Ellington. Both were born in 1899, the year after the United States went to war with Spain in Cuba and the Philippines, and three years after the Supreme Court's *Plessy* decision ushered in the harshest phase of Jim Crow segregation. Dorsey and Ellington grew up first-born sons in notably stable nuclear families; both absorbed major influences from their fathers and maintained extremely close ties to doting mothers. Etta Dorsey seems to have been a model of piety and provided constant musical stimulation within the family through her singing and organ playing. Dorsey's father was an itinerant Baptist preacher who had studied for a time at Atlanta Baptist College but who was forced to work as a sharecropper to support his family. Through him young Dorsey was exposed to the respect and hospitality showered on ministers in the African-American South, an initiation that would fuel Dorsey's own drive for attention. One of his earliest memories was of "playing church" under his family's front porch, hanging up a small cane just as his father did and addressing an imaginary congregation.[6]

Ellington likewise absorbed his fabled rakish bonhomie from his father, a coachman and butler for a white physician and occasional butler at the White House and embassy functions. In contrast to her husband's flair, Daisy Ellington was like Etta Dorsey a pianist, and also notably pious; she took charge of her son's religious upbringing, bringing him each Sunday to the Nineteenth Street Baptist church of her family and the John Wesley A.M.E. Zion church favored by her husband's side of the family. From Sunday school Ellington remembered getting a "wonderful feeling of security" and a narrative imagination shaped by vivid Bible stories. In an essay titled "Mother," Dorsey captured a sentiment that runs through Ellington's own writings about his family: "Mother in her office holds the key of the soul, and she it is who stamps the coin of character and makes the being, who would be a savage but for her gentle cares, a Christian man."[7]

There was, however, a major difference in the economic standing of the Dorsey and Ellington families. The Ellingtons were relatively affluent members of Washington, D.C.'s thriving bourgeoisie. Edward never lacked for whatever material and educational advantages were available to the capital's African-American population. The Dorseys were from rural Georgia and, despite the fact that Etta had purchased some land (probably with a settlement from the death of her first husband, a railroadman killed by a train), were driven to sharecropping and eventually, in 1908, to migrate from rustic Villa Rica to Atlanta. A displaced country boy in the city, Dorsey eventually carved out a modicum of social standing through his piano playing, hanging around theaters and developing his skills of improvisation at house parties and bordellos. The quest for musical opportunities led Dorsey to join the wartime migration of rural southern blacks to Chicago in 1916, though the severity of Chicago winters drove him back to Atlanta for parts of the next two years. Ellington also discovered the urban demimonde as a teenager, hanging around poolrooms and burlesque shows, playing piano at house parties and dances. By the age of twenty he was successful enough at music and other enterprises to have married and bought a house, but like Dorsey he aspired to a larger musical stage, making his first forays to Manhattan in 1923 (with periodic retreats back to the District of Columbia). Ellington established the nucleus of his big band under the name the Washingtonians, which played at a cabaret in Times Square; permanent national fame came four years later, with the move to Harlem's Cotton Club and its invaluable radio hookup.

Dorsey's career trajectory can't help appear desultory in comparison to Ellington's meteoric rise, but by ordinary standards it was dramatic. His twenties were punctuated by a series of psychological crises. Dorsey also faced the challenge of adjusting his southern blues stylings to a musical culture dominated by the showier sounds of vaudeville and what was coming to be called jazz. Fortunately for Dorsey, blues was just beginning to emerge as a major commercial music. He developed his skills as an arranger and copyrighted his first composition, a blues titled "If You Don't Believe I'm Leaving, You Can Count the Days I'm Gone," in 1920. But late that year he had overextended himself to the point of collapse, and had to be rescued in Chicago and taken home to Atlanta by his mother. Back in Chicago the next year, Dorsey was inspired by the performance at the National Baptist Convention of the famous recording preacher "Professor" W. M. Nix. He was "born again" and vowed to recommit his life to Christ by dropping the blues; but soon he was back at it. Dorsey's big break, the equivalent of Ellington's Cotton Club gig, came when he debuted with blues singer Ma Rainey at Chicago's Grand Theater in 1924. The following year he married Nettie Harper. But for the second time Dorsey suffered a nervous breakdown, this time after completing a successful tour with Rainey; again he swore off the blues but found himself creeping back to the commercial success it offered. This time Dorsey teamed up with the guitarist Hudson Whitaker to record a series of salacious-sounding novelty blues with titles like "Somebody's Been Using That Thing," "It's All Worn Out," and, most famously, "It's Tight like That," lighthearted doggerel for which Dorsey earned $2,400 in the first royalty check alone. However, Dorsey soon lost his royalty earnings through a bank failure, which he and Nettie took as a sign of divine displeasure with the blues.[8]

Determined never again to backslide, Dorsey studied and applied the success of recorded sermons by preachers like Nix and the even more commercially successful Reverend J. M. Gates, from Atlanta. To sell his sheet-music gospel songs, Dorsey needed a singer with the power and authority of a preacher like Gates or Nix (or of a blues singer like Bessie Smith). He found one in the Reverend E. H. Hall. Their collaboration led to Dorsey's breakthrough at the National Baptist Convention in Chicago in 1930. His composition "If You See My Savior" became a huge success after its performance at a morning service, selling thousands of copies at the meeting and cementing his reputation with influential national figures responsible for music in the Baptist hierarchy. But it was "Precious Lord" that fulfilled the potential of the gospel idiom Dorsey had helped pioneer. The song marked the transition in Dorsey's approach from *showing* how an individual might struggle to be saved rather than *preaching* about salvation; from a composer of rather conventional paeans to Christian salvation to one who demonstrated the desperate call of those in need of faith. Moreover, it was the song that enabled, or at least coincided with, Dorsey's breaking free of the destructive whipsaw of his ambitions for worldly success and his calling to a Christian life.

In August 1932 Dorsey was at a gospel convention in St. Louis, accompanied by a vocalist and the assistant director of the newly formed gospel chorus at Pilgrim Baptist Church. Nettie Dorsey was expecting their first child any day. The business trip had begun inauspiciously, with Dorsey forgetting the sheet music he had hoped to market. While directing a concert that night, Dorsey received a telegram announcing that Nettie was very ill. Just after the concert he was informed by telephone that she had died while giving birth to a son. The infant, to be named Thomas Andrew Jr., died during the night. As the full devastation set in, Dorsey felt that he could not go on alone. "I needed help; my friends and relations had done all they could for me," he recalled. "I was failing and did not see how I could live." A colleague invited him to walk over to a nearby beautician's school whose common room had a piano. Dorsey sat down and began noodling on the piano, working through a familiar Baptist hymn. He called his friend. "I said, 'Come on Frye! Listen to this. Come over here to this piano! I got this tune and I'm trying to put words with it.'" Dorsey played and sang the piece. "It's all right, sounds good," was the initial response.

> I went over it again. He said, "No man, no. Call Him 'precious Lord.' Don't call him 'blessed Lord'; call him 'precious Lord.'"
> "Why, why? He *is* a blessing."
> "Call Him 'precious Lord.'"
> And that thing like something hit me and went all over me, see. I said, "That does sound better! That's it." And that hooked right in there. The words dropped just like drops of water . . . from the crevice of a rock.[9]

Dorsey finished the song in the next "day or two." The hymn on which Dorsey had improvised his soon-to-be gospel classic was, of all things, an old English hymn. The text, written by an Anglican-turned-Nonconformist named Thomas Shepherd, first appeared in a 1693 hymnbook, one of the few that preceded Watt's collection of 1707. The tune, familiar to Dorsey through the *National Baptist Hymnal,* was of much more recent vintage. Known as "Maitland," it was composed in 1852 by George Nelson Allen, a professor at Oberlin who was much influenced by Lowell Mason's hymn reforms and theories about the "science" of hymn-writing. Allen's revised version of Shepherd's "Must Jesus Bear the Cross Alone?" was quickly absorbed into the canon of leading hymns. The two texts bear some comparison.

Must Jesus bear the cross alone,	Precious Lord, take my hand, lead me on, let me stand,
And all the world go free?	I am tired, I am weak, I am worn:
No, there's a cross for every one,	Through the storm, through the night, lead me on to the light:
And there's a cross for me.	Take my hand, precious Lord, lead me home.
How happy are the saints above,	When my way grows drear, precious Lord, linger near
Who once went sorrowing here!	when my life is almost gone,
But now they taste unmingled love	Hear me cry, hear my call, hold my hand, lest I fall:
And joy without a tear.	Take my hand, precious Lord, lead me home.
The consecrated cross I'll bear	When the shadows appear and the night draws near,
Till death shall set me free;	and the day is past and gone,
And then go home my crown to wear,	At the river I stand, guide my feet, hold my hand:
For there's a crown for me.[10]	Take my hand, precious Lord, lead me home.

Shepherd's hymn, like Dorsey's earlier gospel songs, assumes that salvation is achieved, and looks ahead to coming reward. "Precious Lord" has no such assurance; rather than an announcement of solidarity with Christ and the saints, Dorsey's text is a moan of raw need. It is wordier; Dorsey substitutes three-syllable anapests for Shepherd's iambs. Moreover, "Precious Lord" reverses a convention of gospel song by placing the refrain first. In order to mirror the rhetorical structure of black preaching, a goal he had taken up in his songwriting, Dorsey needed to find a way to reach a climax in the verse rather than in the refrain. Since the first eight bars (two lines) are harmonically interchangeable with the second eight (AA in effect), Dorsey signals the song's climax not through a cadence of chords leading to harmonic resolution but by placing the sort of melodic material usually associated with refrains—high notes, melodic leaps, melisma, and blue notes—in the verse. "Now the melody's an old melody, but they couldn't turn it around, twist it as much as I could," Dorsey pointed out. "They can't handle it with the embellishments and the beauty, you know, the trills and the turns that I put in it, see?"[11]

In effect, Dorsey had "raised a Dr. Watts" while plunking at the piano—not quite literally, but at least a near contemporary and spiritual fellow traveler of Isaac Watts. He had signified on—ornamented—an old chestnut of Christian hymnody, transforming a product of Anglo dissenting Protestantism into a recognizably African-American sacred song. The musical impact of the hymn had been altered, but so had its message and its theology. Whereas the spirituals of enslaved African Americans had emphasized the inscrutable God of the Old Testament and identified themselves with characters and scenarios out of the Hebrew Bible, the new urban gospel drew those singing the music into close contact with a far more comforting and approachable Lord Jesus.

The story of Dorsey and the creation of his most lasting gospel song joins a larger narrative about social class and cultural hierarchy in Chicago's black churches. The African-American population of the city swelled by nearly 150 percent between 1910 and 1920, from about 44,000 to 109,000; it would more than double again by 1930, to 234,000.[12] The tens of thousands of southern African Americans who like Dorsey migrated to Chicago during World War I entered a social milieu in which they were "scorned and 'buked," regarded as uncouth and disreputable by a black middle class jealous of whatever small steps toward acceptance by white Chicago they had been able to achieve. Protestant church life was sharply divided between "old-line" established churches, mainly Baptist and Methodist (Ebenezer Baptist, Metropolitan, Pilgrim Baptist), and the storefront holiness and Pentecostal churches that catered to recent arrivals from the South. Worshippers at the storefronts could expect to "have church" with the customary demonstrative congregational participation they were accustomed to from southern rural church life. Worship at the old-line sanctuaries was in contrast markedly subdued: calling out in response to preaching was discouraged, and in place of gospel shouts churchgoers were expected to sing decorously from the canon of Anglo-American hymnody. Musical worship was important, but took the form, apart from the congregational hymns, of elaborate "musicales" performed by trained choirs whose repertoire was either masterworks of the European sacred art tradition or carefully arranged "concert spirituals" of the sort pioneered half a century earlier by the Fisk Jubilee Singers. Sacred music should be uplifting, and to be uplifting it needed to conform to the genteel codes of urban white middle-class Protestants. Only in this way would the "race" improve itself.[13]

Dorsey and his cohorts had another sort of uplift in mind. "I wrote to give them something to lift them out of that Depression," he said. "They could sing at church but the singing had no life, no spirit . . . We intended gospel to strike a happy medium for the downtrodden." Gospel choruses of the sort organized in 1931 at Ebenezer Baptist Church by Dorsey in collaboration with its new pastor, Dr. James Howard Lorenzo Smith, shook the hierarchy of the African-American church in Chicago. Worshippers accustomed to more emotional and participatory worship would no longer feel marginalized by unfamiliar music performed by trained choirs who deployed music to assert their perceived educational and social advantages. The gospel choruses would provide crucial sites for participation by women in the largely patriarchal institutions of the old-line churches. Women had found greater latitude in storefront churches, and as gospel choruses brought some of the ethos of that music into old-line churches, women found their possibilities expanded. Excluded from the pulpit during regular services (revival meetings were more liberal on this score), women could lead gospel choirs and "preach" through the medium of song. Dorsey in fact sought a strong female vocalist to complement his abilities as a composer-arranger, a kind of sanctified version of blues singer Ma Rainey. Throughout the 1930s Dorsey had worked and recorded with Sallie Martin, possessor of a powerful sermonic technique, of whom Dorsey said, "Sallie can't sing a lick, but she can get over anywhere in the world." Martin was also an effective business manager for Dorsey's expanding gospel-music business, tightening up the lackadaisical marketing and distribution of his sheet-music songs.[14]

More significant than Martin as an icon of gospel song was a teenager Dorsey met in 1928, just a year after she arrived in Chicago from New Orleans. Like Dorsey the child of a Baptist preacher, the young Mahalia Jackson had studied closely the vocal stylings of the great blues singers of the 1920s, but she had kept her distance from secular music (as she would throughout her career). At her aunt's church, Greater Salem Baptist, she met and quickly joined a group of brothers in a quartet that called itself the Johnson Gospel Singers. For their renditions of down-home southern song, the Johnson Singers were sometimes ejected from churches. "One pastor was so offended by the group's singing that he threw them out of his church, saying 'Get that twisting and jazz out of the church,'" reports

Harris. "On her way out of the door, Jackson replied, 'This is the way we *sing* down South!'" She recalled her first and only singing lesson with a Professor DuBois, a "great Negro tenor" with "a very grand way about him" who ran a music salon on Chicago's South Side. After several attempts to coach the young singer, he finally told her bluntly: "The way you sing is not a credit to the Negro race. You've got to learn to sing songs so that white people can understand them."[15]

Jackson responded quickly to the gospel songs of Dorsey, who, she later judged, "is to gospel music what W. C. Handy is to the blues." She provided a major boost to the still-struggling sacred songwriter. "She was the only singer who would take my music, then," recalled Dorsey, "but Mahalia would stand on a street corner and demonstrate it; then we'd sell a batch: 10¢ each. She was actually about the only gospel singer, besides Sallie Martin when she came in." According to Dorsey, Jackson came to him for vocal coaching, and he helped her with timing, dynamics, pacing, and repertoire. He was trying to instill the rhetorical form of the black sermon. Gospel blues replicated in an urban setting the communal experience of the antebellum "hush harbor," where a "caller" would evoke responses among participants as co-worshippers rather than as a subservient flock responding to an authoritative leader. This was the experience of worship that individuals could obtain in the urban storefront churches, and it was a dynamic that could be smuggled into old-line churches through gospel choruses. And with proper training, Dorsey was convinced, Jackson had the talent to serve as such a caller, inspiring a response without dictating it, eliciting and evoking through example rather than through prescription. "She had a voice that nobody ever had or anybody ever will have . . . the trills, tones, the spirit," said Dorsey. "She enjoyed her religion—that was the key, the core."[16]

And Mahalia Jackson in fact became a gospel icon: "The World's Greatest Gospel Singer." She built a national reputation in the 1930s and 1940s, recording her first major hit, "Movin' On Up," for Decca in 1946. The next year, her recording of "Move On Up a Little Higher" sold a million copies for Apollo and launched her as a crossover artist with a substantial white audience. During the 1950s and 1960s she recorded for Columbia, with all its prestige and commercial clout. Soon afterward Jackson was featured on the *Ed Sullivan Show*, invited to give a concert at Carnegie Hall, and made the official soloist for the National Baptist Convention. She was the voice of African-American religion on epochal state occasions like the inauguration of John F. Kennedy and the 1963 March on Washington. Jackson was prominent during the civil rights era, a friend of Martin Luther King Jr., at whose funeral she sang "Precious Lord." Her prodigious talents exposed her to the same pressures that had confronted Cantor Rosenblatt a generation earlier. Beginning in the 1930s, when she was invited to sing in an all-black production of *The Mikado*, Jackson fended off attempts to get her to expand her repertoire to include nonsacred music. "Religion is too important to fiddle around with," she told an interviewer about her decision to turn down a part in a "religious musical" on Broadway. "Now that play might be good. I'm not saying it isn't. But I wouldn't feel right singing in a show."[17] Jackson found herself of interest to scholars starting to probe the origins and formal features of African-American roots music. Invited to an academic symposium on the origins of jazz at a retreat center near Tanglewood, she spent a week fielding queries from professors:

> They backed me up into a corner and asked me about colored church music and the way some congregations clap their hands and tap their feet. They talked about blues singers, and about the field calls and chants the colored people had made up when they were slaves in the fields of the rice plantations. They kept me singing songs for them and analyzing my style and disputing with me about why I did it just that way until I got all heated up, too.
>
> One young professor kept insisting that I didn't even know my own meter. "You tell us you're singing four-four time," he said, "but I tell you you're not. You're singing twelve-twelve time."
>
> "You're telling me wrong," I shouted. "I stand up here tapping my own foot with a four-four beat and you tell me I'm tapping twelve-twelve. One of us is crazy."[18]

A COLLABORATION between the World's Greatest Gospel Singer and Duke Ellington seems a musical odd couple, the profane Saturday Night Function meeting the sacred Sunday Morning Function on ground that couldn't possibly be neutral. Perhaps fittingly, what brought Jackson and Ellington together was the bottom-line material reality of food. Ellington loved to eat, Jackson loved to cook, and according to one story, possibly apocryphal, Ellington worked his legendary charm by finding ways to have Jackson invite him over for meals, than praising her so effusively that she couldn't refuse his request to record with him. His memoir recounts Ellington being approached by a representative from Columbia Records during a party aboard a yacht on Lake Michigan.

> "Say, you must hear this new girl we've got signed up!" he said.
> "Who's that?"
> "Mahalia Jackson."
> "Oh yeah, she's a good cook."
> "No, she's a singer."
> "I know," I said, "but she's a good cook, too."[19]

In 1958 they met in a Columbia recording studio in California to record the piece called "Come Sunday." Billy Strayhorn had sent in his arrangement from Florida. According to the producer, Irving Townsend, "Duke treated this first performance like a kind of divine revelation and would not let Mahalia repeat it until the next day. Then, he asked her to sing it not for records but for him," recalled Townsend. "She sang the never-used Take 2 of *Come Sunday* the following afternoon without a light in the studio and without a sound from the band. It was one of those unpredictable moments which seem to bloom when Ellington is around." Ellington reported the encounter favorably, and in hindsight realized it foreshadowed the major work of his last decade. "This encounter with Mahalia Jackson had a strong influence on me and my sacred music," he would write jauntily in his memoir, "and also made me a much handsomer kid in the Right Light." For Jackson, the session seems to have been fraught with anxiety and ambivalence. Her memoir fails to mention it—although the book contains a snapshot of Jackson and Ellington at the session—and her authorized biography quotes her as saying, "I been wrestling with this thing . . . they want to put me with Duke to sell more for Columbia." In addition to ethical qualms was musical anxiety. According to a friend, "She was scared about the music, she was scared about the big orchestra, and she was scared they were pulling her away from her gospel." On top of that, Ellington caught her by surprise with a request to improvise a sung rendition of a psalm: "'Sing what?' She couldn't believe her ears. 'The 23rd Psalm,' said Duke airily. Halie [Mahalia] grew still. 'I don't know nothing about that.' Duke struck a chord. 'Open your Bible and *sing*, woman.'" Critic Stanley Crouch would describe the result as an "overwhelming masterpiece . . . Ellington brings this beacon of gospel majesty into a context of modern sound far more harmonically complex and thick with dissonance than any she had ever encountered before or would ever be part of again"—undoubtedly a relief to Jackson.[20]

But it is the luscious melody of "Come Sunday," not the Twenty-third Psalm, that musically dominates the 1958 Ellington-Jackson recording. In addition to the vocal rendition by Jackson, there is an instrumental version featuring Ray Nance on violin. The lyrics, which vary slightly among different recordings, are saturated in biblical imagery.

Lord, dear Lord, of love, God Almighty, God of love,
Please look down and see my people through.

Be thou exalted, O God, above the heavens:
and thy glory above all the earth;
That thy beloved may be delivered:
save with thy right hand, and answer me. (Psalm 108:5–6)

I believe the sun and moon will shine
up in the sky.
When the day is gray I know it's
clouds passing by.

Thus saith the Lord,
which giveth the sun for a light by
day,
and the ordinances of the moon and
of the stars for a light by night . . .
(Jeremiah 31:35)

Lilies of the valley, they neither toil
nor spin
And flowers bloom, and springtime
birds sing.

Consider the lilies of the field,
how they grow; they toil not, neither
do they spin. (Matthew 6:28)
For, lo, the winter is past, the rain is
over and gone; The flowers appear
on the earth; the time of the singing
of birds is come and the voice of the
turtle is heard in our land. (Song of
Solomon 2:11–12)

Often we feel weary but he knows
our every care
Go to him in secret he will hear your
every prayer.

O Lord, thou hast searched me,
and known me. (Psalm 139:1)
Come unto me, all ye that labour
and are heavy laden, and I will give
you rest. (Matthew 11: 28)

Up from dawn till sunset man works
all day
Come Sunday, oh Come Sunday,
that's the day.

Man goeth forth unto his work
and to his labour until the evening.
(Psalm 104:23)

"Come Sunday" resembles Dorsey's "Precious Lord" in one important aspect. Its refrain—"Lord, dear Lord, of love, God Almighty, God of love, Please look down and see my people through"—comes before the verse: "I believe the sun and moon will shine up in the sky, When the day is gray I know it's clouds passing by." Both refrain and verse are eight bars long, and as "Come Sunday" was performed in 1958 and in subsequent recordings, it has the unexpected impression of sounding like a standard thirty-two-bar AABA popular song. That's because the refrain not only comes first, but is played twice, followed then by the verse. When the refrain comes up again—"He'll give peace and comfort to every troubled mind, Come Sunday, oh Come Sunday, that's the day"—it sounds like the final, eight-bar A section that appears after the bridge in a thirty-two-bar standard. In this sense "Come Sunday" generates a kind of instability—the listener's sense of being pulled back toward the refrain is foiled by the unexpected return of the verse, which makes its demand for resolution in the refrain.[21]

The genesis of "Come Sunday" is very different from the traumatic origin of Dorsey's "Precious Lord." Nearly from the beginning of his career as a recording artist, Ellington explored the musical and dramatic potential of black sacred music. His early "Black and Tan Fantasy," made into a short film by RKO in 1929, opens with a mournful theme played by trumpeter Bubber Miley, using a plunger mute. The mournful melody is said to be based on an old spiritual that Miley's mother sang to him often when he was a child, possibly "Hosannah" or a white gospel hymn titled "The Holy City." The film story is a kind of morality play, pitting the Saturday night milieu of the nightclub against the sacred space of the church, represented in the film by the Hall Johnson Singers. These figures recur in a second Ellington film, the nine-minute *Symphony in Black: A Rhapsody of Negro Life,* which outlines some of the themes that Ellington would explore later in *Black, Brown and Beige.* Like the latter, it begins with work ("The Laborers"), moves through romance ("A Triangle") in a sequence that marks the film debut of Billie Holiday, and finally to African-American religion ("Hymn of Sorrow"), where mourners gather in a church to lament the death of a baby.[22] The melody that came to be known as "Come Sunday" first appeared in 1943, as part of Ellington's extended work *Black, Brown and Beige,* which was performed in its entirety for the first and only time at a Carnegie Hall benefit concert for Russian war relief held as part of New York City's newly designated "Ellington Week." "Come Sunday" was the suite's dominant melody, appearing at least briefly in all three sections. The song "was intended to depict the movement inside and outside the church, as seen by workers who stood outside, watched, listened, but were not admitted," according to Ellington. "This is developed to the time when the workers have a church of their own. The section ends with promises. I felt that the kind of unfinished ending was in accordance with reality, that it could not be tied, boxed, and stored away when so much else remained to be done."[23]

The exact circumstances and sources of inspiration of "Come Sunday" are unknown. Its melody is difficult to associate with other songs by Ellington or other composers. Some evidence exists in the form of a twenty-nine-page narrative sketch in Ellington's hand describing the experiences of an African man named Boola. Kidnapped from his homeland, Boola is imprisoned and starved on a slave ship bound for America; in "the adjoining cabin a woman is screaming—a symphony of torture," according to Ellington. Probably because of the patriotic imperatives of wartime, Ellington dropped the graphic opening movements, to be titled "Africa" and "Slaveship." He begins instead with "Work Song." "The first thing the Black man did in America was WORK," Ellington wrote, "and there the Work Song was born . . . a song of burden." Boola finds a Bible and laboriously learns to read; scripture provides him with "something to live for—something to work for—something to sing for. Come Sunday, while all the Whites had gone into the church, the slaves congregated under a tree," Ellington continues. "Huddled together, they passed the word of God around in whispers . . . He must enjoy the sweet suffering of this profound internal upheaval of love and joy in silence . . . Good souls praying and singing faithfully, without a word of bitterness or revenge—'I forgive my past suffering, just let my people go.'"[24]

The location of "Come Sunday" is thus the devotional space of the hush harbor. It is a sacred space created by enslaved Africans outside the view and the knowledge of their white masters and mistresses. The Fisk Jubilee Singers had revealed it with enormous effect in "Steal Away." Dorsey had succeeded in capturing the spiritual energy of the urban hush harbors in his gospel choruses, finding in the powerful voices of Mahalia Jackson and others the authority of the caller, able to elicit responses from worshippers without dominating them. Ellington's sacred imagination was turning on the same social location, a site saturated in Christianity yet physically and spiritually worlds apart from it.

After performances of the suite in the mid-1940s, "Come Sunday" seems to have lain dormant until 1958. It was in the years after the collaboration with Mahalia Jackson, as Ellington entered his sixties, that he came to plumb the spiritual aspects of his music to the exclusion of nearly everything else. "Come Sunday" would recur frequently in Ellington's final decade. For the centennial of the Emancipation Proclamation, in 1963, Ellington composed, choreographed, and helped direct a musical revue, *My People*, at the McCormick Theatre in Chicago. Drawing on themes he had explored earlier, Ellington developed a revised up-tempo version of "Come Sunday" featuring tap dance and words from 2 Samuel. He composed several new gospel songs—"Ain't But the One," "Ninety-nine Percent," "Will You Be There?"—and a tribute to Martin Luther King Jr., titled "King Fit the Battle of Alabam," which staged Martin Luther King as Joshua in Bull Connor's Jericho.

Many of these pieces went into the Concert of Sacred Music commissioned and first performed in 1965 at the Episcopal Grace Cathedral on Nob Hill in San Francisco, and at year's end at the Fifth Avenue Presbyterian Church in Manhattan. That concert opened with the overture to *Black, Brown and Beige* as reworked by Ellington for *My People*, followed by a new composition based on the first four words of the Bible: "In the Beginning God" (which won a Grammy the next year). "Come Sunday" appeared no fewer than four times: an instrumental version featuring alto player Johnny Hodges (who had debuted the melody at Carnegie Hall in

1943); a choral version by the Herman McCoy Choir; a Mahalia-esque gospel version sung by Esther Marrow; and the up-tempo version featuring tap dancer Bunny Briggs and a text from 2 Samuel 6:14:

> David up and danced,
> David danced before the Lord;
> He danced before the Lord with all his might.
> Trumpets, cymbals, harps and cymbals rang out loud and clear
> Shouting, singing, trumpets bringing,
> Joy to every ear.[25]

Ellington went on to write two more sacred concerts, one performed at the Cathedral of St. John the Divine in Manhattan, in January 1968, and the final one at Westminster Abbey in 1973, a year before his death. Surprisingly little musical material was recycled in successive concerts. ("Come Sunday" was the last piece performed at Ellington's funeral at St. John the Divine, played on violin by Ray Nance, the only Ellington sideman to perform at the service.) In all, Ellington and his orchestra performed more than 100 sacred concerts around the world, and he repeatedly referred to them as his most important musical work. "Now I can say openly what I have been saying to myself on my knees," he would write later of his response to the invitation to write sacred music.[26]

The challenge of reconciling the Christian piety that Ellington had absorbed as a child with show-business aspirations was similar to the one Dorsey had faced and resolved thirty years earlier, through the medium of gospel blues. Evidence suggests that Ellington was a lifelong reader of religious literature; his estate, which was obtained by the Smithsonian, included many versions and translations of the Bible, along with myriad church bulletins and clippings of newspaper articles by clergy carefully underlined by Ellington. "I know he was quite religious," said Alexandre Rado, a European who first met Ellington in 1948 and worked with him in the 1950s. "I know he was reading the Bible from the influence of his mother. He was keeping his mother's faith." Jazz critic–turned–professor Barry Ulanov, who knew Ellington over many years, called the composer "a naturally Christian soul. And he had it, quite apart from anything to do with his culture, anything to do with his upbringing. There was something in Duke that just gravitated to the figure of Jesus. I don't mean that he said the name often. I just mean that he understood what an incarnational religion was about." One occasion when Ellington did allude to Christ came during the Red Scare, when Ellington was accused of being a fellow traveler for signing the antinuclear Stockholm Peace Petition. "The only 'communism' I know of is that of Jesus Christ," he insisted, in a classic Elling-

THE CATHEDRAL CHURCH  OF ST. JOHN THE DIVINE

By invitation of the Bishop of New York

DUKE ELLINGTON AND HIS ORCHESTRA

PRESENT

A SACRED CONCERT

FRIDAY, JANUARY 19, 1968

8:15 P.M.

THEY WILL BE ASSISTED BY:

ALEC WYTON, ORGANIST AND MASTER OF
CHORISTERS OF THE CATHEDRAL CHURCH

AND

THE CHOIR OF MOTHER A. M. E. ZION CHURCH
Solomon Herriot, Jr., *Director*

THE CHOIRS OF ST. HILDA'S AND ST. HUGH'S SCHOOL
William Toole, *Director*

THE MEN OF THE CATHEDRAL CHOIR

A BENEFIT FOR EXODUS HOUSE

10. Duke Ellington's second sacred concert premiered in Manhattan on 19 January at the world's largest Gothic cathedral before touring the United States and Europe. Courtesy of Virginia Ware Stowe.

tonian double entendre. In the concerts themselves, the name is rarely invoked.[27]

When asked what prompted his turn toward sacred music, Ellington replied that it was not "a matter of career, but in response to a growing understanding of my own vocation, and with the encouragement of many people," mainly clergyman of multiple denominations. "I think of myself as a messenger boy," he reflected, "one who tries to bring messages to people, not people who have never heard of God, but those who were more or less raised with the guidance of the Church."[28] That category would include most Americans, certainly the majority of the audience at his three sacred concerts. In contrast to the evangelical tone of Dorsey's gospel songs, though, Ellington's musical imagination was notably wide-ranging and ambitious; and his sacred concerts strike a wildly eclectic chord. Both the first and second concerts begin with extended interpretations of the Creation, based on Genesis ("In the Beginning God" and "Supreme Being"). Clearly, he took inspiration from references to music and dance in the Psalms and scriptural accounts of David, as both concerts also end with celebrations of dance. In between there are invocations of the glory of creation, statements of praise, exhortations to forgive, live righteously, and obey the Ten Commandments, alongside songs that take a decidedly ecumenical view of religious truth.

Though Ellington rejected the suggestion that he include liturgical elements, the second concert included a collective confession of sin performed by soloist and choir. There are reveries about heaven alongside a paean to freedom ("Freedom is sweet, on the beat, / Freedom is sweet to the reet complete, / It's got zestness and bestness, / Sugar and cream on the blessedness") that ends with choir members reciting the word in twenty-one languages. Ellington's libretto contains everything from doggerel to a kind of hipster's ontological proof of the existence of God ("Silliest thing ever read, / Was that somebody said, / 'GOD is dead.' / The mere mention of the first word, / Automatically eliminates / The second and the third"). There is a tribute to Lutheran pastor John Gensel, a veritable patron saint of the New York jazz community ("The Shepherd [Who Watches Over the Night Flock]"). "Every man prays in his own language," Ellington wrote famously in his notes to the first concert, "and there is no language that God does not understand." A critic judged it "a most remarkable religious synthesis . . . of Western Christianity . . . with African roots and Pantheism, gospel singing, the chronicles of the Bible, the aspirations of the New Testament and, not least, the extra problems faced by mankind in our modern society."[29]

The cultural distance traveled by Ellington in bringing his music to the metropolitan sanctums of mainline Christianity was in some respects greater than Dorsey's movement into old-line black Chicago churches. Unlike Dorsey and his early comrades, who initially were barred or ejected from churches, Ellington found himself courted, through commissions and invitations, to appear not in old-line African-American churches, but in mainline, primarily European-American sanctuaries. (The Washington,

D.C., Baptist Ministers Conference did pass a resolution objecting to the performance of Ellington's sacred concert at Constitution Hall on grounds that Ellington's life "is opposed to what the church stands for.") The 1960s were far more conducive to musical experimentation, of course, and witnessed many attempts to recast sacred or liturgical music in a jazz idiom. Beginning in 1958, a succession of lesser-known composers and jazz artists, including Vince Guaraldi, tried their hand at jazz masses. A 1967 Carnegie Hall program, *Praise the Lord in Many Voices,* featured new works in the folk and rock mode by several Catholic composers and musicians, including a bona-fide jazz figure, Mary Lou Williams, who had walked off a stage in Paris in 1954 before undergoing a profound conversion to Catholicism. As late as 1967 the Vatican was issuing edicts in opposition to "jazz masses," but by 1969 St. Patrick's Cathedral had commissioned a mass by Williams. The same year saw the premier of Ronald Roullier's *Jazz Requiem for Martin Luther King Jr.* at the New York Society for Ethical Culture.[30] The distance traveled from storefront holiness or Pentecostal churches to these sorts of elite venues could not have been greater. And Ellington had occupied a much more prominent association with jazz for much longer than Dorsey had with the blues at the time he set about reconfiguring black church music. Through the gospel choirs and vocalists he included in the sacred concerts, Dorsey's gospel blues was only one of myriad musical ingredients that Ellington tapped.

But obviously their goals were quite different. Dorsey sought to change the nature of congregational worship, bringing back into the singing of laypeople some of the vernacular elements of movement and expression that had been deliberately sifted out by pastors concerned with "race improvement." Ellington had no such goal of changing how worship was acted out in the pews on a weekly basis. His concern was spectacle, not participation; performance, not ritual. He conceived his sacred music as an offering to God that was also an ecumenical message transmitted through his orchestra and singers from God to the audience gathered reverently in rows before the altar. Through the music he assumed the last of his many earthly roles: "Harlem Renaissance piano tickler; bandleading king of the Cotton Club; romantic composer of sensuous ballads; orchestrator of moods of swing which catapulted jitter-hoppers to manic frenzy; sonic painter of lush soundscapes; transcendent artist; African American cultural icon; world citizen. And on top of that jali, muezzin, cantor, mwalimu, kapelmeister, ecumenist and deacon."[31]

ELLINGTON has been famously described as "beyond category," and his unique array of talents and ambitions made it unlikely that he would

have musical heirs. His forays into sacred jazz seem particularly sui generis, produced by a combination of Ellington's need in his final decade to
resolve a lifetime of spiritual reflection and the general cultural ferment of
the 1960s and early 1970s. The gospel blues of Dorsey and Jackson, on the
other hand, have obviously been wildly successful and eminently repro-
ducible. African-American gospel has become a musical genre unto itself, a
musical formula whose techniques and stylings have long since filtered
through the sacred into the realm of popular through a host of major figures: Willie Mae Ford Smith, Sister Rosetta Tharpe, James Cleveland,
Clara Ward, Ray Charles, Shirley Caeser, James Brown, Aretha Franklin,
Sam Cooke, the Edwin Hawkins Singers, Wilson Picket, Otis Redding, and
Al Green. As the list suggests, male singers have been more likely than
women to make the crossover from sacred to secular music. A few, like
Tharpe, Franklin, and Green, have crossed and recrossed repeatedly.

Dorsey's contributions in composing songs were matched by his innovations in creating an institutional support for gospel, principally through
the National Convention of Gospel Choirs and Choruses, with its capacity for training singers and for publishing and distributing sheet music.
Dorsey's success encouraged other gospel workers to organize, including
Willie Mae Ford Smith and Sallie Martin, who joined forces with Kenneth
Morris, another savvy composer of gospel music, and later James Cleveland, who organized the Gospel Music Workshop of America. In contrast
to this hive of musical entrepreneurialism, Ellington seems to have died
without heirs or successors. (In literal terms, of course, he had both in his
son, Mercer, who took over the reins of Ellington's orchestra until his own
death in 1996.) There are, however, a few figures who have consciously
sought to emulate the multifaceted achievements of Ellington in composing, arranging, bandleading, and improvisation. Charles Mingus, who
wedded the Pentecostal energy of his childhood with Vedanta Hindu beliefs, is one. Wynton Marsalis is another.

The New Orleans–born trumpet prodigy Marsalis has made no secret of
his admiration for Ellington, and his career resembles Ellington's own.
Marsalis' two most ambitious extended works, *Blood on the Fields* and *In
This House, On This Morning,* reveal most clearly his debt to Ellington,
not just formally or musically but also in his conception of the role that
music might play in the cultural life of the nation. The work for which
Marsalis received the Pulitzer that famously eluded Ellington, *Blood on
the Fields,* is in important ways a re-visioning of *Black, Brown and Beige.*
Like Ellington's narrative about Boola, it is a diasporic story about becoming African American. It chronicles the struggles of two Africans as they
are captured in their homeland, transported to America, sold at market,

marched to a cotton plantation, and struggle to achieve a relationship and freedom. Jesse is a prince, himself a former slave owner. Leona is a commoner who struggles to help Jesse overcome his debilitating hubris. In the end, after painful struggle, they achieve both companionship and freedom. Two other characters appear in the work, both sung by Jon Hendricks: a slave buyer and Juba, an elder wise man whose advice to Jesse is ultimately vindicated.[32]

In *Blood*, the most prominent figure of Africa is the drum. For Leona, it serves as metonym for the spiritual connection to Africa severed by the Middle Passage. Lying in the ship's hold in the first scene, Leona urges Jesse to move over—to make room for her. But what she believes is the sound of a drum turns out to be the mechanical beat of the ship.

> I think I hear a drum, think I hear a drum . . .
> That must be those drums singing on the wind
> Take a me back my home
> That's the little one with the ringing tone
> Slowly swaying
> Taking me back, far away back my home.

In a bitter voice, Jesse mocks Leona's hopes:

> Woman you don't hear no drum
> All you hear, the clattering of broken bones and homes.

Leona's yearning for the drum persists through her sale, brutal coffle march, and fourteen years' bondage in the cotton fields. Several scenes later she again hears an echo of the drum, and again Jesse punctures her hopes. Immediately following comes a representation of Christianity offered from two perspectives: the Christian piety of the master ("Ol' Massa is a good and righteous man. He likes for his Negroes to worship and honor a merciful and just God"), who preaches a gospel of resignation, forgiveness, and comfort in the hereafter, followed by the militant liberation theology of the slaves. Titled "Oh We Have a Friend in Jesus," with its echo of the Sankey-era classic "What a Friend We Have in Jesus," the Ol' Massa piece begins with a shout-band march whose clean gospel chords begin to stagger under the weight of dissonance in the brass. Then Leona enters, singing a Dorsey-like piano-vocal duet reminiscent of "Precious Lord." The slaves' rejoinder, "God Don't Like Ugly" ("They, however, interpret the word of God quite differently"), offers the rawer sound of a ring-shout spiritual, played over a taut brassy waltz, punctuated by tambourine claps and rolls. Again sung by Leona, this time with a rawer edge of a slave spiritual, the text reiterates two points: "God don't like ugly," "And the last shall be first."

Whereas *Blood on the Fields* is Marsalis' analogue to *Black, Brown and Beige,* a musical expression of the African diaspora in America, the two-hour suite *In This House, On This Morning* is his sacred concert. Dealing explicitly with African-American Protestant worship, it is based on the casual ethnography that takes place among musicians who spend weeks together on the road. "Almost everyone in the band grew up playing church music and what truly spurred my desire to write this music was the many hymns and shouts that they sing on the bus as we travel, at sound checks before concerts, and after meals," Marsalis explains. "Listening to all of them made me want to put that feeling in a long piece and reassert out here the power that underlies jazz by constructing a composition based on the communal complexity of its spiritual sources."[33] His own Catholic upbringing failed to secure his loyalty: "too harsh for a little boy," intolerant of differences. "Now, I go into homes of different spiritual people all over the world," he adds. "I think there's truth in all their traditions. I consider myself a spiritual person." Sounding nearly indistinguishable from Ellington, Marsalis observes: "It all starts with God. It's the same with all musicians. Bach, Beethoven, Duke Ellington, John Coltrane. Even the philosophy of jazz has its underpinning in Christianity. Jesus Christ brought democracy to the world. All are equal. There's no aspect of your birth that makes you superior to another person. We are all part of God's oneness. It's the same with jazz music. Equality is in the music. And it returns to God. It's a matter between the musician and God just as it's a matter between the listener and God."[34]

Like Ellington, Marsalis undertook his major work of sacred, or at least sacred-inspired, music as a commission, not by an Episcopal cathedral but by Lincoln Center. But in contrast to Ellington's ecumenical theism, Marsalis' work reflects a more orthodox trinitarian outlook, namely in the three-part "Prayer" ("Introduction to Prayer," "In This House," and "Choral Response") and the twenty-eight-minute "Sermon," which is split into "Father," "Son," and "Holy Ghost." But overall the work is less theological than ethnomusicological; rather than an act of musical worship, *In This House* evokes the sounds and sights of "doing church." "I wanted to express the full range of humanity that arises in a church service, from deep introspection to rapture to extroverted celebration," Marsalis explains. "So *In This House* has a wide range of things, beginning with 'Devotional' and ending with that country feeling of community when the food comes out after all the aspects of the ceremonial have been completed." With this in mind, pieces are given titles like "Call to Prayer," "Processional," Representative Offerings," "Local Announcements," "Altar Call," "Recessional," "Benediction," and "Pot Blessed Dinner."

The piece is a dense interweaving of musical themes and variations, with an overarching musical unity that contrasts with Ellington's more loose-knit sacred concerts. Marsalis' borrowings are eclectic—certain passages evoke Bach, ancient liturgical chants, and even Arab modes—but the structure within which he positions these motifs is quite formal. Marsalis decided to work with the form of an African-American church service, which, in the model provided him by a minister from Chicago named Jeremiah Wright, happened to have twelve parts. The black church service is "a dialogue with God," Wright explained. "Sometimes you're petitioning God, sometimes God is speaking through his representative, and other times we offer things to God," Marsalis elaborates. "It was like a call and a response, which is a musical device we use." Fortuitously, the blues is also based on units of twelve—three groups of four measures—which is more or less the structure Marsalis uses for his three-movement suite.[35] Like Ellington's first sacred concert, which features a six-note melody setting for "In the Beginning God," *In This House* opens with a six-note melody, played on the soprano saxophone. The first three pieces—"Devotional," "Call to Prayer," "Processional"—introduce the melodic themes and chord progressions that are recapitulated in succeeding pieces and movements. Drummer Herlin Riley's use of tambourine instead of drum set in several pieces conjures up sounds of sanctified church; it's a sound Marsalis would come back to in his next work, *Blood on the Fields*. For example, "Recessional" features an unusual 7/4 meter; band members blend their syncopated handclaps and chanting with the tambourine over a bass and piano vamp, over which solos an alto saxophone.

In This House has only a few lyrics, including the refrain chanted by band members: "In the sweet embrace of life." The major exception, an eleven-line hymn titled "In This House," is performed by Marion Williams, who as much as any contemporary gospel singer has inherited Mahalia Jackson's mantle.[36] Williams' text highlights two purposes of worship: "To praise Thy vast creation, / and ring the bells whose melody / Affirms." In contrast to "Come Sunday," there is little biblical language. The emphasis is less on praising God, Ellington's dominant theme, than on the bells as symbols of the struggle for freedom. In the very opening of *In This House,* bells are sounded on piano by Eric Reed, and recur several times during the piece, usually by piano but also by horns, bass, and bell of a cymbal. They are church bells, summoning congregants to worship. But they are also, the hymn tells us, "Bells which sing of sweet love, / Rebellion lost." Williams repeats the word "rebellion" more than half a dozen times, with increasing urgency, evoking both slave uprisings and the various Old Testament rebellions of the Israelites. Thematically, the bells of *In This*

House function as an analogue to the traditional West African drums of *Blood on the Fields;* Leona continually imagines she hears them when in fact they have been severed by the Middle Passage and replaced with the hybrid American figure of the Mardi Gras Indian. Another parallel to the later work: as does Williams' lyric, Jesse and Leona through their actions interweave the themes of "rebellion" and "sweet love."

Like Ellington and Dorsey before him, Marsalis negotiates a number of boundaries that have customarily marked the distinction between sacred and secular. Both he and Ellington have performed their sacred works in both churches and concert halls. Like Ellington, Marsalis sacralizes black history and culture by placing religion at the forefront of his musical depictions of African-American life. And both historicize Protestant Christianity in the narratives they create, treating the church not as an unchanging given but as a form of practice that responds and adapts to the social conditions of the people who carry it forward. The fit between black culture and Protestant Christianity seems nearly effortless for both composers. Only one short motif from *In This House* suggests that there is anything other than Christianity in African America. "Call to Prayer" opens with Marsalis playing distinctly Arab-sounding modal arpeggios, with a deliberately dirty, warbling trumpet tone and microtones simulating a human voice. The listener is reminded that Protestant services don't feature calls to prayer, and what is evoked is the *adhan*, traditionally performed five times a day to summon Muslims to prayer. As Sun Ra, another bandleader of nearly Ellingtonian longevity, reveals, there is a much larger legacy of ideas through which to explore the possibilities of African-American spirituality.

CHAPTER NINE

From Ephrata (F-Ra-Ta) to Arkestra

> The earth cannot move without music. The earth moves in a certain rhythm, a certain sound, a certain note. When the music stops the earth will stop and everything upon it will die.
>
> —SUN RA

NINETEEN FIFTY-TWO saw the election of President Dwight Eisenhower, the release of Hank Williams' "Your Cheatin' Heart," the publication of Ralph Ellison's *Invisible Man,* and the explosion of the first hydrogen bomb by the United States on Eniwetok Atoll. Less than three weeks before the nuclear test, an obscure Chicago jazz musician named Herman Poole Blount changed his name to Le Sony'r Ra, registering the change at the Cooke County Circuit Court. The newly christened Ra developed a new genealogy for himself, refusing to acknowledge any connection to his biological family or his upbringing in Birmingham, Alabama. Long known by the nickname Sonny, he took the new name from the Egyptian sun god, and the spelling was chosen to give the full name a complement of nine letters, for good luck. In his new genealogy, Ra was a citizen of Saturn, birthdate unknown and irrelevant, sent by the Creator to redeem Earthlings with a musical message. He would go on to become famous in jazz circles under his stage name, Sun Ra, leading a big band called the Arkestra for some forty years, nearly as long as Duke Ellington kept his celebrated orchestra on the road.

Ra's earlier life was typical of many musicians of what has come to be called the swing era. Born in 1914 into one of the most segregated cities in the United States, in a particularly harsh period of oppression of African Americans, Sonny grew up in a house across the street from the post office and within sight of an enormous sign that welcomed railway passengers to

"The Magic City." From an early age he showed academic and musical talent as both a pianist and an arranger. Sonny read constantly, earned top grades, and soaked up the sounds of the Tabernacle Baptist Church to which his grandmother took him, along with the gospel quartets and nationally known big bands that regularly passed through Birmingham: Fats Waller, Duke Ellington, and Fletcher Henderson, among others. Alabama apartheid created a strong and self-reliant African-American community. Sonny received a good education from the city's Industrial High School, and musical guidance from John T. "Fess" Whatley, the reigning patriarch of the Birmingham music scene, an exacting instructor and bandleader who mentored an entire generation of instrumentalists. By the time he graduated from high school Sonny was subbing in local bands and immersing himself in the big-band jazz recordings of the early 1930s, especially the Fletcher Henderson band. In 1934 he took over an Alabama territory band that briefly made it as far as Chicago; known as the Sonny Blount orchestra, it lasted for a decade. Meanwhile he attended Alabama A&M University in Huntsville, where he majored in music education for one year before funds ran out.[1]

After a series of awkward run-ins with the draft board during World War II, Sonny bought a train ticket to Chicago and joined the tail end of the century's second great migration of African Americans out of the South. This migration was twice as large as the earlier one, with some three million African Americans leaving the South between 1940 and 1960. In Chicago alone the African-American population grew by nearly 80 percent—from 277,000 to 492,000 between 1940 and 1950, and another 65 percent over the subsequent decade. Reactivating the union membership he had established during his first visit to Chicago in 1934, Sonny found work almost at once. He traveled to Nashville with rhythm-and-blues singer Wynonie Harris for a time and then with a society band that wore Revolutionary War uniforms complete with wigs. Almost before he knew it, he was playing piano for the bandleader he had idolized as a teenager, Fletcher Henderson, who was appearing at Club DeLisa, Chicago's answer to the Cotton Club. For several years he appeared with a number of bands at a variety of venues, backing rhythm-and-blues singers and other headliners, providing musical backdrops for floor shows. Sonny had become as securely established as most professional musicians ever do, with a respectable if quirky reputation among his peers.[2]

Sonny's musical and intellectual bearings began to shift in the early 1950s. Together with a precocious teenager named Alton Abraham, who acted as agent and longtime booster, Sonny became part of a loose-knit reading and discussion group. He began to read exhaustively in alternative histories of Western civilization, books that questioned the primacy of Greek civilization, proposing instead Egypt as the original source. One author led to another, and the titles give a sense of what Sonny was absorbing: *The Egyptian Book of the Dead; The Children of the Sun* (1918); *The Ruins, or, Meditation on the Revolutions of Empires: and the Law of Nature* (1791); *The Anacalypsis, an Attempt to Draw Aside the Veil of the Saitic Isis; or an Inquiry into the Origin of Languages, Nations and Religions* (1833); *God Wills the Negro: An Anthropological and Geographical Restoration of the Lost History of the American Negro People, Being in Part a Theological Interpretation of Egyptian and Ethiopian Backgrounds* (1939); *Stolen Legacy, the Greeks Were Not the Authors of Greek Philosophy, but the People of North Africa, Commonly Called the Egyptians* (1954). The Nation of Islam was germinating in Chicago during these years, and shared similar interests but drew different conclusions. There was much overlap but also keen schisms among the intellectual legacy Sonny was unpacking. "Anglo-Israelites, Pyramidologists, Edomites, Pre-Adamites, Khazars, Pentecostalists—it was a maelstrom of rival ideologies like out of William Blake's time," observes Ra biographer John Szwed.[3]

Sonny read tirelessly, annotating the texts "in copious notes of red, green, and yellow ink, circling, underlining, arrowing, echoing what he read with comments and cross-references, sometimes with arcane symbols from the world's religions." He learned of the legendary Greek Gnostic thinker Hermes Trismegistus ("Thrice-great"), founder of the Hermetic tradition, whose writings bridged religion and science, music and magic, and promised to reconcile the esoteric wisdom of Egypt and Greece. In time the reading group discovered the work of Madame Helena P. Blavatsky—the dominant nineteenth-century figure of the Theosophical Society—and people she influenced like the composer Scriabin, Rudolph Steiner and eurythmy ("visible speech and song"), Pyotr Demianovitch Ouspensky's writings *(A New Model of the Universe),* and Georgei Ivanovitch Gurdjieff, who synthesized numerology, Pythagorean musicology, Kabbalah, physics, esoteric Christianity, and Blavatsky's theosophy. "The key ideas he received from his readings in theosophy were those which reinforced ideas he already held," writes Szwed: "that the Bible must be demythologized, decoded, and brought in tune with modern life; that it was possible to unify all knowledge; that the universe was organized hierarchically, with forces or spirits which moved between the levels and affected life on Earth; and that there were charismatic leaders who had the means to come to know these secrets." Twenty years later Ra was invited to teach a course at Berkeley, and his knowledge emerged as a kind of synthesis. "In a typical lecture, Sun Ra wrote biblical quotes on the board and then 'permutated' them—rewrote and transformed their letters and syntax into new equations of meaning." His lectures ranged from Egyptology, Neoplatonism, and biblical hermeneutics to how ancient religious texts might speak to contemporary problems of race, war, and pollution.[4]

In a word, Ra was drawn to esoteric knowledge, a kind of parallel tradition to orthodox Christianity, a world of excluded knowledge and hidden teachings: mysteries revealed, intricate correspondences between individual and cosmos, body and spirit, a sense that everything is connected and ordered, provided one has the tools and sensibility to decode the world. Music was the crucial key to understanding the universe, because the universe itself was musical: the planets and stars were governed by musical principles, vibrated with the "music of the spheres." Ra was fascinated by history, but believed it had been distorted or suppressed, whether by professionals or in the Bible, which he came to believe had been badly warped by its earthly compilers. He liked to draw a contrast between history ("his story") and mystery ("my story"). At the same time, he showed a developing fascination with the utopian potential of outer space, with Afrofuturism—a technological future that explicitly included African America. Numbers and letters were important clues to what held this ordered universe together.

Beginning in the early 1950s, Ra became a master of puns and word games. They became the dominant method of his utterances: poems, liner notes, interviews. "I'm very interested in names, and 'Ra' is older than history itself," he reflected. "It's the oldest name known by man to signify an extra-terrestrial being. It's very interesting to note that there is 'ra' in the middle of 'Israel': Is-ra-el. Take away the 'ra' [and] there is no more Israel. It's very interesting. And there is 'ra' in France as well." And, it's worth pointing out, two "ra"s (the first running backward, the second forward) in the new name he chose for his ensemble: the Arkestra. With this new name and new forms of knowledge and meaning came a new sense of life mission: to be a "secret agent of the Creator." Writes Szwed: "With music he would reach across the border of reality into myth; with music he could build a bridge to another dimension, to something better; dance halls, clubs, and theaters could be turned into sacred shrines, the sites of dramas and rituals, and though people would be drawn to hear the music, it was they who would become the instrument on which it would resonate, on which he would create the sound of silhouettes, the images and forecasts of tomorrow . . . all of it disguised as jazz."[5]

"Ancient Aiethopia," a recording made by the Arkestra in 1958, suggests how Ra translated these ideas into music for a ten-man ensemble. String bass and tom-toms maintain a steady swaying vamp throughout the nine-minute piece, which restricts itself to minimal chord changes. After a percussive piano introduction, played over drums and rolling cymbals, the theme sounds: a foreboding four-measure phrase repeated six times by somber-sounding brasses, somehow evoking a caravan. A few measures of drumming segue into a flute duet played over a rocking tom-tom pattern, interspersed with percussion scratches played on a ribbed guiro. Occasionally a gong sounds. As the drums fade to a whisper, the flutes are replaced by a very deep, clean-toned trumpet that explores the opening theme above occasional gongings. The piano reappears for a brief but densely played two-handed solo, which is followed by a percussion interlude of bells and guiro scratches over the continuing bass and tom-tom vamp. After some tentative saxophone squawks in the background, an interlude begins of spooky-sounding and wordless antiphonal chanting by two male voices. The piano signals the return of the twenty-four-measure brass theme, which comes to a slow ritard over repeated sounding of the gong. "Ancient Aiethopia" appeared on an early Arkestra album, *Jazz in Silhouette,* which billed itself as "Magic Music of the Spheres." The cover is a surrealistic painting of female figures hovering above one of Saturn's cratered moons depicted from several hundred miles away. "In tomorrow's world, men will not need artificial instruments such as jets and space ships," the liner notes declare. "In the world of tomorrow, the new man will 'think' the place he wants to go, then his mind will take him there."[6]

THERE is no indication that Sonny had knowledge of the Ephrata commune formed near Philadelphia in the early eighteenth century by a German mystic named Conrad Beissel; if he had he would have been delighted but not surprised. One can imagine what Ra would have done with the name itself. "Ephrata" would yield up "Eph-Ra-ta," for starters. Then musical puns—"Ephrat(a)" would suggest "E-flat," a key signature dear to Freemasons, whose three flats represent the Triad, a number revered as far back as Pythagoras. Or possibly "Ephrata" to "F-flat," a way of naming "E," the third tone in the C major scale, which corresponds to the third planet, Earth. Beyond this wordplay there is a series of unlikely but uncanny congruences between these two musical mystics, separated by two centuries. Conrad Beissel and Le Sony'r Ra shared an intellectual heritage, a similar orientation toward what they considered a fundamentally musical universe. They were propelled to their life work by analogous social forces and shared similar goals for the communities they established. Beissel and Ra make for an unlikely historical pairing, but in doing so they illustrate a link between American sacred music (defined broadly) and one of the most ancient streams of thinking about music and the cosmos, of connecting the body and the spirit through the medium of sound.

Both shared an experience of exodus. Sun Ra had been both pushed out of Alabama and pulled toward Chicago, making an exodus from the known realities of southern Jim Crow to the unknowns of a northern city promoted by black newspapers like the Chicago *Defender* as a kind of African-American Promised Land. Likewise, Beissel had joined a substantial migration to Pennsylvania, a colony that under Quaker leadership was encouraging the immigration of religious sects persecuted in Europe. Born about 1690, Beissel grew up in distressed circumstances in the Neckar Valley of Germany, a region deeply scarred by the Thirty Years' War and conquests by France under Louis XIV. His father drank himself to death shortly before he was born, and his mother died when he was eight or nine. Beissel was taken on as a baker's apprentice and developed some skill on the violin. His credentials as a baker took him to a number of important German cultural centers in the 1710s. In Strasbourg Beissel imbibed the teachings of the great German mystic Jakob Böhme (1575–1624), possibly through the missionary efforts of the Philadelphians, a secret mystical society that had originated in England under the leadership of the visionary Jane Leade. At Mannheim, after a sexual contretemps with his master's wife, Beissel was forced to flee to Heidelberg, thereafter forsaking sexual congress with "mortal women." Beissel became active among radical Pietist groups that were flourishing on the periphery of the great university. Appointed treasurer of the bakers' guild, he had a falling out over guild practices and, after a series of trials, was banished from the Palatinate. With his *Wanderbuch*—the record of his baker's experience—confiscated, Beissel wandered adrift through the countryside, eventually landing in Schwarzenau and taking up with yet more underground sects, including the Baptist Brethren, the Inspirationists, and the Awakened. One group of Baptist "Dunkers" had embarked for Pennsylvania in 1719. The following year Beissel and a group of like-minded spiritual dissidents set out for the colony whose capital was named for the brotherhood of love.[7]

To confuse wartime Chicago with a city of brotherly love would be a huge stretch, but in fact it held some of the same possibilities for Ra that Philadelphia did for Beissel. Both men were motivated in their movements by the desire to follow the route of a respected precursor. For Ra, it was Fletcher Henderson, the bandleader who, along with Ellington, most inspired the fledgling musician in Birmingham (and whose compositions Ra would revive much later in his career as a bandleader of the Arkestra). "Fletcher was really part of an angelic thing," Ra would later say. But he was pushed as well as pulled North. Like any other professional musician of color, he encountered his share of daily indignities and humiliations. Along with a number of fellow jazz artists—Lester Young and Dizzy Gillespie come to mind first—his sense of estrangement was exacerbated by his encounter with the wartime state. Between October 1942 and March 1943 he sought conscientious-objector status, pleading his case in letters and hearings with various boards and officials, often citing scripture. "The judge granted Sonny his knowledge of the Bible, but found his lack of church membership all the more puzzling," according to Szwed. "The outcome became clear within minutes, however, and so Sonny upped the ante, threatening that if he was forced to learn to kill, he would use that skill without prejudice, and kill one of his own captains or generals first. The judge now grew tired of the byplay. 'I've never seen a nigger like you before.' 'No,' Sonny said, 'and you never will again.'"[8] He was held for a time in the county jail, and finally sent to a Civilian Public Service Camp run by the Church of the Brethren (descendants of the German Baptists Beissel had associated with) in rural northwest Pennsylvania, where he was inspired by the interracial mix of principled pacifists. By March he was discharged 4-F on account of his hernia. But the experience left him embittered, and he found it even more difficult to resume life with a family and fellow musicians that had trouble understanding his reluctance to serve.

A number of religious groups that made important innovations in sacred music faced similar hardships for their resistance to the state, usually manifested in pacifism: the eighteenth-century Moravians, German-speakers who found themselves caught in the crossfire of the French and Indian War and the American Revolution; Shakers, whose unwillingness to serve in the Civil War generated hostility among neighboring "worldlings"; and Latter-day Saints intent on creating their own New Israel. The problem was acute for Conrad Beissel and those who sought to follow him. Negotiating a social space for survival was especially urgent for Protestant sects that faced the horrific confessional conflicts flashing through Europe beginning in the early seventeenth century, with state-sanctioned massacres of dissenting groups, repression by both Catholics and established Protestant churches that lasted well into the eighteenth century. The trauma of religious civil war was long in healing in central Europe, inspiring dreams of a religious sanctuary in the New World, just as the dramatic failure of postbellum Reconstruction created a system that made life for African Americans nearly unbearable for decades around the turn of the twentieth century.

Like Anabaptists and other spiritual forebears who modeled themselves upon the early church, Ephrata's communalists understood themselves as existing apart from and above the state; they rejected oaths, military service, land patents, and even the institution of the natural family. Like the Moravian Unitas Fratrum, their pacifism was severely tested, first during the French and Indian War of the 1750s and later during the Revolution, when their neutrality was often construed as support for the opposition (a quandary that also afflicted the Moravians). Perhaps because they were located farther from the sort of backwoods anarchy that threatened the Moravians of North Carolina, the Ephrata Kloster faced less overt hostility. But the Brothers and Sisters had no choice but to accept American survivors of the Battle of the Brandywine, fought in September 1777, an intrusion that greatly disrupted the small community.[9]

When Sonny Blount left Birmingham and his wartime tribulations for Chicago in 1946, he couldn't have known he would be playing with Fletcher Henderson within a few years. Beissel, on the other hand, was clearly motivated by a desire to join cause with a like-minded group of mystics who in 1694 had migrated to Pennsylvania under the leadership of Johannes Kelpius. Born in Transylvania in 1673, Kelpius was of a much more privileged background than Beissel, and had taken a *Magister* degree from University of Altdorf, in Bavaria. But the two shared a set of spiritual convictions. Kelpius had fallen under the influence of Edward Spener's radical pietism (sometimes referred to as chiliasm, and also associated with Philadelphianism), with its emphasis on mystical knowledge, miracles, the impending millennium, and speculation based on numbers and letters. "This Penn is too dull to express the Extraordinary Power the Pietists & Chiliasts among the Protestants in Germany," Kelpius wrote in his enthusiasm before listing a series of preternatural manifestations: "Ecstases, Revelations, Inspirations, Illuminations, Inspeakings, Prophesies, Apparitions, Changings of Minds, Transfigurations, Translations of their Bodys, wonderful Fastings for 11, 14, 27, 37 days, Paradysical Representations by Voices, Melodies & Sensations." Especially powerful for Kelpius was the idea that God originally had contained both sexes, but that the divine feminine Sophia had been separated from the godhead at the Fall, only to be received as a separate being in the form of Eve. Reunion with Sophia was possible only through a life of rigorous devotion and celibacy.[10]

Responding to the lure of Quaker Pennsylvania, Kelpius' group sailed via England, where they spent time with Jane Leade, whose ideas, developed through the Society of Philadelphians, had first reached Beissel in Strasbourg when he was a journeyman baker. Departing from "these Babilonish Coasts, to those American Plantations, being led therunto by the guidance of the Divine Spirit," Kelpius established a celibate commune on the Wissahickon River near Germantown; it became known as the Society of the Woman in the Wilderness. By the time Beissel arrived there in 1720, Kelpius (who composed music for his commune and is thought to have lived in a cave) had been dead for more than a decade, his followers dispersed. Although he aspired to solitude, Beissel's charismatic spiritual gifts attracted disciples. The loose-knit settlement gradually evolved into a full-fledged Protestant monastery that somewhat resembled a Shaker community of a century later. Though some of Beissel's followers, called the Householders, lived with their families and owned property, a majority of the men and women lived separately and celibately, dedicated to spiritual perfection through collective labor and rigorous spiritual exercises.

The complex history of Beissel and Ephrata is richly narrated in the *Chronicon Ephratense,* first published in 1786, two decades after Beissel's death. Given the challenges of physical survival, let alone those of maintaining a spiritual utopia in the face of suspicious or hostile outsiders, the amount of attention Beissel devoted to music was extraordinary. "All Ephrata endeavours were dedicated to the goal of perfect life lived in union with God in the image of the divine Sophia," writes historian Peter Erb, "and song was no exception. Perfect song was the enactment of the union itself, for in it the singer was angelic, returned in his primal image to paradise to praise his maker in a perfect harmony of intellect and will. The lyrics are not properly to be separated from the music, in fact, are subordinated to them. The music dictates the thought."[11] It took time for Beissel to move beyond the Lutheran and Reformed chorales he had known in Germany and the homophonic psalm-singing of pietists and Dunkers.

A musical watershed occurred in May 1727, when at a gathering of German Brethren Beissel introduced antiphonal choral singing, probably polyphonic, in place of homophonic psalms. Beginning in 1730, Beissel began to have hymnbooks printed, usually by Philadelphia printer Benjamin Franklin. *Göttliche Liebes und Lobes Gethöne* (Melodies of Love and Praise) appeared in 1730, and two years later *Vorspiel der Neuen Welt* (Prelude to the New World), featuring dozens of mystical hymns, many by Beissel himself. The first manuscript hymnbook, *Paradiesische Nachts Tropffen* (Teardrops of a Night of Paradise), with its distinctive *Fraktur-schriften* lettering, was painstakingly illuminated by the Solitary over the winter of 1733–34. The name "Ephrata" was first used to refer to the Cocalico River commune in one of these hymnbooks, printed by Franklin in 1736 under the title *Jacobs Kampff- und Ritter-Platz* (Jacob's Place of Struggle and Elevation). "This Beisselian title in its curious way signified to Conrad that the birth struggle of his little Israel had ended in peace at last," writes E. Gordon Alderfer. "The imagery is suggestive. One must remember that the Ephrata of the Old Testament was the pre-Israelite name for what became Bethlehem. It was on the way to Ephrata that Rachel, wife of Jacob, died giving birth to Benjamin. And it was Rachel who 'did build the house of Israel.' Perhaps Conrad Beissel dreamt that the Spiritual Virgins were building a new Israel in a new world in which the Brothers of Zion could find peace."[12]

Jewish language and images were in fact crucial components of Beissel's vision. Probably he was exposed to knowledge of the Kabbalah during his baker's *Wanderjahre* in Europe; those notions had penetrated the secret societies that shaped his thought before he left Europe. Though evidence is scanty, a small Jewish community is thought to have existed on the Pennsylvania frontier in the early years of the eighteenth century, with Orthodox Jews trading with Indians. In any event, Jewish ideas seem to have had some currency among early settlers. Soon after relocating to Pennsylvania Beissel decided to observe the scriptural Jewish Sabbath— Saturday rather than Sunday—as the commune's holy day. "Judaic ideas played an important if secretive role in his spiritual development," writes Alderfer, "and his decision regarding Sabbatarianism was of deep psychological importance to him—as it was to Boehme and many another mystic."[13]

It was not until the 1740s that Beissel fully synthesized his musical and spiritual strivings, in the first hymnbook published by the new press at Ephrata. The decade was a particularly tumultuous period for the cloister. A new hymnal, *Zionitic Weyrauchs Hügel* (Zionist Hill of Incense), published in 1739, generated conflict when its printer, Christopher Sauer, whose wife had left him for several years to follow Beissel, accused Beissel of heresy on the basis of new hymns that appeared to elevate him to the status of Christ. The offending text was a complex weaving of Christian and esoteric imagery, including astrological symbolism, and ran to forty-four stanzas of Doctor Seuss–sounding verse. Its thrust was to draw an analogy between the Israelites in Exodus and the Ephrata community. The hymn begins:

> While the cloud-like pillar gleams,
> Which through God for Israel beams,
> So that they may easily know
> Where 'tis time for them to go.
>
> Leave your camp now out of sight
> Fix your eyes upon the light,
> Follow in your journey's course
> Promptings from the highest source.

The cautionary story of the Exodus and Aaron's follows, then the lesson:

> This which happened long ago
> Is a warning for us now;
> An example that we may
> Show the Israel of today.
>
> How he made a promise dear
> Which was made entirely clear,

When he healed the serpent's bite,
When he raised within their sight.

Like Israel, Ephrata had frequently lost the way and fallen short of its covenant. But a messiah stood by to rescue its faithful. Seeming to equate Beissel with Christ, these were the stanzas that outraged Sauer:

Sehet, sehet, sehet an!
Sehet, sehet, an der Mann!
Der von Gott enhötet ist
Der is unser Herr und Christ.

Look!—behold, behold the man!
Look!—behold him if you can!
He is exalted by God's word,
He is indeed the Christ and Lord!

He is saying constantly:
"Come you here and follow me;
I am your most helpful friend;
I can save you in the end."

He is the uplifted snake
By the Way which we must take;
Through Him we may surely know,
How that we may better grow.

Only with a perfect cure,
Will the Camp be clean and pure;
And the presence of the Lord
On the Way will help afford.

Israel! Then rejoiced anew,
Steadfast be and good and true
To this emblem hold you fast,
Canaan you will reach at last.[14]

The heresy controversy unfolded alongside many changes in Ephrata's social and economic organization during the late 1730s and 1740s. At this time the total population of the cloister probably numbered 200, with approximately 35 brothers, the same number of sisters, and roughly forty families living as Householders. Beissel found himself fending off Moravians, including David Nitschman and Count Zinzendorf himself (who would soon cross paths with the Wesleys farther south), who were making aggressive efforts to recruit the Solitary of Ephrata to the more family-friendly communes of the Unitas Fratrum. A trained musician named Ludwig Blum arrived in 1738, with ambitions to form a singing school; Blum lasted only two years before the sisters pushed him out in favor of Beissel.

The sisters took over the communal structure where the Solitary of both sexes had lived, and males relocated to separate cabins on the periphery (where they would eventually organize their own communal building). A new three-story *Saal*, or chapterhouse, was erected. A group calling itself the Zionitic Brotherhood, a coterie of zealous adepts influenced by Egyptian notions transmitted through Freemasonry, began rigorously uprooting any vestiges of private property in Ephrata. Not long afterward a group of brothers named Eckerling attempted to remake the community as a sort of for-profit production factory based on essentially unpaid labor. Beissel managed to reassert his control and oust the Eckerlings in 1745, at which point Ephrata was rededicated to its original, more spiritual purposes: the Way of Peace, based on rejection of unclean foods, commitment to poverty and celibacy, practice of the scriptural Sabbath, and the achievement of mystical states through singing of hymns.[15]

Two years later Ephrata's press brought out Beissel's musical masterwork, a collection titled *Das Gesäng der einsamen und verlassenen Turtel-Taube* (The Song of the Lonely and Forsaken Turtle Dove, the Christian Church) containing 279 hymns, two-thirds by Beissel. One of them is perhaps the best known of Beissel's hymns: "Gott ein Herrscher aller Heiden" (God a Ruler of All Heathen), which appeared in *Weyrauchs Huegel and Turtel-Taube* and can be heard in modern recordings (which do not of course provide a reliable guide to what Ephrata's choir of the mid-eighteenth century sounded like).

> Gott ein Herrscher aller Heiden,
> der sein Volk bald wird herzlich leiten,
> und ihr recht lassen hoch hergehn.
> Wenn er Zion schön wird schmücken
> ihr Heil wird lassen näher rücken,
> so wird man Freud und Wonne sehen
> an seinem Eigenthum,
> das nun giebt Preiss und Ruhm
> Gott dem König,
> der sie erhöht, ihr Völker seht!
> Wie Gottes Braut nun einhergeht.

> God a ruler of all heathen,
> Who His people soon will lead,
> And let them claim their place on high
> When Zion He beautifully adorns,
> And their salvation day nearer brings,
> Then will joy and gladness be
> In His Kingdom manifest,
> Where praise and glory are given

To God the King,
Who raises them up, You peoples! See
How God's bride now enters in.[16]

Like so many of Beissel's hymns, this one floats by with few musical surprises. His melody glides up and down a major scale, pausing at the tones of the triad. The rhythm is a stately series of quarter and half notes whose unexpected holds defy conventional meter (the hymn is actually constructed of sets of three-line phrases, 8.9.8). The same harmonic cadences appear in most of the hymns, which are sung homophonically, all voices uttering the same words in unison, creating the most basic harmonies. Beissel's compact musical vocabulary makes it difficult to distinguish one hymn setting from the next. The melodies seem almost deliberately nondescript. This is why the hymns have struck hearers as "the Aeolian harp harmonized," referring to the simple stringed instrument that plays itself, as it were, when the wind passing over it causes the strings to vibrate.[17]

Clearly, Beissel had a strong sense of what musical principles were appropriate for the Kloster choir. Predating Billings' Boston-published tunebooks by decades, Beissel's *Turtel-Taube* includes a detailed exposition of harmonic principles along with practical advice for performing the hymns. "In a general sense," Beissel wrote, "the hymns contained in this selection, may be looked upon as roses which have grown forth from among the piercing thorns of the cross, and consequently are not without some beauty of color and pleasantness of fragrance." Each note, each letter, has its own distinctive characteristics, which singers must be taught to know and appreciate, a process that "requires such diligence and costs so much labor that we cannot here describe it."[18] Only after mastering this esoteric knowledge can the choir turn its attention to mastering tone production, which is achieved through proper diet and mental discipline.

Finally Beissel outlines the harmonic principles underlying his four-part hymns, all lines but the bass being sung by women. The four principal notes—the tonic, third, fifth, and octave—he describes as the "masters and lords that dominate from beginning to end," while the other intervals (second, fourth, sixth, and seventh) are "servants," which must "be told how he must serve his fellow-servants, so that they may harmonize." Beissel's system takes the guesswork both out of creating melodies and of harmonizing them, since each "ruler" note has its corresponding "servants" in the alto, tenor, and bass lines; composing is like following an algorithm. For example:

If the melody is in the key of C, E is the note in the *Barrir* (tenor), and G in the *Toener* (alto). Thus the alto and the bass begin on G. This order may, however, be inverted . . . Nevertheless these letters (notes) must remain together and begin and end the tune . . . As regards the four remaining letters (notes), F, A, B, D, which we shall designate servants, let each be told how he must serve his fellow-servants, so that they may harmonize . . . If F occurs in the melody it is served by D in the tenor and bass, and by A in the alto; A demands D in the tenor and bass, and A in the alto, sometimes also in the bass; B calls for D in the tenor, and G in the alto and bass; D asks for B in the tenor, and G in the alto and bass. In this manner a melody in C may be harmonized in four parts.

Rhythmically, Beissel simply keyed the duration of notes to the cadence of the words; accented syllables received longer notes, unaccented shorter ones. Meter was flexible, floating freely without regard for bar lines. The result was unique: "The music of the Ephrata Kloster is entirely unlike the ancient church music," writes Sachse, "and it has none of the rhythm and swing of either the religious or secular folk-song of the Reformation."[19]

This sort of melodic-harmonic formula is exactly what Billings would argue against two decades later in the famous introduction to *The New-England Psalm-Singer,* where he insisted that "*Nature is the best Dictator,* for all the hard dry studied Rules that ever was prescribed, will not enable any person to form an Air any more than the bare Knowledge of the four and twenty Letters, and strict Grammatical Rules will qualify a Scholar for composing a Piece of Poetry, or properly adjusting a Tragedy, without a Genius . . . I think it is best for every *Composer* to be his own *Carver.*"[20] And the formula reveals yet another intellectual source for Beissel's musical imagination: the long-standing traditions of theosophic thought articulated by Jakob Böhme. The great German mystic had lived a century before Beissel and drew together various alchemical, Hermetic, and mystical traditions of thinking about the cosmos, music, language, geometry, and numbers that can be traced (whether or not Böhme was aware of the genealogy) through Hermes Trismegistus and Pythagoras to their ostensible source in Egypt, where Pythagoras is thought to have studied. More specifically, historian Jan Stryz has argued, Beissel's harmonic scheme was a form of sonic alchemy, characterized by "proper relationships between elements treated as living entities . . . just as in alchemy, where essential substances such as Mercury and Sulpher, as well as planetary energies like Sol and Luna, are spoken of as characters that interact with one another." The same alchemical principles were at work not just in composition, but in strict dietary regulations imposed on choir members, and in the social relations among Beissel and the singers, which "were tinctured with the drama of the alchemical love and war that played out within him."[21]

As he narrated it, Beissel's life was a harrowing battle with his own "fiery male power," which he sought to humble "after the manner of women" in order to achieve union with the Sophia. The struggle was often a losing one: "as often as my industry brings forth a flower of paradise, a sword is drawn against me, as if I had committed the greatest crime. This has been going on for many years already and it will continue until my sinful body will perish." In addition to the distressing separation of masculine from feminine, the Fall had brought another result, leaving humans further estranged: a loss of the knowledge of how words are related to what they signify—an inability, in other words, to read the "Book of Nature." "Boehme and the various hermetic groups subscribing to this view of language held that man had suffered a second, linguistic fall resulting in a 'Babylonical Confusion,' as the Rosicrucian tract *Confessio* phrases it," writes Stryz. "What prevents man from seeing the divine presence in nature is the inability to read Nature's Book properly." Words are necessarily connected to what they signify, and the knowledge of those connections had been lost. The sonic dimension, and by extension music, is essential, because language is aural as well as visible. "Sound, then, participates in the work of creation by supplying a signature to each thing, which signature in turn enables each thing to serve as an instrument of the divine. Sound subsequently becomes an expression of both God and creation."[22]

The following passage by Böhme gives a sense of how his influential rendering of Christian theosophy could underscore Beissel's harmonic method, which hinges on the alchemical balance of master and servant tones. (The convergence with Sun Ra's much later experiments with numerology and Christology, his notion of discord ended through a melting into "the eternal sun," is striking.) Böhme wrote that:

> The tree, understand the life, is divided into seven forms; now the curse of God is come into the seven forms, so that they are in strife and enmity, and one form annoys the other, and can never agree unless they all seven enter into death, and die to the self-will. Now this cannot be, unless a death comes into them, which breaks all their will, and be a death to them; as the deity in Christ was a death to the human also: The human will was changed in Christ into the eternal sun, viz. into the resignation in God; so must all the forms in the philosophic work be changed into one, viz. into Sol: Seven must become one, and yet remain in seven, but in one desire, where each form desires the other in love, and then there is no more any strife and contest.[23]

Both Kelpius and Beissel were deeply affected by their association with the Philadelphians, English mystics who discovered and applied Böhme's writings. A groundbreaking treatise on music appeared in 1697, just after Kelpius had sojourned in England on his way to Pennsylvania. It was written by Dr. Francis Lee, a specialist in Hebrew and the Kabbalah who joined the Philadelphian community that coalesced around Jane Leade near London, and published in the society's journal. Marveling at the efflorescence of music produced "by some extraordinary Genius's in this last Age" (he singles out Purcell), Lee sought to use nature as the means of understanding musical art. Again, he rearticulated a theory of music that stretches back over two millennia.

> Musick is an outward Representation of the Harmony of the Divine Powers and Properties in the Nature of God: who exists and manifest himself in infinite variety and multiplicity, all in perfect Concord and Unity . . . And thus the One Ground Note, or Bass contains in it self all the whole Scale above it; not only the Artificial Scale, but all as high as we can imagine; and its Tone is an Aggregate of them all; as the roaring of the Sea is made up of the noise of each particular Wave contain'd in it. Out of the Bass then all the other Notes proceed, as a Birth from it; and together make up its adequate proportion and Image.

Lee went on to construct a sort of interlocking chain of musical harmony, showing how each note in the scale, when taken together with those that precede and follow, occupied a relationship of concord. He moved up the scale from a bass note of G, then to A, B (related to G), C (related to both G and A), and so on. "And thus we see the first great Discord Harmonized with all the other arising from it," Lee observed. "That which went out First, must come in Last: the Great Breach or Division cannot be made up and restored to Unity, till by a Progress forwards and backwards through the whole Circle of alienation it has begun, it has work'd off the contrariety of Disproportion; and by degrees gather up the Proportion it lost, it returns again into its own Original. The Circle is here compleat, and the End has found its Beginning, the Multiplicity received into Identity and Unity."[24]

In good Hermetic style, numerological correspondences abound: the seven notes to the seven planets; the six days of the week ending in the Sabbath; the first six millennia of the world, "in Labour and Misery ending, as is supposed, in the 7000th Year, as its Sabbatical Jubilee"; and the "Seven Working Spirits of God" working toward perfection "through the whole Creation." Lee drew several conclusions. Dissonance was impossible. A set of relationships so perfect as music should not be "debased and prostituted to the vanity of common Amours," but treated with reverence. Finally, all human speech necessarily shared the artfulness of music: "Natural Pronunciation, or the Tone, Accent, and Emphasis, which we use in speaking our Words; and that variety of it that appears in the Expression of our Passions; is nothing else but Musick; it is True and Natural Harmony; and may be prick'd down and perform'd in Comfort; running in

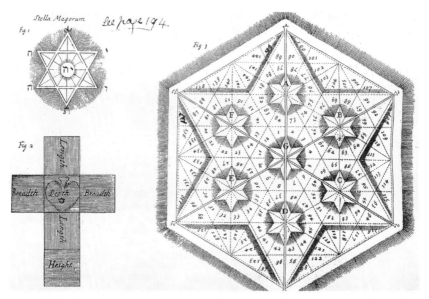

11. Published in 1697, Dr. Francis Lee's diagrams invoke the correspondences between geometry, number, letter, and sound that have characterized esoteric approaches to music since the time of Pythagoras. Courtesy of Arthur Versluis.

minute and swift Division." Hence the secret of Purcell's genius: he composed his music "by listning to Nature," finding notes that unfolded in "Natural Harmony."[25]

Of course, transferring the perfection of nature to the flesh-and-blood of an endlessly mutating spiritual community required a severe discipline, which Beissel was willing to provide to choir members. First of all, rigorous discipline of the body was required. "Care must be taken of the body, and its requirements reduced to a minimum, so that the voice may become angelic, heavenly, pure and clear, and not rough and harsh through the use of coarse food, and therefore unfit to produce the proper quality of tone, but on the contrary, in place of genuine song, only an unseemly grunting and gasping." All meat, milk, cheese, eggs, and honey were proscribed, and beans discouraged. Wheat and buckwheat were recommended as "producing cheerfulness of disposition and buoyancy of spirit"; potatoes and beets were deemed "useful." "As concerns *drink*, it has long been settled that nothing is better than pure, clear water, just as it comes from the well, or as made into soup to which a little bread is added."[26] Choir members wore spare white garments resembling the habits of Capuchin monks for all rehearsals and performances. Beissel's rehearsals ran for four hours, concluding a very taxing workday around midnight, when the choir would process across a meadow through the misty darkness to the *Nachmetten*, or midnight watch, where the Solitary would mix worship and penitence for some two hours.

Beissel himself was a very exacting director, prone to harshly upbraiding his singers when they fell short of his standards, sometimes haranguing for more than an hour. Sisters were frequently reduced to tears, while Brothers fumed. But the singing was, by all accounts, otherworldly. According to an account written in 1835, long after Beissel's time but presumably about music that remained faithful to his musical principles, "The tones issuing from the choir imitate very soft instrumental music; conveying a softness and devotion almost super-human to the auditor." The only part sung by males, the bass, was divided into two parts, "the latter resembling the deep tones of the organ, and the first, in combination with one of the female parts, is an excellent imitation of the concert horn. The whole is sung on the *falsetto* voice." The most detailed description comes from an Anglican minister from Philadelphia named Jacob Duché, who visited the cloister a few years after Beissel's death. The sisters sang with "sweet, shrill and small voices, but with a truth and exactness in time and intonation that was admirable." He continued: "The music had little or no air or melody; but consisted of simple, long notes, combined in the richest harmony . . . The performers sat with their heads reclined, their countenances solemn and dejected, their faces pale and emaciated from their manner of living, their clothing exceedingly white and quite picturesque, and their music such as thrilled to the very soul. I almost began to think myself in the world of spirits, and the objects before me were ethereal."[27]

Beissel's musical goals and methods, not to mention his cosmo-harmonic principles, had some uncanny parallels to those of Sun Ra, who had renamed his band the Arkestra at the time he changed his own name and gradually built it into a big band over the 1950s. Being an Arkestra member entailed almost permanent rehearsals; it was an eight-hour-a-day, five-day-a-week job. No band had a more lopsided ratio of rehearsal to performance. "We'd rehearse all day and right up till you performed, get off at 4 A.M., rehearse at 12 until 4, then back again," recalled one musician.[28] Even in his Birmingham days Sonny had had a propensity for unremitting rehearsals. But in Chicago his goals focused and his ambitions broadened. When the Arkestra relocated to Manhattan's Lower East Side in 1961 (a move that came about almost by accident), relatively high rents impelled a move toward communal living, an arrangement that would continue for the remaining decades of the Arkestra. Fittingly, after spending a few years in the East Village, the Arkestra pushed on to the Germantown section of Philadelphia, the initial New World stomping grounds of both Kelpius and Beissel, where Ra would reside until nearly the end of his life.

Like Beissel, Ra was troubled by sexuality; he was bothered throughout his life by a hernia and undescended testicle, and some have speculated that he was gay, though he never acknowledged it. Beissel, on the other hand, seems to have been plagued by a surfeit of sexual potency. His career resembled a series of periodic attempts to free himself from disruptive social entanglements—particularly with women, who were powerfully attracted to him throughout his life, and the men who resented and suspected Beissel's motives—in order to live a pure hermit's life. Sun Ra faced the opposite problem: highly trained musical comrades escaping his orbit to pursue relationships, usually with women. Ra would have been happy if the Arkestra had functioned as a male monastery; Beissel had the challenge of managing a monastery and a convent existing side by side, even in the same building. (Some of Ephrata's faithful were even married to each other.) Though Ra didn't require his musicians to emulate his celibacy, he maintained a kind of vigilance against what he perceived as the tendencies of women to distract the band from its musical-spiritual goals. He was even less tolerant of drugs or alcohol, a stance that audiences would find incongruous during the 1960s, when the Arkestra seemed so conspicuously attuned to a psychedelic ethos. As at Ephrata, these restrictions existed not in order to comply with some moral code but in order to heighten the spiritual potentialities and musical sensibilities in the service of a larger communal good. "Sonny sought to make his musicians his friends, his community," Szwed observes, "a community he would recruit and train, who would live together and devote themselves entirely to his music and teaching, musician-scholars whom he would tear free from outside interests and worldly distractions to be on twenty-four-hour musical and spiritual call."[29] For both communities, spiritual and artistic goals required a separation from the world, but survival entailed a participation in the commercial marketplace that generated constant centrifugal forces within the community.

One effect of this goal of creating a self-sufficient musical community was Sun Ra's decision in the mid-1950s to maintain artistic and financial control of his work by creating his own recording company. With Alton Abraham, in 1956, Ra registered a company under the name El Saturn Research, which released the great majority of Arkestra recordings over the decades. (Ra also recorded doo-wop quartets like the Cosmic Rays for a time, a genre he had known well growing up in Birmingham, where gospel quartets flourished.) The company was a sort of cottage industry, but over the years it released dozens of Ra's recordings, essentially homemade, pressed in small batches and sold by band members, cash only, at gigs. "The mastering and pressing were crude (even vinyl maniacs admit that Saturns sound much better in CD reissues)," writes Robert L. Campbell.

"At first the covers were hand-decorated, and when printed covers appeared they had a distinctly amateurish appearance." The spiritual realm the Arkestra invoked through music was developing distinctive visual dimensions. Ra's interest in Egypt and esoteric knowledge generated a kind of recognizable (though infinitely variable) iconography on the hand-decorated record jackets. The cover to *The Heliocentric Worlds of Sun Ra* features a row of portraits of famous early astronomers: da Vinci, Copernicus, Galileo, Brahe. In the middle are images of Sun Ra and Pythagoras. Coming out of an era when big bands presented themselves in formal uniforms, the Arkestra began to favor more eclectic costumes, achieving a break from the tuxedoed look when they bought a collection of costumes from a local opera company; by the 1960s they were dressing like the cast of *Godspell.* Ra had read about the symbolism of color among Egyptians, Greeks, and Tibetans, so characteristically there was a method to Ra's apparent visual madness in choosing costumes for the Arkestra.[30]

That music was the underlying but not the sole manifestation of a larger field of spiritual activity that might take visual or verbal forms was a conviction held equally by Beissel. In Ephrata as much as in the Arkestra, poetry was indistinguishable from music. Both leaders composed music according to their own unified systems, and both wrote poetry constantly, Sun Ra's often packaged as part of recordings as well as in published books. Saturn Records had its counterpart in the Ephrata printing press, which freed it from reliance on printers like Franklin, who though he handled many of Beissel's projects during the 1730s was never on cordial terms with the German mystic, and Sauer, who accused Beissel of heresy on the basis of a hymn text that he published. Like other, later spiritual communes in the United States, Ephrata was remarkable for its vertical integration. "In the schools of writing and calligraphy the Solitary were trained to write, copy, design and decorate score-books, hymnals and chorale folios," writes James Ernst. "Moreover, singing, dieting and copying were means of sanctification. Publishing brought into play printing press, bindery, papermill, oil press, mission propagandists and sales—all adding to those who mortified flesh and praised God in song." Ephrata was particularly famed for its *Frakturschriften,* highly ornate lettering in the tradition of illuminated manuscripts. The first hand-decorated manuscript hymnbook of this sort was produced by the Solitary during the winter of 1733–34. These visual symbols had significance. As Stryz suggests, "if we imagine the letter to represent an essential expression of the spirit, rather than an arbitrary sign, then labor over the sound of the musical 'letter' or the form of the written one both comprise instruction in the reading of divine script."[31]

Nowhere are Beissel and Ra more closely aligned than in the way they understood numbers, letters, words, and notes as timeless, inextricably connected, and constitutive of the universe at every level of its structure. Ra summarized this view succinctly. "The earth cannot move without music," he wrote in 1972. "The earth moves in a certain rhythm, a certain sound, a certain note. When the music stops the earth will stop and everything upon it will die." The esoteric traditions that Beissel absorbed from Böhme, Leade, and the Philadelphians are the same ones that Ra absorbed via slightly different channels in his voluminous reading and study-group activity of the early 1950s, and in both cases converged around the venerable figures of Pythagoras, Plato, Hermes Trismegistus, and the Kabbalists. These concepts were part of the common coin of European intellectual life in Beissel's day; what is remarkable is Ra's appropriation of them in the atomic age. In a treatise that accompanied an Arkestra recording released in 1957, Ra explained his method in terms very close to Beissel's emphasis in *Turtel-Taube* on training his singers to appreciate the unique properties of each individual note before using them in sequence. "My rule is that every note played must be a living note," he wrote. "In order to achieve this, I use notes like words in a sentence, making each series of sounds a separate thought. My watchword is precision. I never forget that a 'sound' is just as important as a sound doctrine in a nonmusical field." One Arkestra member recalls the bandleader exhorting him in language that could have come almost directly from Londoner Francis Lee's "New Theory of Musick" of 1697. "You know how many notes there are between C and D?" Ra said. "If you deal with those tones you can play *nature,* and nature doesn't know notes. That's why religions have bells, which sound all the transient tones. You're not musicians, you're *tone scientists.*" The alchemical principle so crucial to Beissel's work at Ephrata was strongly marked in Sun Ra. "If you mix two chemical products you produce a reaction," he wrote in reference to his poetry. "In the same way if you put together certain words you'll obtain a reaction which will have a value for people on this planet."[32]

In all its ambiguous majesty, the Bible was an essential text for both Beissel and Ra, but for neither was it sufficient. Streams of esoteric knowledge from Egypt and Greece provided a necessary complement to Christian scripture. Jewish ideas and images, particularly Kabbalism, provided another tributary feeding into Beissel and the mystics who preceded him. "The New Theory of Musick" was permeated by Kabbalistic mysticism, made visually explicit in the diagram, with its six-pointed "Seal of Solomon" and intricate intermapping of numbers and letters. Identifying as he did with Saturn, Ra made much of these homologies. "Jews worship a six-pointed star, and Saturn's the sixth planet from the Sun," he observed; "also Jews worship on Saturday, which is really Saturn's Day." Ra's intellectual quest in Chicago had begun, after all, with the conviction that the Bible had been mistranslated and misassembled, possibly deliberately, in ways that erased or distorted the role of African peoples in sacred history. The "Good Book," Ra believed, was actually a *code book,* which he set about in the 1950s finding methods of penetrating. Learning Hebrew was one possibility. "But the Kabbalists said that knowing Hebrew was not enough, that every character in the Hebrew alphabet would have to be pored over, investigated, understood as an element of the design of creation itself."[33] And so Ra found himself challenged by a kind of receding hermeneutical horizon with which he could keep pace only by rigorous study.

To equip himself for the study of etymology, Ra obtained Bibles, concordances, and dictionaries in several languages. "This was a dizzying business, endless, where even the simplest of words might have another meaning, and even the spoken word could conceal other words and meanings," writes Szwed. "The most innocuous of exchanges had to be scrutinized: he might respond to a simple greeting of 'good morning' by asking whether it was 'morning' or 'mourning' you meant." For this reason Ra refused to talk about his date of birth, preferring to speak of having arrived on planet Earth at some past time. "B-i-r-t-h" equated with "b-e-r-t-h," in the sense of a final resting place, an idea that didn't square with his ideas of eternity; it was more accurate to talk about "arriving" than about "being born." Through his fascination with puns and homophones, Ra had internalized the antagonism between spoken and written language characteristic of many religious traditions. "Only when the word had been activated by speech, and sounded out (what Rastafarians call 'word-sound-power') could the true meaning be known. It was something those Baptist preachers had known when they began by reading from the Bible in front of their congregations, and then went on, through chant and song and improvisation, to activate the text and transform the Bible's meaning."[34]

Apart from its emphasis on the spiritual significance of numbers and language, Kabbalism shared another affinity with Ephrata and the Arkestra. Unlike the mainstream of Jewish thought, with its ingrained suspicions about the place of music in religious practice, Beissel and Ra stressed music's centrality not just in the structure and workings of the cosmos, but in human expressions of reverence for the divine. Beissel had been shaped enough by the ambivalence about music that early Protestants had absorbed from their reading of the Bible that he felt compelled to write a rationale for the place of music in worship, in the form of eleven questions and answers:

> *Is it consistent with the Word of God that we sing?*
> Yes, as we find in both Old and New Testaments commands and examples. Psalm lxvii. 5, 33; Matthew xxvi. 30; Eph. v. 19; James v. 13 . . .
> *Cannot the godless sing a hymn in a manner acceptable to God?*
> Oh, no, for, like unto the prayer of the wicked, so also is their song abhorrent unto God. The bawling of their hymns pleaseth Him not. Amos v . . .
> *How shall the heart be qualified when we want to sing?*
> As it has been crushed under the law and made pensive after God, then comes the Holy Ghost and brings peace and joy into the heart, that the mouth overflows to the praise of God.

Most of Beissel's answers would have satisfied even Calvin, though his esoteric propensities show through toward the end.

> *What is meant by the psaltery with ten strings, of which David speaks?*
> As the tenth number is a perfect number (when one has counted ten, one begins again and commences with one), therefore is Christ our psaltery with ten strings, whose perfection is continually in our hearts and to be sung with our lips.
> *Who therefore teaches us to sing aright?*
> The Holy Spirit, as the true singing-master, can turn the heart into a celestial harp and divine instrument, so that it can be used without outward instrument and sound, and often also without any audible voice.[35]

Grounded as he was from childhood in the African-American church, Ra showed none of this fastidiousness about the place of music in religious experience (though black gospel continued to worry about such things). Ra did, however, have an argument with perhaps the major theme of both African-American Christianity and religious music: the message of freedom from bondage—the analogy between the Israelites in bondage in Egypt and blacks in bondage in America. This was the point on which the Bible had gone most tragically awry, Ra thought, as he reflected on the glory of Egypt. "Moses said, fear the Creator. Why should a person fear the Creator, be afraid to express themselves? . . . That man [Moses] was a murderer, a liar, and a deceiver. Moses wasn't good for this planet . . . The Egyptian government, they contributed so much to humanity—he ain't left no art, no beauty, no alphabets . . . He learned magic along with the Ra priests and then he took it and used it against them. Bit the hand that fed him. Turned against Pharaoh."[36]

Since most of African-American theology and sacred song was founded on the Exodus story, it was fundamentally incommensurable with Ra's vision. Ra set about constructing a countermyth to the orthodox mythology

12. Sun Ra in a promotional still for *Space Is the Place,* a 1973 film that, like Ra's music, blended elements of biblical allegory, science fiction, and commentary on contemporary race relations. © 1973 Jim Newman

of the Bible, one that recognized the glories of ancient Egypt but also posited a liberating future promised by the Space Age. As Ra and his Arkestra moved into the 1960s and 1970s, they came to emphasize the utopian possibilities of a technological future more than the glories of the past. Space, rather than Egypt, Zion, or Canaan, came to stand for the potential of collective liberation from worldly bondage. And so Ra and the Arkestra took up their position at what Szwed describes in a splendid passage as "a strange intersection where the passivity of New Age, the aggressiveness of science fiction, the coolness of mathematics, the oppositionality of mysticism, and echoes of the mythos of the Nation of Islam all come together. Some might call this black science fiction, focusing on the interplay of the themes of freedom, apocalypse, and survival; or maybe 'Afrofuturism,' where the material culture of Afro-American folk religions are used as sacred technologies to control virtual realities."[37]

But even as Ra rejected an orthodox Christian reading of the Bible, he appropriated forms from the black church. In Arkestra performances, "space chants" were both modeled on and fulfilled the function of spirituals. The following lines, for example, from an album titled *Beyond the Purple Star Zone,* echo the spiritual "No Hiding Place":

"No Hiding Place"	Arkestra chant
Dere's no hidin' place down dere,	The space age is here to stay
Dere's no hidin' place down dere,	Ain't no place that you can run away
Oh I went to de rock to hide my face,	If you run to the rock to hide your face
De rock cried out, "No hidin' place,"	The rock'll cry out, no hiding place.
Dere's no hidin' place down dere.	It's gonna be just like your ancestors said
	Even though they're cold and dead.[38]

The old spiritual "Ship of Zion" provides the model for another space chant:

"Ship of Zion"	Arkestra chant
De Gospel ship is sailin,'	You're on the spaceship Earth
Hosann-sann	And you're outward bound
O, Jesus is de captain,	Out among the stars
Hosann-sann	Destination unknown
De angels are de sailors,	But you haven't met the captain of the
Hosann-sann	spaceship yet, have you?
O, is your bundle ready?	You'd better pay your fare now

Hosann-sann	You'll be left behind
O, have you got your ticket?	You'll be left hangin'
Hosann-sann	In the empty air
	You won't be here and you won't be there[39]

The Arkestra performed these space chants in the manner of ring shouts, the distinctive counterclockwise shuffling, handclapping, call-and-response chants of the South Carolina Sea Islands that evoke some of the earliest practices of African worship in America. "So, just as the slaves' 'sacred world' brought together past and future, time and space, in the eternal now of the ring shout," writes Graham Lock, "so Sun Ra united ancient Egypt and outer space in his myth-world and celebrated the union in his sacred arena, the concert, where costumes and instruments alike linked the worlds of Africa and science fiction, and the entire spectrum of black creative music was enacted in ceremonious and colorful spectacle."[40]

AT LAST, then, some space begins to open up between Arkestra and Ephrata. Despite their common experience of exodus and the uncanny intellectual overlaps in their theorizing and creating of music, Ra and Beissel were, at the risk of stating the obvious, shaped by vastly different historical circumstances. Neo-Pythagoreans they may have been, but they drew on different reserves of popular culture, and they also appropriated them differently. Though in his own life they were inextricable, one can divide the sources of Sun Ra's spiritual and artistic life into separate categories, one deriving from reading and discussion of esoteric texts, the other from African-American popular culture. As Szwed observes, "no one in the Arkestra appeared to be in ecstatic possession, or in deep mimesis; rather they seemed to be modeling a certain kind of social and spiritual order, eclectically drawing theatrics from many sources other than the Afro-Baptist church: the flash of black cabaret, bar-walking saxophonists, nightclub routines, vaudeville and tent shows, as well as from the big bands themselves, which often had their own resident comics, dancers, skits, and parodies which reflected their early experiences in vaudeville and tent shows."[41] Even European opera provided inspiration.

Beissel too had a heritage of popular culture, the fiddling and dancing he excelled in as a young apprentice, but which he rejected as decisively as he renounced "mortal Women." Or perhaps more accurately, the hidden knowledge he picked up through Böhme and the Philadelphians was Beissel's popular culture, but it was suffused with the sacred in a conspicuous way that twentieth-century black popular culture wasn't always. In effect, Beissel as composer and choir leader drew on two intermingled but theologically distinct realms of culture—Christianity and esoteric thought —while Ra had at his disposal a third: secular popular culture (which, as we've seen, is itself accented with stylings and techniques developed for the sacred).

And Ra's was a popular culture not just of music and stage, but of science fiction and alien abduction stories. A turning point in Ra's life had taken place in 1936, at college, when he dreamed of being visited by space beings, transported through a giant light beam, berobed and invested with wisdom, warned that earthly chaos lay ahead, and commanded to return to Earth as a kind of messiah. He continued to retell the dream story throughout his life, with little variation. The vision has much in common with the UFO abduction stories that began to appear in the early 1950s, which in turn followed patterns found in conversion narratives told by enslaved African Americans in the nineteenth century. "Whether Ra's trip to 'another planet' was physical or psychic, visionary or imaginary," proposes Lock, "its significance perhaps lies more in the way he represented it, not in biblical terms but as a science fiction scenario, as if to signal to African Americans that the only way to define a personal identity, to experience a spiritual rebirth, to be 'saved,' in fact, was not by following the old ways of the Christian church but by embracing the future and traveling to outer space."[42]

Beissel, not surprisingly, showed less interest in a future defined by technology and intertwined with beings from other worlds. Though interested in the millennium and thereby reunion with Virgin Sophia, he conceptualized it, like so many others, in the images and metaphors of the Hebrew Bible. In his indifference to the blessings of science, Beissel shaped a community different from subsequent American sects: the Shakers, with their technological wizardry, and the Latter-day Saints, whose revealed scriptures can strike the uninitiated as having a science-fiction, Tolkienesque aesthetic. But of course, Ra's understanding of science and technology had little to do with what the engineers of NASA or of IBM were undertaking. At some point the post-Enlightenment begins to circle back to the pre-Enlightenment.

The Arkestra's race consciousness, on the other hand, had no clear counterpart in the Ephrata experience. Ra was willing to challenge the authority of the Bible in ways unimaginable to Beissel. Not that this is a move that is ever undertaken lightly or without risk. In rejecting the Hebrew Bible as a deliberate mistranslation, Ra was moving against one of the strong currents of his times. Articulated by Baptist ministers like Martin Luther King Jr., much of the rhetoric of the civil rights movement was heavily indebted to the language of Exodus, and the movement inspired some of its loyalty by appealing to what it hoped was the Christian conscience of the nation. In the pursuit of a transformed social order, the social movements of the mid-twentieth century would pluck out of obscurity some of the most traditional of sacred songs, but not without transforming them along the way.

CHAPTER TEN

The Nation with the Soul of a Church

> When we colonize the moon there will be little green people join-
> ing their antennae together and they'll be singing (or chirping)
> something. And it will be "We Shall Overcome."
>
> —JULIAN BOND

FOR AMERICANS, there are a handful of songs that people turn to almost reflexively at moments of national trauma and tragedy. Most can
be found in Protestant hymnals. One could generate a substantial list of
occasions when these songs have been performed at major junctures in the
civic life of the United States, and sometimes outside the country as well.
There are moments when the relentless centrifugal pressures of American
society are relaxed in public spectacles that provide a welcome sense of *e
pluribus unum.* "Amazing Grace" has sounded at the memorial for victims
of the Challenger space shuttle disaster in 1986, at services for victims of
the Oklahoma City bombing in 1994, and at the mass for John F. Kennedy
Jr. in 1999. "We Shall Overcome" has sounded at countless rallies, demonstrations, and memorials around the world, from the 1963 March on
Washington to the 1989 protest at Tienanmen Square, from anti-apartheid
rallies in South Africa to a massive outdoor celebration of Nelson Man-
dela's seventieth birthday in London. Both were heard at key moments in
the aftermath of the destruction of the World Trade Center on 11 September 2001.

"Amazing Grace" and "We Shall Overcome" have become paradigmatic musical expressions of what is sometimes called the "civil religion"
of the United States: the body of quasi-sacred beliefs and rituals that constitute a sort of secular creed that unites American citizens and binds them
to the nation. Gunnar Myrdal famously called it "the American Creed";

its distinctive ideology led G. K. Chesterton to describe the United States as "a nation with the soul of a church," a phrase that Sidney Mead would appropriate for the title of a book analyzing American ideology.[1] Civil religion emerged as a blending of Puritan ideas about America as a New Israel with themes drawn from the Enlightenment and the American Revolution: it features national saints like Washington, Jefferson, and Martin Luther King Jr.; sacred spaces like Mount Vernon, Independence Hall, Ground Zero, and the District of Columbia's proliferating monuments; sacred times and rituals like the Fourth of July, Washington's birthday, Memorial Day, Thanksgiving, and the Pledge of Allegiance; sacred objects like the original copies of the Declaration of Independence and the Constitution.[2] Civil religion expresses itself in the "God bless you" of politicians and "In God We Trust" of currency; in "My Country 'Tis of Thee," "O Beautiful for Spacious Skies," and "God Bless America."

"Amazing Grace" and "We Shall Overcome" occupy an important spot on this national soundtrack. Ironically, despite their evangelical origins neither song makes explicit reference to Christ, or even to God for that matter, at least in the commonly used verses. Yet both songs sound perfectly at home in sacred or quasi-sacred settings, at times of spiritual moment. Though deeply rooted in evangelical Protestant religion, the songs, like so many others we have considered, are deeply indebted to the language of the Hebrew Bible. And though many would undoubtedly consider "Amazing Grace" and "We Shall Overcome" quintessentially American, both songs are the products of a transnational circulation of ideas and musics, both in their histories and in their contemporary uses.

Though they have much in common, these secular spirituals reveal quite different histories, and gesture at different social goals. "Amazing Grace" has come to be a song of the *individual* subject seeking solace in the face of suffering and adversity. Like Dorsey's "Precious Lord," it conveys its spiritual message not through a didactic injunction but by evoking within the singer the kind of universal experience that might lead to a recognition of the need to seek a similar state of spiritual grace or solace. "We Shall Overcome" by contrast seems above all a song of *communal* identity, of solidarity based on collective action. It has a different political valence; its history has given the song undeniable associations with the left. It's hard to imagine Young Americans for Freedom singing "We Shall Overcome," unless as a parody. "Amazing Grace," on the other hand, seems distinctly apolitical (itself a kind of politics). However, these associations and affiliations are contingent on time and place. "Amazing Grace" began its career as a song less about the isolated individual than about the individual within a divine covenant, while "We Shall Overcome" started out as a song of the first-person singular. Both songs developed markedly new associations and meanings during the 1960s.

Only a few hymns have managed to transcend their Christian origins and become secular spirituals of American civil religion. How can we account for the careers of "Amazing Grace" and "We Shall Overcome"? Perhaps by comparing them to another hymn of cosmopolitan origin and potential appeal to an interreligious audience, we can better understand how a hymn can become a secular spiritual. Through an extraordinary series of historical encounters and transformations, "How Great Thou Art" has become one of the most widely known Protestant hymns in the world, and is sometimes identified as the single most popular Christian hymn among Americans. But it has never become a secular spiritual, and it's difficult to imagine it gaining much traction outside evangelical Christian circles. The reason has to do with the hymn's theology, of course, but also with the context in which it became famous and the restrictions governing the circulation of music that is not in the public domain.

THE GENEALOGY of "Amazing Grace" is probably better known than that of any other American sacred song. Its words have been widely accepted as autobiographical for its author, John Newton, a seafaring man of the eighteenth century who underwent a famous conversion experience during a terrible storm in the North Atlantic. Popular accounts of "Amazing Grace" depict Newton "wiping the brine from his forehead as he wrote the hymn, with the breakers still crashing over the gunwales," observes Newton scholar Bruce Hindmarsh. In fact Newton almost certainly composed the hymn twenty-five years after his near-annihilation at sea. The process by which Newton the self-described "infidel and libertine" became Newton the evangelist hymnwriter was a protracted one. Through his twenties, Newton was a citizen of the Atlantic "hydrarchy" vividly described by historians Peter Linebaugh and Marcus Rediker: an unruly, loose-knit, transatlantic network of sailors, African slaves, dispossessed English peasants, radical evangelists, repatriated prisoners, indentured servants, and religious radicals that ranged across the Atlantic world beginning around the middle of the seventeenth century. These diverse groups represented a threat to the newly emerging capitalist economic order and were ruthlessly put down by the Herculean state as, hydralike, they reared their many heads in periodic rebellions staged in England, western Africa, the Americas, and the oceans in between.[3]

Newton, though, unlike a great majority of the hydrarchy, had social advantages; his father was a sea captain. Born in London in 1725, Newton joined the merchant marine as a teenager with the expectation of advancing to his father's station. Like so many sailors, he was press-ganged into the British Navy in 1743, attempted to desert, was brutally handled, and was eventually transferred to a ship involved in the African slave trade. For two years Newton languished on the Guinea coast of Africa before joining a ship completing its triangular route to England in 1748 via Brazil and Newfoundland. In March a savage storm hit the ship off Newfoundland, and Newton, who had been idly reading Thomas a Kempis' *Imitation of Christ*, found himself praying. An account Newton wrote later, in 1764, the year he was ordained by the Church of England, identifies that storm as his moment of conversion.[4]

But his path to the parish priesthood in Olney, a small town in the Midlands, was far from direct. After completing his perilous voyage, Newton returned to sea as a mate and again as a captain and married before leaving the sea to settle in Liverpool. He worked for the customs service as a tide inspector, studied theology, and became active in a church. Without attending university he learned to read Hebrew, Greek, Latin, and Syriac. He became active in evangelical circles that included John Whitefield, the Wesleys, and various Moravians living in England. For several years he had trouble obtaining ordination orders, ostensibly because he lacked a university degree but also because of his association with Dissenters. He finally joined the priesthoood and took a parish in Olney, a market town of some 2,000 inhabitants; its commons had recently been enclosed by an act of Parliament. "The people here are mostly poor—the country low and dirty," Newton observed; his friend William Cowper, with whom he would later write hymns, described Olney as "inhabited chiefly by the half-starved and the ragged of the Earth." Perhaps as a result of his worldly and nonconformist background, the new curate developed a close rapport with his parishioners, a capacity to empathize with the daily struggle of tradespeople buffeted by ruinous market fluctuations.[5] Newton began writing hymns for specific occasions and contexts in the life of the parish. In 1779 many of these would be collected in *Olney Hymns,* the hymnbook in which "Amazing Grace" first appears.

Though Newton left no explicit evidence, by comparing Newton's manuscript sermon notebooks and his diary, Hindmarsh is able to pin down the day on which the hymn was first used at Olney: New Year's Day 1773. In fact the six stanzas of "Amazing Grace" track closely the argument of the sermon. Originally titled "Faith's Review and Expectation," both the hymn and sermon were based on 1 Chronicles 17:16–17, which conveys David's response to a prophet's announcement of the covenant: "And David the king came and sat before the Lord, and said, Who am I, O Lord God, and what is mine house, that thou hast brought me hitherto?

And yet this was a small thing in thine eyes, O God; for thou hast also spoken of thy servant's house for a great while to come, and hast regarded me according to the estate of a man of high degree, O Lord God." "Amazing Grace" originated, like so many psalms and hymns, as an imitation of the original Hebrew psalmist, an attempt to clarify and dramatize the idea of a divine covenant with God's chosen people. In short, "We are singing a paraphrase of the words of King David when we sing 'Amazing Grace.'" The model of exegesis available to Newton would have him interpreting Christ as the son of David—a fulfillment of divine promise, and an extension of God's grace to Newton and his Olney congregation. While pointing to the individual's experience of saving grace, the broader context of the hymn is inescapably social: it is about a promise extended to a group, and fully realized only within the corporate body of Christ. "'Amazing Grace' was a didactic hymn of biblical theology written for a society of believers within an evangelical Anglican parish," explains Hindmarsh. "In the mouth of the singer, 'I' and 'me' and 'mine' [were] autobiographical only within the larger context of salvation history."[6]

Writing in his diary exactly ten years after introducing the hymn in worship at Olney, Newton amplified his understanding of how grace had operated in his own life, in a way that has encouraged speculation about the autobiographical nature of his most famous hymn. "Few living can have more cause than myself to say, What am I—that thou hast brought me hitherto," he wrote on New Year's Day 1783 (seven months before the Salem Moravians would launch their musical celebration of American independence). "Brought me from Africa, from the house of bondage, saved me from sinking in the Ocean & from a thousands deaths—raised me from a state of contempt & misery beyond the common lot of mortals—to admit me among thy children, thy servants, to know & preach thy Gospel, And this in a situation of honor & eminence."[7]

> Amazing grace! (how sweet the sound)
> That sav'd a wretch like me!
> I was once lost, but now am found,
> Was blind, but now I see.
>
> 'Twas grace that taught my heart to fear,
>   And grace my fears reliev'd;
> How precious did that grace appear,
>   The hour I first believ'd!
>
> Thro' many dangers, toils and snares,
> I have already come;
> 'Tis grace has brought me safe thus far,
> And grace will lead me home.

The Lord has promis'd good to me,
His word my hope secures;
He will my shield and portion be,
As long as life endures.

Yes, when this flesh and heart shall fail,
And mortal life shall cease;
I shall possess, within the vail,
A life of joy and peace.

The earth shall soon dissolve like snow,
The sun forbear to shine;
But God, who call'd me here below,
Will be for ever mine.

The hymn begins with wonder, and with "the stark contrasts that evoked the initial cry of wonder," Hindmarsh notes in a fine reading of the hymn. "The second stanza, ringing changes on the thrice repeated 'grace,' harks back to the first exclamation while developing the paradox in evangelical theology that the preaching of the law, and the remorse which it provokes, is itself a part of the very grace which brings powerful psychological release from the guilt of sin and the fear of damnation." He continues: "Of the danger and toil of stanza three, both Newton and his poor parishioners had had much, but the last half of the stanza becomes a pivot upon which the whole hymn turns, gathering the past up once more into the word 'grace' and then turning with faith to face the future."[8] The final three stanzas, less commonly used now, follow the believer through the rest of life, death, and the end of time.

Set in common meter, with alternating eight- and six-syllable lines, "Amazing Grace" can be sung to any number of psalm and hymn tunes. We have no way to know what setting was used in Newton's parish; the first recorded tune associated with it was the now-obscure "Hephzibah," in a British collection of hymns published in 1808. "Amazing Grace" fell quickly out of use in Britain. It would have a far greater impact in America, where it first appeared in a Dutch Reformed hymnbook published in New York in 1789. It appeared in unofficial songbooks as well, including the *Hartford Selection* (1789) and *Village Hymns* (1824), important musical resources for the Second Great Awakening in New England, which Timothy Dwight had labored so zealously to promote as president of Yale. In the southern and western revival frontiers, "Amazing Grace" appeared in a Baptist collection published in Virginia in 1793 and in the *Dover Selection* (1828), where it was placed in the category of spiritual songs "for popular use." The first edition of the Methodist *Zion Songster*, published in 1829 and reprinted numerous times over the following decades, contained "Amazing Grace." That collection was probably the source for Harriet Beecher Stowe's Uncle Tom, who, to the consternation of Simon Legree, persists in singing Methodist hymns, including "Amazing Grace."[9]

BOTH American religious allegiances and musical technologies were changing rapidly during the decades when "Amazing Grace" established itself in the evangelical repertoire. Sects like the Shakers, Mormons, and Seventh-Day Adventists and many others flourished during what historians call the Second Great Awakening, but membership among established Protestant churches was also skyrocketing. Along with a dramatic increase in the land mass of the United States came an increase in both population and church membership. In 1790 there were approximately 4 million people living in the United States, with only one in twenty west of the Appalachians. By the Civil War, the population had increased to more than 30 million, with half settled in the trans-Appalachian West. Church membership increased even more dramatically, tenfold between 1800 and 1850; in 1800 one in fifteen was a Protestant church member, by 1850 one in seven. The number of churches showed comparable growth; in 1780 there were around 2,500 congregations, which increased to 11,000 in 1820 and 52,000 in 1860. Much of this growth was attributable to Methodists, who by 1850 were by far the largest American denomination. What had been roughly 50 Methodist congregations in 1783 had reached nearly 20,000 in 1860, compared with 12,150 for Baptists, the second-largest denomination. "American Methodism was truly a national phenomenon, unmatched in the breadth of its appeal by any other religious movement," writes historian John Wigger. It was "the largest, most geographically diverse movement of middling and artisan men and women in the early republic."[10] An 1807 long-meter hymn captures some of the militant spirit of Methodism during its Awakening bloom:

> The world, the devil, and Tom Paine,
> Have tried their force, but all in vain.
> They can't prevail, the reason is:
> The Lord defends the Methodist.
>
> They pray, they sing, they preach the best,
> And do the Devil most molest;
> If Satan had his vicious way,
> He'd kill and damn them all today.
>
> They are despised by Satan's train,
> Because they shout and preach so plain;
> I'm bound to march in endless bliss,
> And die a shouting Methodist.[11]

Alongside skyrocketing numbers and fervor were innovations in preaching, prayer, and music; the Methodists, Baptists, and other newly revived churchfolk were worshipping differently. The legendary camp meetings that began in Kentucky in 1801 drew a significant proportion of the state's population into gatherings that sometimes lasted several days; during those days, worshippers spent nearly all their waking hours preaching, praying, or singing. Incredulous observers were astonished by the spectacle of people sighing, moaning, jeering, barking, jerking, jumping uncontrollably, and falling into trances. The "singing exercise," wrote Barton Stone, a minister who helped organize the gathering at Cane Ridge, "is more unaccountable than any thing else I ever saw. The subject in a very happy state of mind would sing most melodiously, not from the mouth or nose, but entirely in the breast, the sounds issuing from thence. Such music silenced every thing, and attracted the attention of all. It was most heavenly. None could ever be tired of hearing it."[12]

Camp meetings called for new types of music, more direct and emotional than the familiar psalms and hymns of Watts and his Calvinist kin. Lyrically, the themes remained largely the same. Hymns placed the evangelical believer in the role of an apostle progressing through a spiritual journey of conversion, perseverance, Christian witness, and to heaven, always acknowledging the profound distance separating even the most pious believer from God, and used familiar metaphors usually drawn from the Hebrew Bible. But the musical vehicles changed to fit the circumstances of the new forms of social worship. Participants needed new songs with catchy, memorable melodies and refrains that could be picked up immediately. Fortuitously, shape-note books provided a torrent of such tunes. Of the spiritual hothouse of the Second Awakening among New England Baptists, camp-meeting Methodists, Mormons, Shakers, and African Americans, historian Nathan Hatch writes, "Never has the Christian church been blessed with such a furious and creative outpouring of vernacular song."[13]

The antebellum years saw the popular acceptance of the "fasola" method, which began as part of an elite effort to improve congregational singing in Massachusetts but ended up democratizing musical notation and producing a distinctively American idiom of sacred song. Singing schools went hand in hand with the development of simplified systems of musical notation. As early as 1714, a music educator named John Tufts had published *A Very Plain and Easy Introduction to the Singing of Psalm Tunes,* which indicated different notes by placing letters on a five-line staff: F for *fa,* S for *so,* L for *la,* M for *mi.* More popular and influential was the method published at the end of the eighteenth century by William Little and William Smith of Philadelphia, who developed shape-note heads: in their system, *fa* appeared as a triangle, *so* as a circle, *la* as a square, and *mi* as diamond. Because the diatonic scale contains seven notes, *fa, so,* and *la* could designate either of two notes, depending on their placement on the staff; *mi* could designate only the seventh step of the scale. Scorned as "dunce notes" in cultured circles, the new technology migrated during the first decades of the nineteenth century through western New England and Pennsylvania into backwoods Virginia, North Carolina, and Kentucky, where it joined forces with the celebrated camp-meeting revivals of Gasper River, Cane Ridge, and other backwoods settlements.

Through shape-note notation, the hymns of Watts and the increasingly popular Charles Wesley could be joined to new tunes of secular origin, mainly Celtic ballads and fiddle tunes. New tunebooks using shape notes were scored for three lines, with tenor carrying the melody (as for Billings' compositions), generating a distinctive modal, "high lonesome" sound. In practice, the community of singers would work through the tune singing the tones as "fa," "so," "la," and so on, to fix the individual lines before repeating with the actual text. At least thirty-eight tunebooks using shape notes were published between 1798 and 1855, when *The Social Harp* appeared. The pathbreaking *Southern Harmony* was the most popular tunebook of the nineteenth century, selling some 600,000 copies between its release in 1835 and the end of the Civil War. In it, "Amazing Grace" was paired for the first time with a new tune, the now-familiar "New Britain." The origins of the new tune are uncertain. It is thought to have migrated to the Shenandoah Valley from Scotland or the Hebrides, and appeared in print for the first time in 1831, in *The Virginia Harmony*. One scholar has linked it to an old Scottish ballad called "Fair Helen of Kirkconnel."[14] Despite this famously intimate fit between text and tune, "New Britain" was used as the setting for other famous hymns, including Watts's "Alas and Did My Savior Bleed" and Cowper's "There Is a Fountain Filled with Blood." Likewise, "Amazing Grace" found itself set to dozens of different melodies throughout the nineteenth century. For example, in Sankey's 1895 edition of *Gospel Hymns,* "Amazing Grace" is set to the tune "Warwick," attributed to Samuel Stanley. The hymn was also published with a variety of wandering refrains—choruses that could be used interchangeably with several hymns. This refrain, for example, was attached to "Amazing Grace":

> Shout, shout for glory,
> Shout, shout aloud for glory;
> Brother, sister, mourner,
> All shout glory hallelujah.[15]

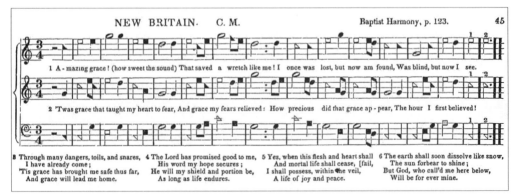

13. The text of "Amazing Grace" was first paired with the now-familiar tune "New Britain" in one of the many shape-note tunebooks that appeared in the first half of the nineteenth century. Courtesy of Fine Arts Library, Michigan State University.

Though the singing schools had sought to replace the increasingly unruly method of lining-out hymns with the more disciplined reading of music, the call-and-response technique worked too well in camp meetings to be jettisoned. An early Methodist hymnbook included this call-and-response song:

Call:
O brothers will you meet me,
O sisters will you meet me,
O mourners will you meet me
On Canaan's happy shore.

Response:
By the grace of God I'll meet you
By the grace of God I'll meet you
By the grace of God I'll meet you
Where parting is no more.[16]

There was another body of short, catchy songs developed for specific functions and performed as call-and-response: work songs of enslaved African Americans. Out of this vast, intensively researched but still and always mysterious repertoire emerged what we now call "We Shall Overcome." "Amazing Grace" epitomizes one type of song genealogy, in which the origin and circumstances are reasonably clear—in this case, practically to the day, and with accompanying scripture—while its subsequent development, especially as it entered the repertoire of camp-meeting and revival songs, becomes more difficult to trace. In contrast, "We Shall Overcome" has no clear point of origin; like all work songs and spirituals, it springs autochthonously, its circumstances of creation unknown. Asked about their version of the song, performed with the words "I'll Overcome Someday" as a shout at an all-night prayer vigil, worshippers in Johns Island, South Carolina, identified it as "an old slave song," used as a work song by field hands. Some accounts link the song to a spiritual, "No More Auction Block for Me," which was set to a tune called "Sicilian Mariners." A film documentary on "We Shall Overcome" shows blues artist Taj Mahal performing a version on guitar using the phrase, "I'll be all right." Reportedly this version was popular in black Baptist churches by the end of the nineteenth century.[17] Only in 1900 did the song enter the written record, in a version arranged by Charles Tindley for a song collection titled *New Songs of the Gospel,* compiled by C. Austin Miles.

Tindley was a renowned preacher in Philadelphia. In an era of iron-clad segregation, the Bainbridge Street Methodist Episcopal Church (popularly called "Tindley Temple") attracted substantial numbers of white worshippers in addition to its African-American base. Tindley was pushing worship in the direction in which Dorsey and his associates would prod Chicago's old-line black churches within a generation. His church encouraged more emotional and expressive worship during services, more like a storefront holiness church than the dignified and staid comportment that Methodists were associated with by the turn of the twentieth century. Philadelphia had long figured as an important place for black worship and music. A century earlier, free blacks like Absalom Jones and Richard Allen had become exasperated by discrimination against African Americans in Methodist churches and had founded several new churches in Philadelphia, including the African Methodist Episcopal (A.M.E.) Church, also known as "Mother Bethel." For use in the new church, Allen in 1801 compiled the first African-American hymn collection, which included mainly texts by Watts, Wesley, and Newton. But the hymnbook also featured hymns tailored to African-American tastes, including ones from the oral tradition, and pioneered the transcription of "wandering refrains" long before they were published in white gospel collections like Sankey's. Tindley was a kind of link between Allen and Dorsey. Born into slavery, he became a charismatic and hugely successful minister in Philadelphia. As a composer of gospel songs, he influenced the direction of Dorsey. His songs were included in collections like *Gospel Pearls,* which Dorsey and later Mahalia Jackson admired (it was the collection she first used in Chicago).

But Tindley's "I Will Overcome" has very little in common with the version of "We Shall Overcome" familiar since the 1960s. That song is not a standard meter at all: 5.5.7.4.4.7 is sui generis. But it is supremely suited for lining-out by a songleader, since each verse is entirely constructed from a three- or four-word phrase ("We shall overcome," "I am not afraid," "We'll walk hand in hand," etc.) that is then repeated throughout the verse, with "Deep in my heart I do believe" as a sort of bridge. And its melody corresponds nicely to the text. The first two identical phrases ("We shall overcome") attempt unsuccessfully to rise, but are pulled down. In the third phrase ("We shall overcome some day"), the melody pulls away, reaching its highest point of the song on the note (a ninth) that accompanies "some." In the second eight bars, a slow falling-off of the melody occurs. There are two four-syllable parallel falling phrases ("Deep in my heart, I do believe"), the second beginning a minor third below the first. The final phrase follows the same words as the final phrase of the first eight bars ("We shall overcome some day") but resolves downward to the tonic. What the musical setting depicts is a struggle to rise, accomplished on the third attempt at the midpoint of the song, then a slow falling back to harmonic resolution.

Tindley's "I'll Overcome Some Day" is quite different. It is also sixteen measures long, but in a 3/4 time signature rather than 4/4. The first eight bars consist of two identical musical phrases and are in common meter (8.6.8.6), with an ABAB rhyme scheme; the second eight measures are a chorus (6.6.6.8) that might function as a wandering refrain for other songs. The text echoes both martial hymns like "Hold the Fort!" ("This world is one great battlefield" is how Tindley's hymn begins) and "Amazing Grace" ("A thousand snares are set for me"). Tindley's "I'll Overcome Some Day," in other words, has more in common with "Amazing Grace" than with the more familiar, civil rights–era variation of "We Shall Overcome." As set to "New Britain," "Amazing Grace" offers a textbook example of the bourgeois song form in terms of its harmonic cadence and its pitch contour, which follows a classic arch pattern, rising and falling. The song's melodic phrases form complementary pairs, observes musicologist Richard Middleton, which neatly mirror the symmetrical pairing of words (grace/wretch, lost/found, blind/see).[18]

In short, Tindley's version remained squarely in the fold of evangelical Christianity, emphasizing the individual's struggle to withstand worldly temptations. Not until the middle of the century did "We Shall Overcome" take on any of the political inflections for which it is known. The roots of the civil rights struggle of the 1950s and 1960s lie in the interracial labor movement that began a generation earlier, in what Michael Denning has called the "Age of the CIO"; so does the emergence of "We Shall Overcome" as a secular spiritual. Actually, the use of Protestant hymns by workers and labor organizers extends well back into the nineteenth cen-

14. One source for "We Shall Overcome" was a gospel hymn written by Philadelphia minister Charles Tindley, though both words and tune are notably different from the familiar version. Source: C. Austin Miles, *New Songs of the Gospel* (Philadelphia: Hall-Mack, 1900).

tury, when union organizers began borrowing Christian images and hymn tunes in order to contest what seemed a clear preference on the part of the established churches for the interests of business over labor. Especially popular were the Gilded Age gospel songs of Ira Sankey and Philip Bliss, including "The Ninety and Nine" and even the much-loved, much-maligned "Sweet Bye and Bye," target of Mark Twain and Joe Hill. "Hold the Fort!" supplied the most widely used tune for all these labor song-poems. An 1886 version by James Tallmadge included these stanzas:

> How the mighty host advances,
> Labor leads the van;
> The Knights of Labor are rallying by the thousands
> On the labor plan.

> Strong entrenched behind their minions,
> Sit the money kings;
> Slavery grabbers, thieves, and traitors
> Join them in their rings . . .

> Storm the fort, ye Knights of Labor
> 'Tis a glorious fight:
> Brawn and brain against injustice—
> God defend the right.[19]

The Wobblies also had a well-known version—"Hold the fort for we are coming— / Union men, be strong. / Side by side we battle onward, / Victory will come"—which was republished in a wide range of union songbooks. The Southern Tenant Farmers' Union used it during its difficult organizing campaigns in the 1930s. Out of this milieu was born "We Shall Overcome" as protest song.

In 1945 African-American tobacco workers in Charleston, South Carolina (site of so much social turmoil during the Wesleys' brief sojourn there in the 1740s), went on strike against the American Tobacco Company, which was paying them forty-five cents an hour. Strikers slowed the tempo of a gospel song usually sung to the words "We will see the Lord someday," sung rapidly and accompanied by handclapping. "We will win our rights someday" became the strike version. "When we first started singing I thought it was kind of silly," recalled one worker. "But as the strike went along it gave me a whole lot of encouragement. And believing that we would overcome, it made me fight that much harder, and we did overcome—we won." By the following year the song had migrated to the Highlander Folk School of Monteagle, Tennessee, northwest of Chattanooga. Highlander was an integrated training center for labor organizers and social-justice activists founded in 1932 by Myles Horton, who had begun as a Presbyterian missionary and Young Men's Christian Association organizer before attending Union Theological Seminary. The song helped create solidarity among students during trying times. Jamila Jones, then a teenager, tells of singing the song in the dark with about fifty other Highlanders as armed deputies searched the compound, ostensibly for moonshine; she spontaneously created the line "We are not afraid today." "It unnerved them," she recalled; "If you have to sing, do you have to sing so loud?" she recalled one of the thugs asking her. (The school was closed by a Tennessee court in 1960 for being integrated and allegedly selling beer, but quickly reopened.) Highlander students fanned out across the South, carrying the song to strikes and demonstrations in which they were involved.[20]

Horton's wife, Zilphia, taught it to Pete Seeger, who modified the rhythm of the song and added some verses. Seeger explained why he changed the wording from "We Will Overcome," as he first heard it in 1947, to "We Shall Overcome." "I changed it to 'We shall,'" he said. "Toshi [his wife] kids me that it was my Harvard grammar, but I think I like a more open sound; 'We Will' has alliteration to it, but 'We shall' opens the mouth wider; the 'i' in 'will' is not an easy vowel to sing well."[21] Martin Luther King Jr. heard this at a twenty-fifth anniversary celebration for Highlander. The next day, as he worked over the song's lyrics in the backseat of a car, King remarked to Ralph Abernathy, "That song really sticks with you, doesn't it." Two years later, Seeger helped recruit a banjo picker named Guy Carawan as music director at Highlander. Though he gave the appearance of being a hillbilly—a "California beach guy," in the words of Julian Bond—Carawan knew roots music well and innovated in the use of black vernacular music like "Eyes on the Prize" in the struggle for racial equality.[22] In 1960 Carawan performed the song at Shaw University in Nashville at a regional meeting to plan the campaign of sit-ins at segregated facilities, further associating song and movement.

In 1962, during action in Albany, Georgia, Seeger was impressed by a singing quartet that included a young Bernice Johnson and urged that the Student Nonviolent Coordinating Committee enlist the group for publicity and fundraising. Billed as the Albany Freedom Singers, the quartet was booked on a fundraising tour across the North, helping recruit at northern universities and colleges for Freedom Summer voter-registration work of 1964. They sang at a workshop attended by Schwerner and Goodman, later killed in Mississippi. By that point tensions had developed between white and black civil rights workers. "The left, dominated by whites, believed that in order to express the group you should say 'we,'" recalled Bernice Johnson Reagon. "In the black community if you want to express the group, you have to say 'I,' because if you say 'we,' I have no idea who the 'we' is . . . There are many black traditional collective expressions songs where it's 'I,' because in order for you to get a group you have to have 'I.' You have to have people willing to stand up and name themselves."[23] Thus "We Shall Overcome" was the focus of a complex negotiation. The song had been borrowed for mutually agreeable political reasons, and adapted to make explicit a social understanding implicit among the originators of that song. The African-American originators accepted those changes, according to Reagon, because they understood why they mattered and appreciated the assistance that the borrowing group brought to the struggle. There is a sense in Reagon's remarks that Newton's use of the first person in "Amazing Grace" was not really about the individual subject in isolation because it assumes the existence of a covenant between God and community.

Moreover, at this crucial juncture in the Second Reconstruction, as the civil rights movement is sometimes known, there are echoes of the Fisk Jubilee Singers some four-score years earlier. African-American singers were performing vernacular songs for the purposes of fundraising and what would later be called consciousness raising, being coached and managed (with varying degrees of success) by well-intentioned and politically allied white cultural entrepreneurs. Inevitably there was tension, but for the most part harmony was maintained, at least before 1965. There was broad overlap between the civil rights constituency and the primarily white audience of the folk revival of the early 1960s. Invited to perform at the Newport Folk Festival in 1963, the Albany Freedom Singers were joined onstage for "We Shall Overcome" by such revival luminaries as Seeger, Joan Baez, Bob Dylan, and Peter, Paul, and Mary. Most of these performed a few weeks later at the March on Washington, where Baez was chosen to lead the singing of "We Shall Overcome" and King delivered his "I Have a Dream" speech. (Mahalia Jackson gave a historic performance as well.)

The racial crossover of "We Shall Overcome" was not limited to enthusiasts of folk music or fellow travelers in the civil rights and later antiwar movements. By 1965 organizers could hear their trope being articulated at the highest levels of state. "What happened in Selma is part of a far larger movement that reaches into every state in America," President Johnson told Congress in a nationally televised address calling for a voting rights act. "Because it's not just Negroes, but really, it's all of us, who must overcome the crippling legacy of bigotry and injustice. And we *shall* overcome." Julian Bond recalls feeling slightly "used" by Johnson's appropriation of the phrase. On the other hand, Johnson's address represented "the words of a statesman, and more, they were the words of a poet," according to John Lewis. "Dr. King must have agreed. He wiped away a tear at the point when Johnson said the words, 'we shall overcome.'" The song was sung the night before King's assassination, when he delivered his "Been to the Mountaintop" sermon at a church in Memphis.[24]

In hindsight, Johnson was mistaken in limiting the "far larger movement" to the United States. In the same years it was becoming a canonized civil rights anthem, Pete Seeger was bringing it to an international audience. He sang it in thirty countries during his 1963 world tour. Film footage shows schoolchildren in Moscow learning the song from Seeger's recording. Various versions of "We Shall Overcome" have been sung in social movements in Korea, Thailand, Indonesia, China (at Tienanmen Square), Lebanon, northern Ireland, and South Africa, where Bishop Tutu commented: "It's a song that speaks about how you actually are not looking for the elimination of an enemy; you are looking for winning over a new friend." Julian Bond joked about the song's universality in predicting that "when we colonize the moon there will be little green people joining their antennae together and they'll be singing (or chirping) something. And it will be 'We Shall Overcome.'"[25]

AMAZING GRACE" arrived at the same cultural orbit, at approximately the same time and for many of the same reasons, as did "We Shall Overcome." In the second Star Trek film, *The Wrath of Khan* (1982), Dr. Spock knowingly sacrifices his life by exposing himself to a radioactive engine room in order to save the *Enterprise* and, by extension, the known universe. A familiar melody plays on the soundtrack as the ship's crew holds a funeral and releases Spock's casket into space, bound for a new planet created by the same device for which he risked his life. The film "offers a picture of redemption replete with biblical allusions but reset within a secular cosmology and indeed a secular eschatology—and with Spock as the Messiah figure," Hindmarsh notes.[26] A subtle bagpipe quotation from "Amazing Grace" fits like a glove; the melody is universally known, and it has all the right connotations of hope and healing. But for the hymn to have such resonance, the ears of American and other film viewers had to be prepared. The cultural preparation for "Amazing Grace" followed much the same pattern as that which elevated "We Shall Overcome" from an obscure Protestant hymn of uncertain origin to one of the most familiar of songs in less than a decade. Both songs were pushed into the secular mainstream by the civil rights movement.

Ironically, the hymn had enjoyed a moment of maximum cultural exposure over a century earlier. In Harriet Beecher Stowe's 1855 novel, the best-selling American book of the nineteenth century, Uncle Tom persists in singing Methodist hymns despite the violent reprisals of Simon Legree. After one nearly homicidal beating near the end of his life, Tom, alone and dejected, sings the final two verses of "Amazing Grace," along with a new stanza that was joined to the hymn in the nineteenth century:

> When we've been there ten thousand years
> Bright shining like the sun,
> We've no less days to sing God's praise
> Than when we first begun.[27]

The hymn would find its way into increasing numbers of hymnbooks over the century that followed, but only within the confines of Protestant worship.

In 1947, poised on the brink of racial and commercial crossover success, Mahalia Jackson recorded "Amazing Grace" for Apollo Records and continued to sing the song at demonstrations in the early 1960s. The legendary organizer Fannie Lou Hamer also regularly sang it. During the summer of 1964—"Freedom Summer"—exactly the same time that "We Shall Overcome" was being widely publicized by the Albany Freedom Singers, Judy Collins heard Hamer singing in Mississippi the hymn she herself had learned as a child in a Methodist church. "During those days of turmoil," she would later write, "I sang 'Amazing Grace' as a rune to give magical protection—a charm to ward off danger, an incantation to the angels of heaven to descend. I had left the choir loft of the Methodists and was not sure the magic worked outside of church walls . . . in the open air in Mississippi. But I wasn't taking any chances."[28] By the time Collins recorded the song in 1970, and it reached the Billboard Top 40 shortly afterward, it had picked up associations not just with the black freedom struggle but with the anti–Vietnam War movement as well. Again, there was some of Newton's original notion of the I-for-we, an individual acquiring identity through a social covenant. The ex-slaver had spent his last years in London, where he was a friend and spiritual adviser to William Wilberforce (1759–1833), the leading British abolitionist. In 1972 "Amazing Grace" made an unexpected triumphal homecoming, recrossing the Atlantic to become a major popular hit in Britain: a bagpipe version by the Royal Scots Dragoon Guards actually reached Number 1 in England and Europe. "In the book shop the young man was singing 'Day by Day' from *Godspell*; in the Food Hall it was 'Jesus Christ, Superstar,' recalled a British woman; "all the other departments were broadcasting 'Amazing Grace.' The bus conductor was whistling it . . . Why was this the only hymn-tune we had ever heard of?" Perhaps more surprisingly, the tune was adopted by fans of a British football club, to which they would bawl, "Ar-se-nal! Ar-se-nal! Ar-se-nal!"[29]

More importantly, the song was acquiring a powerful therapeutic resonance. Collins herself had used the song in an "encounter group" she was part of in 1968, because it was the only song everyone seemed to know. With the ascendance of an individual-centered therapeutic ethos in the 1970s, "Amazing Grace" found itself pressed into a variety of settings: twelve-step recovery programs (Collins herself alluded to her struggles with alcohol) and gay and lesbian liberation, out of which emerged a revision called "Amazing Gays, how sweet the sound." Bill Moyers' widely viewed PBS documentary emphasized the redemptive power of "Amazing Grace" among, for example, convicted felons at Huntsville Prison in Texas. The inmates, looking almost angelic in their gleaming white uniforms and well-coiffed hair, had turned to the song to help them survive the prospect of a lifetime of incarceration. One of the inmates, we learn, was a Baptist deacon and choir member at the time he arranged to have his wife murdered. Moyers' film brings out another contemporary resonance of the song: its connection to traditional values reproduced through families. We meet two extended southern families, one white, one black, who sing "Amazing Grace" as part of their reunions and for whom the song serves as a cynosure of collective memory. Johnny Cash managed to tie both prison and family together. He proudly mentioned that his album *Folsom Prison Blues* was endorsed by a convict, and reflected on the song's ability to free individuals from prisons, both real and figurative. But Cash himself associated the song with his own family, particularly singing with his mother and siblings as they worked in Arkansas cotton fields after the death of his brother in 1944.[30]

There is little Christian theology or explicit God-talk among the people Moyers interviews. Collins' own spirituality is New Age eclectic, and the other subjects interviewed appear more comfortable talking about family and memory than about anything that could be construed as evangelical. The song makes no mention of God during the first three, most commonly sung verses (though of course its Christian theology has been unmistakable for a majority of those actually singing the song over the generations, hence God goes without saying). "The hymn is simply a celebration of the experience of grace," observes Hindmarsh, "and in principle could be sung by a Christian, Jew, Muslim, or a person of no particular faith." American religion, whether Christian or civil, has long carried a political charge, and after the 1960s the dictum "the personal is the political" became a familiar slogan. The expanded range of "Amazing Grace" suggests a corollary to both these claims: *the personal is the religious.* Or at least religion can both begin and end with the personal and still be considered legitimate. As such "Amazing Grace" made perfect sense as a musical choice for the interfaith service held near Ground Zero six weeks after September

11 and attended by 9,000 people, mainly relatives of people killed in the collapse of the Twin Towers of the World Trade Center. Mayor Giuliani, Governor Pataki, and Senator Clinton were present, but only clergy spoke: a Catholic cardinal, a rabbi, an imam, and the son of Billy Graham. Music was central to the event. Americans tend to privatize incidents of terrorism, responding to them less as political attacks against the United States than as personal assaults on individuals who happen to be Americans.[31] The first-person singular that has come to dominate "Amazing Grace" since the 1960s meshes as well with such a service as it did with Spock's funeral onboard the U.S.S. *Enterprise*.

MANY are called but few are chosen. The extraordinary transnational genealogy of another would-be secular spiritual that remains firmly contained by evangelical Christianity points out some of the qualities that make possible the rare instances of crossover from the sacred realm into a broader public one. The hymn "How Great Thou Art" has a history nearly as well documented as "Amazing Grace," but compressed into a much shorter time span. It is preeminently a song of the twentieth century, created out of the successive traumas of two world wars, the Russian Revolution, and the Cold War, before becoming the greatest revival hymn of what Henry Luce would dub the American Century. Its great fame stems from a chance encounter in London during the 1954 Billy Graham crusade between George Beverly Shea, Graham's longtime musical sidekick—a sort of Ira Sankey to Graham's Dwight Moody—and George Gray, an acquaintance of Shea's from the British religious publishing house Pickering & Inglis. Running into each other on Oxford Street, Gray handed Shea a four-page leaflet with a new hymn that included words in both English and Russian and, according to Shea, "a very strong and worshipful title." Another copy ended up in the possession of Cliff Barrows, Graham's musical director, who worked up a rendition for the 1955 crusade at Toronto's Maple Leaf Garden. "But it was in Madison Square Garden in 1957 that 'How Great Thou Art' really became a crusade favorite, the unofficial theme song of the Billy Graham Crusade," recalls Shea. "We sang it about a hundred times at the insistence of the New York audiences. From then on it became a standard at most of the crusades."[32] Through Graham's revival meetings the hymn became widely known among evangelicals throughout the world and is by some estimations the most beloved of all gospel songs.

The strange career of "How Great Thou Art" began in 1885, when a young Swedish pastor named Carl Boberg was caught in a terrific thunderstorm. The storm, and the rainbow and the brilliant light reflected on the sea inlet that followed, inspired Boberg to compose a nine-stanza poem meditating on the power and beauty of nature in relation to his wonder at Christian salvation. Born in 1859 in the coastal town of Mönsterås, Boberg became a religious editor in addition to a minister and later served in the Swedish Parliament for thirteen years. His poem, "O Store God" (O Great God), became known throughout Sweden; set to a folk melody, it was first published in 1891. From that point began a remarkable transatlantic migration. A German translation produced by an Estonian appeared in 1907 under the title "Wie gross bist Du" (How Great Thou Art). Working from that version, a Russian pastor named Ivan Prokhanoff, a prolific hymn translator often compared to Martin Luther, published in 1912 in St. Petersburg a Russian version that was included in a volume of spiritual songs he had collected from different languages. A decade later, after the Russian Revolution, a large collection of Prokhanoff's sacred songs, including his translation of "Wie gross bist Du," was published in New York City by the American Bible Society—in Russian. About that time, it turns out, the hymn reached the United States by another route as well; in 1925 a man named E. Gustav Johnson translated the several verses of the original Swedish version into English, using the original folk tune, but it failed to catch on among American worshippers. It was the Russian route that led the hymn to worldwide popularity.[33]

Prokhanoff's New York collection was republished in the Soviet Union in 1927 in a hymnbook called *Kimvali* (Cymbals). It came to the attention of an English missionary named Stuart K. Hine, who with his wife had arrived in 1923 to proselytize the rugged backcountry of western Ukraine and later the Carpathian Mountains of Czechoslovakia and Romania, traveling mainly by bicycle. The Hines used the Russian hymn in their missionary work but gradually developed an English translation as well. To a hymn whose first two stanzas expressed a sense of wonder at nature, in the spirit of Psalm 8 or 19 ("I see the stars, I hear the rolling thunder, Thy power throughout the universe displayed . . . When I look down from lofty mountain grandeur, And hear the brook and feel the gentle breeze"), Hine added a third stanza of atonement theology, professing his astonishment that God would sacrifice his son on the Cross: "my burden gladly bearing, He bled and died to take away my sin." The onset of World War II forced the Hines' return to London, where Hine continued evangelizing among a population hammered by the German blitz. He reported later that his fourth verse was inspired by the plaintive query of war refugees in London: "When are we going home?" The final stanza anticipates in no uncertain terms the Second Coming, when Christ will appear with a "shout of acclamation And take me home," "to bow in humble adoration" and proclaim, "my God, how great Thou art!"

The speed with which "How Great Thou Art" spread after World War II demonstrates the efficiency of missionary communications networks. With his translation now complete, Hine in 1949 published it in a magazine that went out to refugees in fifteen countries, prompting requests for reprints of the hymn. Missionaries visiting Britain brought it back to New Zealand in 1950 and to both central Africa and the United States in 1951, where its fame continued to spread. Staff for Inter-Varsity heard the hymn at a conference in India in 1953 and transmitted it for use in Canada and the United States. Hine received a letter from India. "Near the sacred city of Nasik I heard a choir of Naga tribespeople from the jungles of Assam sing the hymn 'How great Thou art,'" wrote a missionary named J. Edwin Orr in 1954, the same year the hymn came to the attention of the Graham crusade. "It was a great blessing to missionaries and nationals alike, but most of all to me. That night I could not sleep for elation of spirit, but spent the time in praise and adoration of God." Orr further popularized the hymn during tours of the United States. Through Orr the hymn came to the attention of Manna Music, Inc., a Christian publishing company based in Hollywood that has closely guarded the rights to the song since obtaining copyright in 1953.[34] Until then the hymn had basically been in the public domain, with Hine himself making many thousand copies for free distribution. By the time it reached Madison Square Garden in 1957, then, "How Great Thou Art" was already well known by evangelicals.

It seemed that the hymn might acquire the kind of public standing accorded to a secular spiritual. Hine himself was surprised at hearing his hymn sung at Grand Central Station in Manhattan as he got off a train in 1958. "Emerging into the vast station hall, I saw a lady singing it, up in the gallery, where a pipe organ had been installed," he recalled. "She sang all four verses (in conversation afterwards, I learned she was a professional opera singer), and the great crowd below, mostly with upturned faces, were listening with rapt attention, and joining in the singing. New York knew it!" Elvis Presley was drawn to "How Great Thou Art," recording it in 1966 and again, in a live performance, in 1974, both versions winning Grammy awards. The song was requested by American G.I.s in Vietnam, and used to drown out a noisy demonstration by protesters at a London revival meeting in 1971 (as "Hold the Fort!" had been deployed a century earlier).[35] Its melody, only slightly revised from the original Swedish folk song, is compelling, with a soaring chorus and a kind of unexpected syncopation in its rhythmic sway that brings to mind a song of southern Africa.

But as "Amazing Grace" and "We Shall Overcome" established a secure standing in secular society, "How Great Thou Art" remained a hymn about and for Christian evangelicals. Its copyright is tightly controlled and costly to license, its theology too direct for rites of American civil religion. In contrast, Katherine Lee Bates's "O Beautiful for Spacious Skies" fuses celebration of natural beauty ("amber waves of grain," "purple-mountain'd majesty") with a perfect epitome of American civil religion in its social-gospel incarnation (pilgrims who beat a "thoroughfare for freedom" "across the wilderness"; heroes who loved country more than self, "mercy more than life"; a God who "shed his grace on thee," crowned "thy good with brotherhood," mended "thine every flaw," and confirmed "thy liberty in law"). In none of the secular spirituals is there a cross, a bloody sacrifice, a second coming. As Graham himself explained, "The reason I liked 'How great Thou art' was because it glorified God: it turned a Christian's eyes toward God rather than upon himself, as so many songs do."[36] A successful secular spiritual can imply God, even invoke him directly (as in Irving Berlin's "God Bless America"); however, it must focus not on the divine, but on the nation's human citizenry. With its ecumenical leveling impulse, civil religion chokes on the piety of a hymn like "How Great Thou Art."

In the aftermath of September 11, the practice of civil religion remained a touchy business, even at its most sanctified public rituals. When New Yorkers gathered at Yankee Stadium for the "Prayer for America," they heard an extraordinary sequence of sacred sounds: a Muslim call to prayer; the blowing of a shofar; Placido Domingo singing "Ave Maria"; a Sikh prayer; "Lift Every Voice and Sing" by a children's choir; benedictions from a Greek Orthodox archbishop and a Hindu priest. Afterward one of the participants was suspended from his position as president of the Atlantic region of the Lutheran Church–Missouri Synod, a denomination of 2.6 million members. Because he had appeared and prayed publicly alongside a Muslim, a Hindu, a Sikh, and a Jew, the Reverend David H. Benke was accused by other Lutheran pastors of breaking two of the Ten Commandments and committing heresy, syncretism (mixing with other faiths), and unionism (mixing with other Christian denominations). "Instead of keeping God's name sacred and separate from every other name," read the complaint against Benke, "it was made common as it was dragged to the level of Allah." Said one minister: "We don't hate the Muslims, the Jews, the Sikhs. We love them, therefore we want to let them know they are lost, they are eternally lost, unless they believe in Jesus."[37] After offering prayers at the Ground Zero memorial service, the Reverend Franklin Graham, eldest son of Billy, found himself at the center of a different controversy. Though he had also appeared with an interfaith gathering, including the same Muslim imam who had appeared at Yankee Stadium, he opined in a televised interview that the God of Islam is "a different God, and I believe it is a very evil and wicked religion." He also accused the Koran of "preaching violence," and identified terrorism as a feature of even "mainstream" Islam.[38]

Neither controversy was unprecedented or even particularly surprising; it is only their eruption at a moment when the United States was so conspicuously clamoring for national unity that makes them noteworthy. Since 1965 the United States has been coming to terms with religious diversity on a different scale than before. The question frequently arises, as it did at the World Parliament of Religions in 1893: On whose terms will interreligious dialogue be allowed to take place? Musical exchange begins to look like the kinder, gentler face of religious encounter, a site where hard boundaries appear to soften only to reassert themselves when the crowd breaks up, the sense of communal solidarity dissipates, and religious leaders so inclined are free to withdraw from the public square to their own spiritual fortresses to await the history-ending "shout of acclamation."

CHAPTER ELEVEN

Coltrane and Beyond

> I'd like to point out to people the divine in a musical language that transcends words. I want to speak to their souls.
>
> —JOHN COLTRANE

IN 1957, the year Sun Ra recorded "Sun Song" and "Call for All Demons," tenor saxophonist John Coltrane underwent one of the fabled religious transformations in the history of American music. Throughout much of the 1950s he had been addicted to heroin and alcohol and, despite his enormous musical contributions, had been fired by his most important employer, Miles Davis, who grew tired of Coltrane's "nodding off on the bandstand." Two years earlier it had appeared that Coltrane was putting some distance between his musical career and the substance abuse that was more rule than exception among jazz musicians who came of age during the late 1940s and 1950s. After an apprenticeship in ensembles led by Dizzy Gillespie and Johnny Hodges, he had been hired by Davis into perhaps the best-paying, most prestigious group in jazz. He also met and married his first wife, a practicing Muslim who took the name Naima; like Coltrane she had moved from rural North Carolina to Philadelphia during the war. Beginning in the late 1940s, several prominent jazz artists had embraced Islam, including Yusef Lateef, Ahmad Jamal, Sahib Shihab, Idrees Sulieman, and, most famously, drummer Art Blakey, who took the name Abdullah ibn Buhaina. Philadelphia had both a thriving jazz scene and a relatively prominent Muslim presence during Coltrane's years there. He played and socialized with many Muslims. But despite the stabilizing influence of his wife and others, Coltrane, suffering from painful dental problems, continued to suffer from alcohol and heroin abuse.

"During the year 1957, I experienced, by the grace of God, a spiritual awakening which was to lead me to a richer, fuller, more productive life," Coltrane would later write. "At that time, in gratitude, I humbly asked to be given the means and privilege to make others happy through music. I feel this has been granted through His grace. ALL PRAISE TO GOD."[1] For the next decade, until his death from liver cancer at age forty-one, Coltrane proceeded to record some of the canonical jazz albums with Miles Davis and, beginning in 1961, as a leader of his own quartet. Many of his own recordings had an unmistakable spiritual inflection in their mood, musical stylings, and most obviously their titles: "Spiritual," "Dear Lord," "Om," "Hymn of Praise," "The Father and the Son and the Holy Ghost." It was on the record jacket of the most celebrated of these recordings that Coltrane made public his spiritual awakening of eight years earlier.

Released early in 1965, the album, *A Love Supreme,* is a four-part suite performed by a quartet. The movements describe a sort of spiritual progression or pilgrimage: "Acknowledgement," "Resolution," "Pursuance," and "Psalm." The last track is a remarkable performance by Coltrane, playing in free time, in which he plainly and clearly narrates, word for word, the four-stanza prayer by himself that appears on the record jacket. It begins:

> I will do all I can to be worthy of Thee O Lord.
> It all has to do with it.
> Thank you God.
> Peace.

The second stanza offers a vision of the unity of material and immaterial reality in and through the divine:

> Words, sounds, speech, men, memory, thoughts, fears and emotion—time—
>   all related . . . all made from one . . . all made in one.
> Blessed be His name.
> Thought waves—heat waves—all vibrations—all paths lead to God. Thank
>   you God.
> His way . . . it is so lovely . . . it is gracious.
> It is merciful—Thank you God.
> One thought can produce millions of vibrations and they all go back to God
>   . . . everything does.
> Thank you God . . .

Finally:

> God breathes through us so completely . . . so gently we hardly feel it . . . yet,
>   it is our everything.

Thank you God.
ELATION—ELEGANCE—EXALTATION—
All from God.
Thank you God. Amen.[2]

With passionate articulation, Coltrane issues this prayer on the saxophone, rising above the tympani and cymbal rolls played by Elvin Jones and the church-bell-like chiming of McCoy Tyner's piano. Earlier, toward the end of "Acknowledgement," there is some mantralike chanting of the phrase "a love supreme," which echoes a four-syllable phrase Coltrane has just explored on tenor saxophone through a series of modulations. He guides the listener to a point where the phrase seems to emerge seamlessly from the music. "He's telling us that God is everywhere—in every register, in every key—and he's showing us that you have to discover religious belief," Coltrane scholar Lewis Porter has written. Of the chanting, "It's as if he's saying, 'It doesn't matter what we think we play that's man-made,'" observes Alice Coltrane, his widow. "'God, you gave all of us an instrument. We can also offer you praise with the use of the voice that you created in us.'" Other listeners have heard the phrase "a love supreme" blending aurally into "Allah Supreme"—Allahu Akbar in Arabic—and imagined the quartet as "a roving band of sufi mendicants singing their *dhikr.*"[3]

This is a different sort of spirituality from that in the works that were beginning to issue from Duke Ellington, whose first sacred concert took place the same year *A Love Supreme* was released—less Judeo-Christian, more Eastern-mystical. Critic Gary Giddens wrote of Ellington's sacred works that rather than injecting elements of church music into a jazz show, Ellington in effect "brought the Cotton Club revue to the pulpit."[4] Coltrane's approach was different—we could say he brought the ashram to the Village Vanguard. Exploring the modes and musical structures of India and Africa, he pioneered approaches to what is now called world music long before the genre existed. Coltrane's explorations opened up sonic and intellectual horizons both within the world of jazz, where Eastern modes and spirituality would later become almost commonplace, and within the larger and more visible realm of popular music, where groups like the Beatles were experimenting with the same musical sources. And because for non-European cultures the links between music and the divine are deep and inextricable, Coltrane was inevitably at work within the sacred. To play world music with any degree of seriousness is *ipso facto* to engage the world religions alongside which those musics have sprung.

In a book titled *Noise: The Political Economy of Music,* Jacques Attali has argued that changes in the organization of music, both its form and the way it is produced and consumed, have anticipated changes in society. "Music is prophecy," he insists. "Its styles and economic organization are ahead of the rest of society because it explores, much faster than material reality can, the entire range of possibilities of a given code. It makes audible the new world that will gradually become visible, that will impose itself and regulate the order of things." Viewed in a certain light, this is the kind of argument that makes empirically attuned and causally minded historians roll their eyes and glance at their watches. (It's worth pointing out that Attali is a French economist.) But the timing of Coltrane's investment and incorporation of nonwestern musics fits Attali's model well. The 1965 Immigration Act was a watershed event in the evolution of the religious landscape of the United States, opening the way to immigration by people from Asia, Africa, and the Middle East, many of them practitioners of religions like Hinduism, Buddhism, and Islam that were proportionally quite rare in the United States, creating what one observer of American religion has called a new religious landscape.[5]

Celebrants of world religion in America are not the only ones to lay claim to Coltrane. He was linked to as well as lionized by important figures among African-American cultural nationalists of the 1960s, seen as a militant musical voice of black rage and radical social criticism. "He has come to stand for a disciplined mind-set, a desire for spiritual ecstasy, a vision of music as ritual and of performance as a holy rite," observes jazz critic Francis Davis. "Depending on what a listener wants from it, Coltrane's music is a cry for black liberation, the soundtrack of a spiritual quest, a backdrop for tripping, or merely (merely!) the next evolutionary step for jazz after bebop." Coltrane's playing was undeniably and deeply fired by the blues; two of his early musical opportunities came with bluesmen, Earl Bostic and Eddie "Cleanhead" Vinson. But it was animated also by a distinctively African-American religious fervor that underlay spirituals and gospel blues, a sensibility honed in holiness and Pentecostal churches. Harvey Cox draws an extended analogy between Christian Pentecostalism and jazz: both developed among racially mixed subcultures in urban areas, share a sense of spirit possession and trance, challenge the distinction between composer and performer, enjoy an uneasy relationship with the "mainstream" culture of the United States. "Both jazz and pentecostalism," he insists, "stand as powerful reminders that who we are as Americans—though we often try to deny it—is a direct result of the unique mixture of black and white which has shaped us." Coltrane's powerfully jarring vocalized saxophone plays a clear analogue to Pentecostalism's defining worship practice, glossolalia, or speaking in tongues. And Coltrane has been adopted as a kind of patron saint of a Christian congregation in

San Francisco.[6] These two profiles of Coltrane are not mutually exclusive, of course. Understanding the sources of both his spirituality and his music—the way in which his composing and improvising can sonically embody traditions of nonwestern religion and African-American Pentecostalism—suggests a religious future for both the United States and the world that holds in balance many of the same apparent tensions.

COLTRANE was born in 1926 in Hamlet, North Carolina, and grew up in the small town of High Point, near the center of the state. Both of his grandparents were Methodist ministers. Coltrane remembered his maternal grandfather as "the dominating cat in the family. He was the most well versed, active politically . . . pretty militant, you know." His own religious upbringing, he said, "wasn't too strict," but he did attend church regularly. His cousin Mary Alexander, who grew up with Coltrane, remembers him responding to an altar call, known as "opening the doors of the church." "Out of the clear blue sky John went up to join the church," she said. "I didn't even know what he was doing, he was so little." The death of his close male relatives, including his father, when Coltrane was a young adolescent drew him closer to his mother and cousin. Coltrane began playing saxophone, went out for football, worked as a soda jerk, was voted "Best Dressed Boy" and "Most Musical," and, shortly after graduating from high school in 1943, moved to Philadelphia, where his mother then lived. A short stint in the Navy just after the war brought him to Hawaii, where he played some saxophone. Then Coltrane returned to the flourishing jazz subculture of Philadelphia, where he began practicing and studying with the almost obsessive diligence for which he became famous. When neighbors got tired of the sound, Coltrane would practice in the nearby A.M.E. Zion church attended by his family, using a key the pastor had given him.[7]

Because his grandfathers were A.M.E. Zion rather than one of the more demonstratively ecstatic Baptist or holiness denominations, Coltrane had little direct contact with the jazz-inflected shout music that was entering black churches through the Pentecostals. Particularly strong in Coltrane's region—the Carolinas, the Virginias, and the Georgia Piedmont—was the United House of Prayer for All People, a Pentecostal church founded in the 1920s by an African-Portuguese immigrant from Cape Verde named Marcelino Manoel daGraca, popularly known as "Daddy Grace." DaGraca hailed from the multiethnic community around the old whaling town of New Bedford, Massachusetts, and established his first church in West Wareham. His work as a cook on the Southern Railway gave him mobility, and he conducted revivals along the railway routes. Grace wore long robes and let his fingernails grow. Some followers thought he looked "just like Jesus." At a time when a distrust of musical instruments lingered among Christian believers, whatever Psalm 150 might say, Grace was fearless in opening worship to brass and even reeds. "He had to bait his hook to bring in his catch," explained one House of Prayer pastor. The sociologist Arthur Huff Fauset recorded this account of worship at a Philadelphia church in the 1940s, when Coltrane lived in the city. "The service usually begins with unison singing, accompanied by piano or band," he wrote. "Then there is testimony. The singing is interlarded with shrieks, handclapping, stamping, and frequently concludes with the wholesale spectacle of a number of followers advancing to the front of the auditorium where they dance on the sawdust-covered floor. Other members flit about singly through the aisles and passageways. From time to time someone will collapse and fall prostrate to the floor . . . All the while there is much calling out in tongues, which is said to be the Holy Spirit speaking through the human form."[8]

As was true of the earliest Pentecostal gatherings on Azusa Street in Los Angeles in 1906, these revivals often breached racial boundaries, and as a result Grace was often prosecuted for breaking segregation laws. The South Carolina Supreme Court closed a church in 1938, citing evidence "that there is dancing carried on in the church, weird noises and music, shouting, stamping of feet, unearthly sounds, use of drums, trombones, horns, and scrubbing boards." But as a House of Prayer musician explains, these sounds are the audible sign of the presence of the spirit: "Once you are in one accord, then the Holy Ghost can come in . . . when everybody is on that level, and I can feel it, and the members can feel it. And when we feel it, it changes us. We have to get out of self and walk in spirit, not flesh. We feel the Holy Ghost's power then, and the music comes through our horn, and no more is it the average music you'd hear in a night club or a jazz radio station. It's actually music given to us through the spirit of God, through the brass, and the people can feel the radiation of the horns . . . it's like fire shut up in the bones!"[9]

The House of Prayer established its base on the coastal regions of the Southeast that were in proximity to the South Carolina and Georgia Sea Islands, where the West African–derived custom of the "ring shout" persisted the longest among rural congregations. Over the nineteenth century African-American musicians developed proficiency on European brass instruments, filling a niche in playing dance music that many whites discouraged their children from pursuing and that was more lucrative than other employment opportunities. At the end of both the Civil War and the Spanish-American War quantities of surplus instruments flooded the market, putting horns within reach of many. Slide trombones, with their ability to produce vocalized tone—growls, slides, and melisma—became the favored instruments of the "shout bands," whose name conveys the kinship that existed with the tradition of the ring shout.

As in southern cities like Memphis, Chicago in the 1920s was an incubator for the cross-pollination of African-American Pentecostal spirituality with jazz instrumentation and idioms. The city attracted migrants from the Southeast and Southwest in the population flows that brought Thomas Dorsey and Mahalia Jackson. The Reverend Ford Washington McGee was born in Tennessee but grew up east of Dallas. He attended college in Oklahoma, where he was called to be an evangelist and faith healer, building a large congregation of the Pentecostal Church of God in Christ in Oklahoma City. After moving to Chicago in 1925, he established what he called a temple and began recording his sermons and music for Okeh, a leading "race record" label, in 1927. "Fifty Miles of Elbow Room," recorded for Vocalion in 1930, features a jubilantly shouted performance by Reverend McGee and a vocal group accompanied by piano, guitar, handclapping, and a trumpet player thought to be jazz great Red Allen.

> Twelve hundred miles its length and breadth the four-square city stands
> Its gem-set walls of jasper shine, not made with human hands
> One hundred miles its gates are wide, abundant entrance there
> With fifty miles of elbow room on either side to spare
> When the gates swing wide on the other side just beyond the sunset sea
> There'll be room to spare as we enter there, room for you and room for me
> For the gates are wide on the other side where the flowers ever bloom
> On the right hand, and on the left hand, fifty miles of elbow room[10]

An even bigger ensemble was fielded for a recording of "I'm in the Battlefield for My Lord," by the Reverend D. C. Rice and his Sanctified Congregation: trumpet, trombone, piano, bass, drums, and a triangle. The piece features New Orleans–style collective improvisation behind the vocals and a sixteen-bar trumpet solo. Alternating sixteen-bar verses and choruses, it would be covered by such major gospel figures as James Cleveland, the Dixie Hummingbirds, Thomas A. Dorsey, and the Five Blind Boys of Alabama.

> I'm on the battlefield for my Lord
> I'm on the battlefield for my Lord
> I promised the Lord that I would serve until I die
> I'm on the battlefield for my Lord[11]

Rice had been raised as a Baptist in Alabama before moving to Chicago in 1916, where he joined and soon became the pastor of a Pentecostal church on the South Side. After hearing the recorded sermons of F. W. McGee and J. M. Gates, Rice contacted producer Jack Kapp, who hired him for a series of recordings for Vocalion. His recording career cut short by the Depression, Rice returned to Alabama, where he pastored several holiness churches and became bishop of the Apostolic Overcoming Holy Church of God.[12]

Whether or not Coltrane heard recordings of this sort as he was growing up is unknown. No horns would have been allowed in the Methodist churches he attended as a child; by the 1950s, when Coltrane was honing his style, the race records of the 1920s had been long since forgotten. But at least in urban-based holiness and Pentecostal churches, space had been established not just for the use of brass instruments but for the bluesy inflections and improvised choruses of jazz. Across the country, many were impressed by the level of musicianship and musical freedom on display in houses of worship. As a teenager in Chicago during World War I, Langston Hughes was "entranced by their stepped-up rhythms, tambourines, hand clapping, and uninhibited dynamics, rivaled only by Ma Rainey singing the blues at the old Monogram Theater." At about the same time, in New York, clarinetist Garvin Bushell recalled, "They sang the blues in church; the words were religious, but it was the blues. They often had a drummer and a trumpet player." In Washington, D.C., bassist Pops Foster "used to hurry to finish our theater job so we could go listen to them play. They really played some great jazz on those hymns they played." Zora Neale Hurston found the same musical crossovers in the Deep South. "In Jacksonville there is a jazz pianist who seldom has a free night; nearly as much of his business comes from playing for 'Sanctified' church services as for parties," she wrote of her stint as a Works Progress Administration folklorist during the Depression. "Standing outside of church, it is difficult to determine just which kind of engagement he is filling at the moment." Coltrane's contemporary and fellow tenor player Sonny Rollins was brought up Moravian, which he remembers as musically "very straight-laced, with an organ playing hymns and Bach Cantatas. But my grandmother used to take me to a church run by a woman named Mother Horn right there on Lenox Avenue. It was one of these real sanctified churches that had band instruments playing, and it made a big impression—I remember hearing a trumpet player who was really swinging." After moving to Chicago in 1949 Rollins regularly attended a sanctified church where his friend played trumpet "because the music was so animated."[13]

Actually, by the mid-1950s both "Fifty Miles of Elbow Room" and "I'm in the Battlefield for My Lord" were back in circulation, thanks to the herculean efforts of Harry Smith, the folklorist and record collector who compiled the *Anthology of American Folk Music*. For years Smith had scoured collections of old 78s, assembling a kind of subterranean history of American popular music that circulated commercially with the recording boom of the 1920s but whose cultural roots seemed much deeper, reaching back to European songs that had accompanied early waves of settlement—"the old, weird America," as Greil Marcus has termed it in his brilliant interpretation of the collection. Released in 1952 by Moses Asch at Folkways Records, Smith's collection became a cult classic and inspiration for the folk revival that achieved its most prominent expression through Bob Dylan. One of the six sides Smith compiled featured all church music, mainly African American: gospel shouts, sermon fragments, shape-note songs, ecstatic choruses by sanctified and holiness singers, all of which added up to a more vigorous and musically adventuresome recollection of American church music than anyone could have expected.[14]

Some of this religio-musical sensibility began finding its way into the repertoire of modern jazz. In 1947, about the time he converted to Islam, Art Blakey had formed a big band called the Messengers, a name with both Muslim and African-American accents. Several years later he formed a quintet called the Jazz Messengers with pianist Horace Silver, recording in 1955 "The Preacher," a popular piece with a gospel-drenched fervor missing from the predominantly cool jazz of the period. Then there were the exertions of bassist Charles Mingus, a virtuoso instrumentalist *cum* composer-bandleader in the tradition of Ellington. Born four years before Coltrane, Mingus had grown up in the Watts section of Los Angeles right around the corner from the A.M.E. church his family regularly attended. A few years later he enthusiastically attended a bona fide holiness church with a musical family he befriended, an experience Coltrane apparently never had (though Sun Ra did, growing up in Birmingham). His first exposure to secular music came at age twelve, listening to remote broadcasts of the Ellington band. Coming up musically through swing bands and bebop, he began drawing on all styles and periods of jazz when he assembled his own bands beginning in the 1950s. Pieces like "Wednesday Night Prayer Meeting" and "Better Get It in Your Soul," both from 1959, evoked the handclapping, shouting fervor of his Pentecostal upbringing; Mingus' own voice is audible exhorting the band above the torrid 6/8 tempo. John Handy's alto sax solo in "Better Get It," riding above the stop-time handclapping of the band, has all the fervor of a revival testimonial. It's not hard to hear the echoes of Reverend McGhee's version of "Fifty Miles of Elbow Room." But in terms of his own spirituality, Mingus began departing from his evangelical Christian background as a seventeen-year-old. By then he was playing professionally, and a road trip brought him into contact with a bohemian painter in San Francisco who introduced the young bassist to Vedanta Hinduism. It became his spiritual orientation for the rest of Mingus' life, and when he died his wife took his ashes from Mexico to India and scattered them in the Ganges.[15]

In his own way, Coltrane shared in the roots music aesthetic, although his musical borrowings were obviously different from those of Dylan and Baez. "It's like a big reservoir, that we all dip out of," he said of his musical sources. His choice of the English folksong "Greensleeves" for *Africa/Brass* (1961) was a nod to the British music that featured so prominently in Smith's anthology. The same session, Coltrane's first for the Impulse label, saw him experimenting with African ideas about rhythm and organizing musical units into an ensemble whole. "I have an African record at home and they're singing these rhythms, some of their native rhythms, so I took part of it and gave it to the bass," he told an interviewer. Two other major recordings, "Spiritual" and "India," reveal how Coltrane was expanding his musical network beyond the ordinary sources of the jazz canon in ways that contributed to his gathering spiritual awareness. Both were recorded in 1961, the first year of Coltrane's leaving Miles Davis and assembling the quartet that would go on to record his most influential work in the 1960s for Impulse. In order to capture the intensity and spontaneity of live performance, Coltrane recorded four nights of a two-week engagement at the Village Vanguard from which LPs were later pressed. The ominous C-minor theme of "Spiritual" was borrowed from a lesser-known melody to the spiritual "Nobody Knows de Trouble I Seen" that Coltrane apparently came across in James Weldon Johnson's *Book of American Negro Spirituals* (1925).[16] At the Vanguard, Coltrane played a sixteen-bar interpretation of the traditional dirgelike melody with Eric Dolphy's accompaniment on bass clarinet before the band launched into a jazz waltz vamp of alternating Cm7 and F9 chords.

"India" reveals Coltrane pushing further into world music. In this case Coltrane borrowed from Indian ragas and chants that appeared on a Folkways recording, *Religious Music of India* (1952). After the basses (both Jimmy Garrison and Reggie Workman appear on the track) set up a rhythmic vamp with drummer Jones, Coltrane enters on soprano saxophone, the most Eastern-sounding of his instruments; he is joined by Eric Dolphy on bass clarinet. Though the simple four-note melody resembles one of the Vedic chants on the Folkways album, "India" sounds most similar to a track titled "Raga Bhairavi," performed by two flutes with percussion accompaniment as a purifying ritual at temples before weddings and other ceremonial functions. The nearly fourteen-minute performance rests on one chord, a G major pedal point. As the liner notes to the album explain:

> In Indian music all scales, all intervals are established by relation to one fixed sound, the tonic . . . The tonic is the unmoving center, the fundamental unity in relation to which all the descriptive or expressive elements are evolved. The performers and hearers gradually identify themselves with the tonic. It is only when the tonic ceases to be heard as a note but becomes the unnoticed norm of our perception of melody—just as the beats of the heart are the unnoticed rhythm which defines our relation to time—that we begin to perceive the music. This identification with the tonic, the reduction of all the world of music to its basic unmanifest unity is the essential factor which allows the utilization of music as one of the forms of Yoga, one of the ways of spiritual attainment.[17]

The move away from multiple chord changes toward more extended improvisations on simple chords using modal scales had begun a couple of years earlier, most prominently on the Miles Davis album *Kind of Blue* (1959), but on recordings like "India" the saxophonist takes the impulse toward harmonic streamlining to its logical conclusion.

Coltrane had begun studying North Indian music intensively in 1961, and manuscripts exist of various nonwestern scales that he wrote out to guide his study of Indian modes. One sheet provides the labels that Coltrane attached to various scales, which in Indian fashion ascend and descend slightly differently: "Night, Power and Majesty"; "Morning, Sad"; "Evening & Night, Praise"; "Evening, Gay"; "Night, Melancholy." In Indian music, these diurnal terms refer to specific ragas. Coltrane was particularly impressed by the work of sitarist Ravi Shankar (Coltrane would name one of his sons Ravi), who had been gaining an audience in the United States since the mid-1950s. "When I hear his music, I want to copy it—not note for note of course, but in his spirit," he explained. He was drawn to the modal aspect of Shankar's music, which Coltrane was beginning to see as a common thread in world music (the same insight that the Fisk Jubilee Singers evoked during their tour of Great Britain in the 1870s). "There's a lot of modal music that is played every day throughout the world," he observed. "It's particularly evident in Africa, but if you look at Spain or Scotland, India or China, you'll discover this again in each case . . . Certainly, the popular music of England is not that of South America, but take away their purely ethnic characteristics—that is, their folkloric aspect—and you'll discover the presence of the same pentatonic sonority, of comparable modal structures. It's this universal aspect of music that interests me and attracts me; that's what I'm aiming for."[18] Coltrane studied other scales as well: Algerian, Chinese, Japanese, and so on. But he was particularly drawn to North Indian music.

The study of music brought Coltrane unavoidably into contact with the spiritual traditions on which Indian music rested. Sound vibrations were thought to be inextricably linked to the spiritual realm such that the faulty performance of sacred songs could have consequences not just for the ritual at hand but for the universe itself. Coltrane became fascinated by the potential of music to bring about tangible emotional and physical effects. "I would like to bring to people something like happiness," he said. "I would like to discover a method so that if I want it to rain, it will start right away to rain. If one of my friends is ill, I'd like to play a certain song and he will be cured . . . The true powers of music are still unknown. To be able to control them must be, I believe, the goal of every musician."[19] Coltrane read extensively in a variety of traditions, often books recommended by friends. Of Indians, he was particularly struck by the writings of Ghandi, Jiddu Krishnamurti, and Paramahansa Yogananda, author of *Autobiography of a Yogi,* which became a counterculture classic. He is supposed to have been studying the Kabbalah at the time he conceived *A Love Supreme,* and he took an interest in Sonny Rollins' accounts of Rosicrucianism.

Out of it all emerged the panreligious blend that Coltrane for the first time makes explicit in *A Love Supreme.* Recorded less than a year later, the album *Om* included group chanting from the *Bhagavad Gita:* "I, the oblation and I the flame into which it is offered. I am the sire of the world and this world's mother and grandsire. I am he who awards to each the fruit of his action. I make all things clean. I am Om-OM-OM-OM!" The recording also featured a range of nontraditional jazz instruments, including bells, gongs, a thumb piano, and wooden flutes. Shankar, who saw Coltrane perform late in his life, described the music as "fantastic" but also somewhat distressing. "There was a turbulence in the music that gave me a negative feeling at times, but I could not quite put my finger on the trouble," Shankar said. "Here was a creative person who had become a vegetarian, who was studying yoga and the Bhagavad-Gita, yet in whose music I still heard much turmoil. I could not understand it."[20]

Coltrane's ideas about the music's essential active role in the workings of the cosmos bring to mind Sun Ra, who also warned of dire consequences if music fell out of synch with the natural world. Since 1956, when they played together on the same bill, the two musicians had an ongoing interest in each other's musical and philosophical developments. At one of their first meetings Ra gave Coltrane a copy of one of his visionary leaflets, titled "Solaristic Precepts." Coltrane had a passionate interest in astrology,

15. Raised in the black church, John Coltrane made extensive studies of spirituality and its musical expression between his religious awakening in 1957 and his death ten years later. Courtesy of Prints and Photographs Division, Library of Congress.

and fully expected to die young. "I also have my moon in conjunction with Mars in Taurus, in direct opposition with Saturn, the deadly planet, in Scorpion, the sign of death!" he pointed out. "Also I have my ascendant and my Venus in the sign of Virgo; three bad aspects of my birth chart. I won't live to be very old!"[21] Ra was a pioneer in the use of free musical forms by larger jazz ensembles, an approach to which Coltrane was drawn in his last years. Coltrane was a great admirer of Ra's leading saxophone player, John Gilmore, to whom he was sometimes compared. "I listened to John Gilmore kind of closely before I made 'Chasin' the Trane,' too," he told an interviewer. "So some of those things on there are really direct influences of listening to this cat." Coltrane often attended Arkestra shows when they played at Birdland in New York City, and after Ra's troupe relocated to New York from Chicago he began dropping by the band's rehearsal studio, discussing saxophone techniques with Gilmore and esoteric knowledge with Ra. "Trane really wanted to play more avant-garde music, but he didn't get the foundation until he listened to Sun Ra a lot," Gilmore is quoted as saying. "I think we helped him get his Oriental and African music together, too." Both were friends of the Nigerian drummer and performance artist Babatunde Olatunji, who had come to the United States on a Rotary scholarship before establishing himself in New York City as a composer and leader of a pan-Africanist musical-dance troupe that appeared on television, at the New York World's Fair, and in leading Manhattan nightclubs. In 1967 Olatunji established the Center of African Culture on 125th Street in Harlem, the venue where Coltrane would make his very last recording, in April, three months before his death.[22]

There were also affinities to Sun Ra in Coltrane's earlier musical experiments. The album *Giant Steps*, recorded within a few months of *Kind of Blue* but with Coltrane as leader of his own group rather than sideman, was an extended exploration of the possibilities for jazz of using the interval of the third rather than the more commonly used fourth as the structural basis for the harmonic progression. (The I-IV-V progression—built on the root, fourth, and fifth intervals of the scale—is the basis of blues harmony, and the great majority of popular songs on which jazz musicians traditionally improvised used variations of the cycle of fourths.) Other musicians had experimented with a thirds-based approach, but Coltrane brought it to a new level, particularly by making the chord changes at nearly superhuman speed. The sources of this type of musical structure were various, but Porter speculates that esoteric relationships of the sort that so interested Sun Ra had something to do with Coltrane's attraction. "During the late 1950s [Coltrane] would draw the circle of fifths and then connect the twelve key centers with lines," according to Porter. "Sometimes he'd place an equilateral triangle within the circle, creating a 'magic' triangle" whose three points "connect key centers a major third apart."[23]

But before long Coltrane had exhausted the possibilities of thirds-based progressions and moved on, in the direction of simplified chord sequences and the use of modal and sometimes nonwestern scales. If the music of his quartet of the early to mid-1960s had a trademark interval, it was the fourth, which sounded especially clearly in the piano work of McCoy Tyner, whom Coltrane had known in Philadelphia and who converted to Islam. (Naima Coltrane was a friend of the older sister of Aisha Davis, who married Tyner in 1959; both Davis sisters were Muslims deeply involved in the jazz community.) Tyner's technique of emphasizing the interval of the fourth rather than the familiar triad in his chord voicings became a signature sound of the quartet (and enormously influential on other jazz artists) and lent to the music an abstract, mysterious, ethereal, and to some ears spiritual sound that underscored Coltrane's explicitly spiritual ambitions.[24]

Coltrane's music evolved rapidly from the mid-1960s until his death in

1967. After 1965 he made a number of personnel changes, shifting further away from a steady rhythmic pulse in favor of a freer rhythmic approach and a looser structure of tonal centers rather than chord or modal based. The same years were arguably the peak of Coltrane's explicit engagement with sacred and spiritual themes in his music. There was of course *A Love Supreme,* Coltrane's most explicit statement of religious principles and most sustained exploration of spiritual themes, which came at the beginning of this period. The fourth part of the suite, "Psalm," finds Coltrane reciting nearly word for word on saxophone the prayer he wrote for the album jacket, with musical phrases that perfectly complement the words they narrate. Coltrane's six-minute recitation, like African-American intonational chant, is divided into several units, each of which follows an arched shape, with ascending phrase, recitation on one note, and descending phrase. As Lewis Porter notes, each successive section moves to a higher recitation tone, thereby increasing the intensity as the chant moves toward its climax. Coltrane's saxophone prayer is also punctuated with the phrase "Thank you, God," which he intones as either a minor third or a fifth descending to the tonic, as would a black preacher for similar phrases embedded in the sermon.[25] This rhetorical structure, refined during the twentieth century in holiness and Pentecostal churches, is exactly the one that so impressed Thomas A. Dorsey in the recorded sermons of Nix and Gates, and shaped his approach to composing gospel blues. And by converting speech into music, Coltrane inverts the move made in the first movement of the suite, "Acknowledgement," where he spontaneously switches from exploring the four-note phrase on saxophone to chanting it.

A Love Supreme was only the beginning of Coltrane's explicit engagement with religious themes during the last two years of his life. The album *Transition* features a suite of movements, including three versions of "Prayer and Meditation," for day, evening, and four in the morning. *Meditations* includes a piece titled "The Father and the Son and the Holy Ghost." In addition to *Om,* with its chanting of the *Bhagavad Gita,* there are albums containing pieces with titles like "Song of Praise," "Amen," and "Dear Lord," one of Coltrane's more jubilant performances, based on a three-note melody that sounds like a theme Ellington might have used in one of the sacred concerts. The group recorded a piece titled "Reverend King," which began with a Sanskrit chant—"A-um-ma-ni-pad-me-hum" —said to represent "the seven breaths of life." ("Alabama," which Coltrane recorded after the death of four young girls in the infamous bombing of a Birmingham church in 1963, opens with a saxophone recitative by Coltrane claimed to be based on remarks by Martin Luther King Jr.)[26]

In the summer of 1966 his band spent two weeks in Japan, where they were lionized by audiences who were at times taken aback by the forms his music had taken. In a lengthy interview conducted in Japan he reflected on the relation between his Christian upbringing and his mature beliefs about religion. "Now, as I look out upon the world—and this has always been a thing with me—I feel that all men know the truth, see?" Coltrane said. "I've always felt that even though a man was not a Christian, he still had to know the truth in some way. Or if he was a Christian, he could know the truth, or he could *not*." Asked at a Tokyo press conference what he would like to be in ten years, Coltrane responded: "I would like to be a saint." A few days later he visited and prayed at the Nagasaki War Memorial. He was moved by Japanese traditional music, the instrumental sounds of *shakuhachi* and *koto,* and especially by the sounds of Buddhist worship, like temple bells, which he included in some of his final recordings. "My goal is to live the truly religious life and express it in my music," he told an interviewer in 1966. "If you live it, when you play there's no problem because the music is just part of the whole thing . . . My music is the spiritual expression of what I am—my faith, my knowledge, my being . . . I'd like to point out to people the divine in a musical language that transcends words. I want to speak to their souls."[27]

B y t h e m i d - 1960s this kind of sentiment had begun to filter through the world of popular music in the work and words of performers able to reach a vastly larger audience than Coltrane (who by jazz standards was a commercial success during the 1960s). Many of the most successful rock and pop stars of the decade explored the Asian spirituality and musical forms that Coltrane had been the first to probe. Most directly influenced was the folk-rock group the Byrds, which had developed its style in Los Angeles folk clubs as an attempt to combine the electrical energy and vocal stylings of the British Invasion rock bands with the musical and songwriting sensibilities of the American folk revival: Bob Dylan meets the Beatles, in a word. The Byrds followed up their 1965 debut album *Mr. Tambourine Man,* titled after the Dylan song, with a chart-topping cover that reflected the spiritual undercurrents of the folk revival: Pete Seeger's "Turn! Turn! Turn!" whose text was a famous passage from Ecclesiastes. Next the group turned toward Coltrane and the East, recording "Eight Miles High," a song that blended psychedelic lyrics with musical forms directly inspired by Coltrane's music. Reportedly the Byrds had been touring the United States in a mobile home in which they listened to only two tapes, one of Ravi Shankar playing ragas and the other featuring Coltrane's "Africa" and "India." Lead vocalist and songwiter Roger McGuinn was inspired by the latter song to fashion a melody almost directly from it (which Coltrane had in turn borrowed from a Folkways recording), which he played on his distinctive Rickenbacker twelve-string guitar. "The first break is a direct quote from a Coltrane phrase, and throughout the rest of the song we try to emulate the scales and modes that Trane was using," said McGuinn. "Especially his spiritual feeling, which got me into transcendental meditation not long afterwards."[28] The Byrds, in effect, were the product of two independent but related tributaries of folk-revival music: the music of Woody Guthrie, Robert Johnson, and the old-time sound recordings as filtered through Harry Smith and Bob Dylan, and the folk music of India as filtered through Moses Asch and John Coltrane.

"Eight Miles High" would be the Byrd's last Top 20 single, although the group would continue to enjoy success both as a group and as individuals on their own. In 1966 Indian music and spirituality were raised to the highest possible mass-culture prominence through the efforts of the Beatles. The sitar had been sounded as early as "Norwegian Wood," from the 1965 album *Rubber Soul*. During the summer and fall of 1966 George Harrison studied sitar with Shankar in Bombay, where he lived in the Taj Mahal Hotel. The Beatles' next album, *Revolver*, featured sitar-playing and Asian spirituality in the songs "Love You To" and "Tomorrow Never Knows," in which John Lennon recites passages said to be from the Tibetan *Book of the Dead* over what sounds like hallucinatory electronic gibbering. Several Indian-based songs appeared over the next two years, mainly by George Harrison, including "Within You Without You" *(Sergeant Pepper),* "Blue Jay Way" *(Magical Mystery Tour),* "The Inner Light," and "Across the Universe." The Beatles became famously involved with Maharishi Mahesh Yogi, popularizer of transcendental meditation in the summer of 1967, bringing unprecedented attention to Indian religious practices, and in February 1968 traveled to Rishikesh (the city where in 1979 Charles Mingus would have his ashes scattered into the Ganges) to continue their explorations of Indian spirituality with a cohort that included Donovan, Mia Farrow, and Mike Love of the Beach Boys. "He had such thirst for the knowledge and wisdom of Indian traditions," Shankar wrote in a eulogy of Harrison. "In many ways he was more Indian than many Indians."[29]

Nowhere did the Beatles allude to any Coltrane influence in their turn toward the East, although Ravi Shankar was their major source of Indian musical expertise, as he had been Coltrane's. (Shankar gave Harrison a copy of *Autobiography of a Yogi,* just as someone had passed the book along to Coltrane.) The late 1960s vogue for "raga rock" might well have occurred without Coltrane's involvement. But beyond doubt he contributed to a cultural climate receptive to Indian music and spirituality, and did serve as an important influence in his own right on musicians and composers as disparate as Eric Clapton, Philip Glass, and Bono of U2. Keyboardist Ray Manzarek had first heard Coltrane's "My Favorite Things" in 1960 and was "completely blown away"; five years later in California he met another fan, drummer John Densmore, and they resolved to incorporate some of the "freedom" they heard in Coltrane's music into their new group, the Doors. One result was their 1967 number-one hit, "Light My Fire," which used a minor two-chord vamp modeled directly on "My Favorite Things"; Manzarek called it "our tribute to Coltrane."[30]

Other musicians spoke more directly of Coltrane's spiritual impact. "I haven't heard anything higher than 'The Father and the Son and the Holy Ghost' from the *Meditations* album," said guitarist Carlos Santana, in the ecstatic tone often adopted in discussing Coltrane. "I would often play it at four in the morning, the traditional time for meditation . . . I could hear the Supreme One playing music through John Coltrane's mind." Guitarist John McLaughlin recalled going into a "kind of trance" while listening to the uncompromisingly intense collective improvisations of *Ascension*, again from 1965, and feeling himself "flying over Africa. I could feel the spirit of the entire continent and its pulsating, teeming life; I could hear African music and Coltrane's music simultaneously," McLaughlin recalled. (McGuinn also spoke of the "feeling of flying" he got from Coltrane's music.) Jerry Garcia of the Grateful Dead also acknowledged Coltrane's influence, albeit in a more measured tone: "I've been impressed with that thing of flow, and of making statements that to my ears sound like paragraphs— he'll play along stylistically with a certain kind of tone, in a certain kind of syntax, for X amount of time, then he'll change the subject, then play along with this other personality coming out, which really impressed me." Coltrane's influence was not limited to purveyors of rock or jazz. Minimalist composers Philip Glass, Steve Reich, and Terry Riley have cited Coltrane's influence on their compositions, especially in their use of polyrhythmic cycles and Eastern harmonic drones. Glass in particular has commented extensively on the relationship between his musical works and the ideas and practices he developed through his study of yoga and Buddhism. His 1979 opera, *Satyagraha,* took Gandhi as its subject and is infused with themes of Indian spirituality.[31]

The popular music of the Atlantic world in this era had a fascinating, almost surreal transcontinental dimension. British pop music was deeply shaped by the African-American roots music of its former North American colony, as groups like the Animals, the Rolling Stones, and the Beatles developed their own soundings of black music; it then promptly recrossed the Atlantic in what is called the British Invasion. A few years later many of the same British artists "discovered" the music of another former colony, India, and assimilated elements of it piecemeal into rock, from which it became a major popular source and inspiration for the genre that has come to be called world music. As a result, musicians as disparate as Muddy Waters and Ravi Shankar became pop icons. (Every two years Shankar was booked at what would turn out to be a major American musical event: the Monterey Pop Festival in 1967, Woodstock in 1969, and the Concert for Bangladesh in 1971.)

Not a few musicians burned out like Roman candles in these years. Coltrane's death in 1967, just short of his forty-first birthday and at the height of the African-American uprising in Newark, New Jersey, devastated the jazz community. His funeral took place at St. Peter's Church in Manhattan, where the Reverend John Gensel, the Lutheran pastor close to many pillars of the New York jazz scene, conducted the service. Ornette Coleman's and Albert Ayler's quartets played one number each, and some of Coltrane's relatives who had traveled up from North Carolina were nonplussed to see jazz at a funeral. Sun Ra was stricken. "The Arkestra played at a memorial for Coltrane at the University of Pennsylvania shortly after his death," notes John Szwed, "and for years afterwards Sun Ra would suddenly bring up Coltrane's passing in conversations as an object lesson—whether to himself or to others was not always clear."[32] But Coltrane's musical legacy was sustained and carried forward by myriad musicians, both by former sidemen—Tyner, Jones, Garrison, Pharoah Sanders, Rashied Ali—and by many who knew him only through recordings.

Alice Coltrane was particularly important in maintaining his legacy, an achievement all the more remarkable in the 1960s milieu, where jazz was particularly charged with aggressive masculine energy. Born Alice McLeod, she had grown up in Detroit, where she played piano in churches and studied classical music before moving to Europe and playing with major expatriate musicians. After returning to Detroit she joined a quartet led by vibraphonist Terry Gibbs, with whom she made her first recording, *Terry Gibbs Plays Jewish Melodies in Jazztime,* in 1963 (which included, not surprisingly, a version of "Bei Mir Bist Du Schön"). Alice began traveling with Coltrane later that year, gave birth to the first of their three sons in August 1964, and became the pianist in Coltrane's final, most free-form group when McCoy Tyner left at the beginning of 1966. She had developed a fine bebop style, but Coltrane encouraged her to develop the flowing harplike effect on the piano, playing arpeggios over the full range of the instruments. (She would study and later record on harp.) After John's death, Alice perpetuated his spiritual legacy as well, becoming an ad-

vanced student of Swami Satchidananda and establishing a religious retreat called the Vedantic Center in California. She has published a variety
of spiritual writings and released collections of spiritual chants. On one of
her few jazz recordings, she contributed a piece called "One for the Father," which, she writes, "exemplifies my fond remembrance of the father,
John Coltrane; and at such time of remembering, I see the father, his three
sons, and the Holy Ghost, or Nilakantha who is Lord Siva, the Destroyer
of Ignorance." Hers is an eclectic Hinduism, blending elements of Christianity and Egyptian mythology into the sort of panreligious vision that
John himself favored.[33]

Given Coltrane's aspiration to sainthood, it seems fitting that he has
been canonized, after a manner, by a congregation in San Francisco. Located in a storefront near Haight Street, St. John's African Orthodox
Church traces its apostolic succession to Ignatius Peter III, patriarch of
Antioch. Its founding pastor, Franzo Wayne King, was struck as a high
school student by jazz artists as a kind of royal fraternity in marked contrast to the grim portrayals of African-American history prevalent at the
time. A recording of "My Favorite Things" piqued his interest in Coltrane,
whom he first saw in 1965 at the San Francisco Jazz Workshop. "The only
thing I could liken it to was the Pentecostal experience, when the Holy
Ghost was falling and the spirit of the Lord was not only in the place, but
in the people." King underwent a conversion experience while hearing "A
Love Supreme" performed in "a den of iniquity, where liquor was being
poured and cigarettes being smoked. John Coltrane was the call back to
God, back to self-discipline," King asserts. "The scriptures say, 'And Jesus
breathed on them, and said, "Receive ye the Holy Ghost."' Well, John
breathed on me, and I've been obedient to the spirit of God ever since. But
it was the mind of God that sent John here—and his sound is the voice of
God."[34]

For King, Coltrane's challenging art is an important reminder that "faith
is not accomplished without coming to the crucifixion of ourselves," that,
in the words of Job, "Yea though he slay me, yet will I trust him." Beginning in 1971 as the One Mind Evolutionary Transition Church of Christ
(it joined the African Orthodox Church a decade later), the congregation
created an eclectic liturgy blending Eastern Orthodox elements with the
sounds of the black church and of Coltrane's music. "When you come in,
you're going to find drums, bass, a piano, organ and saxophones. We're
blessed to have some very gifted and anointed musicians, and some of
them are part of the clergy . . . I just integrate myself into the music just
like everybody else. I might come out and play saxophone; I might open up
the confession. I might open the Bible and teach from that, or I might teach

from a John Coltrane quote. It depends how the spirit leads me. But there will be a heavy amount of John Coltrane's music and improvisation on that music."[35] Next to the altar is a Byzantine-style painting of Coltrane, his head encircled by a halo, holding a saxophone with flames flickering in the bell in one hand, in the other a scroll inscribed with the words "Let us sing all songs to God. Let us praise Him in the right path. Yes it is. 'Seek and ye shall find.'" Along with the Orthodox and Pentecostal elements, there is an ecumenical flavor to the theology of St. John's. "We don't hold a monopoly on John Coltrane," Reverend King has said, "because John is a saint among Buddhists; he is a saint among Moslems. He is a saint among Jews. And I think there are even a few atheists who are leaning on that anointed sound."[36]

Epilogue

THE YEAR that saw the release of *A Love Supreme* and the first experiments with Indian music by the Beatles and the Byrds also brought the most sweeping change in immigration law since the 1920s. America's ethnic and religious landscape was irrevocably altered on the Fourth of July 1965, when President Johnson chose the Statue of Liberty as the site to sign into law the Immigration and Naturalization Act. Immigration for Asians had been almost completely shut off beginning in 1882, and 1924 legislation had instituted a stringent quota system designed to drastically curtail entry to the United States from Africa, the Middle East, and most of Europe. The new law replaced geographic criteria with considerations of occupation and family reunification. The demographic face of the nation has changed rapidly as a result. At the beginning of the twenty-first century, the United States had about 30 million immigrants, over 10 percent of the population, with about one million arriving each year. Some 13 million arrived during the 1990s, meaning that 5 percent of the population has been in the United States for a decade or less. The percentage of American citizens born overseas is at an all-time high, surpassing even the great wave of European migration that occurred between 1880 and 1920. During the 1990s the Latino population of the United States increased nearly 40 percent, producing a population of 35 million by 2000, a majority of Mexican descent. The Asian population grew by over 40 percent to nearly 12 million in 2000.[1]

The impact on American religion has been dramatic. "We are surprised to find that there are more Muslim Americans than Episcopalians, more Muslims than members of the Presbyterian Church USA, and as many Muslims as there are Jews—that is, about six million," writes Diana Eck. "We are astonished to learn that Los Angeles is the most complex Buddhist city in the world, with a Buddhist population spanning the whole range of the Asian Buddhist world from Sri Lanka to Korea, along with a multitude of native-born American Buddhists."[2] Though statistics about religious adherence are notoriously difficult to verify, Buddhists may now number about four million, Hindus perhaps one million. This influx has altered the country's visible religious landscape in conspicuous ways, with exotic-looking mosques, temples, and gurdwaras punctuating the landscape not just on the cosmopolitan coasts but across the suburbs and open plains of the heartland.

Invisible to the eye are the equally dramatic changes in the American soundscape, both the sacred songs that accompany worship in these diverse sanctuaries and the broader range of music that sounds in ethnic festivals and through recordings marketed as world music. Through his composing and playing, his public statements, and the influence he exerted on other musicians to attune themselves to musics and ideas beyond the customary scope of American popular song, John Coltrane contributed to this proliferation of music. More significant than any single artist in complicating the religious soundscape were the reforms of the Second Vatican Council of 1962–1965, which made possible an infusion of vernacular world musics into the Catholic mass.[3] That this was taking place in the same few years in the 1960s may have been a historical accident; but one might just as reasonably point to it as corroborating evidence for Attali's claims about music as prophecy.

There are different ways of interpreting the demography of post-1965 immigration and its spiritual consequences, though. Some have questioned whether increased immigration and ethnic diversity necessarily translate into increased religious diversity. Many Asian immigrants come from countries where Christianity predominates, such as the Philippines, while others—South Korea and Vietnam, for instance—have sizable Christian minorities. Regardless of the dominant religion of the home country, immigrants to the United States are often anomalous groups within the population; they are more likely to be highly educated and Christian, for one thing. Moreover, religious identities, whether collective or individual, aren't primordial or ingrained. They are easily shaped and altered by different circumstances and contexts. Statistically at least, the United States is still overwhelmingly a Christian nation, and this fact undoubtedly has an effect on the religious identities of its immigrants. Recent surveys of public opinion show that more than 80 percent of Americans identify themselves as Christian, down just slightly from the results of 1947, when the question was first asked. More than half claim to attend church at least once a month, compared with 10 percent in the United Kingdom, 20 percent in Italy. (Even in Israel, only one-quarter of the population regularly attends Jewish worship services).[4] They may feel pressure to identify religiously with the mainstream by converting or at least submerging non-Christian practices.

Even if they don't, religion in America is subject to what R. Stephen Warner calls "processes of institutional isomorphism toward congregationalism": newcomers tend to adapt their beliefs and especially practices to conform to a more American Protestant church-centered model. This has certainly been the case for sacred music, as we've seen, where the Protestant hymn form has worked its way into the services of American Indians, Jews, Buddhists, and Roman Catholics. Warner proposes that we interpret the changes under way in American population and religion as "a process of the de-Europeanization of American Christianity, not the de-Christianization of American society." Philip Jenkins has made much the same argument in a number of prominent venues. Scholars who emphasize American religious diversity, he asserts, have an ideological rationale for underestimating the ongoing popularity and vitality of Christianity in the United States, and for overstating the inroads made by other religions. The subtitle of Eck's book—*How a "Christian Country" Has Become the World's Most Religiously Diverse Nation*—would thus more accurately read: *How Mass Immigration Ensured That a Christian Country Has Become an Even More Christian Country.*[5]

Gestures toward syncretism and interfaith solidarity in the United States invariably provoke dissent and resistance, especially in the wake of traumas like September 11. There has been much soul-searching among Muslims as well as among members of other faiths uncertain how to understand the position of Islamic fundamentalists amid the broader historical and geographical sweep of Islam. If Islam came under new scrutiny as a religious rationale for terrorism, Buddhism seemed to have lost its currency in a climate in which the major Abrahamic faiths circled each other warily. The case of folk rocker Steve Earle nicely captures these tensions. Raised in Bible Belt Texas, where his great-great-grandfather Elijah erected a Methodist chapel that still stands, Earle has been drawn to biblical themes. In 1995 he recorded "Waters of Babylon," a version of the 137th Psalm written by the Melodians, a Jamaican reggae band. His album *Jerusalem*, released amid moral panic over the war on terror, is unmistakably a jeremiad directed at the United States. The album's most controversial track is "John Walker's Blues," a first-person reflection on the "American Taliban" captured in Afghanistan and sentenced to prison, complete with Arabic chanting from the Qur'an. But the title track, "Jerusalem," invokes Isaiah's ancient language of peaceful coexistence, the same image with which William Billings welcomed American independence, to imagine an end to conflict in the Middle East, and perhaps in the United States as well: "But I believe there'll come a day when the lion and the lamb / Will lie down in peace together in Jerusalem."[6]

If music often presages broader social and cultural changes, what does America's sacred soundscape augur? What role might music play in the ominous possible global scenarios in which Christianity and Islam face off across swathes of the global South in a replay of the twelfth and thirteenth centuries, or Christendom finds itself pulled between the liberalizing North and orthodox South in reenactment of the Reformation that wracked Europe for centuries after the Crusades? Of the three Abrahamic religions, fundamentalist Islam has been easily the most hostile to music; it was one of the many activities banned by the Taliban, for example. (This is not to overlook the rich musical traditions of some varieties of Islam—Sufi, for instance.) Interestingly, the specific forms of Christianity that have been growing the most rapidly and are expected to become increasingly prevalent—not only in the United States but across Africa, Latin America, and parts of Asia where Christianity is burgeoning—are the aggressive, culturally conservative, emotionally and physically demonstrative styles associated with Pentecostalism and evangelical fundamentalism. And these churches have been among the most liberal in their attitudes toward music—both its emphasis within worship and the nearly promiscuous variety of styles and genres that have been accepted into its sacred spaces. Musically, it's the Christianity of African-American holiness preaching, of gospel blues, handclaps, and tambourines, of trombone shout bands, and of the amplified, almost rock-concert ambience of the praise-and-worship music that predominantly white evangelical congregations have adopted, following the lead, whether consciously or not, of the black church.

Coltrane's music as sacralized by St. John's African Orthodox Church suggests one sort of religious future. Even as Coltrane moved through a number of musical genres—rhythm and blues, big-band jazz, bebop, modal, and atonal avant-garde—his playing never lost the Pentecostal fire that he somehow brought to it, whether its source was the African Methodist church of his upbringing or some other source. Yet in his extreme musical and spiritual eclecticism—"I believe in all religions," he said on the back of his album *Meditations*—Coltrane embodied the sort of tolerant and respectful pluralism that Eck sees well under way in the United States. While no one could describe Coltrane as a Pentecostal Christian, he clearly has been a source of inspiration for those who would describe themselves in those terms. Of course, in all but a handful of churches one is much more likely to hear the praise music of Contemporary Christian Music than anything remotely resembling Coltrane. "Proselytizers are forever lifting recent pop styles and attaching pious lyrics," complains critic Jon Pareles, "though labeling as 'sacred' the music of soft-rockers like Bob Carlisle or grunge rockers-come-lately like Creed pushes the word past any useful meaning." But the music is reshaping the experience of worship. As Pentecostalism continues its rapid expansion both in the United States and through the global South, one is reminded of perhaps the most prominent Pentecostal musician active in the United States: John Ashcroft, noted gospel composer, pianist, and singer. Will the theology and song of the future resemble that of John Coltrane or John Ashcroft? How compatible are those variations on the Christian faith?[7]

Music has served historically as a powerful solvent of religious differences, but it is by no means all-powerful. It tends to operate most effectively among ordinary worshippers concerned more with the experiential aspects of religion than with creedal or dogmatic differences. In the view of many believers, however, especially those charged with religious authority, there remain hard-and-fast distinctions and boundaries that no amount of musical exchange will dissolve. Music is after all only one form of religious practice; its syncretic impulses can be outmatched by prayers, sermons, and collective litanies, not to mention positions adopted by ecclesiastical councils and synods. Sacred sound represents spiritual impulses at their most mercurial and universal, but language has a way of erecting boundaries through such areas of aural common ground. With their pervasive Old Testament phrases and metaphors, America's sacred songs have tended to reinforce religious exclusions. The moral grandeur of an Israel— whether Jewish, Christian, Mormon, or other—commonly depends on the existence of an Egypt or a Babylon, oppressors and captors whose identity is readily assignable to populations located outside the religious community, denomination, or even nation.

Sacred music tends to generate its own loyalties and its own glacial tempo of change; Luther himself remained fond of much of the musical legacy of the Catholic church. Music is the preeminent art form of memory. Probably this fact is the key to its roles in America's religious cultures: like no other form of spiritual expression, music ties participants to the religious experiences of childhood, rife as they often are with the most indelible memories. Nurtured as it usually is in the bosom of the family, sacred song shares childhood's characteristic mixture of openness tempered by a longing for the verities of tradition. Innovation in religious music seems to take place more easily during periods of ecumenical tolerance and easing of sectarian tensions. Ears and larynxes seem to open up when pressure to conform to orthodoxy is lifted. The ability to move freely, whether between states, regions, or continents, is also important. No doubt the creativity of sacred music in the United States is a by-product of the same democratizing impulses of market competition that have encouraged such a proliferation of forms of faith and have kept rates of religious participation higher than in comparable North Atlantic societies. Musical innovation in North America has peaked during periods of spiritual revival: the mid-eighteenth century, the early nineteenth century, the decades after the Civil War, and the years following World War II. The entire planet seems well into such a phase now, a heterophonous awakening with no end in earshot.

Note on Method

Notes ✦ Index

Note on Method

THIS BOOK relies heavily on the methods and published work of ethnomusicologists, but it is a work of history, not of musicology or ethnography. Its goal is to understand the historical processes by which religious belief and sacred music have become established and evolved in North America. How should historians analyze music, particularly that for which sound recordings do not exist and documentary evidence is meager? A flexible approach is required, one that honors the injunction to write what is possible to write about while being candid about areas where the historian must traverse particularly thin empirical ice. Much of the study is based on the traditional stuff of historiography—published and unpublished writings, letters, journalistic accounts—and on the work of historians who have labored over these materials. Invaluable for all periods are reports by ear-witnesses and participant-observers. For my purposes, it isn't always as important to reconstruct what tones people actually heard in the seventeenth and eighteenth centuries as to describe and analyze what they thought about those sounds—how they participated in the process of creating and performing it, how they reacted to what they heard or created.

This work builds on the pioneering work done by collectors and scholars in a variety of disciplines: ethnomusicology, folklore studies, anthropology, hymnology, and others. But it is grounded in the aural data of sacred music as well: sound recordings when possible, notation when appropriate, and examples of music that appear in film and video. My project has benefited enormously from the many fine collections produced by Smithsonian-Folkways and others who have kept historic or obscure recordings in circulation. In analyzing these recordings I use an eclectic toolkit drawn from the realm of ethnomusicology and music criticism, although extended formal musical analysis is beyond the scope of this book (and of dubious utility to the sort of analysis I am attempting). Historians who work with music have an obligation to their readers to help them make sense of the musical text: what it sounds like, how it works both as a set of lyrics and as the product of tones and rhythms.

Sound recordings date back only slightly over a century, but published accounts and sheet music date back to earliest European settlement. In some cases it is useful to describe basic rhythmic, melodic, or harmonic features, in other cases to focus on the text, on both its meaning and its formal arrangement into verses or stanzas. The use of sound recordings raises an unavoidable question: What use are they for reconstructing the performance and sound of music that predates the 1890s, the decade from which my earliest examples come? There is the temptation to engage in ethnographic "upstreaming," using observations of modern practices to interpret practices of the more distant past. In some instances sheet music survives, in other cases detailed prose descriptions. In many cases I assume a degree of cultural continuity in performance practices when that seems warranted by other clues in the historical record. By triangulating among different kinds of sources it is possible to arrive at reasonable conclusions regarding historical soundscapes. But it is important not to lose sight of the difficulties posed by music, both its material impermanence and the thorny questions it raises about how to interpret a nonrepresentational cultural form. "It is the mark of an educated person to look for precision in each class of things just so far as the nature of the subject admits," wrote Aristotle near the beginning of the *Nicomachean Ethics,* in words that seem designed for this kind of study; "it is evidently equally foolish to accept probable reasoning from a mathematician and to demand from a rhetorician scientific proofs."

The reader will have long since noticed that this account of American sacred music is selective and interpretive rather than exhaustive or comprehensive. Any number of important religious-musical styles, works, or performances might have been included as case studies but weren't; the symbiotic relationship between sacred and popular music since World War II in particular will be the subject of a future work. The examples chosen here were ones that caught my attention over the course of trolling and sifting through a much larger body of religion and sound. They speak to each other and to the broad themes of the book. I chose them, of course, but in a sense they also chose me, by capturing my attention and my historical imagination. By the time I had nearly finished the manuscript I came across a passage by musicologist Richard Crawford that nicely conveys this dynamic. "In the gap between specific events and the broader processes we recognize as historical lie the wellsprings of narrative energy," writes Crawford. "As one thinks hard about why certain details refuse to be forgotten, their place in the larger scheme of things may start to reveal itself."[1] As a description of method, that seems as apt an observation as any on which to end.

Notes

Introduction

Epigraph: Benjamin F. Crawford, quoted in Jon Michael Spencer, *Protest and Praise: Sacred Music of Black Religion* (Minneapolis: Fortress, 1990), 61.

1. Frederick Douglass, *Narrative of the Life of Frederick Douglass, An American Slave, Written by Himself,* ed. David W. Blight (Boston: Bedford, 1993), 142.
2. Ibid.
3. Natalie Angier, "Sonata for Humans, Birds and Humpback Whales," *New York Times,* 9 January 2001, D5. On historical soundscapes, see Leigh Eric Schmidt, *Hearing Things: Religion, Illusion, and the American Enlightenment* (Cambridge: Harvard University Press, 2000); Mark M. Smith, *Listening to Nineteenth-Century America* (Chapel Hill: University of North Carolina Press, 2001); Alain Corbin, *Village Bells: Sound and Meaning in the Nineteenth-Century French Countryside,* trans. Martin Thom (New York: Columbia University Press, 1998).
4. Works that have been especially useful in helping me think about how to connect nation, religion, and music, respectively, are Thomas A. Bender, ed., *Rethinking American History in a Global Age* (Berkeley: University of California Press, 2002); and the NYU Organization of American Historians' La Pietra reports that preceded it; Thomas A. Tweed, ed., *Retelling U.S. Religious History* (Berkeley: University of California Press, 1997); Walter H. Conser Jr. and Sumner B. Twiss, eds., *Religious Diversity and American Religious History: Studies in Traditions and Cultures* (Athens: University of Georgia Press, 1997); Ronald Niezen, *Spirit Wars: Native North American Religions in the Age of Nation Building* (Berkeley: University of California Press, 2000); David D. Hall, ed., *Lived Religion in America: Toward a History of Practice*

(Princeton: Princeton University Press, 1997); Jon Butler, *Awash in a Sea of Faith: Christianizing the American People* (Cambridge: Harvard University Press, 1990); Nathan Hatch, *The Democratization of American Christianity* (New Haven: Yale University Press, 1989); R. Laurence Moore, *Religious Outsiders and the Making of Americans* (New York: Oxford University Press, 1986); Lawrence E. Sullivan, *Enchanting Powers: Music in the World's Religions* (Cambridge: Harvard University Press, 1997); Lawrence A. Hoffman and Janet R. Walton, eds., *Sacred Sound and Social Change: Liturgical Music in Jewish and Christian Experience* (Notre Dame: University of Notre Dame Press, 1992); Joyce Irwin, ed., *Sacred Sound: Music in Religious Thought and Practice* (Chico, Calif.: Scholars Press, 1983); Ellen Koskoff, ed., *Women and Music in Cross-Cultural Perspective* (New York: Greenwood, 1987); Peter Van der Merwe, *Origins of the Popular Style: The Antecedents of Twentieth-Century Popular Music* (Oxford: Oxford University Press, 1989); John Storm Roberts, *Black Music of Two Worlds: African, Caribbean, Latin and African-American Traditions,* 2d ed. (New York: Schirmer, 1998); Christopher Small, *Music of the Common Tongue: Survival and Celebration in African American Music* (Hanover, N.H.: Wesleyan University Press, 1987); Jon Michael Spencer, ed., *Theomusicology: A Special Issue of Black Sacred Music* 8 (Durham, N.C.: Duke University Press, spring 1994).

5. Flavia Waters Champe, *The Matachines Dance of the Upper Rio Grande: History, Music, and Choreography* (Lincoln: University of Nebraska Press, 1983), 1; Sylvia Rodríguez, *The Matachines Dance: Ritual Symbolism and Interethnic Relations in the Upper Río Grande Valley* (Albuquerque: University of New Mexico Press, 1996), 6; Brenda Mae Romero, "The Matachines Music and Dance in San Juan Pueblo and Alcalde, New Mexico: Contexts and Meanings" (Ph.D. diss., University of California at Los Angeles, 1993), 11–47.

6. Champe, *Matachines Dance,* 1; Romero, "Matachines Music and Dance," 67–70; Rodriguez, *Matachines Dance,* 156.

7. Ramón A. Gutiérrez, *When Jesus Came, the Corn Mothers Went Away: Marriage, Sexuality, and Power in New Mexico, 1500–1846* (Stanford: Stanford University Press, 1991), 48–50; Brenda Mae Romero, "Cultural Interaction in New Mexico as Illustrated in the Matachines Dance," in *Musics of Multicultural America: A Study of Twelve Musical Communities,* ed. Kip Lornell and Anne K. Rasmussen (New York: Schirmer, 1997), 179; Gutiérrez, *When Jesus Came,* 83–85.

8. The subtitle to Rodriguez's introduction is "The Beautiful Dance of Subjugation"; *Matachines Dance,* 1–15; Gutiérrez, *When Jesus Came,* 48–49.

9. Gutiérrez, *When Jesus Came,* 337–40; Rodríguez, *Matachines Dance,* 17.

10. Rodríguez, *Matachines Dance,* 2, 93–95.

11. Romero, "Matachines Music and Dance," 27–30, 60–62.

12. Romero, "Cultural Interaction in New Mexico," 179; Rodríguez, *Matachines Dance,* 111–15, 98–99.

13. Romero, "Cultural Interaction in New Mexico," 177.

14. Comments one informant from Picuris Pueblo: "So it's a form of worship, like going to church. It's a religious order. And anything like that, well, we probably don't look at it any different than going through the chapters in the Bible. Just, you know, one big package, like"; Rodríguez, *Matachines Dance,* 80.
15. Rodríguez, *Matachines Dance,* 36–40, 57–61.
16. See *The La Pietra Report: A Report to the Profession,* available at http://www.oah.org/activities/lapietra/final.html; Thomas Bender, "Historians, the Nation, and the Plenitude of Narratives," in *Rethinking American History,* 1–22.
17. See Walter Johnson, "Time and Revolution in African America: Temporality and the History of Atlantic Slavery," in Bender, *Rethinking American History,* 148–167.

1. O for a Thousand Tongues to Sing

Epigraph: Martin Luther, quoted in Michael Hicks, *Mormonism and Music: A History* (Urbana: University of Illinois Press, 1989), 1.

1. John Wesley, *The Journal of the Rev. John Wesley, A.M.,* ed. Nehemiah Curnock, vol. 1 (London: Epworth, 1938), 110; John L. Nuelsen, *John Wesley and the German Hymn: A Detailed Study of John Wesley's Translations of Thirty-three German Hymns,* trans. Theodore Parry, Sidney H. Moore, and Arthur Holbrooke (Yorkshire: Calverley, 1972), 17.
2. Nuelsen, *Wesley and the German Hymn,* 15, 16, 17.
3. Wesley, *Journal,* 142–143.
4. Nuelsen, *Wesley and the German Hymn,* 21.
5. Ibid., 108.
6. Wesley, *Journal,* 169, 151, 160.
7. Louis F. Benson, *The English Hymn: Its Development and Use in Worship* (1915; reprint, Richmond, Va.: John Knox, 1962), 225.
8. Sylvia R. Frey and Betty Wood, *Come Shouting to Zion: African American Protestantism in the American South and British Caribbean to 1830* (Chapel Hill: University of North Carolina Press, 1998), 88; on "motley crew" see Peter Linebaugh and Marcus Rediker, *The Many-Headed Hydra: Sailors, Slaves, Commoners, and the Hidden History of the Revolutionary Atlantic* (Boston: Beacon, 2000), 212–213. Wesley, *Journal,* 345–346.
9. Wesley, *Journal,* 284–285, 396–397.
10. John R. Tyson, ed., *Charles Wesley: A Reader* (New York: Oxford University Press, 1989), 66–81, quotation on 78.
11. Frey and Wood, *Come Shouting to Zion,* 90; Linebaugh and Rediker, *Many-Headed Hydra,* chap. 6.
12. Tyson, *Charles Wesley,* 66–81, quotation on 66; Wesley, *Journal,* 263–264, 316; Nuelsen, *Wesley and the German Hymn,* 34, 39–40.
13. Wesley, *Journal,* 385–86; Frey and Wood, *Come Shouting to Zion,* 91.
14. Wesley, *Journal,* 418; Whitefield quoted in ibid., 400–401, n. 1; Frey and Wood, *Come Shouting to Zion,* 91.

15. Wesley, *Journal*, 475–476; Nuelsen, *Wesley and the German Hymn*, 32; Tyson, *Charles Wesley*, 21.

16. Nuelsen, *Wesley and the German Hymn*, 81; Tyson, *Charles Wesley*, 221.

17. Nuelsen, *Wesley and the German Hymn*, 55, 84, 82.

18. Benson, *English Hymn*, 19–26.

19. Rochelle A. Stackhouse, *The Language of the Psalms in Worship: American Revisions of Watts' Psalter* (Lanham, Md.: Scarecrow, 1997), 30, 31; Benson, *English Hymn*, 27–30, 48–50; Mather quoted in Sandra S. Sizer, *Gospel Hymns and Social Religion: The Rhetoric of Nineteenth-Century Revivalism* (Philadelphia: Temple University Press, 1978), 64–65.

20. Stephen Marini, "Rehearsal for Revival: Sacred Singing and the Great Awakening in America," in *Sacred Sound: Music in Religious Thought and Practice,* ed. Joyce Irwin (Chico, Calif.: Scholars, 1983), 80; Stephen Marini, "Hymnody as History: Early Evangelical Hymns and the Recovery of American Popular Religion," *Church History* 71 (June 2002), 280–281.

21. Benson, *English Hymn*, 109.

22. Watts quoted in Stackhouse, *Language of the Psalms*, 36.

23. Benson, *English Hymn*, 162–163; Henry Wilder Foote, *Three Centuries of American Hymnody* (Cambridge: Harvard University Press, 1940), 65–66.

24. Edwards quoted in Benson, *English Hymn*, 163.

25. Edwards quoted in Foote, *Three Centuries,* 148; Benson, *English Hymn*, 255–261, 340–357; Foote, *Three Centuries,* 146–168.

26. Nym Cooke, "Sacred Music to 1800," in *The Cambridge History of American Music,* ed. David Nicholls (Cambridge: Cambridge University Press, 1998), 85.

27. Examples taken from *The Whole Booke of Psalmes* (commonly known as the *Bay Psalm Book*) (Cambridge, 1640).

28. The best brief account of the singing reform movement is found in the "Prologue" to David P. McKay and Richard Crawford, *William Billings of Boston: Eighteenth-Century Composer* (Princeton: Princeton University Press, 1975), 3–29; see also chap. 2 of Gilbert Chase, *America's Music: From the Pilgrims to the Present,* 3d ed. (Urbana: University of Illinois Press, 1987), 19–37; Esther Rothenbusch Crookshank, "'We're Marching to Zion': Isaac Watts in America," paper presented at Hymnody in American Protestantism conference, Wheaton, Ill., May 2000, 3–8.

29. Marini, "Rehearsal for Revival," 71–91.

30. Eileen Southern, *The Music of Black Americans: A History* (New York: Norton, 1971), 31–37, 58–61, quotations on 36, 59.

31. Ibid., 59.

32. Ritter quoted in Crookshank, "'We're Marching to Zion,'" 11.

33. Watts quoted in Stackhouse, *Language of the Psalms,* 67.

34. Ibid., 59–69.

35. Benson, *English Hymn*, 111–112.

36. Stackhouse, *Language of the Psalms,* 141–149; Mycall, Barlow, and Dwight quoted on 143.

37. Ibid., 115–125.
38. Crookshank, "'We're Marching to Zion,'" 18.

2. Singing Independence

Epigraph: William Billings, *The Complete Works of William Billings,* ed. Hans Nathan (vol. 2) and Karl Kroeger (vols. 1, 3, and 4) (Boston: American Historical Society and the Colonial Society of Massachusetts, 1977), 2: 136–137.

1. Marilyn Gombosi, *A Day of Solemn Thanksgiving* (Chapel Hill: University of North Carolina Press, 1977), 42.
2. Ibid., 13–14.
3. Ibid., 7, 15.
4. Ibid., 65–69.
5. Ibid., 43–48.
6. Ibid., 63–64.
7. Ibid., 91–93.
8. Ibid., 93–94.
9. Ibid., 143–48.
10. Ibid., 13. For recent historiography on (mainly nineteenth-century) soundscapes, see Leigh Eric Schmidt, *Hearing Things: Religion, Illusion, and the American Enlightenment* (Cambridge: Harvard University Press, 2000); Mark M. Smith, *Listening to Nineteenth-Century America* (Chapel Hill: University of North Carolina Press, 2001); Alain Corbin, *Village Bells: Sound and Meaning in the Nineteenth-Century French Countryside,* trans. Martin Thom (New York: Columbia University Press, 1998).
11. Sylvia R. Frey and Betty Wood, *Come Shouting to Zion: African American Protestantism in the American South and British Caribbean to 1830* (Chapel Hill: University of North Carolina Press, 1998), 83–87.
12. J. Taylor Hamilton, *A History of the Church Known as the Moravian Church, or The Unitas Fratrum, or The Unity of the Brethren, during the Eighteenth and Nineteenth Centuries* (1900; reprint, New York: AMS Publishing, 1971), 108–110, 141–143, 170–176, 242–247, 292–296; Daniel K. Richter, *Facing East from Indian Country: A Native History of Early America* (Cambridge: Harvard University Press, 2001), 204–206, 221–222.
13. Gombosi, *Day of Solemn Thanksgiving,* 18–19, 14.
14. Benjamin Franklin, *A Benjamin Franklin Reader,* ed. Nathan G. Goodman (New York: Crowell, 1945), 182.
15. Gombosi, *Day of Solemn Thanksgiving,* 8–9.
16. Ibid., 16.
17. Ibid.; Hunter James, *The Quiet People of the Land: A Story of the North Carolina Moravians in Revolutionary Times* (Winston-Salem, N.C.: Old Salem, 1976), 121.
18. Gombosi, *Day of Solemn Thanksgiving,* 17.
19. Billings, *Complete Works,* 2: 244–255.

20. William Billings, *Peace: An Anthem,* ed. Gillian Anderson (Washington, D.C.: C. T. Wagner, 1974), 3; David P. McKay and Richard Crawford, *William Billings of Boston: Eighteenth-Century Composer* (Princeton: Princeton University Press, 1975), 133.

21. Billings, *Complete Works,* 3: 257–275.

22. Campbell quoted in Nathan Hatch, *The Democratization of American Christianity* (New Haven: Yale University Press, 1989), 71. On civil religion, see Catherine L. Albanese, *America: Religions and Religion,* 3d ed. (Belmont, Calif.: Wadsworth, 1999), 438–445.

23. Nathaniel D. Gould, *Church Music in America, Comprising Its History and Its Peculiarities at Different Periods, with Cursory Remarks on Its Legitimate Use and Its Abuse* (Boston: A. N. Johnson, 1853), 46.

24. McKay and Crawford, *William Billings,* 47–48, 53; program notes, William Billings, *Wake Ev'ry Breath,* William Appling Singers and Orchestra (New World Records 80539-2, 1998).

25. McKay and Crawford, *William Billings,* 60.

26. Billings, *Complete Works,* 1: 32–33.

27. McKay and Crawford, *William Billings,* 41.

28. "Africa" is performed in Billings, *Wake Ev'ry Breath,* and in *"A Land of Pure Delight": Anthems and Fuging Tunes by William Billings,* His Majestie's Clerks, Paul Hillier, conductor (Harmonia Mundi 907048, 1992). Perhaps the most widely recorded Billings composition is the anthem "I Am the Rose of Sharon," based on the Song of Solomon, from *The Singing-Master's Assistant,* in Billings, *Complete Works,* 2: 216–225.

29. Billings, *Complete Works,* 4: 33.

30. Ibid., 3: 5. Crawford draws the comparison to Fielding in McKay and Crawford, *William Billings,* 81.

31. Billings, *Complete Works,* 3: 29–31.

32. Ibid., 4: 29–30.

33. Ibid., 2: 72–73.

34. Ibid., 1: 74.

35. Ibid., 316.

36. Gould, *Church Music in America,* 44; McKay and Crawford, *William Billings,* 221–230.

37. Quoted in McKay and Crawford, *William Billings,* 167.

38. Ibid., 124–129.

39. Richard Crawford, *American Studies and American Musicology: A Point of View and a Case in Point* (New York: Institute for Studies in American Music, 1975), 27–31.

3. Marching to Zion

Epigraph: British Mormon Joseph Beecroft on his first Christmas in Utah, 1856, in Michael Hicks, *Mormonism and Music: A History* (Urbana: University of Illinois Press, 1989), 45.

1. Daniel W. Patterson, *The Shaker Spiritual* (Princeton: Princeton University Press, 1979), 62–63.
2. Ibid., 18, 19; Edward D. Andrews, *The Gift to Be Simple: Songs, Dances, and Rituals of the American Shakers* (1940; reprint, New York: Dover, 1962), 3, 61.
3. Patterson, *Shaker Spiritual*, 150; see also Andrews, *Gift to Be Simple*, 29–30.
4. Patterson, *Shaker Spiritual*, 13, 456.
5. Ibid., 99–130, 245–315, 377–396; quotation on 100.
6. I. Neighbours, "The Spiritual Sailor," in *The Sacred Harp,* ed. B. F. White and E. J. King (Philadelphia: S. C. Collins, 1860), 150.
7. Andrews, *Gift to be Simple*, 99–100; Patterson, *Shaker Spiritual*, 157.
8. Patterson, *Shaker Spiritual*, 162.
9. Ibid., 136, 189.
10. Ibid., 164, 142–44, 140.
11. Ibid., 185, 178, 208.
12. Andrews, *Gift to be Simple*, 23–27.
13. Ann Taves, *Fits, Trances and Visions: Experiencing Religion and Explaining Experience from Wesley to James* (Princeton: Princeton University Press, 1999), 121–249; Patterson, *Shaker Spiritual*, 316–318, quotation on 39; Andrews, *Gift to Be Simple*, 22.
14. Patterson, *Shaker Spiritual*, 198, 320.
15. Ibid., 324, 342–345; program notes to Joel Cohen, *The Golden Harvest: More Shaker Chants and Spirituals* (Hamburg: Pure Classics 779 020-2, 2000), 34.
16. Andrews, *Gift to Be Simple*, 30.
17. Patterson, *Shaker Spiritual*, 320–321.
18. Ibid., 378, 353.
19. Ibid., 356; Andrews, *Gift to Be Simple,* 75.
20. Patterson, *Shaker Spiritual,* 354–355.
21. Ibid., 352.
22. Ibid., 356–58; program notes to Cohen, *The Golden Harvest,* 35–36.
23. *Independent Mechanic* (1811), quoted in Mark M. Smith, *Listening to Nineteenth-Century America* (Durham, N.C.: University of North Carolina Press, 2001), 102–103.
24. Patterson, *Shaker Spiritual*, 401–402.
25. *Sacred Hymns and Spiritual Songs for the Church of Jesus Christ of Latter-day Saints*, 14th ed. (Salt Lake City: George Q. Cannon, 1871), 58–59.
26. Hicks, *Mormonism and Music*, 69, 65; Grant Wacker, *Heaven Below: Early Pentecostals and American Culture* (Cambridge: Harvard University Press, 2001).
27. Catherine L. Albanese, *America: Religion and Religions,* 3d ed. (Belmont, Calif.: Wadsworth, 1999) 218–222.
28. Hicks, *Mormonism and Music*, 35–36, 3.
29. Ibid., 10–20, 29; quotation on 10.
30. Ibid., 22; *Sacred Hymns and Spiritual Songs,* 341–342.

31. David J. Whitaker, "Mormons and Native Americans: A Historical and Bibliographical Introduction," *Dialogue: A Journal of Mormon Thought* 18 (winter 1985), 34; Hicks, *Mormonism and Music,* 7; Whitaker, "Mormons and Native Americans," 44.

32. Whitaker, "Mormons and Native Americans," 35, 36; see also Keith Parry, "Joseph Smith and the Clash of Sacred Cultures," *Dialogue: A Journal of Mormon Thought* 18 (winter 1985), 65–80.

33. Jan Shipps, *Mormonism: The Story of a New Religious Tradition* (Urbana: University of Illinois Press, 1985), 122.

34. *Sacred Hymns and Spiritual Songs,* 73, 89.

35. Shipps, *Mormonism,* 122.

36. Young quoted in Leonard J. Arrington and Davis Britton, *The Mormon Experience: A History of the Latter-day Saints* (New York: Knopf, 1979), 148; Stanley B. Kimball, "The Captivity Narrative on Mormon Trails, 1846–65," *Dialogue: A Journal of Mormon Thought* 18 (winter 1985), 82, 74; Richard White, *The Middle Ground* (Cambridge: Cambridge University Press); Whitaker, "Mormons and Native Americans," 42.

37. Hicks, *Mormonism and Music,* 28, 65, 59–60; *Sacred Hymns and Spiritual Songs,* 337–338.

38. Hicks, *Mormonism and Music,* 65.

39. Ibid., 58, 60, 64, 46; Shipps, *Mormonism,* 123–128.

40. Hicks, *Mormonism and Music,* 80, 85.

41. Ibid., 98–104, 124–125.

42. Ibid., 166.

43. Ibid., 157.

44. Olin Thomas, "Come, Come Ye Saints," Affirmation Conference, Salt Lake City, Utah, 24 August 1997, available at http://www.affirmation.org/olin.htm.

4. Holding the Fort

Epigraph: W. E. B. Du Bois, *The Souls of Black Folk,* ed. David W. Blight and Robert Gooding-Williams (Boston: Bedford, 1997), 150.

1. Paul J. Scheips, *"Hold the Fort!" The Story of a Song from the Sawdust Trail to the Picket Line* (Washington, D.C.: Smithsonian, 1971), 20.

2. "John Brown's Body," in *The New Oxford Companion to Music,* ed. Denis Arnold, vol. 1 (New York: Oxford University Press, 1983), 1001–02; "Patriotic Music," in *The New Grove Dictionary of American Music,* ed. H. Wiley Hitchcock and Stanley Sadie, vol. 3 (London: Macmillan, 1986), 487; Andrew Ward, *Dark Midnight When I Rise: The Story of the Jubilee Singers* (New York: Farrar, 2000), 216; David W. Blight, *Race and Reunion: The Civil War in American Memory* (Cambridge: Harvard University Press, 2001), 65–69.

3. Ward, *Dark Midnight When I Rise,* 216, 225, 219–20, 304; Gustavus D. Pike, *The Singing Campaign for Ten Thousand Pounds; or, the Jubilee Singers in Great Britain* (New York: American Missionary Association, 1875), 76.

4. Pike, *Singing Campaign,* 50; Ward, *Dark Midnight When I Rise,* 220, 239, 216.

5. Pike, *Singing Campaign,* 53–54.
6. Jon Cruz, *Culture on the Margins: The Black Spiritual and the Rise of American Cultural Interpretation* (Princeton: Princeton University Press, 1999), 181, 185.
7. Dena J. Epstein, *Sinful Tunes and Spirituals: Black Folk Music to the Civil War* (Urbana: University of Illinois Press, 1977), 246.
8. Cruz, *Culture on the Margins,* 144–145.
9. Thomas Wentworth Higginson, "Negro Spirituals," *Atlantic Monthly* 19 (June 1867), reprinted in *African American Religious History: A Documentary Witness,* ed. Milton C. Sernett, 2d ed. (Durham, N.C.: Duke University Press, 1999), 113.
10. Ibid., 135.
11. On "imperialist nostalgia," see Renato Rosaldo, *Culture and Truth: The Remaking of Social Analysis* (Boston: Beacon, 1989), 68–87.
12. William G. McLoughlin Jr., *Modern Revivalism: Charles Grandison Finney to Billy Graham* (New York: Ronald, 1959), 166; Pike, *Singing Campaign,* 150; Gamaliel Bradford, *D. L. Moody: A Worker in Souls* (Garden City, N.Y.: Doubleday, 1928), 145. On the popularity of Sankey's gospel hymns on the Continent, particularly the Netherlands, see Jan Smelik, "The Gospel Hymn in the Low Countries," in *Sharing the Reformed Tradition: The Dutch-North American Exchange, 1846–1996,* ed. George Harinck and Hans Krabbendam (Amsterdam: VU Uitgeverij, 1996), 79–96.
13. McLoughlin, *Modern Revivalism,* 234; Ian Bradley, *Abide with Me: The World of Victorian Hymns* (London: SCM Press, 1997), 180; Louis F. Benson, *The English Hymn: Its Development and Use in Worship* (1915; reprint, Richmond, Va.: John Knox, 1962), 487; Bradley, *Abide with Me,* 182–183.
14. Scheips, *"Hold the Fort!"* 18–21, 16; Sandra S. Sizer, *Gospel Hymns and Social Religion: The Rhetoric of Nineteenth-Century Revivalism* (Philadelphia: Temple University Press, 1978), 135.
15. Scheips, *"Hold the Fort!"* 1–14.
16. Sizer, *Gospel Hymns and Social Religion,* 152–159, quotation on 175 n. 1; Scheips, *"Hold the Fort!"* 18.
17. Ward, *Dark Midnight When I Rise,* 372; Blight, *Race and Reunion,* 73–74.
18. Scheips, *"Hold the Fort!"* 30–45; Daniel W. Patterson, *The Shaker Spiritual* (Princeton: Princeton University Press, 1979), 451, 453.
19. June Hadden Hobbs, *"I Sing for I Cannot Be Silent": The Feminization of American Hymnody, 1870–1920* (Pittsburgh: University of Pittsburgh Press, 1997), 70–142; Sizer, *Gospel Hymns and Social Religion,* 47–48. See also Esther Rothenbusch, "The Joyful Sound: Women in the Nineteenth-Century United States Hymnody Tradition," in *Women and Music in Cross-Cultural Perspective,* ed. Ellen Koskoff (New York: Greenwood, 1987), 177–194.
20. Hobbs, *"I Sing for I Cannot Be Silent,"* 103, 145–146; Sizer, *Gospel Hymns and Social Religion,* 83–89.
21. Hobbs, *"I Sing for I Cannot Be Silent,"* 104–111; quotations on 13, 11.
22. Bradford, *D. L. Moody,* 153–154.
23. Pike, *Singing Campaign,* 150–151.

24. Sizer, *Gospel Hymns and Social Religion*, 83–137.
25. Frederick Douglass, *My Bondage and My Freedom* (1855; reprint, New York: Dover, 1969), 279; George P. Rawick, ed., *The American Slave: A Composite Autobiography* (New York: Greenwood, 1979), 4243.
26. Robert Johnson, "Hellhound on My Trail," in program guide to *The Smithsonian Collection of Classic Jazz*, ann. Martin Williams (Washington, D.C.: Smithsonian Institution, 1973), 16–17; Peter Van der Merwe, *Origins of the Popular Style: The Antecedents of Twentieth-Century Popular Music* (Oxford: Oxford University Press, 1989), 131–132.
27. Pike, *Singing Campaign*, 151; Ward, *Dark Midnight When I Rise*, 213, 288, 383–384, 391.
28. Ward, *Dark Midnight When I Rise*, 390.
29. For example, Gwendolin Sims Warren, *Ev'ry Time I Feel the Spirit: 101 Best-Loved Psalms, Gospel Hymns, and Spiritual Songs of the African-American Church* (New York: Henry Holt, 1997), 86.
30. Ward, *Dark Midnight When I Rise*, 160–161.
31. Ibid., 136.
32. Pike, *Singing Campaign*, 33–34. Thanks also for astute comments on "Steal Away" by an anonymous reader of the manuscript.
33. Ward, *Dark Midnight When I Rise*, 157, 135, 164, 175; Pike, *Singing Campaign*, 61.
34. Harriett Beecher Stowe, *Uncle Tom's Cabin*, ed. Elizabeth Ammons (New York: Norton, 1994), 2, 24–25.
35. Ibid., 287.
36. Ibid., 297.
37. Ibid., 324, 342, 380.
38. Robert S. Levine, "Uncle Tom's Cabin in Frederick Douglass' Paper: An Analysis of Reception," in ibid., 523–542; Du Bois, *The Souls of Black Folk*, 186, 193, 149.
39. Tim Brooks, "'Might Take One Disc of This Trash as a Novelty': Early recordings by the Fisk Jubilee Singers and the popularization of 'Negro Folk Music,'" *American Music* 18 (fall 2000), 278; Pike, *Singing Campaign*, 206; Higginson, "Negro Spirituals," 112.
40. Van der Merwe, *Origins of the Popular Style*, 288–290; see also John Storm Roberts, *Black Music of Two Worlds: African, Caribbean, Latin, and African-American Traditions*, 2d ed. (New York: Schirmer, 1998).
41. Pike, *Singing Campaign*, 124, 126–129.
42. Ibid., 108–109, 52–53, 198–199.
43. Yvonne Chireau, "Black Culture and Black Zion: African American Religious Encounters with Judaism, 1790–1930, an Overview," in *Black Zion: African American Religious Encounters with Judaism*, ed. Yvonne Chireau and Nathaniel Deutsch (New York: Oxford University Press, 2000), 20.

5. Dances with Ghosts

Epigraph: James Mooney, *The Ghost-Dance Religion and Wounded Knee* (1896; reprint, New York: Dover, 1991), 657.

1. Shalom Goldman, ed., *Hebrew and the Bible in America: The First Two Centuries* (Hanover, N.H.: University Press of New England, 1993), especially Richard H. Popkin, "The Rise and Fall of the Jewish Indian Theory," 70–90.

2. Francis Fletcher, chaplain to Sir Francis Drake, observed in 1579 in northern California, quoted in Henry Wilder Foote, *Three Centuries of American Hymnody* (Cambridge: Harvard University Press, 1940), 29.

3. Raymond J. DeMallie, "The Lakota Ghost Dance: An Ethnohistorical Account," in *Religion in American History: A Reader*, ed. Jon Butler and Harry S. Stout (New York: Oxford University Press, 1998), 260.

4. James Mooney, *Ghost-Dance Religion*, 798; for a historical analysis of how Catholicism has interacted with Lakota spirituality, see Christopher Vecsey, "A Century of Lakota Sioux Catholicism at Pine Ridge," in *Religious Diversity and American Religious History: Studies in Traditions and Cultures*, ed. Walter H. Conser Jr. and Sumner B. Twiss (Athens: University of Georgia Press, 1997), 262–295.

5. Daniel Richter, *Facing East from Indian Country: A Native History of Early America* (Cambridge: Harvard University Press, 2001), 1–10.

6. Mooney, *Ghost-Dance Religion*, v–vi; L. G. Moses, *The Indian Man: A Biography of James Mooney* (Urbana: University of Illinois Press, 1984), 1–22.

7. Mooney, *Ghost-Dance Religion*, 653–654.

8. Ibid., 766, 765.

9. Ibid., 765, 771–772, 773.

10. Ibid., 780–781.

11. Ibid., 777.

12. Ibid., 926–927. On Tenskwatawa, see Richter, *Facing East*, 228–230.

13. Judith Vander, *Shoshone Ghost Dance Religion: Poetry Songs and Great Basin Context* (Urbana: University of Illinois Press, 1997), 55–71; Ronald Niezen, *Spirit Wars: Native North American Religions in the Age of Nation Building* (Berkeley: University of California Press, 2000), 132.

14. Ibid., 777, 953, 921.

15. Ibid., 1072, 953, 918; Moses, *Indian Man*, 84. Moses doesn't mention Mooney's recording any songs apart from Caddo Ghost Dance songs.

16. Mooney, *Ghost-Dance Religion*, 657–763.

17. Ibid., 928–952; quotation on 928.

18. Ibid., 782–783.

19. Ibid., 828, 922.

20. Lawrence G. Coates, "The Mormons and the Ghost Dance," in *Dialogue: A Journal of Mormon Thought* 18 (winter 1985), 91, 94.

21. Mooney, *Ghost-Dance Religion*, 793.

22. *Sacred Hymns and Spiritual Songs for the Church of Jesus Christ of Latter-day Saints*, 14th ed. (Salt Lake City: George Q. Cannon, 1871), 371–373.

23. Coates, "The Mormons and the Ghost Dance," 89–111.

24. Jon Cruz, *Culture on the Margins: The Black Spiritual and the Rise of American Cultural Interpretation* (Princeton: Princeton University Press, 1999), 175–188.

25. Joan Mark, *A Stranger in Her Native Land: Alice Fletcher and American Indians* (Lincoln: University of Nebraska Press, 1988), 256.

26. Alice C. Fletcher with Francis La Flesche, *A Study of Omaha Indian Music* (1893; reprint, Lincoln: University of Nebraska Press, 1994), 7–8.

27. Mark, *Stranger in Her Native Land,* 220.

28. Helen Myers, "Introduction," in Fletcher, *Omaha Indian Music,* xviii; Mark, *Stranger in Her Native Land,* 223–224, 229–230.

29. Fletcher, *Omaha Indian Music,* 61.

30. Ibid., 76, 71, 62, 66, 68.

31. Ibid., 10.

32. Ibid., 56.

33. John F. Kasson, *Amusing the Million: Coney Island at the Turn of the Century* (New York: Hill and Wang, 1978), 24; Mark, *Stranger in Her Native Land,* 233–245.

34. For Densmore's life, see Charles Hofmann, ed., *Frances Densmore and American Indian Music* (New York: Museum of the American Indian Heye Foundation, 1968), quotation on 1–2; Nina Marchetti Archabal, "Frances Densmore: Pioneer in the Study of American Indian Music," in *Women of Minnesota: Selected Biographical Essays,* ed. Barbara Stuhler and Gretchen Kreuter (St. Paul: Minnesota Historical Society Press, 1998), 94–115; on Geronimo, see Hofmann, *Frances Densmore,* 19–20.

35. Hofmann, *Frances Densmore,* 1–2, 4, 97.

36. Mark, *Stranger in Her Native Land,* 231; Frances Densmore, *The American Indians and Their Music* (New York: Womans Press, 1926), 132, 125.

37. Hofmann, *Frances Densmore,* 119–120.

38. Ibid., 10, 40.

39. Archabal, "Frances Densmore," 99; David P. McAllester, *Peyote Music* (New York: Viking, 1949), 44–45; Fletcher, *Omaha Indian Music,* 12.

40. Mooney, *Ghost-Dance Religion,* 1047.

41. Vander, *Shoshone Ghost Dance Religion,* 16.

42. McAllester, *Peyote Music,* 44–45.

43. Niezen, *Spirit Wars,* 142; Frederick E. Hoxie, ed., *Talking Back to Civilization: Indian Voices from the Progressive Era* (Boston: Bedford/St. Martin's, 2001), 21.

44. Hoxie, *Talking Back to Civilization,* 83.

45. Omer C. Stewart, *Peyote Religion: A History* (Norman: University of Oklahoma Press, 1987), 221. Niezen, *Spirit Wars,* 142.

46. Episcopal Bishop Henry B. Whipple, quoted in Michael D. McNally, *Ojibwe Singers: Hymns, Grief, and a Native Culture in Motion* (New York: Oxford University Press, 2000), 81; Michael D. McNally, "The Practice of Native American Christianity," *Church History* 69 (December 2000), 842; see also idem, "The Uses of Ojibwa Hymn-Singing at White Earth: Toward a History of Practice," in *Lived Religion in America: Toward a History of Practice,* ed. David D. Hall (Princeton: Princeton University Press, 1997), 133–159.

47. John Wesley, *The Journal of the Rev. John Wesley, A.M.,* ed. Nehemiah Curnock, vol. 1 (London: Epworth, 1938), 35; McNally, *Ojibwe Singers,* 64.

48. McNally, *Ojibwe Singers,* 191.

49. Luke E. Lassiter, Clyde Ellis, and Ralph Kotay, *The Jesus Road: Kiowas,*

Christianity, and Indian Hymns (Lincoln: University of Nebraska Press, 2002).

6. Onward Buddhist Soldiers

Epigraph: Mahaprajnaparamita Sastra (Treatise on the Perfection of Great Wisdom), "Sounds of the Dharma: Buddhism and Music," available at www. blia.org/english/publications/booklet/pages/38.htm.

1. "Beastie Boys: The Big Show," *Tricycle*, winter 1994, available at http://www. tricycle.com/interviews/yauchinterview.html.
2. Beastie Boys, *Ill Communication* (Capitol 28599, 1994).
3. For the larger intellectual context of esoteric and theosophical thought in which Carus thought through the links between Christianity, science, and Eastern religions, see Joscelyn Godwin, *The Theosophical Enlightenment* (Albany: SUNY Press, 1994), esp. 277–379.
4. For details on Carus' life, see Harold Henderson, *Catalyst for Controversy: Paul Carus of Open Court* (Carbondale: Southern Illinois University Press, 1993); and Martin J. Verhoeven, "Americanizing the Buddha: Paul Carus and the Transformation of Asian Thought," in *The Faces of Buddhism in America*, ed. Charles S. Prebish and Kenneth K. Tanaka (Berkeley: University of California Press, 1998), 207–227.
5. Henderson, *Catalyst for Controversy,* 20.
6. Thomas A. Tweed, *The American Encounter with Buddhism, 1844–1912* (Bloomington: Indiana University Press, 1992), 10; Henderson, *Catalyst for Controversy,* 116; Verhoeven, "Americanizing the Buddha," 216, 222.
7. Verhoeven, "Americanizing the Buddha," 207–208; Henderson, *Catalyst for Controversy,* 154–155.
8. Paul Carus, *Sacred Tunes for the Consecration of Life: Hymns of the Religion of Science* (Chicago: Open Court, 1899), 3–4.
9. Ibid.; John Greenleaf Whittier, *The Complete Poetical Works of John Greenleaf Whittier* (Boston: Houghton Mifflin, 1894), 449–450; *The Methodist Hymnal* (New York: Methodist Book Concern, 1935), 342.
10. Carus, *Sacred Tunes,* 3.
11. Ibid., 45. Biographical details on hymn composers drawn mainly from Stanley Sadie, ed., *The New Grove Dictionary of Music and Musicians,* vols. 1–20 (London: Macmillan, 1980).
12. Carus, *Sacred Tunes,* 43.
13. Henderson, *Catalyst for Controversy,* 106.
14. Verhoeven, "Americanizing the Buddha," 209, 222.
15. Ibid., 220, 221; Diana L. Eck, *A New Religious America: How a "Christian Country" Has Now Become the World's Most Religiously Diverse Nation* (New York: HarperCollins, 2001), 172; Henderson, *Catalyst for Controversy,* 115.
16. Richard Hughes Seager, *Buddhism in America* (New York: Columbia University Press, 1999), 56.
17. Teshirogi Shunichi, "Hymns, the Site of Cultural Encounters," unpublished

paper in author's possession; Susan Miyo Asai, "Transformation of Tradition: Three Generations of Japanese American Music Making," *Musical Quarterly* 79:3 (1995), 431; Tetsuden Kashima, *Buddhism in America: The Social Organization of an Ethnic Religious Institution* (Westport, Conn.: Greenwood, 1977), 218.

18. Louise Hunter, *Buddhism in Hawaii* (Honolulu: University of Hawaii Press, 1971), 131.

19. On the history of the *Vade Mecum*, see George J. Tanabe Jr., "Glorious Gathas: Americanization and Japanization in Hongangi Hymns," in *Engaged Pure Land Buddhism: Challenges Facing Jodo Shinshu in the Contemporary World*, ed. Kenneth K. Tanaka and Eisho Nasu (Berkeley: WisdomOcean Publications, 1998), 221–237, quotation on 226. I am indebted to Professor Eisho Nasu for bringing this article to my attention.

20. Paul Carus, *Buddhist Hymns: Versified Translations from the Dhammapada and Various Other Sources Adapted to Modern Music* (Chicago: Open Court, 1911), 5.

21. Carus, *Buddhist Hymns*, 6–7.

22. Ibid., 9, 6.

23. Ibid., 10.

24. Ibid., 9.

25. Mark Slobin, *Chosen Voices: The Story of the American Cantorate* (Urbana: University of Illinois Press, 1989), 46; *Jōdoshinshū Hongwangji-ha* (n.p.: Shenshin Buddhist Temple, 1991); *Shin Buddhist Gathas Disc 1* (BCA Records, 1994).

26. Eck, *New Religious America*, 172–173.

27. Susan Miyo Asai, "Sansei Voices in the Community: Japanese American Musicians in California," in *Musics of Multicultural America: A Study of Twelve Musical Communities*, ed. Kip Lornell and Anne K. Rasmussen (New York: Schirmer, 1997), 264–271.

28. Henderson, *Catalyst for Controversy*, 160.

29. Thomas A. Tweed and Stephen Prothero, eds., *Asian Religions in America: A Documentary History* (New York: Oxford University Press, 1999), 172–77.

30. Philip Kapleau, "Transmitting the Dharma," in *The Life of Buddhism*, ed. Frank E. Reynold and Jason A. Carbine (Berkeley: University of California Press, 2000), 212.

31. Ibid.

32. Charles S. Prebish, *Luminous Passage: The Practice and Study of Buddhism in America* (Berkeley: University of California Press, 1999), 18–19; Kapleau, "Transmitting the Dharma," 213.

33. G. Victor Sogen Hori, "Japanese Zen in America: Americanizing the Face in the Mirror," in Prebish and Tanaka, *Faces of Buddhism in America*, 55; Kapleau, "Transmitting the Dharma," 212, 213.

34. Tweed and Prothero, *Asian Religions in America*, 193, 192.

35. "Taking Chances: Laurie Anderson Talks to John Cage," available at www.tricycle.com/interviews/cageinterview.html; John Cage, *Silence: Lectures and Writings* (Middletown, Conn.: Wesleyan University Press, 1961), 262.

36. Interview with John Cage on *4'33"*, *NPR 100*, available at www.npr.org/pro-
    grams/specials/vote/100/list.htmlfrom.
37. The "one hand clapping" koan is attributed to Hakuin Ekaku (1686–1769),
    one of the most celebrated masters of Zen Buddhism in Japan. As a teacher,
    Hakuin placed special emphasis on the study of koans as the most effective
    path to spiritual enlightenment.
38. Tweed and Prothero, *Asian Religions in America*, 346–347; Ted Panken, "Ap-
    proaching Enlightenment," *Down Beat* 68 (February 2001), 27.
39. Yauch quoted in "Beastie Boys: The Big Show"; David Peissner, "The Beastie
    Boys: The Well Rounded Interview," available at www.well-rounded.com/mu-
    sic/reviews/beastieboys_intv.html.
40. Seager, *Buddhism in America*, 113–118.

7. Yossele, Yossele!

Second Epigraph: B. F. White and E. J. King, *The Sacred Harp* (Philadelphia:
S. Collins, 1860), 78.
 1. Samuel Rosenblatt, *Yossele Rosenblatt: The Story of His Life as Told by His
    Son* (New York: Farrar, Straus and Young, 1954), 287–290.
 2. Krin Gabbard, *Jammin' at the Margins: Jazz and the American Cinema* (Chi-
    cago: University of Chicago Press, 1996), 25–63.
 3. Arthur Hertzberg, "The New England Puritans and the Jews," in *Hebrew
    and the Bible in America: The First Two Centuries*, ed. Shalom Goldman
    (Hanover: University Press of New England, 1993), 105–108; Goldman, *He-
    brew and the Bible*, xxii; Sacvan Bercovitch, *The Puritan Origins of the Amer-
    ican Self* (New Haven: Yale University Press, 1975).
 4. John Cage, *Silence: Lectures and Writings* (Middletown, Conn.: Wesleyan
    University Press, 1961), x.
 5. Luís León, "Born Again in East LA: The Congregation as Border Space," *in
    Gatherings in Diaspora: Religious Communities and the New Immigration*,
    ed. R. Stephen Warner and Judith G. Wittner (Philadelphia: Temple University
    Press, 1998), 163–196, quotation on 171.
 6. Lawrence W. Levine, *Black Culture and Black Consciousness: Afro-American
    Folk Thought from Slavery to Freedom* (New York: Oxford University Press,
    1977), 50–51.
 7. Yvonne Chireau, "Black Culture and Black Zion: African American Religious
    Encounters with Judaism, 17–90–1930, an Overview," in *Black Zion: African
    American Religious Encounters with Judaism*, ed. Yvonne Chireau and
    Nathaniel Deutsch (New York: Oxford University Press, 2000), 15–32.
 8. Ellen Koskoff, "The Sound of a Woman's Voice: Gender and Music in a New
    York Hasidic Community," in *Women and Music in Cross-Cultural Perspec-
    tive*, ed. Ellen Koskoff (New York: Greenwood, 1987), 217–218; Eliyahu
    Schleifer, "Jewish Liturgical Music from the Bible to Hasidism," in *Sacred
    Sound and Social Change: Liturgical Music in Jewish and Christian Experi-
    ence*, ed. Lawrence A. Hoffman and Janet R. Walton (Notre Dame: University
    of Notre Dame Press, 1992), 23, 24.

9. Amnon Shiloah, *Jewish Musical Traditions* (Detroit: Wayne State University Press, 1992), 74–75.

10. Schleifer, "Jewish Liturgical Music," 45.

11. Rosenblatt, *Yossele Rosenblatt,* 11–12.

12. Ibid., 6–7, 148–149.

13. Patricia Erens, *The Jew in American Cinema* (Bloomington: Indiana University Press, 1984), 29; Harry M. Geduld, *The Birth of the Talkies: From Edison to Jolson* (Bloomington: Indiana University Press, 1975), 193–194; Carringer, *The Jazz Singer,* 20. For reviews, see Geduld, *Birth of the Talkies,* 175–183.

14. Geduld, *Birth of the Talkies,* 170.

15. Andrew Sarris, *"You Ain't Heard Nothin' Yet": The American Talking Film, History and Memory, 1927–1949* (New York: Oxford University Press, 1998), 33.

16. *Masterpieces of the Synagogue, Volume 2: The Art of Cantor Josef Rosenblatt* (RCA Camden, CAL-507, n.d.).

17. *Jewish Heritage Online Magazine,* available at www.jhom.com/calendar/tishrei/kolnidrei.html (several versions of Kol Nidre can be downloaded at this site); Schleifer, "Jewish Liturgical Music," 39; conversation with Professor John Eulenberg, 6 May 2002.

18. Michael Rogin, *Blackface, White Noise: Jewish Immigrants in the Hollywood Melting Pot* (Berkeley: University of California Press, 1996), 73–120.

19. Jeffrey Melnick, *A Right to Sing the Blues: African Americans, Jews, and American Popular Song* (Cambridge: Harvard University Press, 1999), 178, 172, 170.

20. For the Ozick reference and on melancholy more generally, see ibid., 181–188.

21. Benjie-Ellen Schiller, "The Hymnal as an Index of Musical Change in Reform Synagogues," in Hoffman and Walton, *Sacred Sound and Social Change,* 198.

22. Mark Slobin, *Tenement Songs: The Popular Music of the Jewish Immigrants* (Urbana: University of Illinois Press, 1982), 184–185, quotation on 182.

23. Mark Slobin, *Fiddler on the Move: Exploring the Klezmer World* (New York: Oxford University Press, 2000), 118.

24. Deborah Dash Moore, "Social History of American Judaism," in *The Encyclopedia of the American Religious Experience: Studies of Traditions and Movements,* ed. Charles H. Lippy and Peter W. Williams, vol. 1 (New York: Scribner's, 1988), 294–295; Charles E. Hall, *Negroes in the United States, 1920–1932* (1935; reprint, New York: Arno, 1969), 55.

25. Jeffrey Melnick, "Tin Pan Alley and the Black-Jewish Nation," in *American Popular Music: New Approaches to the Twentieth Century,* ed. Rachel Rubin and Jeffrey Melnick (Amherst: University of Massachusetts Press, 2001), 29–45.

26. Schleifer, "Jewish Liturgical Music," 49; Shiloah, *Jewish Musical Traditions,* 17; Schleifer, "Jewish Liturgical Music," 35–36.

27. Joseph A. Levine, *Synagogue Song in America* (Crown Point, Ind.: White Cliffs, 1989), 44–46.

28. Schleifer, "Jewish Liturgical Music," 45; Shiloah, *Jewish Musical Traditions,* 67.

29. Slobin, *Tenement Songs,* 19–20; Geoffrey Goldberg, "Jewish Liturgical Music in the Wake of Nineteenth-Century Reform," in Hoffman and Walton, *Sacred Sound and Social Change,* 60; Schiller, "Hymnal as Index of Musical Change," 188, 199.

30. On the Jewish Awakening, see Jonathan D. Sarna, "The Late Nineteenth-Century American Jewish Awakening," in *Religious Diversity and American Religious History: Studies in Traditions and Cultures,* ed. Walter H. Conser Jr. and Sumner B. Twiss (Athens: University of Georgia Press, 1997), 1–25, quotations on 18, 14; Wise quoted in Mark Slobin, *Chosen Voices: The Story of the American Cantorate* (Urbana: University of Illinois Press, 1989), 45.

31. Slobin, *Tenement Songs,* 19–20; Rosenblatt, *Yossele Rosenblatt,* 129–132.

32. Rosenblatt, *Yossele Rosenblatt,* 237–238.

33. Slobin, *Chosen Voices,* 69–74; idem, *Tenement Songs,* 37.

34. Slobin, *Tenement Songs,* 195; Henry Sapoznik, *Klezmer! Jewish Music from Old World to Our World* (New York: Schirmer, 1999), 77, 119.

35. Slobin, *Fiddler on the Move,* 7; idem, *Tenement Songs,* 21.

36. Slobin, *Fiddler on the Move,* 7. See also Sapoznik, *Klezmer!* chap. 1.

37. Slobin, *Fiddler on the Move,* 68.

38. Henry Sapoznik, "Klezmer Music: The First One Thousand Years," in *Music of Multicultural America: A Study of Twelve Musical Communities,* ed. Kip Lornell and Anne K. Rasmussen (New York: Schirmer, 1997), 49–71, quotation on 56.

39. Andrews quoted in Yiddish Radio Project, available at www.yiddishradioproject.org/exhibits/ymis/sheet_music.php3?pg=2; John Sforza, *Swing It! The Andrews Sisters Story* (Lexington: University Press of Kentucky, 2000), 29; Sapoznik, *Klezmer!* 133–140, quotation on 140.

40. Melnick, *A Right to Sing the Blues,* 179–181; Sapoznik, *Klezmer!* 133–140; www.yiddishradioproject.org; Sforza, *Swing It!* 26–32. There are some discrepancies over dates and other details among the various accounts.

41. Sforza, *Swing It!* 26–32.

42. James Lincoln Collier, *Benny Goodman and the Swing Era* (New York: Oxford University Press, 1989), 13–15.

43. Slobin, *Fiddler on the Move,* 9; Schiller, "Hymnal as Index of Musical Change," 205; Slobin, *Tenement Songs,* 22.

44. *Bird,* dir. Clint Eastwood (Warner Brothers, 1988).

8. Come Sunday

Epigraph: Dorsey quoted in Lawrence W. Levine, *Black Culture and Black Consciousness: Afro-American Folk Thought from Slavery to Freedom* (New York: Oxford University Press, 1977), 182.

1. As Morris tells it, he first heard the song performed by a choir at a conference in Kansas City. "I asked them where they heard it, and they asked their choir director . . . where they had gotten it from," Morris recalled. "He didn't know; he had heard it all of his life. I had never heard it before. I am the one who made the arrangement." After the song was pirated by a white publisher,

Morris began to copyright all his compositions; Bernice Johnson Reagon, ed., *We'll Understand It Better By and By: Pioneering African American Gospel Composers* (Washington, D.C.: Smithsonian, 1992), 336–337.

2. Henry Gariepy, *Songs in the Night: Inspiring Stories behind 100 Hymns Born in Trial and Suffering* (Grand Rapids: Eerdman's, 1996); Gwendolin Sims Warren, *Ev'ry Time I Feel the Spirit: 101 Best-Loved Psalms, Gospel Hymns, and Spiritual Songs of the African-American Church* (New York: Henry Holt, 1997).

3. Horace Clarence Boyer, "'Take My Hand, Precious Lord, Lead Me On,'" in Reagon, *We'll Understand It Better By and By,* 142–143; Warren, *Ev'ry Time I Feel the Spirit,* 167–168.

4. Edward Kennedy Ellington, *Music Is My Mistress* (Garden City, N.Y.: Doubleday, 1973), 261.

5. *Love and Theft* is the title of both an influential book by Eric Lott (1993) and an acclaimed recording by Bob Dylan (2001).

6. Michael W. Harris, *The Rise of Gospel Blues: The Music of Thomas Andrew Dorsey in the Urban Church* (New York: Oxford, 1992), 17.

7. Ibid., 10–46, quotation on 18; Ellington, *Music Is My Mistress,* 6–37.

8. Harris, *Rise of Gospel Blues,* 47–150, quotation on 150.

9. Ibid., 228, 237–238.

10. *The Methodist Hymnal* (New York: Methodist Book Concern, 1935), 276.

11. Harris, *Rise of Gospel Blues,* 237.

12. Charles E. Hall, *Negroes in the United States, 1920–1932* (1935; reprint, New York: Arno, 1969), 55.

13. Harris, *Rise of Gospel Blues,* 106–125; see also interviews in *Say Amen, Somebody,* dir. George T. Nierenberg (First Run Features, 1982).

14. Dorsey quoted in Levine, *Black Culture and Black Consciousness,* 183; Harris, *Rise of Gospel Blues,* 257. For vivid evidence of female dominance in gospel organizations coupled with the struggle to carve out careers amid patriarchal churches, see *Say Amen, Somebody.*

15. Harris, *Rise of Gospel Blues,* 258; Mahalia Jackson with Evan McLeod Wylie, *Movin' on Up* (New York: Hawthorn, 1966), 58–59, 62.

16. Laurraine Goreau, *Just Mahalia, Baby* (Waco: Word Books, 1975), 56; Harris, *Rise of Gospel Blues,* 257–261.

17. Nat Hentoff, "You Can Still Hear Her Voice When the Music Has Stopped, *The Reporter,* 27 June 1957, 34.

18. Jackson, *Movin' on Up,* 87–89.

19. Ellington, *Music Is My Mistress,* 255–256.

20. Townsend and Crouch quoted in Mark Tucker, *The Duke Ellington Reader* (New York: Oxford University Press, 1993), 320, 444; Ellington, *Music Is My Mistress,* 255–256; Goreau, *Just Mahalia,* 250–251.

21. Duke Ellington, *Black, Brown and Beige* (Columbia CK 64274, n.d.); idem, *Duke Ellington's Concert of Sacred Music* (1966; reissue, RCA 74321 32334 2, 1995).

22. Janna Tull Steed, *Duke Ellington: A Spiritual Biography* (New York: Crossroad, 1999), 53–54, 71.

23. Ellington, *Music Is My Mistress*, 181.
24. John Edward Hasse, *Beyond Category: The Life and Genius of Duke Ellington* (New York: Simon and Schuster, 1993), 261–262.
25. Ellington, *Music Is My Mistress*, 197–198; idem, *Concert of Sacred Music.*
26. Steed, *Duke Ellington*, 19; Ellington, *Music Is My Mistress*, 261.
27. Steed, *Duke Ellington*, 21–22, quotations on 94, 25; Ellington quoted in Michael Denning, *The Cultural Front: The Laboring of American Culture in the Twentieth Century* (London: Verso, 1996), 318; Duke Ellington, program notes for *Second Sacred Concert*, 19 January 1968, in author's possession.
28. Ellington, *Music Is My Mistress*, 267–268.
29. Duke Ellington, *Second Sacred Concert* (1974; reissue, Prestige 24045-2, 1990); Raymond Horricks quoted in Hasse, *Beyond Category*, 358.
30. John S. Wilson, "Jazz and Church: Oil-Water Mix?" *New York Times*, 15 January 1967; idem, "For the Masses, Jazz Masses," *New York Times*, 13 February 1966, 26X; *Carnegie Hall Program* 75: 6 (1967); "Mass Meetings," *New Yorker*, 14 May 1979, 29–31; John S. Wilson, "A Jazz Requiem for Dr. King Really Swings," *New York Times*, April 7, 1969, 48.
31. Jay Hoggard quoted in Steed, *Duke Ellington*, 137.
32. Juba refers both to a dance resembling the ring shout featuring rhythmic clapping and stomping performed by African-American slaves, and to William Henry Lane, "Master Juba," a celebrated antebellum dancer from Manhattan's Five Points district who is thought to have invented the tap dance.
33. Stanley Crouch, program notes to Wynton Marsalis, *In This House, On This Morning* (Columbia C2K 53220, 1994), 4.
34. Robert A. Becker, "Blues Jazz and Spirituality: Jazz Great Wynton Marsalis Shares His Thoughts on Religion and Music," publication unknown, 1997, 16, clipping in author's possession.
35. Crouch, program notes to *In This House, On This Morning*, 6.
36. Dorsey scholar Michael Harris named gospel singer Marion Williams as the singer whose rendition of "Precious Lord" comes closest to what he thought Dorsey intended; interviewed in "Precious Lord," *NPR 100*, available at www.npr.org/programs/specials/vote/100/list.html.

9. From Ephrata (F-Ra-Ta) to Arkestra

Epigraph: Sun Ra, "The Air Spiritual Man," quoted in John F. Szwed, *Space Is the Place: The Lives and Times of Sun Ra* (New York: Pantheon, 1997), 329.
1. Szwed, *Space Is the Place*, 3–37; Robert L. Campbell, "From Sonny Blount to Sun Ra: The Birmingham and Chicago Years," available at www.dpo.uab.edu/~moudry/camp1.htm.
2. James R. Grossman, *Land of Hope: Chicago, Black Southerners, and the Great Migration* (Chicago: University of Chicago Press, 1989), 19; Benjamin Filene, *Romancing the Folk: Public Memory and American Roots Music* (Chapel Hill: University of North Carolina Press, 2000), 105; Szwed, *Space Is the Place*, 37–61; Campbell, "From Blount to Ra."
3. Szwed, *Space Is the Place*, 72.

4. Ibid., 109, 295.

5. Ibid., 86, 109 (ellipsis in original).

6. Sun Ra, *Jazz in Silhouette* (1958; reissue, Evidence 22012-2, 1991).

7. E. G. Alderfer, *The Ephrata Commune: An Early American Counterculture* (Pittsburgh: University of Pittsburgh Press, 1985), 14–26. See also Jan Stryz, "The Alchemy of the Voice at Ephrata Cloister," *Esoterica* 1 (1999), 133–159, available at www.esoteric.msu.edu/Alchemy.html.

8. Ra quoted in Szwed, *Space Is the Place*, 57, 44.

9. Alderfer, *Ephrata Commune*, 10–11, 164–165.

10. Albert G. Hess, "Observations on *The Lamenting Voice of the Hidden Love*," *Journal of the American Musicological Society* 5 (1952), 213, 214. Thanks to Jon Butler for alerting me to this article.

11. Peter C. Erb, ed., *Johann Conrad Beissel and the Ephrata Community: Mystical and Historical Texts* (Lewiston, Maine: Edwin Mellon Press, 1985), 34.

12. Alderfer, *Ephrata Commune*, 42, 60.

13. Ibid., 35.

14. James E. Ernst, *Ephrata: A History* (Allentown: Pennsylvania German Folklore Society, 1963), 154–158.

15. Alderfer, *Ephrata Commune*, 44–106.

16. Gloriae Dei Cantores, *Music of the Americas, 1492–1992* (Paraclete GDCD 010, 1992). This hymn appears in modern notation in Julius Friedrich Sachse, *The Music of the Ephrata Cloister* (Lancaster: Pennsylvania German Society, 1903), 90–91, described as "the celebrated seven-part motet," "artistically rendered by Mrs. Frank Binnix" in 1901. Thanks to Professor Patrick McConeghy for assistance in translation. On the Aeolian harp, see Ernst, *Ephrata*, 247.

17. Consider, for example, the Ephrata Cloister Chorus, *Anticipating Paradise: Music of Hope and Praise from Early Communities* (Ephrata Cloister Associates, 2000).

18. Beissel, quoted in Sachse, *Music of the Ephrata Cloister*, 57, 71–72.

19. Ibid., 71–73, 14.

20. David P. McKay and Richard Crawford, *William Billings of Boston: Eighteenth-Century Composer* (Princeton: Princeton University Press, 1975), 53–55.

21. Stryz, "Alchemy of the Voice," 145.

22. Beissel quoted in ibid., 138–139, 141–142.

23. Böhme quoted in ibid., 146.

24. Francis Lee, "A New Theory of Musick," reproduced in Arthur Versluis, "Mysticism and Spiritual Harmonics in Eighteenth-Century England," *Esoterica* 4 (2002), 102, available at www.esoteric.msu.edu/VolumeIV/Harmonic.htm.

25. Lee, "New Theory of Musick," 103.

26. Beissel quoted in Sachse, *Music of the Ephrata Cloister*, 67, 68, 14.

27. William M. Fahnestock quoted in Alderfer, *Ephrata Commune*, 114; Duché quoted in Erb, *Beissel and the Ephrata Community*, 34; Alderfer, *Ephrata Commune*, 115.

28. Unnamed musician quoted in Szwed, *Space Is the Place*, 119.

29. Ibid., 41, 45–46, 346–347, quotation from 97. On Ra's sexuality, see also Ajay Heble, *Landing on the Wrong Note: Jazz, Dissonance, and Critical Practice* (New York: Routledge, 2000), 135.
30. Campbell, "From Blount to Ra"; Szwed, *Space Is the Place*, 217, 172.
31. Ernst, *Ephrata*, 246; Stryz, "Alchemy of the Voice," 145.
32. Quoted in Szwed, *Space Is the Place*, 329, 156, 112, 319.
33. Ibid., 351.
34. Ibid., 103–104; Campbell, "From Blount to Ra."
35. Sachse, *Music of the Ephrata Cloister*, 24–25.
36. Graham Lock, *Blutopia: Visions of the Future and Revisions of the Past in the Work of Sun Ra, Duke Ellington, and Anthony Braxton* (Durham, N.C.: Duke University Press, 1999), 20–21.
37. Szwed, *Space Is the Place*, 137; see also Lock, *Blutopia*, 13–74; Heble, *Landing on the Wrong Note*, 117–138.
38. James Weldon Johnson and J. Rosamond Johnson, *The Book of American Negro Spirituals* (1925; reprint, New York: Viking, 1969), 74–75; Lock, *Blutopia*, 35.
39. Thomas Wentworth Higginson, "Slave Songs and Spirituals," in *African American Religious History: A Documentary Witness*, ed. Milton C. Sernett (Durham, N.C.: Duke University Press, 1999), 129; Szwed, *Space Is the Place*, 261.
40. Lock, *Blutopia*, 40.
41. Szwed, *Space Is the Place*, 262.
42. Lock, *Blutopia*, 55; see also Szwed, *Space Is the Place*, 29–32.

10. The Nation with the Soul of a Church

Epigraph: Julian Bond, interview with Bill Moyers in the PBS documentary *Amazing Grace* (Newbridge Communications, 1994)
1. Sidney E. Mead, *The Nation with the Soul of a Church* (New York: Harper and Row, 1975), 48–77.
2. On civil religion, see Catherine L. Albanese, *America: Religions and Religion*, 3d ed. (Belmont, Calif.: Wadsworth, 1999), 432–460; Robert N. Bellah, "Civil Religion in America," *Daedalus* 96 (winter 1967), 1–21; on the "American Creed," see Gunnar Myrdal, *The American Dilemma: The Negro Problem and Modern Democracy* (New York: Harper and Row, 1944), 3–12, 24–25.
3. D. Bruce Hindmarsh, "Amazing Grace, How Sweet It Has Sounded: The History of a Hymn and a Cultural Icon," paper presented at Hymnody in American Protestantism conference, Wheaton, Ill., May 2000, 3; Peter Linebaugh and Marcus Rediker, *The Many-Headed Hydra: Sailors, Slaves, Commoners, and the Hidden History of the Revolutionary Atlantic* (Boston: Beacon, 2000).
4. D. Bruce Hindmarsh, *John Newton and the Evangelical Tradition between the Conversions of Wesley and Wilberforce* (Oxford: Oxford University Press, 1996), 16–23.
5. Ibid., 169–220, quotations on 171, 172.

6. Hindmarsh, "Amazing Grace," 8.

7. Quotation from ibid., 8, n. 21.

8. Ibid., 6.

9. Ibid., 11–12, 17; Harriet Beecher Stowe, *Uncle Tom's Cabin*, ed. Elizabeth Ammons (New York: Norton, 1994), 340.

10. Albanese, *America*, 159–160; Jon Butler, *Awash in a Sea of Faith: Christianizing the American People* (Cambridge: Harvard University Press, 1990), 270; John H. Wigger, *Taking Heaven by Storm: Methodism and the Rise of Popular Christianity in America* (New York: Oxford University Press, 1998), 3–21, quotation on 6.

11. "The World, the Devil, and Tom Paine," in Albert Christ-Janer, Charles W. Hughes, and Carleton Sprague Smith, eds., *American Hymns Old and New* (New York: Columbia University Press, 1980), 368.

12. Stone quoted in Elliott J. Gorn, Randy Roberts, and Terry D. Bilhartz, eds., *Constructing the American Past: A Source Book of a People's History*, vol. 1 (New York: Longman, 1999), 153. On camp meetings, see Ellen Eslinger, *Citizens of Zion: The Social Origins of Camp Meetings Revivalism* (Knoxville: University of Tennessee Press, 1999); Dickson D. Bruce Jr., *And They All Sang Hallelujah: Plain-Folk Camp-Meeting Religion, 1800–1845* (Knoxville: University of Tennessee Press, 1974).

13. On persistent themes of early evangelical hymns, see Stephen Marini, "Hymnody as History: Early Evangelical Hymns and the Recovery of American Popular Religion," *Church History* 71 (June 2002), 286–287; Nathan Hatch, *The Democratization of American Christianity* (New Haven: Yale University Press, 1991), 160.

14. Ron Pen, "Triangles, Squares Circles, and Diamonds: The 'Fasola Folk' and Their Singing Tradition," in *Musics of Multicultural America: A Study of Twelve Musical Communities*, ed. Kip Lornell and Anne K. Rasmussen (New York: Schirmer, 1997), 216; "Two Notes from Scotland," Hymn Society *Bulletin* 7 (n.d.), 219 (photocopy in author's possession); Richard Crawford, *America's Musical Life: A History* (New York: Norton, 2001), 167; Hindmarsh, "Amazing Grace," 14.

15. George Pullen Jackson, *White Spirituals in the Southern Uplands: The Story of the Fasola Folk, Their Songs, Singings, and "Buckwheat Notes"* (Chapel Hill: University of North Carolina Press, 1933), 134, 225.

16. Hatch, *Democratization of American Christianity*, 152.

17. *We Shall Overcome: The Song That Moved a Nation*, dir. Jim Brown (California Newsreel, 1989).

18. Richard Middleton, *Studying Popular Music* (Milton Keynes: Open University Press, 1990), 16–18.

19. Michael Denning, *The Cultural Front: The Laboring of American Culture in the Twentieth Century* (London: Verso, 1996); Clark D. Halker, *For Democracy, Workers, and God: Labor Song-Poems and Labor Protest, 1865–1895* (Urbana: University of Illinois Press, 1991), 182–184; see also 191, n .53; Paul J. Scheips, *"Hold the Fort!" The Story of a Song from the Sawdust Trail to the Picket Line* (Washington, D.C.: Smithsonian, 1971), 34–45.

20. Worker interviewed in *We Shall Overcome;* also quoted on "We Shall Overcome," *NPR 100,* available at www.npr.org/programs/specials/vote/100/list.html. Details on Highlander also drawn from www.nl.edu/ace/Resources/Horton.html.

21. Seeger quoted in Benjamin Filene, *Romancing the Folk: Public Memory and American Roots Music* (Chapel Hill: University of North Carolina Press, 2000), 198.

22. Interviews with Andrew Young and Julian Bond, "We Shall Overcome."

23. Interview with Bernice Johnson Reagon, ibid.

24. Interviews with Julian Bond and John Lewis, ibid.

25. Interviews with Desmond Tutu and Julian Bond, ibid.

26. Hindmarsh, "Amazing Grace," 21.

27. Stowe, *Uncle Tom's Cabin,* 340. The new verse apparently is one of dozens that evolved as part of the hymn titled "Jerusalem, My Happy Home." Hindmarsh identifies its first published appearance in a hymn collection published by evangelist Edwin Othello Excell in 1910, but Stowe's citation of it predates that by more than half a century; Hindmarsh, "Amazing Grace," 17.

28. Quotation from Hindmarsh, "Amazing Grace," 18–19.

29. Margaret Dickie quoted in "Two Notes from Scotland," 217. Richard Middleton shows how through a minor adjustment to the tune of "New Britain" by Arsenal football fans, "'Spiritual lyricism' is transformed into an unending, circling chant of collective support for the team"; Middleton, *Studying Popular Music,* 17–18.

30. Hindmarsh, "Amazing Grace," 20; Moyers' *Amazing Grace.* Even Jerry Garcia of the Grateful Dead felt drawn to "Amazing Grace" before his death. A rendition he recorded in 1993 was recently released with a volume of the guitarist's brightly colored paintings, with the text of "Amazing Grace" printed over the painting. Jerry Garcia, *Jerry Garcia's Amazing Grace* (New York: William Morrow, 2002).

31. Hindmarsh," Amazing Grace," 22; Melani McAlister, "A Cultural History of the War without End," *Journal of American History* 89 (September 2002), 439–455.

32. Cliff Barrows, Billy Graham, and Donald Hustad, eds., *Crusader Hymns and Hymn Stories* (Chicago: Hope Publishing, 1967), 9–11; *Then Sings My Soul,* dir. Dick Ross (World Wide Pictures, 1982); John Pollock, *Billy Graham: The Authorized Biography* (New York: McGraw-Hill, 1966), 154.

33. Stuart K. Hine, *The Story of "How Great Thou Art": How It Came to Be Written* (London: Florentina, 1958), 2–6; Stuart K. Hine, *Not You, But God: A Testimony of God's Faithfulness* (n.p., 1973), 95–105; Barrows, Graham, and Hustad, *Crusader Hymns,* 9–11.

34. Hine, *Not You, But God,* 96. There are indications that exorbitant fees for permission to reprint the hymn have discouraged its use in hymn collections; correspondence from John S. Andrews, 7 November 2002.

35. Hine, *Not You, But God,* 95, 97, 103; Elvis Presley, *Amazing Grace: His Greatest Sacred Performances* (RCA 07863 66421-2, 1994).

36. Hine, *The Story of "How Great Thou Art,"* 6.

37. "Pastor Is under Fire for Interfaith Prayers," *New York Times,* 8 February 2002, B1; "Preparing to Take on His Church," ibid., 10 July 2002, B3.

38. Harvey Cox, "Religion and the War against Evil," *The Nation,* 6 December 2001; "Preparing to Take on His Church," *New York Times,* 10 July 2002, B3; "A Nation Challenged: The Evangelist; Muslim Group Seeks to Meet Billy Graham's Son," ibid., 20 November 2001; "Evangelist Says Muslims Haven't Adequately Apologized for Sept. 11 Attacks," ibid., 15 August 2002, accessed at www.nytimes.com.

11. Coltrane and Beyond

Epigraph: Lewis Porter, *John Coltrane: His Life and Music* (Ann Arbor: University of Michigan Press, 1998), 232.

1. Liner notes to John Coltrane, *A Love Supreme* (Impulse, 1964).

2. Coltrane, *A Love Supreme.*

3. Porter, *John Coltrane,* 242; Ashley Kahn, *A Love Supreme: The Story of John Coltrane's Signature Album* (New York: Viking, 2002), 104; Mustafa Bayoumi, "East of the Sun (West of the Moon): Islam, the Ahmadis, and African America," *Journal of Asian-American Studies,* October 2001, 261. Thanks to Christopher Chase for bringing this article to my attention.

4. "Gary Giddins on the Sacred Concerts," in *The Duke Ellington Reader,* ed. Mark Tucker (New York: Oxford University Press, 1993), 376.

5. Jacques Attali, *Noise: The Political Economy of Music,* trans Brian Massumi (Minneapolis: University of Minnesota Press, 1985), 11; Diana L. Eck, *A New Religious America: How a "Christian Country" Has Now Become the World's Most Religiously Diverse Nation* (New York: HarperCollins, 2001).

6. Francis Davis, "Coltrane at 75: The Man and the Myths," *New York Times,* 23 September 2001, Arts section, 25; Harvey Cox, *Fire from Heaven: The Rise of Pentecostal Spirituality and the Reshaping of Religion in the Twenty-first Century* (Reading, Mass.: Addison-Wesley, 1995), 143–155, quotation on 145.

7. Porter, *John Coltrane,* 11–84, quotations on 11–13; Kahn, *A Love Supreme,* 223, quotation on 224.

8. Nick Spitzer, program notes to *Saints' Paradise: Trombone Shout Bands from the United House of Prayer* (Washington, D.C.: Smithsonian Folkways, 1999).

9. Spitzer, program notes to *Saints' Paradise.*

10. Rev. F. W. McGee, "Fifty Miles of Elbow Room," in *Anthology of American Folk Music* (Washington, D.C.: Smithsonian Folkways, 1997).

11. Rev. D. C. Rice and his Sanctified Congregation, "I'm in the Battlefield for My Lord," ibid.

12. "A Booklet of Essays, Appreciations, and Annotations Pertaining to the *Anthology of American Folk Music*" (Washington, D.C.: Smithsonian Folkways, 1997), 55.

13. Lawrence W. Levine, *Black Culture and Black Consciousness: Afro-American Folk Thought from Slavery to Freedom* (New York: Oxford University Press,

1977), 180–181; Ted Panken, "Approaching Enlightenment," *Down Beat* 68 (February 2001), 27.

14. *Anthology of American Folk Music;* Greil Marcus, *Invisible Republic: Bob Dylan's Basement Tapes* (New York: Holt, 1997).

15. Ingrid Monson, "Art Blakey's African Diaspora," in *The African Diaspora: A Musical Perspective,* ed. Ingrid Monson (New York: Garland, 2000), 336; Gene Santoro, *Myself When I Am Real: The Life and Music of Charles Mingus* (New York: Oxford University Press, 2000), 9–11, 20, 29, 43–45. One of Mingus' best-known albums was titled *Ah-Um,* a clear allusion to sacred Hindu chant.

16. Porter, *John Coltrane,* 205, 213, 262.

17. Alain Danielou, "Introduction," *Religious Music of India* (Folkways F-4431, 1952).

18. Porter, *John Coltrane,* 211.

19. Quotation from ibid.

20. Ibid., 259, 265, 274. See also Eric Nisenson, *Ascension: John Coltrane and His Quest* (New York: St. Martin's, 1993), 153, 167. In an interesting example of the kind of slippage that can take place when discussing Asian religion, Porter identifies the chanting as from the *Bhagavad Gita,* while Nisenson attributes it to the Tibetan *Book of the Dead.*

21. John Szwed, *Space Is the Place: The Lives and Times of Sun Ra* (New York: Pantheon, 1997), 148; Porter, *John Coltrane,* 255–256.

22. Porter, *John Coltrane,* 205–206; John Fraim, *Spirit Catcher: The Life and Art of John Coltrane* (West Liberty, Ohio: GreatHouse, 1996), 142; Szwed, *Space Is the Place,* 202–203.

23. Porter, *John Coltrane,* 150.

24. Ibid., 177, 216.

25. Ibid., 246–247.

26. Ibid., 331, n. 11.

27. Ibid., 260, 232; Fraim, *Spirit Catcher,* 194–196.

28. Fraim, *Spirit Catcher,* 182.

29. Greg Panfile, "Inner Lite: The Beatles and the Maharishi, 1967–68," available at www.trancenet.org/news/beatles.shtml; Ravi Shankar, "George Harrison, World-Music Catalyst and Great-Souled Man; A Childlike Simplicity, Full of Love and Fun," *New York Times,* 9 December 2001.

30. Porter, *John Coltrane,* 296; interviews with Manzarek and Densmore on "Light My Fire," *NPR 100,* available at www.npr.org/programs/specials/vote/100/list.html.

31. Fraim, *Spirit Catcher,* 181–182; Nisenson, *Ascension,* 230–231; "First Lesson, Best Lesson: An Interview with Philip Glass," available at www.tricycle.com/interviews/glassintissue2.html.

32. Szwed, *Space Is the Place,* 248.

33. Porter, *John Coltrane,* 270–274, 297–298.

34. Cox, *Fire from Heaven,* 153–154; Porter, *John Coltrane,* 296–297; Franzo Wayne King, "'I Just Integrate Myself into the Music,'" *New York Times Magazine,* 18 June 2000, 102.

35. King, "'I Just Integrate Myself,'" 102.
36. Cox, *Fire From Heaven*, 153–154.

Epilogue

1. Diana L. Eck, *New Religious America: How a "Christian Country" Has Become the World's Most Religiously Diverse Nation* (New York: Harper-Collins, 2001), 2–3; Philip Jenkins, *The Next Christendom: The Coming of Global Christianity* (New York: Oxford University Press, 2002), 100.
2. Eck, *New Religious America*, 2–3.
3. Thomas Day, *Why Catholics Can't Sing: The Culture of Catholicism and the Triumph of Bad Taste* (New York: Crossroad, 1996).
4. Gregg Easterbrook, "Still a Christian Nation," available at www.beliefnet.com/story/81/story_8198.html.
5. R. Stephen Warner, "Religion and New (Post-1965) Immigrants: Some Principles Drawn from Field Research," *American Studies* 41 (summer/fall 2000), 276–279; Jenkins, *Next Christendom*, 99–105; "Christianity's New Center" (interview with Philip Jenkins), *Atlantic Unbound*, 12 September 2002, available at www.theatlantic.com/unbound/interviews/int2002–09–12.htm; Jenkins, "A New Religious America," *First Things*, August/September 2002, 25–28.
6. Barbara Crossette, "A Tough Time to Talk of Peace; Buddhists Find Nonviolence Out of Fashion after Sept. 11," *New York Times*, 29 October 2002; Steve Earle, *Jerusalem* (Artemis 751147-2, 2002); Lauren St. John, *Hardcover Troubadour: The Life and Near Death of Steve Earle* (London: Fourth Estate, 2003), 4–5.
7. Jon Pareles, "Music Moved by the Spirit Thrives," *New York Times*, 21 June 1998. On Ashcroft the musician, see Laurie Goodstein, "Moderato Non Troppo," ibid., 14 January 2001.

Note on Method

1. Richard Crawford, *America's Musical Life: A History* (New York: Norton, 2001), 859.

Index